NEURODEVELOPMENTAL DISORDERS

Interest in the field of neurodevelopmental disorders has grown exponentially in recent years across a range of disciplines, including psychology, psychiatry, education and neuroscience. The research itself has become more sophisticated, using multidisciplinary methods to probe interdisciplinary questions. *Neurodevelopmental Disorders: Research Challenges and Solutions* provides a thorough overview of the key issues involved in researching neurodevelopmental disorders.

The volume includes fourteen chapters, arranged over three sections. Chapters in the first section address general research challenges for the study of neurodevelopmental disorders. The second section draws upon specific disorders (such as Williams syndrome, Autism Spectrum Disorders, Down syndrome, Fragile X syndrome, ADHD and Language Disorders) to consider the syndrome-specific issues or challenges that may be crucial to advancing our understanding of aspects of cognition and behaviour associated with them. The final section considers how research evidence may be translated into practice to begin making an impact upon the lives of individuals who have neurodevelopmental disorders and their families. Each chapter in the book also includes 'practical tips' for either conducting research with individuals who have neurodevelopmental disorders or considering wider practical issues.

The book will be indispensable reading for advanced students, researchers and practitioners in the fields of developmental psychology, developmental psychopathology, special needs education, neuropsychology and neurodevelopmental disorders.

Jo Van Herwegen is a senior lecturer in the Department of Psychology at Kingston University, UK. She is coordinator of the Child Development and Learning Difficulties Unit. Her research focuses on language and number development in both typical and atypical populations, including Williams syndrome, Autism Spectrum Disorders, Down syndrome, and Specific Language Impairment.

Deborah Riby is a senior lecturer in the Department of Psychology at Durham University, UK and is an honorary lecturer at Monash University, Melbourne, Australia. She is coordinator of the Developmental Psychology Research Group and head of the North East Williams Syndrome Research Group. Her research focuses on syndrome-specific signatures of cognition and behaviour, primarily focusing on the developmental disorders Williams syndrome and Autism.

Research Methods in Developmental Psychology
A Handbook Series

Research Methods in Developmental Psychology is a series of edited books focusing on research challenges for conducting research in developmental psychology. Ideally suited to both students coming to this area for the first time and more experienced researchers, each volume provides an invaluable overview of research in this growing field, and how it can inform both education and interventions. Volumes include research challenges in neurodevelopmental disorders, child development and gerontology.

Published titles:

Neurodevelopmental Disorders: Research challenges and solutions
Edited by Jo Van Herwegen and Deborah Riby

NEURODEVELOPMENTAL DISORDERS

Research challenges and solutions

*Edited by Jo Van Herwegen
and Deborah Riby*

Psychology Press
Taylor & Francis Group
LONDON AND NEW YORK

First published 2015
by Psychology Press
27 Church Road, Hove, East Sussex BN3 2FA

and by Psychology Press
711 Third Avenue, New York, NY 10017

Psychology Press is an imprint of the Taylor & Francis Group, an informa business

British Library Cataloguing in Publication Data
A catalogue record for this book is available from the British Library

Library of Congress Cataloging in Publication Data
Neurodevelopmental disorders (Riby)
Neurodevelopmental disorders : research challenges and solutions / edited by Deborah Riby and Jo Van Herwegen.
p. ; cm.
Includes bibliographical references and index.
I. Riby, Deborah, editor. II. Van Herwegen, Jo, editor. III. Title.
[DNLM: 1. Developmental Disabilities--etiology. 2. Child Development Disorders, Pervasive--psychology. 3. Child Development. 4. Developmental Disabilities--psychology. 5. Intellectual Disability. 6. Neuropsychological Tests. WS 350.6]
RJ506.D47
616.85'88--dc23
2014027253

ISBN: 978-1-84872-328-3 (hbk)
ISBN: 978-1-84872-329-0 (pbk)
ISBN: 978-1-315-73531-3 (ebk)

Typeset in Bembo and ITC Stone Sans
by Saxon Graphics Ltd, Derby

CONTENTS

FIGURES

LIST OF CONTRIBUTORS

George Ball, Centre for Brain and Cognitive Development, Department of Psychological Sciences, Birkbeck, University of London, UK

Nicola Botting, Division of Language and Communication Science, City University London, UK

Tony Charman, Institute of Psychiatry, King's College London, UK

Brianna Doherty, Attention, Brain and Cognitive Development, Department of Experimental Psychology, University of Oxford, UK

Kevin Durkin, School of Psychological Sciences and Health, University of Strathclyde, UK

Emily K. Farran, Department of Psychology and Human Development, Institute of Education, University of London, UK

Sue Fletcher-Watson, Centre for Clinical Brain Sciences, University of Edinburgh, UK

Rachel George, Institute for Research in Child Development, School of Psychology, University of East London, UK

Victoria Grahame, Northumberland Tyne and Wear NHS Foundation Trust, UK

Brian W. Haas, Department of Psychology, University of Georgia, USA

Mary Hanley, Department of Psychology, Durham University, UK

Jo Van Herwegen, Department of Psychology, Kingston University, UK

Themis Karaminis, Centre for Research in Autism and Education, Institute of Education, UK

Annette Karmiloff-Smith, Centre for Brain and Cognitive Development, Department of Psychological Sciences, Birkbeck, University of London, UK

Victoria Knowland, Division of Language and Communication Science, City University London, UK

Sarah Lloyd-Fox, Centre for Brain and Cognitive Development, Birkbeck, University of London, UK

Derek G. Moore, Institute for Research in Child Development, School of Psychology, University of East London, UK

Harry Purser, School of Psychology, University of Nottingham, UK

Sinead Rhodes, School of Psychological Sciences and Health, University of Strathclyde, UK

Deborah Riby, Department of Psychology, Durham University, UK

Jacqui Rodgers, Institute of Neuroscience, Newcastle University, UK

Gaia Scerif, Attention, Brain and Cognitive Development, Department of Experimental Psychology, University of Oxford, UK

Andria Shimi, Attention, Brain and Cognitive Development, Department of Experimental Psychology, University of Oxford, UK

ABOUT THE EDITORS

Jo Van Herwegen is a Senior Lecturer in the Department of Psychology at Kingston University. She is coordinator of the Child Development and Learning Difficulties Unit and course director for the MSc Child Psychology. After working as a researcher at the Institute of Child Health (UCL) and at the Institute of Education, Jo completed her PhD in 2010 at King's College London in which she investigated metaphor and metonymy comprehension in Williams syndrome. After a short post-doc position at Middlesex University, Jo was appointed as a lecturer at Kingston University in September 2010. Her research focuses mainly on language and number development in both typical and atypical populations, such as Williams syndrome, Autism Spectrum Disorders, Down syndrome and Specific Language Impairment. Linking the aforementioned areas of research activity, she explores individual differences, as well as what cognitive abilities and strategies relate to successful performance in typical populations and how these differ in atypical populations, in order to aid the development of economically valid training programmes. Jo studies cognitive abilities from infancy onwards in order to obtain a better understanding of how they develop over time and how performance across different cognitive areas relate to each other. In her research she employs a range of methods and experimental designs, including spontaneous language samples, preferential looking, experimental tasks and eye-tracking. Lately her research has focused also on the design and validity of new intervention programmes for preschool children. She has obtained funding from the British Academy and Nuffield Foundation to support her research.

Deborah Riby is a Senior Lecturer in the Department of Psychology at Durham University. She is coordinator of the Developmental Psychology Research Group and head of the North East Williams Syndrome Research Group. Dr Riby is also course director for the MSc Developmental Psychopathology and MA Research

Methods (Developmental Psychology). She completed her PhD on face perception in Williams syndrome and Autism at Stirling University in 2007 and then had a one-year post-doc research post at the same institution. From 2008–2013 she held a lectureship in the School of Psychology at Newcastle University before moving to her current position in Durham. Her research focuses on syndrome-specific signatures of cognition and behaviour in the developmental disorders Williams syndrome and Autism. She has largely studied components of social attention and social cognition in these groups, as well as in individuals who are developing typically. As well as using eye-tracking to explore social attention she has used a variety of experimental paradigms to probe social communication styles. Most recently she has taken a holistic view of the individual to consider the impact of anxiety and sensory processing on components of social functioning in these developmental disorders. Deborah has secured research funding from the ESRC, British Academy, Nuffield Foundation and the EPS to support her work. In 2014 Deborah was awarded the Margaret Donaldson Award by the British Psychological Society for outstanding early career contribution to the field of developmental psychology.

PREFACE

Why are we writing this book?

During 2012 and 2013 we ran a series of three seminar days funded by a British Psychological Society seminar series grant and with additional financial support from the Williams Syndrome Foundation UK (http://www.williams-syndrome. org.uk) to explore current issues and future directions in the study of neurodevelopmental disorders. Those seminars, hosted at three different UK universities, attracted over 172 delegates, with 19 invited speakers varying from PhD students to professors, including acclaimed leaders in the field. This showed very clearly that there was a desire to have the opportunity to engage with other academics in this area, to discuss hot topics around research practice and methodological advances in our ability to capture the nature of cognition and behaviour in a range of neurodevelopmental disorders. In this Preface we will not go into a full discussion of the issues addressed in that series but the topics covered throughout the book capture the nature of those discussions, the range of methodological issues addressed and the variety of disorders that were featured. In the second half of the Preface we give a full description of the structure of the book and a taster of how we have tried to capture the issues from the seminar series. Indeed, it was as part of the experience of hosting the seminar series that the idea for this book was born.

It is difficult to put into figures the vast increase in the number of peer-reviewed academic publications reporting components of cognition and behaviour associated with neurodevelopmental disorders, because the field has increased exponentially in the last two decades or so. Just to give a taster, the relatively newly emerged sub-discipline of developmental cognitive neuroscience has sprung into action over the last decade due largely to methodological advances (for example, eye-tracking methodologies and new neuro-imaging techniques that are discussed in this book), creating its own identity and forging its place firmly within (or perhaps alongside) the wider field of neurodevelopmental disorder research. When pondering the question of how to capture the huge growth in the field comes the realisation that this really is a vast area – how do we narrow down which disorders we cover, which areas of cognition and behaviour are we focusing on, which methodological approaches have dominated, and what the future challenges are? Thinking forward, where do we see the field progressing to? Reflecting upon this question for too long only seems to increase the complexities of the issue.

So, let's just give a flavour with an illustration from research in Autism Spectrum Disorders (ASD). Just in the area of ASD between 2000 and 2014 there have been over 13,000 publications that feature the word 'autism' in the title (via Web of Science citations, using only 'articles'). Slightly more specific, within the subdomain of psychology, citation reports indicate over 5,700 articles combining the terms 'autism' and 'behaviour' within this same time period; over 1,400 combining the terms 'attention' and 'autism'; over 1,000 combining the terms 'cognitive' and 'autism'; and over 1,400 combining the terms 'language' and 'autism'. Within this same time period and in the research area of psychology, over 470 articles have featured Williams syndrome in the title; over 1,000 have mentioned Down syndrome, and over 370 the term Fragile X syndrome. This is a mere hint to represent the broad field within the last decade or so, and to provide an illustration of the quantity (let alone the quality) of research evidence.

Alongside these academic peer-reviewed publications, in the current day and age, we must also emphasise the dramatic growth of academic blogs and the use of social media, allowing researchers to engage with, and discuss hot topics with, non-academic partners and a far wider audience. Of course as academics we might have our 'impact' hat on in this respect (after all, it won't be long until REF2020!) but equally the importance of considering the applied nature, the practical applications, and intervention implications of our work for individuals and families is essential (see Part 3 of this book as a mere illustration of this). Keeping this need in mind, each chapter of the book concludes by providing 'practical tips' for either conducting research with individuals who have neurodevelopmental disorders or considering wider practical issues. It is hoped that by paying attention to these tips and hints we can increase the possible impact of our work in the future – not only in terms of theoretical contribution and/or impact, but also in the manner with which we ask important questions within the field.

What about the growth of expertise and building a legacy for developmental psychology and neurodevelopmental disorders research in the UK and further afield? In the UK alone there are far more postgraduate courses dedicated to developmental psychology (child development), neurodevelopmental disorders or developmental psychopathology (of which the editors are course directors of a number at their host institutions) than there were a decade or two ago. We were also hugely impressed by the extensive areas being studied by PhD students within this field, as presented in our previous seminar series. There are a number of lab groups throughout the UK and further afield that are dedicated to the study of atypical development. These labs are a hive of research activity and we hope that the current text will be of relevance to researchers (as well as practitioners) working in this area at any stage of their career.

Having detailed the impetus to embark upon this journey we will spend the remainder of the Preface giving an overview of the chapters and focus of the text, indicating how we aim to pull together core issues and topics across a range of neurodevelopmental disorders.

Structure of the book

We have provided three core sections to pull together the chapters throughout the text. It will be clear that there are a number of issues, challenges and methodological considerations that merge across chapters (as an illustration let's take the two examples of comorbidity and within-syndrome heterogeneity that will feature in at least Chapters 7 and 9). Where this is the case the editors aim to draw the reader's attention to further discussions of similar issues in other chapters. Most importantly, the issues that we aim to address, by their very nature, will not occur in isolation (dramatically increasing the research challenges). Therefore, the text aims to provide a rounded insight into applied/practical issues when studying and conducting research with individuals who have neurodevelopmental disorders; with the ultimate aim of advancing knowledge of cognition and behaviour within- and across- disorder groups.

In **Part I** we address key methodological approaches and general/broad research issues for the study of neurodevelopmental disorders, not specific to one disorder or another, but indicative of methodological advances and reflections of best practice, research aims and future possibilities. **Chapter 1** begins with the authors providing an overview and discussion of a selection of challenges when studying neurodevelopmental disorders – reflecting upon the issues that can provide the biggest challenges for researchers. To pull out an important theme of this chapter, the authors clearly indicate the contribution of neurodevelopmental disorders to our understanding of both typical and atypical cognition and behaviour. Some of the issues addressed in Chapter 1 regarding the nature of 'development' per se also feature as the core focus in the following chapter.

In **Chapter 2** we emphasise the importance of taking a truly developmental perspective to the study of neuro*developmental* disorders which is often underappreciated. Utilising illustrations from Williams-, Down-, and Fragile X-syndrome, the chapter makes a strong theoretical plea for a developmental approach from multiple levels. Section 1 argues that adult neuropsychological models are inappropriate for understanding neurodevelopmental disorders. Developmental change is then highlighted in the context of mapping: genotype to phenotype, brain to cognition, early basic-level underpinnings to cognitive-level outcomes, and of evaluating environmental factors. Brain to cognition links lead us nicely onto further discussion of advances in this field in the following chapter.

Chapter 3 provides a description of why it is valuable to study brain to behaviour links in neurodevelopmental disorders. The previously mentioned advances in the field of developmental neuroscience, and breakthroughs in neuroscience more generally, have provided an unprecedented opportunity to learn about the association between the brain and behaviour. We describe how specific neuroscience approaches can be used to study the link between the brain and behaviour and provide specific examples of research findings on brain–behaviour links in various disorders.

Leading directly on from Chapter 3, **Chapter 4** details the pros and cons of different neuroimaging techniques for studying developmental disorders as well as the specific contribution of functional Near Infrared Spectroscopy. It is noted that researchers should give careful thought with regards to which brain imaging techniques are most relevant to the questions being asked, and especially when working with disorder groups, the needs of the individuals taking part.

Chapter 5 focuses on the use of animal and computational models to gain a better understanding of the causes of developmental disorders. Using examples from Specific Language Impairment it is shown how both types of models can provide a framework to understand the causal links between deficits observed at different levels of description (behavioural, cognitive and neurological) which will lead us into the next chapter.

Chapter 6 introduces ACORNS, an Accessible Cause–Outcome Representation and Notation System. It is proposed that this universal notation system is necessary to allow developmental science to capture and communicate the complexity of the causal links across different levels, as well as the similarities and differences across different neurodevelopmental disorders which will allow the development of more precise cross-disciplinary meta-theoretical accounts of development.

This draws the first section of the book to a close and we move to **Part II** in order to consider specific neurodevelopmental disorders and the challenges that they pose for research (and researchers). This section starts in **Chapter 7** by emphasising the heterogeneous nature of Autism Spectrum Disorders (ASD) both in terms of aetiology and in phenotypic presentation across individuals and across development. For many decades this variability was often treated as 'noise' or a nuisance variable. However, today the clinical and scientific communities have begun to embrace this heterogeneity. We review aspects of variability, including diagnostic criteria and stability of diagnosis, the pattern of common co-occurring conditions, cognitive and behavioural profiles and outcome, and the search for meaningful subgroups.

Chapter 8 continues the discussion of heterogeneity and variability focussing on children with primary language impairment. This chapter is structured around four main questions, including the specificity of the disorder, the existence of subgroups, the stability of language profiles over time and finally how environmental factors and child-internal factors might affect language outcomes. The chapter includes a discussion of theoretical, as well as practical, considerations for practitioners and clinicians.

The boundary between disorders is a crucial issue and in **Chapter 9** we discuss this hot topic. Attention Deficit Hyperactivity Disorder (ADHD) is a common neurodevelopmental disorder that shows high rates of comorbidity with other disorders such as ASD and disruptive behaviour disorders (e.g. conduct disorder). Comorbidity influences the broad psychological profile of individuals with a disorder including cognitive, social and behaviour profiles. The chapter explores the influence of comorbidity on each of these areas. It considers whether the psychological profile (aspects such as executive functions, theory of mind and disruptive behaviours) is influenced by the presence of co-occurring symptoms of other disorders that are commonly observed in these children. While the behavioural diagnostic measures used in ASD might play an important role in distinctions between neurodevelopmental disorders, this is not the case in the next chapter.

Focussing on Fragile X syndrome (FXS) **Chapter 10** discusses evidence spanning genotype, neuroscience, cognition and behaviour. We emphasise the developmental nature of FXS (linking back to core issues of considering development as noted in Chapters 1 and 2), to illustrate a number of broad points emerging from the study of genetic disorders. We use longitudinal data that highlight variability in outcomes in individuals with FXS, and underscore the need to understand diverging developmental trajectories, predictors of greater risk, mechanisms of resilience and environmental protective influences.

We move on to more cognitive aspects and their implications for studying development in individuals with neurodevelopmental disorders in **Chapter 11** with a focus on Down syndrome (DS). This disorder is associated with a broad range of cognitive deficits and we discuss issues of specificity surrounding these deficits. Particular reference is made to task demands when conducting research with this group. The domain of verbal short-term memory is used to illustrate some different approaches in establishing the specificity of a cognitive deficit. Within an analysis of task demands, we discuss some of the most commonly used tests in developmental disorder research, with a view to highlighting difficulties when interpreting task scores of individuals with DS.

The final chapter of this section, **Chapter 12** discusses how eye-tracking is becoming a commonly used tool to measure aspects of attention in various fields within psychology. We review evidence from eye-tracking studies of social attention, focussing on the insights gained from the cross-syndrome comparison of ASD and Williams syndrome (WS). As well as giving an overview of advances in the technology relevant to its use with individuals with neurodevelopmental disorders, the chapter considers what eye-tracking studies have revealed about ASD and WS and what challenges remain for future research in this area. This cross-syndrome discussion of the use of eye-tracking illustrates important issues when comparing and contrasting patterns of cognition and/or behaviour in neurodevelopmental disorders – for example the crucial question of whether the data reveal syndrome-specific patterns or performance indicative of general developmental delay. Such issues are not only important to the use of eye-tracking techniques and research within this area, but more generally within the field of clinical psychology for diagnosis and intervention.

Part III of the book takes a look at applied issues related to the study of neurodevelopmental disorders. We have selected two specific topics for this section to indicate the possible direction of applied work in the future and the implications for understanding some of the complex issues already discussed up to this point.

The ubiquity of new technologies in everyday life necessitates an evidence base for best practice in their uses by those with neurodevelopmental disorders and this is the topic under discussion in **Chapter 13**. Technologies offer both benefits and challenges. We review emerging evidence on how children and young people with ADHD, ASD and Specific Language Impairment access, respond to and learn from technology. Research with each population has tended to focus on very different issues, which are outlined throughout the chapter (again linking back to the challenges of syndrome specificity as discussed in Chapter 11 and to components of cognition addressed for ADHD in Chapter 12 and ASD in Chapter 13). There is a proposal for more coordinated efforts to understand how technology may be harnessed and managed to benefit those with neurodevelopmental disorders.

Last, but by no means least, **Chapter 14** emphasises the evidence that individuals with neurodevelopmental disorders are at increased risk of experiencing mental health difficulties, especially anxiety. We examine prevalence rates of anxiety for children with a range of neurodevelopmental disorders (linking across chapters that have already introduced key components of many of these disorders). Consideration is given to the emotional and behavioural phenotypes associated with anxiety and some of the challenges associated with the identification and assessment of anxiety in children with neurodevelopmental disorders, including some thoughts about the potential overlap between core characteristics and mental health symptoms. Finally, we consider the implications for psychological intervention.

It is hoped that readers of this text will see the value of cross-chapter links and the vast impact of the methodological issues across the various neurodevelopmental disorders addressed in this volume. We hope that the discussion of these key issues will advance the field and make a significant contribution not only to theoretical knowledge but also to the lives of individuals with neurodevelopmental disorders and their families.

ACKNOWLEDGEMENTS

From the editors

We have many people to thank for their contribution to this book. Our chapter contributors have been fantastic and we are hugely grateful to them for enabling us to produce this volume of work. Thank you to all the authors for trying their utmost to keep to our editorial deadlines (sometimes with tight turn-around times!), following our editorial guidelines and reviewing other chapters when requested. We have been immensely pleased that so many of the chapter authors have shared our vision for this book, understanding the links between chapters that are so important to producing a comprehensive volume.

During the process we have had great help with putting together the text from several colleagues and students, including Alea Ruf, Emma Lough, and Valerie Gunn. We thank you for your valuable contribution of both time and effort.

We would also like to thank our publishers, particularly George Russell who has supported the idea, book proposal and concept of book from the very start and who made this book happen. We also thank Michael Fenton and Lucy Kennedy for their valuable support, enthusiasm and advice at all stages in the preparation of the book.

Jo thanks her partner Rob for his patience, support, inquisitive questions and debates.

Deborah would like to take this opportunity to thank her family for their unwavering support – special thanks to Jessica and Amelia.

From the authors

Chapter 2

During the writing of this chapter, Annette Karmiloff-Smith was funded by a Wellcome Trust Strategic Award (Grant No. 098330/Z/12/Z), as well as grants from the Waterloo Foundation, UK and Autour de Williams, France. Substantial sections of the chapter are reproduced from Karmiloff-Smith's Bartlett Lecture (Karmiloff-Smith (2013). Challenging the use of adult neuropsychological models for explaining neurodevelopmental disorders: Developed versus developing brains. *Quarterly Journal of Experimental Psychology,* 66, 1–14) and from Karmiloff-Smith et al., 2012.

Chapter 6

We would like to thank all the leading developmental psychologists we have published and worked with over the years who have inspired and influenced us – Peter Hobson, John Oates, Michael Howe, Julie Dockrell, George Butterworth, Michael Siegel, Annette Karmiloff-Smith, Mark Johnson and Jennifer Wishart – some of whom, sadly, are no longer with us.

Chapter 10

Most of the research overviewed here could not have been carried out without the continued contributions of children and adults with Fragile X syndrome, their families, and their national support groups. We are particularly indebted to the Fragile X Society for facilitating our research efforts. We are grateful to team members, colleagues and collaborators for shaping our thinking about the issues we raise here. B.D. is supported by a Rhodes and Clarendon Scholarship. A.S. and G.S. are supported by a James S. McDonnell Foundation (Understanding Human Cognition) Scholar Award.

PART I
General research challenges

1

NEURODEVELOPMENTAL DISORDERS

Definitions and issues

Jo Van Herwegen, Deborah Riby and Emily K. Farran

1.1 Introduction

Neurodevelopmental disorders are different from acquired disorders in that for the latter the cause or the onset can happen during any time of a person's lifespan. A crucial component of neurodevelopmental disorders is that individuals show difficulties from birth onwards and the cause is often situated during gestation or birth. The term 'neurodevelopmental' disorder has seen an increased use over the past two decades (Bishop & Rutter, 2006), yet it is often used to cover a wide variety of meanings and disorders. Some, for example, have used the term in a very restricted sense to refer only to those conditions that affect children's neurological development with a known genetic or acquired etiology, such as Fragile X syndrome (FXS) or fetal alcohol syndrome. However, others have taken a broader definition of neurodevelopmental disorders and included those conditions presumed to be of multifactorial etiology, such as Autism Spectrum Disorders (ASD), developmental dyslexia and Attention Deficit Hyperactivity Disorder (ADHD). The current DSM 5 criteria are even broader and include all developmental disorders; intellectual disabilities, communication disorders, ASD, ADHD, specific learning disorders, motor disorders (including developmental coordination and movements disorders, Tourette's, and tic disorders), and other specified and unspecified neurodevelopmental disorders. Similarly, ICD-10 refers to disorders of psychological development and includes developmental disorders of speech and language, scholastic skills and motor function. The ICD-10 also includes pervasive developmental disorders (this includes ASD and Rett's syndrome). Therefore, the work that is of relevance to this field is broad in its coverage of atypical development.

In this chapter (and throughout the current text), we will refer to neurodevelopmental disorders as those disorders that are of a genetic or multifactorial origin that result in one or more specific cognitive deficits. These deficits are present early in life and extend into adult life without showing relapse or remission.

This therefore excludes acquired disorders, such as fetal alcohol syndrome, acquired motor disorders, or disorders that are akin to remissions, such as schizophrenia and anti-social behaviours.

1.2 The importance of researching neurodevelopmental disorders

The most important reason to study neurodevelopmental disorders is to obtain a better understanding that can subsequently inform better (more accurate) diagnosis and in turn lead to more successful training programmes or interventions. A more thorough understanding of neurodevelopmental disorders not only requires a description of the behavioural and biological aspects of a disorder, but the cognitive or psychological processes must be examined as these mediate the link between the brain and behaviour (see Chapters 2, 5 and 6 for discussion of some of these issues). One framework that incorporates all three levels (e.g. biological, cognitive and behavioural), as well as environmental factors, is the causal model by Morton and Frith (1995). This model aims to provide full causal explanations for neurodevelopmental disorders, incorporating developmental aspects to allow evaluation of different competing causal accounts for specific disorders. Yet, as we will discuss below there are a number of challenges and complexities typical to most disorders which challenge such causal frameworks.

Second, research in neurodevelopmental disorders is vital in order to advance our theoretical understanding of typical developmental (TD) pathways and cognition in general. For example, it has been argued that infants are born with certain core systems for knowledge (Spelke & Kinzler, 2007). One core domain that has been well-researched in infants is number development. Research has shown that six-month-old infants can discriminate between large numerosities using their approximate number system and that this system is more predictive of number abilities later in life. In contrast, it has been argued that discrimination between small numbers is related to an object file system which is more akin to memory abilities (Feigenson, Dehaene & Spelke, 2004). Yet, as both core systems are already present in TD infants these studies can only show correlations between the early discrimination abilities and number development later in life. In contrast, neurodevelopmental disorders are often associated with uneven cognitive profiles with performance on certain cognitive abilities outperforming others. Therefore, neurodevelopmental disorders provide the perfect opportunity to investigate more subtle associations, or what abilities underlie successful performance on certain tasks. For example, studies have shown that participants with Williams syndrome (WS) perform better on number tasks that include verbal abilities, such as counting tasks, but perform worse on tasks that tap into the magnitude system or approximate number system (ANS). This pattern contrasts with that seen in Down syndrome (DS) where individuals show the opposite pattern (Ansari et al., 2003; Ansari, Donlan & Karmiloff-Smith, 2007; Paterson, Girelli, Butterworth & Karmiloff-Smith, 2006). A recent study by Karmiloff-Smith and colleagues (2012a) showed that, although infants with WS were able to discriminate between two and three dots, they could not discriminate between large numerosities such as eight and sixteen dots. Infants with DS on the other hand showed the opposite pattern. Yet, direct comparisons between older children and adults with DS and WS have demonstrated that those with DS have overall better number abilities compared to those with WS (Paterson et al., 2006). This evidence suggests that the ability to discriminate between large numerosities or the magnitude system is a better predictor for number outcomes later in life than the object file system (but see discussion in Chapter 2). This is important for our understanding of typical development because it can lead to better training and intervention programmes. Indeed, recent studies of TD children and adults have shown that training of ANS abilities positively impacts on overall mathematical abilities (Dewind & Brannon, 2012; Park & Brannon, 2013; Van Herwegen, Costa & Passolunghi, submitted).

Therefore, as illustrated by the area of number development, the study of developmental disorders not only informs knowledge of these disorders per se, but can also inform our understanding of the 'typical' path of development in individuals who do not have a disorder of development. The theoretical contribution that research within the field of developmental disorders can make is vast. However, to make both theoretical and applied contributions to knowledge there are a number of methodological issues that require consideration. These issues will be discussed across a number of chapters within this volume and the discussion below is a summary of some of the main issues to be addressed.

1.3 Critical issues when researching neurodevelopmental disorders

1.3.1 The need to study development and related issues

Research in the field of neurodevelopmental disorders has historically adopted models used for adult brain-damaged patients (for a detailed discussion see Chapter 2). For example, evidence from double dissociations has repeatedly been used to show that certain cognitive abilities can be either spared or impaired and thus, can exist independently from each other – which led to the development of theories of 'modularity of mind' by Fodor (1983). A frequently mentioned example of such a double dissociation in neurodevelopmental disorders is the fact that language abilities outperform non-verbal intelligence abilities in WS, in contrast to individuals with Specific Language Impairment (SLI) who show language difficulties in the absence of any general intelligence deficits (Pinker, 1999; though for further discussion on this issue see Chapter 8). Yet, notions of double dissociations are static and claims that the brain exists of specific modules are based on studies investigating the brain in its mature state. Recently, more subtle matching methodologies have suggested that it is highly unlikely that any area of functioning can be 'intact' and have instead suggested that neurodevelopmental disorders can be described in terms of *relative* proficiencies and deficits.

Additionally, studies that have investigated cognitive abilities in infants have shown that the course/pathway of *development* in neurodevelopmental disorders is often atypical. For example, while typically developing children generally point before they start speaking infants with WS only point after the emergence of their first word (Laing et al., 2002). In addition, it is less clear how the infant brain is structured and how the endstate is the result of developmental processes (Karmiloff-Smith, Scerif & Ansari, 2003). A recent view of cognitive development is that the specialisation of brain structures is the result of brain maturation over development through interaction with the environment, genes, brain and behaviour (Thomas, 2003). Thus, advocates of a neuroconstructivist approach have provided strong evidence that a more developmental approach is required when studying neurodevelopmental disorders (see discussion in Chapter 2; Karmiloff-Smith, 1998, 2009; Farran & Karmiloff-Smith, 2012; Thomas, Baughman, Karaminis & Addyman, 2012).

One reason why a developmental approach is needed is the fact that the brain changes over time. Brain plasticity is often defined as changes to the brain system as a result of external (environmental) or internal (brain damage) factors (Huttenlocher, 2002). Plasticity of the brain is larger in children than in adults, which is evidenced by the fact that children recover better and faster after brain damage compared to adults (but see Thomas, 2003, for a discussion). This means that subtle differences over time can impact the development of cognitive abilities. This is especially true for specialisation of the brain in neurodevelopmental disorders:

> brain volume, brain anatomy, brain chemistry, hemispheric asymmetry and temporal patterns of brain activity are all atypical [...]. How could the resulting system be described as a normal brain with parts intact and parts impaired, as the popular view holds? Rather, the brains of infants with [neurodevelopment disorders] develop differently from the outset, which has subtle, widespread repercussions.
>
> *(Karmiloff-Smith, 1998, p. 393)*

As a consequence, a developmental approach is required to study neuro-developmental disorders.

More developmental approaches have emerged within the field of neurodevelopmental disorders in recent years. First, research studies have started to adopt more developmental research methods, including inclusion of wider age ranges and tracing development back to infancy, and are gradually using fewer matched group designs. For example, in the past studies of neurodevelopmental disorders often investigated narrow age ranges and matched groups of neurodevelopmental disorders to control groups (e.g. typically developing individuals or other neurodevelopmental disorders) based on either chronological age or mental age abilities. Such approaches are common in adult neuropsychology but again they represent a static timepoint in development in that they do not capture any of the changes over time. In addition, matching participants with neurodevelopmental disorders to a typically developing control group based on chronological age (CA) often underestimates the disorder group, as disorder groups rarely perform at their CA level. However, matching groups on mental age requires groups to be matched on a specific standardised task, for example matching groups on their receptive vocabulary using the British Picture Vocabulary Scale (Dunn, Dunn, Whetton & Burley, 1997), or the Ravens Coloured Progressive Matrices task (RCPM: Raven, Court & Raven, 1990). Not only does this mean that the matching is theoretically driven, which can interfere with the findings of the study, depending on what abilities the groups are matched, performance in the disorder group will again be under- or over-estimated, due to the often uneven cognitive profiles of neurodevelopmental disorders (see Thomas et al., 2009 for a discussion). Finally, matching studies often apply the rule that two groups are matched when their performance is not significantly different (or p value is larger than 0.05). Yet, the question is how matched the two groups really are as differences in performance often have to be quite large in order for the statistical result to be significant and statistically non-significant group differences might still include large differences and significance in the real world.

The best developmental solution to a matching approach is to study cognitive changes in neurodevelopmental disorders over development using longitudinal studies. Yet, longitudinal studies are time consuming and often expensive. An alternative method that is becoming frequently used is that of a developmental trajectory or cross-sectional approach in which different participants across a large age range are examined and trajectories of the neurodevelopmental group are compared to those of the control group (see Thomas et al., 2009). Yet, the developmental trajectory approach is not without criticism and recent studies have shown that outcomes from cross-sectional studies differ from those using longitudinal designs (see discussion in Chapter 10; Cornish, Cole, Longhi, Karmiloff-Smith & Scerif, 2013). Cross-sectional studies include snapshots of cognitive abilities across different age groups and thus the individual differences between these individuals might mask any real changes over time across an entire group. As a result, although cross-sectional studies can give an indication of the developmental profile in neurodevelopmental disorders, these studies should be followed up by longitudinal research. In addition, other difficulties for cross-sectional studies include the fact that standardised tasks need to include a wide age range in order to avoid floor and ceiling effects between the two groups (see the discussion in Thomas, Purser & Van Herwegen, 2012) and importantly, this design assumes that individuals with the same disorder will follow the same developmental trajectory (this may not always be the case: see Chapter 7 for a discussion of heterogeneity within disorders and Little et al., 2013 for a study using cluster analysis to explore variability within one disorder group).

A second developmental trend in recent studies is the examination of domain-general abilities (such as eye movement behaviour, attention, processing speed, cognitive control, memory abilities, etc.) and how these building blocks affect the development of cognitive abilities later in life. This is important in that even when development in neurodevelopmental disorders appears to be within the typical range, because of plasticity and compensation strategies in the brain, this behaviour might be reliant upon alternative cognitive strategies or abilities. For example, individuals with WS are often reported to have relatively good face processing abilities on some aspects of recognition, despite their lower general intelligence. Yet studies have shown that they rely upon atypical strategies to complete basic face recognition tasks and that in contrast to TD controls those with WS rely on their local processing abilities rather than global processing (Annaz, Karmiloff-Smith, Johnson & Thomas, 2009; see also Chapter 2 for a detailed discussion). Another trend that has emerged from the understanding that differences in domain-general aspects can result in domain-specific differences is to investigate how these domain-general abilities affect performance on standardised tasks (see also Chapter 11 for a detailed discussion). One study by Van Herwegen and colleagues (2011a) has shown that participants with WS make the same errors and show similar performance strategies on the Ravens Coloured Progressive Matrices as typically developing children, which shows that this task is reliable and can be used to compare performance in WS to TD populations (Van Herwegen, Farran & Annaz, 2011a; however, this might not be the case for individuals with Down syndrome, see Gunn & Jarrold, 2004). Yet, more studies are needed to explore how participants with neurodevelopmental disorders understand task instructions or how domain-general difficulties, such as attention span, short-term memory abilities or problems with planning of eye movements, affect their performance scores (see also Chapter 11). If these domain general difficulties are shown to affect task performance then it questions what the task is still measuring and whether groups can actually be matched or compared based upon these tasks.

Although more recent studies have employed more developmental than static approaches to examine cognitive development in neurodevelopmental disorders, there are a number of challenges that remain. First of all, very few studies have examined brain plasticity directly in neurodevelopmental disorders. One reason for this is the fact that brain-imaging techniques (functional Magnetic Resonance Imaging [fMRI]; see Chapters 3 and 4 for further details) require participants to either be still for a long time, remain in a confined space and be within spaces where there is a lot of noise. These factors cause difficulties for participants with high anxiety or high sensitivity to sounds (e.g. WS) or hyperactivity (e.g. ADHD), especially for very young individuals with these disorders. Currently, Electroencepholegram (EEG) is the dominant neuroimaging technique that has been used to study brain activation in people with neurodevelopmental disorders (although even EEG can be problematic for those who do not like to be touched, such as those with ASD). This is because it tolerates participant movement and is relatively uninvasive. However, whilst this has high temporal resolution, spatial resolution is poor, particularly compared to the knowledge about localisation of brain activation that can be gained from fMRI. Yet, newer technologies such as functional Near Infrared Spectoscopy (fNIRS) are now becoming more widely available. fNIRS, like fMRI, uses haemodynamic response to measure brain activation, and yet it uses a similar experimental set-up to EEG and thus can be tolerated from infancy (a cloth head band with probes attached is worn by the participant). Whilst fNIRS cannot provide structural information, it provides functional information with higher temporal resolution than fMRI and better spatial resolution than EEG, with minimal interference from participants' movements (see Lloyd-Fox, Blasi & Elwell, 2010 for a review; Chapter 4 provides a detailed discussion of the advantages and use of fNIRS). Increased use of this technique might allow more studies to be carried out which will further our understanding about behaviour and plasticity over time in neurodevelopmental disorders. Yet it needs to be ensured that these studies are hypothesis-driven, as just investigating differences in brain activation and brain anatomy are not informative (Filippi & Karmiloff-Smith, 2013).

Second, it is not always possible to investigate which domain-general abilities present early in life can affect cognitive ability later in development due to the fact that some neurodevelopmental disorders cannot be diagnosed very early in development. This is especially the case for those disorders that rely on a behavioural clinical diagnosis such as ASD, ADHD and SLI. However, the fact that these disorders are likely to be genetic, and thus run in families, allows investigation of groups that are at risk of being diagnosed later on in life. For example, research from younger siblings of those already diagnosed with ASD has identified deficits from the second year of life in both social and non-social domains. For example, children who go on to develop ASD show reduced use of, and a reduced repertoire of, gestures during their second year. Similarly, from about six months, the developmental trajectory for social responsiveness (face gazing, social smiling) begins to drop away from the typical trajectory, whilst receptive language delays are observed from 12 months in those who are diagnosed with ASD at 36 months (see Chapter 7 for further discussion on studying at-risk groups). Deficits in executive function and motor skills have also been reported (see Jones, Gliga, Bedford, Charman & Johnson, 2014, for a review). Although studying at-risk groups allows examination of early precursors in development and enables theoretical accounts of the disorder to be refined, which might help to diagnose certain neurodevelopmental disorders earlier than can currently be done, there are a number of children in at-risk groups that do not develop the neurodevelopmental disorder later in life, yet equally do not demonstrate typical performance (see Rogers, 2009 for an overview). Therefore, more research within this area is needed to provide a better understanding of these at-risk children and how their genetic and environmental factors differ from those who do meet the criteria for the neurodevelopmental disorder later in life (see also Chapters 2 and 8).

1.3.2 The need for accurate diagnosis and issues with variability and comorbidity

As mentioned previously, although by definition neurodevelopmental disorders have a genetic origin, the genetic markers for some of the disorders are currently unknown or may be particularly complex and multifactorial. For these disorders, diagnosis relies upon observed behaviours by a clinician and parental reports. This has caused some issues as often different clinicians and researchers use different diagnostic criteria which prevents direct comparison between studies. For example, some researchers categorise individuals with Developmental Coordination Disorder as children with motor abilities at or below the 5th percentile (Tsai, Wilson & Wu, 2008), while other researchers use the 15th percentile as a cut-off (Dewey, Cantell & Crawford, 2007). Another concern is the fact that diagnostic criteria change over time. For example, in the DSM-IV, ASD were specified as a triad of impairments in social interaction, impaired social communication and restricted behaviours. Yet, in the newer DSM-5 this triad has been reduced to impairments in two areas: impaired social interaction and communication are now considered as one area of difficulty, while restricted behaviours form the second area of difficulty. Although this change reflects previous findings that the development of language and social abilities are interdependent, it has lead to concerns about comparability between past and future studies. For example, a study by Worley and Matson (2012) found that of 180 children aged three to sixteen years old who met the diagnosis for ASD using DSM-IV criteria, only 121 met the diagnosis using the DSM-5 criteria. Yet, the children who did not meet the criteria for ASD still scored higher than TD controls on a measure that assessed ASD symptoms and they did not differ from those children who did still meet ASD criteria when using DSM-5. However, children who met diagnosis using DSM-5 showed more severe difficulties for non-verbal communication and socialisation than those who did not meet the ASD diagnosis using DSM-5. In addition, Asperger's syndrome was undiagnosed in the DSM criteria until 1994. The new DSM-5 criteria no longer allow a distinction between those diagnosed with high functioning ASD and those with Asperger's syndrome. Not only do these changes have important clinical implications, they also affect comparisons between studies and the development of causal frameworks for ASD.

Furthermore, even when genetic origins are known, such as is the case in WS and DS, the size of the genetic deletion often varies or the diagnosis can be the result of different genetic mutations. For example, it is well known that in the vast majority of individuals (e.g. 95 per cent of individuals) DS is caused by trisomy on chromosome 21. However, in a few cases DS can also be caused by mosaicism or a translocation of the genes on the same chromosome (Capone, 2001). The impact of these different origins on diagnosis and behavioural outcomes has been the focus of minimal research and is therefore poorly understood. In addition, recent discoveries in the genetic make-up of typically developing individuals have shown that healthy controls show frequent breakages and deletions within their genetic make-up (1000 Genomes Project Consortium, 2012). Yet, these do not necessarily result in any atypical behaviour or cognitive impairment. This demonstrates that discovering the genetic origins of cognitive and behavioural impairments is a complicated issue and implies that the genetic origin of many neurodevelopmental disorders of currently unknown aetiology (such as ASD, ADHD and SLI) are likely to be multifactorial rather than caused by a defect on a single chromosome as is the case in WS or DS (Bishop, 2006; Tripp & Wickens, 2009). In addition, we also know that environmental issues can affect gene expression and cognitive development early on which makes the task of unravelling genetic origins even more complicated (for a further discussion of environmental influences on development see Chapters 2, 5 and 8).

Other issues that complicate diagnosis and affect research are variability and comorbidity (see further discussion in Chapters 7 and 9). One general question related to variability that mainly affects causal frameworks of neurodevelopmental disorders is whether they are qualitatively different from typically developing populations or whether wide variability within the general population is the norm, with the behaviour observed in neurodevelopmental disorders being at different end points of these continuums. A second issue with variability affects research outcomes more directly and includes the suggestion that there is large variability in cognitive and behavioural outcomes within specific neurodevelopmental disorders (e.g. within disorder heterogeneity). For example, studies of ADHD have shown that not all people with ADHD have problems with attentional control (Nigg, Willcutt, Doyle & Sonuga-Barke, 2005). The issue of wide variability has also led to the discussion of different sub-groups. For example, van der Lely and colleagues have often argued that there is a sub-group of children with SLI who show specific grammatical impairments and therefore form a specific sub-sample of SLI (van der Lely & Marshall, 2011). Yet other studies have shown that although SLI form a heterogenous group, sub-groups are not stable over time and children often belong to more than one sub-group over development (Conti-Ramsden & Botting, 1999). In addition, studies that have investigated variability within neurodevelopmental disorders often find conflicting evidence and there is also variability within the TD population. Research has shown that the variability observed within WS for example, is not necessarily larger than the cognitive variability found within the general population (Van Herwegen, Rundblad, Davelaar & Annaz, 2011b). In a typical population problems of variability in research studies are often resolved through inclusion of large sample sizes. However, often large sample sizes are simply not available for neurodevelopmental disorders due to prevalence rates and thus variability might affect research outcomes in studies that include small sample sizes. Still, further research is required to examine whether variability is specific to, or larger in, neurodevelopmental disorders by examining variability in depth within specific disorders as well as across different syndromes. Additional questions that need to be explored include: 1) where the variability comes from and whether it originates from small genetic differences or from differences of environmental factors, or an interaction between the two; and 2) how variability affects diagnosis and whether we should view developmental disorders on a continuum instead of using specific classifications and discrete categories.

Linked to the use and controversy of discrete categories, there is considerable overlap or co-existence of phenotypical outcomes across different neurodevelopmental disorders, which is often referred to as comorbidity (Gillberg, 2010). For example, it is well-known that participants with DS often have memory difficulties, especially for short-term memory, from birth onwards (see Chapter 11 for a detailed discussion). However, recent studies have shown that a number of people with DS as young as 40 years of age develop symptoms that are similar to Alzheimer's disease (AD: Stanton & Coetzee, 2004). This begs the question for older DS participants whether memory problems are still symptomatic of DS itself, or whether these difficulties are caused by the early onset of AD. Another example of comorbidity (see Chapter 9 for a discussion) is the fact that most neurodevelopmental disorders (such as WS, ADHD, ASD and DS) show attention difficulties which in some cases leads to a dual diagnosis (for example WS with ADHD or ASD with ADHD). Finally, recent research has questioned the shared symptomatology of comorbid diagnoses, for example ASD, when paired with different primary disorders. Moss and colleagues (in press, a, b) reported that 65 per cent of their sample with Cornelia de Lange syndrome (CdLS) and 26 per cent of their DS sample met criterion for ASD, but that each group demonstrated subtle differences in ASD characteristics. For example, the individuals with CdLS showed less repetitive behaviour and more gestures than an ASD only group, whilst those with DS were less withdrawn from their surroundings than an ASD only group. This has strong implications for how we conceptualise overlapping symptoms and overlapping diagnoses across disorder groups. Questions of comorbidity are important for the development of causal frameworks but also for the type of training or intervention that should be administered. For instance, if comorbidity is the norm in neurodevelopmental disorders should we use specific categories and classification, or should we talk about a continuum instead (as previously noted)? In addition, comorbidity creates difficulties for finding the cause of neurodevelopmental disorders, as it is unclear in such cases what factors are *causal* to the disorders and which ones solely form risk factors. To obtain a better understanding of comorbidity a more precise description of the similarities and differences between developmental disorders (e.g. increased knowledge of syndrome-specificity) is required. This increased knowledge needs to include investigation of the comorbid symptoms at different levels, including genetic, neurobiological, cognitive, and behavioural similarities/differences.

1.3.3 The need for theoretical-based interventions and issues of complexity and cumulative risk

As discussed, one of the main aims of research within the field of neurodevelopmental disorders is to help people and families diagnosed with a disorder, through the use of training programmes or intervention studies. Before intervention or training programmes can be developed it is important to understand causal factors and syndrome-specific phenomonology of a certain difficulty (see also Chapter 14 for a discussion of intervention studies). One area of development that has been well researched within TD, which has shaped the development of training and intervention studies in neurodevelopmental disorders, is reading ability. For example, a recent study by Burgoyne and colleagues (2012) examined the benefits of a reading programme delivered to over 50 participants with DS via teaching assistants. The training included both reading and language comprehension exercises and results showed that after 20 weeks children in the training group improved on a number of key measures (single word reading, letter–sound knowledge and phoneme blending) compared to those in the control group.

Although it is encouraging to see that training and intervention studies have a positive effect on performance levels in neurodevelopmental disorders, very few training and intervention programmes are based upon clear theoretical predictions. This prevents unambiguous explanations as to why certain children benefit more from training or intervention programmes compared to others, or what the underlying cognitive processes may be for any change that is observed. Further issues that have not yet been the focus of intervention studies are the timing of the interventions (within development), or the fact that different interventions might work better at different ages. For example, causal explanations for figurative language comprehension difficulties in ASD have been linked to: 1) weaker theory of mind abilities; 2) weak central coherence; 3) word knowledge; and 4) executive functioning abilities (Martin & McDonald, 2003). However, there is variable evidence for these four different theories and as a result it is unclear which area should be the focus of intervention or training to support figurative language comprehension in ASD. One possibility that has not been considered is that different abilities may have important impacts on the development of figurative language at different times during development. Seeing the complexity of development, it is rather likely that a number of issues or difficulties will affect the development of a certain cognitive ability or that failure is cumulative.

Related to the issue of cumulative failure is the fact that very few models, and therefore also training and intervention studies, have taken environmental issues into account. For example, studies with TD groups have shown that socio-economic status, parental rearing styles and sleep are factors that affect cognitive development and intervention success (Hackman & Farah, 2009). These factors have almost entirely been neglected within cognitive research and intervention programmes with neurodevelopmental disorder groups. Yet, as discussed within the causal model by Morton and Frith (1995), environmental factors are likely to affect all levels of development and thus they are also likely to affect outcomes for interventions. In addition, investigation of which specific environmental factors affect development will advance theoretical understanding and diagnosis, allowing further discrimination between disadvantage versus impairment.

1.4 Conclusions and future directions

Numerous studies have been carried out within the field of neurodevelopmental disorders, especially over the past decade (Bishop & Rutter, 2006). Although this surge in research has improved our understanding of neurodevelopmental disorders, and consequently has facilitated the development of theoretical and causal frameworks, research faces several methodological difficulties that directly impact on the accurate diagnosis of disorders. We have focussed on issues of variability and comorbidity which often result in issues with diagnosis, with a knock-on effect on causal explanations and intervention programmes, and in practical issues when it comes to using a developmental approach.

One of the research challenges that remains is the fact that neurodevelopmental disorders are often rare and therefore research studies may include a small sample size for practical reasons, such as cost and time efficiency. For example, a review by Martens and colleagues (2008) has shown that the median sample size for studies across different domains of functioning in WS ranged from six to seventeen participants (Martens, Wilson & Reuters, 2008; with the exception of studies using parental reports of behaviour). The authors noted that this issue of small sample size was especially evident in research published prior to 2000. Small sample size is rarely addressed in studies of neurodevelopmental disorders, with the notion that this is 'okay' due to the rarity of some disorders. Yet, researchers ought to ask more questions about how the small sample sizes affect issues of variability and causal explanations, let alone statistics power. One solution researchers in the field might want to consider, is to work together and combine research groups to ensure larger sample sizes can be achieved.

However, there is also a need for more case studies that look into children who have responded and who have not responded to treatments and interventions, in order to get a better understanding of how interventions work and why they do so (see for example Griffiths & Stuart, 2013). Single case designs have a great deal to offer here. In addition, there should also be more focus on the long-term outcomes of intervention programmes to ensure that benefits are maintained over time. In addition, case studies, especially those of partial deletion patients or those who have atypical genetic deletions, will allow a better insight into the genotype–phenotype relations and causal explanation frameworks (Karmiloff-Smith et al., 2012b).

A better understanding of causal models and theoretical explanations, as well as the success of intervention studies, will also require more cross-syndrome comparison studies (see for example Chapter 12). Cross-syndrome comparisons allow investigation of syndrome-specific versus syndrome-general difficulties. For example, FXS and WS both show attention difficulties but comparisons of the error patterns shows clear differences between the two syndromes; with those with FXS making more 'repetitions' and those with WS making more 'distractor errors' (Scerif, Cornish, Wilding, Driver & Karmiloff-Smith, 2004, 2007). Cross-syndrome comparison studies show clear evidence that similar behavioural outcomes can be caused by different underlying problems, which require different remedial strategies and interventions. In addition, advances in computational modelling (see Chapter 5) as well as notational methods (see Chapter 6) will be crucial to further our understanding of neurodevelopmental disorders.

Finally, future studies should also consider looking at environmental differences (see examples in Chapters 2 and 8), including cultural differences, and compare research outcomes across different countries. A number of neurodevelopmental disorders rely upon behavioural diagnoses. These diagnoses depend upon the methods used, as well as the training standards and values of the clinician. These are likely to be culturally different and may explain varying prevalence rates across different countries (see Norbury and Sparks, 2013, for a discussion of cultural approaches to neurodevelopmental disorders). Therefore, cross-cultural studies, especially those that include population studies, will allow for a better understanding of environmental factors and cultural differences that impact on prevalence rates, diagnosis and treatments of neurodevelopmental disorders. However, such studies themselves will involve a number of methodological issues and challenges.

Practical tips

1. Check carefully for variability within data and consider further examination of case studies as these can provide vital information for causal frameworks.
2. Consider environmental differences between groups, as it is possible that even within a certain culture approaches to atypical groups are different to those of typically developing controls – which will impact on developmental outcomes and research results.
3. Importantly, consider collaborations with other researchers to increase sample sizes and reduce methodological issues such as variability, or even to obtain longitudinal results.

References

1000 Genomes Project Consortium (2012). An integrated map of genetic variation from 1,092 human genomes. *Nature, 491*(7422), 56–65.

Annaz, D., Karmiloff-Smith, A., Johnson, M. H. & Thomas, M. S. C. (2009). A cross-syndrome study of the development of holistic face recognition in children with autism, Down syndrome, and Williams syndrome. *Journal of Experimental Child Psychology, 102*, 456–486.

Ansari, D., Donlan, C., Thomas, M. S. C., Ewing, S. A., Peen, T. & Karmiloff-Smith, A. (2003). What makes counting count? Verbal and visuo-spatial contributions to typical and atypical number development. *Journal of Experimental Child Psychology, 85*, 50–62.

Ansari, D., Donlan, C. & Karmiloff-Smith, A. (2007). Typical and atypical development of visual estimation abilities. *Cortex, 43*, 758–768.

Bishop, D. M. V. (2006). What causes Specific Language Impairment in children? *Current Directions in Psychological Science, 15*, 217–221.

Bishop, D. & Rutter, M. (2006). Neurodevelopmental disorders: Conceptual issues. In: D. Bishop, D. Pine, M. Rutter, S. Scott, J. Stevenson, E. Taylor & A. Thapar (eds), *Rutter's Child and Adolescent Psychiatry, Fifth Edition* (pp. 32–41). Oxford: Blackwell.

Burgoyne, K., Duff, F. J., Clarke, P. J., Buckley, S., Snowling, M. J. & Hulme, C. (2012). Efficacy of a reading and language intervention for children with Down syndrome: a randomized controlled trial. *Journal of Child Psychology & Psychiatry, 53*, 1044–1053.

Capone, G. (2001). Down syndrome: advances in molecular biology and the neurosciences. *Journal of Developmental & Behavioral Pediatrics, 22*, 40–59.

Conti-Ramsden, G. & Botting, N. (1999). Classification of children with Specific Language Impairment. *Journal of Speech, Language, and Hearing Research, 42*, 1195–1204.

Cornish, K., Cole, V., Longhi, E., Karmiloff-Smith, A. & Scerif, G. (2013). Mapping developmental trajectories of attention and working memory in fragile X syndrome: Developmental freeze or developmental change? *Development and Psychopathology, 25*, 365–376.

Dewey, D., Cantell, M. & Crawford, S. G. (2007). Motor and gestural performance in children with autism spectrum disorders, developmental coordination disorder, and/or attention deficit hyperactivity disorder. *Journal of the International Neuropsychological Society, 13*, 246–256.

Dewind, N. K. & Brannon, E. M. (2012). Malleability of the approximate number system: effects of feedback and training. *Frontiers in Human Neuroscience, 6*, 1–10.

Dunn, L., Dunn, L., Whetton, C. & Burley, J. (1997). *British Picture Vocabulary Scale II.* Windsor: NFER-Nelson.

Farran, E. K. & Karmiloff-Smith, A. (2012). *Neurodevelopmental Disorders Across the Lifespan: A Neuroconstructivist Approach.* Oxford, UK: Oxford University Press.

Feigenson, L., Dehaene, S. & Spelke, E. (2004). Core systems of number. *Trends in Cognitive Science, 8*, 307–314.

Filippi, R. & Karmiloff-Smith, A. (2013). What can developmental disorders teach us about typical development? In C. R. Marshall (ed.), *Current Issues in Developmental Disorders* (pp. 193–209). London, UK: Psychology Press.

Fodor, J. A. (1983). *Modularity of Mind: An Essay on Faculty Psychology.* Cambridge, MA: MIT Press.

Gillberg, C. (2010). The ESSENCE in child psychiatry: Early symptomatic syndromes eliciting neurodevelopmental clinical examinations. *Research in Developmental Disabilities, 31*, 1543–1551.

Griffiths, Y. & Stuart, M. (2013). Reviewing evidence-based practice for pupils with dyslexia and literacy difficulties. *Journal of Research in Reading, 36*, 96–116.

Gunn, D. M. & Jarrold, C. (2004). Raven's matrices performance in Down Syndrome: Evidence of unusual errors. *Research in Developmental Disabilities, 25*, 443–457.

Hackman, D. A. & Farah, M. J. (2009). Socioeconomic status and the developing brain. *Trends in Cognitive Science, 13*, 65–73.

Huttenlocher, P. R. (2002). *Neural Plasticity: The Effects of Environment on the Development of the Cerebral Cortex.* Cambridge, MA: Harvard University Press.

Jones, E. J. H., Gliga, T., Bedford, R., Charman, T. & Johnson, M. H. (2014). Developmental pathways to autism: a review of prospective studies of infants at risk. *Neuroscience & Biobehavioral Reviews, 39*, 1–33.

Karmiloff-Smith, A. (1998). Development itself is the key to understanding developmental disorders. *Trends in Cognitive Sciences, 2*, 389–398.

——(2009). Nativism versus neuroconstructivism: Rethinking the study of developmental disorders. *Developmental Psychology, 45*, 56–63.

Karmiloff-Smith, A., Scerif, G. & Ansari, D. (2003). Double dissociations in developmental disorders? Theoretically misconceived, empirically dubious. *Cortex, 39*, 161–163.

Karmiloff-Smith, A., D'Souza, D., Dekker, T., Van Herwegen, J., Xu, F., Rodic, M. & Ansari, D. (2012a). Genetic and environmental vulnerabilities: the importance of cross-syndrome comparisons. *PNAS, 190*(2), 17261–17265.

Karmiloff-Smith, A., Broadbent, H., Farran, E. K., Longhi, E., D'Souza, D., … Sansbury, F. (2012b). Social cognition in Williams syndrome: genotype/phenotype insights from partial deletion patients. *Frontiers in Psychology, 3*, 1–8.

Laing, E., Butterworth, G., Ansari, D., Gsödl, M., Longhi, E., Panagiotaki, G., … Karmiloff-Smith, A. (2002). Atypical development of language and social communication in toddlers with Williams sydnrome. *Developmental Science, 5*(2), 233–246.

Little, K., Riby, D. M., Janes, E., Fleck, R., Clark, F. & Rogers, J. (2013). Heterogeneity of social approach behaviours in Williams syndrome. *Research in Developmental Disabilities, 34*, 959–967.

Lloyd-Fox, S., Blasi, A. & Elwell, C. E. (2010). Illuminating the developing brain: The past, present and future of functional near infrared spectroscopy. *Neuroscience and Biobehavioural Reviews, 34*(3), 269–284.

Martens, M. A., Wilson, S. J. & Reuters, D. C. (2008). Research review: Williams syndrome: a critical review of the cognitive, behavioral, and neuroanatomical phonotype. *Journal of Child Psychology and Psychiatry, 49*(6), 576–608.

Martin, I. & McDonald, S. (2003). Weak coherence, no theory of mind, or executive dysfunction? Solving the puzzle of pragmatic language disorders. *Brain and Language, 85*, 451–466.

Morton, J. & Frith, U. (1995). Causal modeling: Structural approaches to developmental psychopathology. In D. Cicchetti & D. Cohen (eds), *Developmental Psychopathology* (pp. 357–390). New York, NY: Wiley.

Moss, J., Howlin, P., Magiati, I. & Oliver, C. (in press, a). Characteristics of Autism Spectrum Disorder in Cornelia de Lange syndrome. *Journal of Child Psychiatry and Psychology*.

Moss, J., Richards, C., Nelson, L. & Oliver, C. (in press, b). Prevalence and behavioural characteristics of autism spectrum disorder in Down syndrome. *Autism: International Journal of Research and Practice*.

Nigg, J. T., Willcutt, E. G., Doyle, A. E. & Sonuga-Barke, E. J. S. (2005). Causal heterogeneity in Attention-Deficit/Hyperactivity Disorder: Do we need neuropsychologically impaired subtypes? *Biological Psychiatry, 57*, 1224–1230.

Norbury, C. F. & Sparks, A. (2013). Difference or disorder? Cultural issues in understanding neurodevelopmental disorders. *Developmental Psychology, 49*, 45–58.

Park, J. & Brannon, E. M. (2013). Training the approximate number system improves math proficiency. *Psychological Science, 24*, 2013–2019.

Paterson, S. J., Girelli, L., Butterworth, B. & Karmiloff-Smith, A. (2006). Are numerical impairments syndrome specific? Evidence from Williams syndrome and Down's syndrome. *Journal of Child Psychology and Psychiatry, 47*, 190–204.

Pinker, S. (1999). *Words and Rules*. New York: Harper Perennial.

Raven, J. C., Court, J. H. & Raven, J. C. (1990). *Manual for Raven's Progressive Matrices and Vocabulary Scales – Section 2: Coloured Progressive Matrices*. Oxford, UK: Oxford Psychologists Press.

Rogers, S. (2009). What are infant siblings teaching us about autism in infancy? *Autism Research, 2*, 125–137.

Scerif, G., Cornish, K., Wilding, J., Driver, J. & Karmiloff-Smith, A. (2004). Visual search in typically developing toddlers and toddlers with fragile X or Williams syndrome. *Developmental Science, 7*, 116–130.

——(2007). Delineation of early attentional control difficulties in fragile X syndrome: Focus on neurocomputational mechanisms. *Neuropsychologia, 45*, 1889–1898.

Spelke, E. S. & Kinzler, K. D. (2007). Core knowledge. *Developmental Science, 10*, 89–96.

Stanton, L. R. & Coetzee, R. H. (2004). Down's syndrome and dementia. *Advances in Psychiatric Treatment, 10*, 50–58.

Thomas, M.S.C. (2003). Limits on plasticity. *Journal of Cognition and Development, 4*, 95–121.

Thomas, M. S. C., Annaz, D., Ansari, D., Serif, G., Jarrold, C. & Karmiloff-Smith, A. (2009). Using developmental trajectories to understand developmental disorders. *Journal of Speech, Language, and Hearing Research, 52*, 336–358.

Thomas, M. S. C., Baughman, F. D., Karaminis, T. & Addyman, C. (2012). Modeling development disorders. In C. Marshall (ed.), *Current Issues in Developmental Disorders* (pp. 93–124). London, UK: Psychology Press.

Thomas, M. S. C., Purser, H. & Van Herwegen, J. (2012). The developmental trajectories approach to cognition. In E. K. Farran & A. Karmiloff-Smith (eds), *Neurodevelopmental Disorders Across The Lifespan: A Neuroconstructivist Approach* (pp. 13–35). Oxford, UK: Oxford University Press.

Tripp, G. & Wickens, J. R. (2009). Neurobiology of ADHD. *Neuropharmacology, 57*, 579–589.

Tsai, C.-L., Wilson, P. H. & Wu, S. K. (2008). Role of visual-perceptual skills (non-motor) in children with developmental coordination disorder. *Human Movement Science, 27*, 649–664.

van der Lely, H. K. & Marshall, C. R. (2011). Grammatical-specific language impairment: A window onto domain specificity. In J. Gouendouzi, F. Loncke & M. J. Williams (eds), *The Handbook of Psycholinguistics and Cognitive Processes: Perspectives in Communication Disorders* (pp. 401–418). New York: Psychology Press.

Van Herwegen, J., Costa, H. M. & Passolunghi, M. (submitted). Improving number abilities in preschoolers: the preschool number learning scheme PLUS.

Van Herwegen, J., Farran, E. & Annaz, D. (2011a). Item and error analysis on Raven's Coloured Progressive Matrices in Williams syndrome. *Research in Developmental Disabilities, 32*(1), 93–99.

Van Herwegen, J., Rundblad, G., Davelaar, E. J. & Annaz, D. (2011b). Variability and standardised test profiles in typically developing children and children with Williams syndrome. *British Journal of Developmental Psychology, 29*, 883–894.

Worley, J. A. & Matson, J. L. (2012). Comparing symptoms of autism spectrum disorders using the current DSM-IV-TR diagnostic criteria and the proposed DSM-V diagnostic criteria. *Research in Autism Spectrum Disorders, 6*, 965–970.

2

WHY DEVELOPMENT MATTERS IN NEURODEVELOPMENTAL DISORDERS

George Ball and Annette Karmiloff-Smith

2.1 Why is the adult neuropsychological model inappropriate for understanding neurodevelopmental disorders?

Paradoxically, numerous studies of infants and children are not developmental at all, because they take static snapshots, targeting a specific age group. A truly developmental perspective embraces a developmental way of thinking, regardless of the age of the population studied (Karmiloff-Smith, 1992, 1998). Even research on infants can be non-developmental, simply examining performance in, for example, five-month-olds, whereas some studies of adults are developmental, because they focus on change over time (Cornish et al., 2008; Tyler et al., 2009).

In other words, neuro-cognitive development is dynamic across the entire lifespan, and there is no static end state. Indeed, to understand ontogenetic development in atypical or typical individuals, it is vital to trace developmental trajectories across time (Karmiloff-Smith, 1998; Cornish, Scerif & Karmiloff-Smith, 2007), to assess progressive change from infancy onwards at the genetic, neural, cognitive and behavioural levels, including the role of the environment, and to pinpoint how parts of the developing system may interact with other parts differently at different times across ontogenesis (Karmiloff-Smith, 1998; Steele, Brown & Scerif, 2012). A process that is vital, say, at Time 2 may no longer play a role at Time 5. Yet, its delay at Time 2 may have been crucial to a healthy developmental trajectory and outcome, because of its interactions with other parts of the developing system (Karmiloff-Smith, 1998). Indeed, developmental timing is among the most important of factors that must be taken into account when trying to understand human development, particularly in the case of neurodevelopmental disorders.

This is why, in our view, the adult neuropsychological model is inappropriate for explaining neurodevelopmental disorders. Adult models tend to be static, whereas neurodevelopmental disorders require a dynamic approach that focuses on trajectories and how they change over time (Thomas et al., 2009). Thus, we need to distinguish between the develop*ed* brain and the develop*ing* brain (Karmiloff-Smith, 2010; Karmiloff-Smith et al., 2012a). Take the case of Williams syndrome (WS), a neurogenetic syndrome involving the hemizygous deletion of some 28 genes on chromosome 7. The fusiform face area (FFA) is particularly large in volume compared to the rest of the WS brain, and adolescents and adults with WS are very proficient at face processing tasks (Karmiloff-Smith et al., 2004). There are two possible explanations, one drawn from the adult neuropsychological approach, the other from a developmental perspective. The first would argue that the large FFA in WS *causes* the face processing proficiency – a brain-to-behaviour explanation. The second, by contrast, would argue that the unusual infant focus on faces in WS influences the enlargement of the FFA over time – a bidirectional brain-to-behaviour-to-brain *interaction*. Only a truly developmental approach can address such alternatives. But where does the WS infant fascination with faces stem from? Could this be 'caused' by an early difference in the FFA? Or, is the following *developmental* scenario more likely? In the last three months of intra-uterine life the foetus does a great deal of auditory processing and recognises the intonation patterns of its mother's voice at birth (Hepper, Scott & Shahidullah, 1993). In the early years, infants with WS tend to pay particular attention to auditory input (Mervis, Morris, Bertrand & Robinson, 1999). What is the first sound that the baby hears at birth? Usually it is its mother's voice. Locating the voice would orient the baby to the mother's face, which would display smiles and other encouraging stimuli. So, it is possible that the WS infant's fascination with faces – a visual stimulus – stems from an earlier fascination with voices – an auditory stimulus – in combination with problems with visual disengagement and a heightened social drive (Frigerio et al., 2006; Riby & Hancock, 2008). Thus, the visual fixation on faces could initially derive from attention to the auditory modality and thence drive the progressive enlargement of the FFA. While this hypothesis may turn out to be inaccurate, we believe that it is an illustration of a vital *developmental* way of thinking when trying to explain neurodevelopmental disorders.

Later in Section 2.4, we provide a second example of how similar data across two syndromes (WS and Down syndrome [DS]) can seem to replicate the double dissociation approach of adult neuropsychology, isolating two numerical systems (see discussion from Chapter 1). However, the explanations for these differing patterns in the two neurodevelopmental disorders are not due to impaired versus intact numerical modules. Rather, they are rooted in differences in earlier, more basic-level processes, such as saccadic eye movement planning and attention, which affect number as well as other cognitive domains over developmental time differently in each syndrome (see Section 2.4 below for more detail). Indeed, we advocate that any time a seeming dissociation is found in adolescents or adults with neurodevelopmental disorders, it is crucial to trace such cognitive-level outcomes back to their basic-level processes in early development and to consider their cascading effects over developmental time.

2.2 Developmental change counts in mapping genotype to phenotype

Many studies map specific genes to specific behavioural phenotypes, but rare are those that take account of changing gene expression over time. Yet, if a gene is expressed widely initially and becomes increasingly confined to certain brain regions, then the mapping from gene to phenotype will change (Karmiloff-Smith et al., 2012b). Developmental time – or what Elman and collaborators called 'chronotopic constraints' (Elman et al., 1996) – plays a crucial role, even in monogenic disorders. Take, for example, Fragile X syndrome (FXS), which is associated with the silencing of a single gene, whose protein product, FMRP, is involved in the regulation of multiple cascading processes leading to activity-dependent changes in dendritic spine morphology and synaptic regulation across cortex. FMRP is highly expressed in both foetal and adult brain tissues, but it interacts with multiple other proteins, a process which changes over developmental time. In adult cerebellum and cerebral cortex, FMRP and two of these proteins are co-localised. In the foetus, as in the adult, FMRP is located in cytoplasm, but in the foetus only one of the collaborating proteins is strongly expressed in the nucleus (Scerif & Karmiloff-Smith, 2005). Thus, FMRP is likely to collaborate with sets of proteins in undifferentiated foetal neurones, which are different from those with which it interacts in differentiated adult neurones. These complex interactions suggest that a single gene dysfunction can initiate multiple cascading effects on cellular, neural and cognitive phenotypes that vary across developmental time (see also Chapter 10 for a detailed discussion of FMRP in FXS).

The importance of considering developmental change in mapping genotype to neural phenotype may also be seen in the phenotypic trajectories of neurogenetic disorders such as Down syndrome (DS). DS, or trisomy 21, is caused in most cases by a non-disjunction after conception, resulting in an extra copy of chromosome 21. It has been argued that the DS genotype particularly impairs the development of late developing neural systems such as the hippocampus and prefrontal cortex (Edgin, 2013; Nadel, 1986). For example, while the density of myelinated fibres in hippocampal regions of neonates is somewhat reduced relative to typically developing controls, this hippocampal difference in density increases progressively throughout childhood and into early adulthood, resulting in much larger relative differences further down the developmental trajectory (Ábrahám et al., 2012). Such developmental findings might explain why, relative to typical controls, no hippocampal volume reduction is reported in the first year of life (Pennington, Moon, Edgin, Stedron & Nadel, 2003) but is routinely identified in older children (Carducci et al., 2013; Jernigan, Bellugi, Sowell, Doherty & Hesselink, 1993; Pinter et al., 2001) and in adults (Aylward et al., 1999; Kesslak, Nagata, Lott & Nalcioglu, 1994; Raz, Torres, Briggs & Spencer, 1995). Thus, when mapping the DS genotype to the DS brain, consideration must be given to changes that occur in the neural profile across developmental time.

Development is also important when mapping genotype to cognitive phenotypic outcomes. Continuing with the above example from DS that reveals progressive delay in hippocampal development, the described neural trajectory also fits with findings in the cognitive domain. Interestingly, hippocampal-dependent processes, such as episodic memory and spatial learning, are severely impaired in adolescents and young adults with DS relative to implicit and working memory processes (Pennington et al., 2003; Vicari, Bellucci & Carlesimo, 2000). Crucially, however, a developmental trajectory approach does not automatically assume that this dissociation at the cognitive level is present in the same form earlier in the developmental trajectory. Indeed, Rast and Meltzoff (1995) found that two-year-olds with DS showed strength in memory for episodically defined events relative to their acquisition of object permanence for instance (see also Paterson, Brown, Gsödl, Johnson & Karmiloff-Smith, 1999, for similar differences between the start and end states for language and number in DS and WS).

Clearly, more in-depth research on the early cognitive profile of each neurodevelopmental disorder would better inform our understanding of their full developmental trajectories, but any account of genotype to phenotype mappings should be sensitive to possible changes in gene expression and cognitive phenotype over developmental time. Snapshots of a cognitive phenotype at Time 6, for instance, may tell the researcher nothing about the state of that cognitive phenotype at Time 1, unless considered within the context of development. Figure 2.1

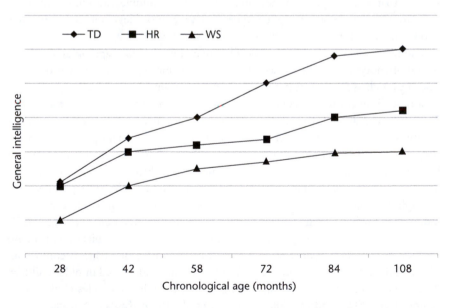

FIGURE 2.1 General intelligence scores of HR, a child with partial deletion WS, average general intelligence scores of typically developing children and of children with WS (full deletion), from chronological ages 28 to 108 months. (Unpublished figure, reproduced from conference presentations by Karmiloff-Smith.)

illustrates this point. It plots the longitudinal trajectory of a child (HR) with a partial deletion of some 23 of the 28 genes in the WS critical region (Karmiloff-Smith et al., 2003, 2012b; Tassabehji et al., 1999, 2005) with respect to her general intelligence scores from chronological age 28 months (Time 1) to 108 months (Time 6), together with the average general intelligence trajectories of typically developing (TD) children and those with the full WS deletion for comparison. It is clear that HR's general intelligence scores were at the same level as typically developing children at 28 months but became progressively impaired over developmental time, such that by 108 months, HR's general intelligence score was markedly below TD children, although still higher than the average child with WS of the same chronological age. Had one taken a snapshot and drawn conclusions about genotype/phenotype relations when HR was 28 months, the conclusion would have been that her deleted genes had no impact on general intelligence. By contrast, examining the graph seven years later at 108 months, it is clear that she is seriously impaired, although not as severely as children with the full WS deletion, highlighting the importance of taking account of full developmental trajectories over time when mapping genotype to phenotype.

2.3 Developmental change counts in mapping brain to cognition

The cognitive phenotype of WS is characterised by relatively skilled language, a strong drive for social interaction, and proficient face-processing abilities, with scores falling within the normal range on standardised face processing tasks, like the Rivermead Face Memory Task (Wilson et al., 2008) and the Benton Facial Recognition Test (Benton, Sivan, Hamsher, Varney & Spreen, 1994), alongside very impaired spatial and numerical cognition (Karmiloff-Smith et al., 2004). The initial excitement about the syndrome stemmed from the identification of this uneven cognitive profile and the possibility that it might represent 'selective deficits of an otherwise normal modular system' (Clahsen & Temple, 2003, p. 347), with the modules for language and face processing considered intact and those for number and spatial cognition selectively impaired.

Electrophysiological studies of the WS brain have pointed to possible developmental arrest compared with the TD brain. Even in domains of relatively proficient behaviour, e.g. in face and language processing, the WS brain fails to become progressively specialised (Karmiloff-Smith, 2009), in contrast to the TD brain. Indeed, the TD brain initially processes incoming input bilaterally but, with development, a progressive specialisation and localisation of brain function emerges, giving rise to a shift to increasingly specialised hemispheric processing (predominantly right hemisphere for faces, predominantly left hemisphere for the morphosyntax of language: Casey, Giedd & Thomas, 2000; Choudhury & Benaisch, 2011; Durston et al., 2006; Johnson, 2001; Mills, Coffey-Corins & Neville, 1997; Minagawa-Kawai, Mori, Naoi & Kojima, 2007; de Haan, Pascalis & Johnson, 2002). By contrast, several studies have now shown that the WS brain tends to continue processing faces and language bilaterally, even in adulthood (Grice et al., 2001,

2003; Karmiloff-Smith et al., 2004; Mills et al., 2000; Neville, Mills & Bellugi, 1994, see also examples in Chapter 3). In other words, whereas the TD brain presents with a gradual specialisation and hemispheric localisation of function over developmental time, this does not seem to occur in the development of the WS brain (Karmiloff-Smith, 2009). Moreover, in TD brains the temporal signature for faces becomes increasingly specific over developmental time, whereas WS brains tend to process faces, cars and other objects with the same temporal signature (Grice et al., 2001; Karmiloff-Smith, 2009; see also Golarai et al., 2010, for similar differences between TD and WS neural processing in fMRI studies).

Therefore, even when individuals with WS score in the normal range, such as on standardised face processing tasks, this does not mean a selective 'sparing', because it has been shown that the cognitive and neural processes underlying the proficient behaviour are different from those of TD controls (Karmiloff-Smith et al., 2004).

2.4 The need to trace higher-level cognitive outcomes back to basic-level processes in infancy

Let us now take a concrete example of a cognitive domain – exact and approximate number – and the demonstration of a possible double dissociation in infancy, typical of the type found in studies of adult neuropsychology. Small exact number discrimination involves the computation of precise differences between one, two, three or four items. Large approximate number discrimination is the capacity to estimate whether two quantities (e.g. eight versus sixteen items) are different, without being able to count them, based on magnitude judgements. For example, studies of adult neuropsychological patients have yielded a double dissociation between numerical abilities, affecting two intra-parietal circuits – one for computing exact number, the other for computing approximate numerical quantities (Butterworth, 2010; Dehaene, 1997; Demeyere, Lestor & Humphreys, 2010).

Research on TD infants also yields two numerical sub-systems that develop at different rates (Brannon, 2006; Izard, Dehaene-Lambertz & Dehaene, 2008; Lipton & Spelke, 2003; Xu, 2003). Indeed, TD infants are able to discriminate small numbers (one, two, three) as early as three months, but it is several months later that they can discriminate large approximate quantities: at six months they differentiate eight from sixteen dots, i.e. a ratio of 1:2, and by nine to ten months they distinguish eight from twelve dots, a ratio of 2:3 (Brannon, Abbott & Lutz, 2004; Xu & Arriaga, 2007). In a series of studies examining small exact number discrimination and large approximate number discrimination in infants with DS and infants with WS (Karmiloff-Smith et al., 2012a; Paterson et al., 1999; Van Herwegen, Ansari, Xu & Karmiloff-Smith, 2008), we found that those with WS performed like TD controls on small number discrimination tasks, but showed significantly weaker discrimination of large approximate quantities. By contrast, infants with DS displayed the opposite pattern: they failed at small number discrimination but showed significant discrimination of large approximate quantities.

So, for the first time in research on infants with different neurogenetic syndromes, our studies yielded a double dissociation between small exact numbers and large approximate numbers, typical of the findings in adult neuropsychological patients. The results might therefore suggest that for WS, one or more of the 28 genes deleted on one copy of chromosome 7q11.23 contribute to a domain-specific deficit in large approximate number discrimination while leaving intact the small number system, and for DS, one or more of the extra genes on chromosome 21 contribute to a domain-specific deficit in small exact number discrimination while sparing the large number system. However, notions like 'double dissociation', 'intact' and 'sparing' are drawn from the adult neuropsychological literature, describing a system in its mature state. Is this an appropriate model for a system in the process of gradual development? Or, as we believe, do these sub-systems *emerge* over time, through early cross-domain/cross-modality interactions, as different brain circuits progressively specialise for different numerical functions (Karmiloff-Smith, 1998, 2009; Simon, 1997)?

It is therefore imperative to assess how other processes might interact over developmental time with infant sensitivity to numerical displays. We thus drew on earlier data on infant/toddler attention and saccadic eye movement planning in the two syndromes (Brown et al., 2003) and related these to the WS and DS numerical findings (Karmiloff-Smith et al., 2012a). The attention studies identified deficits in both syndromes – deficits in attention shifting in WS, deficits in sustained attention in DS. In the saccadic eye movement study, infants/toddlers with DS showed similar patterns to TD infants, i.e. efficient albeit slower saccadic eye movement planning. By contrast, infants/toddlers with WS displayed severe eye movement planning deficits (Brown et al., 2003). We thus predicted that infants/toddlers with WS would be impaired in their scanning of large numerical displays. To examine this further, after the experiment proper, we collected eye-tracking data (Tobii, 2003) from infants with WS and DS while they were viewing numerical displays on the computer screen. A preliminary examination of scanning patterns of the infants who provided useful data indicated that, like in our studies of eye movement planning and attention (Brown et al., 2003), those with DS tended to scan the overall array, whereas those with WS tended to remain fixated on a few individual items (see illustrations of scanning patterns in Karmiloff-Smith et al., 2012a).

Thus, for WS, a serious deficit in rapid saccade planning (Brown et al., 2003; Karmiloff-Smith et al., 2012a) may cause problems in visually disengaging from individual objects in displays. This likely explains why they succeed at small exact number discrimination, yet have difficulty discriminating large approximate quantities because they do not scan them adequately. By contrast, the opposite holds for infants with DS, because they have difficulties with sustained attention (Krakow & Kopp, 1982; Casey & Riddle, 2012), which interferes with their precise individuation of objects in small displays but enhances their rapid global scanning of large displays.

Thus, rather than identifying a double dissociation of spared and impaired modules between the two syndromes, it turns out that a single but different basic-level problem for each syndrome – attention shifting in WS, sustained attention in DS – contributes to the explanation of *both* the numerical deficits *and* the numerical proficiencies in each syndrome. The findings therefore do not require an explanation solely in terms of selective, domain-specific number abilities, as might be the case in adult neuropsychological patients whose brains had by then become specialised in terms of two independently functioning numerical sub-systems. Rather, the syndrome-specific infant differences are likely to be traceable to basic-level deficits and proficiencies in the visual and attention systems early in development, which have cascading effects on cognitive-level outcomes over ontogenetic time. Furthermore, identification of these different basic-level problems in early development may be particularly useful in informing the planning of early syndrome-specific intervention.

2.5 Developmental change counts in understanding the impact of environmental factors

A question to emerge from studies of families with children with neurodevelopmental disorders is why the effects of positive environments are not greater. Indeed, unlike children from low SES environments, many children with neurogenetic syndromes who participate in academic research are well nourished, grow up in a caring environment, receive considerable cognitive stimulation and do not suffer the physical and mental abuses reported in some contexts of early social adversity (Meaney & Szyf, 2005; Liston, McEwen & Casey, 2009; Tomalski et al., 2013; Tottenham et al., 2010, 2011). For instance, we have recently shown that low SES has detrimental effects on the frontal cortex as early as six to nine months of age (Tomalski et al., 2013). So, why do positive environments not compensate for genetic vulnerabilities? Is it just the severity of the genetic mutations that constrains environmental effects? Or is this not only due to mutated genes, but also because early environments for such children differ in more subtle ways than is commonly realised? Indeed, having a neurodevelopmental disorder not only involves genetic mutations; it also changes the environment in which the atypical infant develops in multiple subtle ways. In our view, the moment a parent is informed that their child has a genetic disorder, the parent's behaviour necessarily subtly adapts. As a result, the baby's responses within the dyadic interaction will also be subtly modified, and these interactional effects may increase over time. This is not only true of children with neurodevelopmental disorders. Even for well-stimulated typically developing children, cognitive development can be subtly fostered or hindered by differences in environmental conditions, e.g. in mother/infant interaction styles (Karmiloff-Smith et al., 2010, 2012a).

A couple of examples serve to illustrate the environmental changes that may obtain for children growing up with genetic disorders. The first comes from a study of the process of vocabulary learning in toddlers with DS (John & Mervis, 2010). When TD toddlers start to label things, their parents usually allow them temporarily to overgeneralise (e.g. call all animals 'cat'). By contrast, in the case of toddlers with

DS, parents tend to veto and correct overgeneralisations immediately (John & Mervis, 2010). In our view, this is because of the parents' natural fear that their child with lower intelligence will never learn the right label if allowed to overgeneralise. Yet, initial overgeneralisation in the TD child encourages category formation (e.g. by calling different animals 'cat', the child creates an implicit 'animal' category), and categorisation is known to be impaired in many neurodevelopmental disorders, including DS. The second example comes from motor development. Observational data from our lab reveal that parents of infants/toddlers with genetic syndromes often find it difficult (compared to parents of TD infants) to let their atypically developing offspring use the sensitive nerve endings in their mouth to explore object properties, or to crawl/walk uninhibited around the lab in order to fully discover their environment. This reticence is likely to be due to an understandable greater fear of accidents with respect to vulnerable children. These unconscious assumptions about what atypical children can and cannot learn may unwittingly lead their parents to provide less variation in their linguistic input to their child and in general offer a more cautious, less varied environment – subtle differences that are likely to compound over developmental time.

Thus, a richer notion of 'environment' is required, i.e. how having a neurodevelopmental disorder may subtly change the social, cognitive, linguistic, emotional and physical environments to which the atypically developing child is progressively exposed.

2.6 Conclusions

We started this chapter by highlighting an important difference between adult neuropsychological models and truly developmental approaches to neurodevelopmental disorders, namely that adult models tend to be static and developmental approaches necessarily require a dynamic perspective, which allows for identifying phenotypic changes over developmental time. Section 2.2 stressed how genotype to phenotype mapping depends on developmental time; gene expression, neural and cognitive profiles may differ considerably at different points on the developmental trajectory. Section 2.3 provided an example of how a developmental explanation is needed to map findings of atypical neural processing for faces and language to relatively proficient face and language processing behaviours in *adults* with WS. Unlike the adult neuropsychological model, a developmental approach does not assume the existence of domain-specific neural sub-systems in neurodevelopmental disorders. Indeed, it argues that the atypical genetic profile found in neurodevelopmental disorders affects brain development from the start of ontogenesis, impacting low-level, domain-general processes that cascade over developmental time and affect neural specialisation processes in later development. Section 2.4 provided one such example where cross-syndrome differences in number processing by adults with DS and WS may be partially explained by differences in basic-level attentional processes in very early development. Similarly, in Section 2.5 we suggested that subtle environmental differences for children with neurodevelopmental disorders relative to typically developing children compound over developmental time to affect brain and behaviour in later development.

In conclusion, we reiterate that focussing on the process of development itself is key to a full understanding of any neurodevelopmental disorder (Karmiloff-Smith, 1998). Furthermore, to understand the full implications of having a neurodevelopmental disorder, it is critical to study the disorder at multiple levels (genetic, cellular, neural, cognitive, behavioural and environmental) as well as using the convergence of multiple methodologies (e.g. MEG, fMRI, fNIRS, EEG/ERP, eye-tracking, etc.). Even though plasticity may be reduced in genetic syndromes, it is clear that identifying developmental change remains crucial, whether researching children or adults with neurodevelopmental disorders.

Practical tips

1. We strongly recommend the tracing of full developmental trajectories from infancy onwards. This does not necessarily restrict the researcher solely to longitudinal studies, although it does represent an important approach. Indeed, an optimal design for studying developmental disorders is to combine case studies with initial cross-sectional designs and then longitudinal group follow-up (Thomas et al., 2009). An understanding of underlying mechanisms will be furthered by the richer descriptive vocabulary provided by the trajectories approach (e.g. in distinguishing different types of delay and deviance).

2. We highlight the need for longitudinal studies. However, these should be not only at the cognitive level, but also at the neural level (Karmiloff-Smith, 2010). Understanding the extent to which the brains of children with neurodevelopmental disorders change over time is crucial. And it is just as necessary to identify regressive events as progressive changes, including the extent to which the atypically developing brain shows any indices of circuit specialisation.

3. We recommend examining microdevelopmental change in neuro-developmental disorders. While this has been a relatively lively area of TD research (Karmiloff-Smith, 1984, 2013; Siegler & Svetina, 2002), it has rarely if ever been used for the study of neurodevelopmental disorders. Yet, understanding the processes of change over the very short term is just as important as identifying macro-developmental change.

4. In our view, researchers are still far from understanding how genetic mutations interact with the subtle changes that occur in the environments of children with neurodevelopmental disorders. We thus need a much more in-depth account of environment changes. One avenue of promising research would be the study of twins in which one twin has a neurodevelopmental disorder and the other is typically developing. Subtle differences in the socio-linguistic, cognitive and physical environments of each twin of equivalent chronological age and *seemingly equivalent* environment could be very informative.

References

Ábrahám, H., Vincze, A., Veszprémi, B., Kravják, A., Gömöri, É., Kovács, G. G. & Seress, L. (2012). Impaired myelination of the human hippocampal formation in Down syndrome. *International Journal of Developmental Neuroscience, 30,* 147–158.

Aylward, E. H., Li, Q., Honeycutt, N. A., Warren, A. C., Pulsifer, M. B., Barta, P. E., ... Pearlson, G. D. (1999). MRI volumes of the hippocampus and amygdala in adults with Down's syndrome with and without dementia. *American Journal of Psychiatry, 156,* 564–568.

Benton, A. L., Sivan, A. B., Hamsher, K. deS., Varney, N. R. & Spreen, O. (1994). *Contributions to Neuropsychological Assessment* (2nd ed.). New York, NY: Oxford University Press.

Brannon, E. M. (2006). The representation of numerical magnitude. *Current Opinion in Neurobiology, 16,* 222–229.

Brannon, E. M., Abbott, S. & Lutz, D. (2004). Number bias for the discrimination of large visual sets in infancy. *Cognition, 93,* B59–B68.

Brown, J. H., Johnson, M. H., Paterson, S. J., Gilmore, R., Longhi, E. & Karmiloff-Smith, A. (2003). Spatial representation and attention in toddlers with Williams syndrome and Down syndrome. *Neuropsychologia, 41,* 1037–1046.

Butterworth, B. (2010). Foundational numerical capacities and the origins of dyscalculia. *Trends in Cognitive Sciences, 14,* 534–541.

Carducci, F., Onorati, P., Condoluci, C., Di Gennaro, G., Quarato, P. P., Pierallini, A., ... Albertini, G. (2013). Whole-brain voxel-based morphometry study of children and adolescents with Down syndrome. *Functional Neurology, 28,* 19–28.

Casey, B. J. & Riddle, M. (2012). Typical and atypical development of attention. In M. I. Posner (ed.). *Cognitive Neuroscience of Attention* (2nd ed., pp. 345–356). New York, NY: Guilford Press.

Casey, B. J., Giedd, J. N. & Thomas, K. M. (2000). Structural and functional brain development and its relation to cognitive development. *Biological Psychology, 54,* 241–257.

Choudhury, N. & Benaisch, A. A. (2011). Maturation of auditory evoked potentials from 6 to 48 months: Prediction to 3 and 4 year language and cognitive abilities. *Clinical Neurophysiology, 122,* 320–338.

Clahsen, H. & Temple, C. M. (2003). Words and rules in children with Williams syndrome. In Y. Levy & J. Schaeffer (eds), *Language Competence Across Populations: Toward a Definition of Specific Language Impairment* (pp. 323–352). Dordrecht, Netherlands: Kluwer.

Cornish, K., Scerif, G. & Karmiloff-Smith, A. (2007). Tracing syndrome-specific trajectories of attention across the lifespan. *Cortex, 43,* 672–685.

Cornish, K. M., Kogan, C. S., Jacquemont, S., Turk, J., Dalton, A., Hagerman, R. J. & Hagerman, P. J. (2008). Age-dependent cognitive changes in carriers of the fragile X syndrome. *Cortex, 44,* 628–636.

de Haan, M., Pascalis, O. & Johnson, M. H. (2002). Specialization of neural mechanisms underlying face recognition in human infants. *Journal of Cognitive Neuroscience, 14,* 199–209.

Dehaene, S. (1997). *The Number Sense: How the Mind Creates Mathematics.* Oxford, UK: Oxford University Press.

Demeyere, N., Lestor, V. & Humphreys, G. (2010). Neuropsychological evidence for a dissociation in counting and subitizing. *NeuroCase, 16*, 219–237.

Durston, S., Davidson, M. C., Tottenham, N., Galvan, A., Spicer, J., Fosella, J. A. & Casey, B. J. (2006). A shift from diffuse to focal cortical activity with development. *Developmental Science, 9*, 1–8.

Edgin, J. O. (2013). Cognition in Down syndrome: a developmental cognitive neuroscience perspective. *Wiley Interdisciplinary Reviews: Cognitive Science, 4*, 307–317.

Elman, J. L., Bates, E. L., Johnson, M. H., Karmiloff-Smith, A., Parisi, D. & Plunkett, K. (1996). *Rethinking Innateness: A Connectionist Perspective on Development.* Cambridge, MA: MIT Press.

Frigerio, E., Burt, D. M., Gagliardi, C., Cioffi, G., Martelli, S., Perrett, D. I. & Borgatti, R. (2006). Is everybody always my friend? Perception of approachability in Williams syndrome. *Neuropsychologia, 44*, 254–259.

Golarai, G., Hong, S., Haas, B. W., Galaburda, A. M., Mills, D. L., Bellugi, U., … Reiss, A. L. (2010). The fusiform face area is enlarged in Williams syndrome. *The Journal of Neuroscience, 30*, 6700–6712.

Grice, S., Spratling, M. W., Karmiloff-Smith, A., Halit, H., Csibra, G., de Haan, M. & Johnson, M. H. (2001). Disordered visual processing and oscillatory brain activity in autism and Williams syndrome. *NeuroReport, 12*, 2697–2700.

Grice, S. J., de Haan, M., Halit, H., Johnson, M. H., Csibra, G., Grant, J. & Karmiloff-Smith, A. (2003). ERP abnormalities of visual perception in Williams syndrome. *NeuroReport, 14*, 1773–1777.

Hepper, P. G., Scott, D. & Shahidullah, S. (1993). Newborn and fetal response to maternal voice. *Journal of Reproductive and Infant Psychology, 11*, 147–153.

Izard, V., Dehaene-Lambertz, G. & Dehaene, S. (2008). Distinct cerebral pathways for object identity and number in human infants. *PLoS Biology, 6*, e11.

Jernigan, T. L., Bellugi, U., Sowell, E., Doherty, S. & Hesselink, J. R. (1993). Cerebral morphologic distinctions between Williams and Down syndromes. *Archives of Neurology, 50*, 186–191.

John, A. E. & Mervis, C. B. (2010). Comprehension of the communicative intent behind pointing and gazing gestures by young children with Williams syndrome or Down syndrome. *Journal of Speech, Language, and Hearing Research, 53*, 950–960.

Johnson, M. H. (2001). Functional brain development in humans. *Nature Reviews Neuroscience, 2*, 475–483.

Karmiloff-Smith, A. (1984). Children's problem solving. In M. E. Lamb, A. L. Brown & B. Rogoff (eds), *Advances in Developmental Psychology* (Vol. III, pp. 39–90). New Jersey: Erlbaum.

——(1992). *Beyond Modularity: A Developmental Approach to Cognitive Science.* Cambridge, MA: MIT Press.

——(1998). Development itself is the key to understanding developmental disorders. *Trends in Cognitive Science, 2*, 389–398.

——(2009). Nativism vs neuroconstructivism: rethinking the study of developmental disorders. *Developmental Psychology, 45*, 56–63.

——(2010). Neuroimaging of the developing brain: taking 'developing' seriously. *Human Brain Mapping, 31*, 934–941.

——(2013). 'Microgenetics': no single method can elucidate human learning. *Human Development, 56*, 47–51.

Karmiloff-Smith, A., Grant, J., Ewing, S., Carette, M. J., Metcalfe, K., Donnai, D., ... Tassabehji, M. (2003). Using case study comparisons to explore genotype-phenotype correlations in Williams-Beuren syndrome. *Journal of Medical Genetics, 40*, 136–140.

Karmiloff-Smith, A., Thomas, M., Annaz, D., Humphreys, K., Ewing, S., Brace, N., ... Campbell, R. (2004). Exploring the Williams syndrome face processing debate: The importance of building developmental trajectories. *Journal of Child Psychology and Psychiatry, 45*, 1258–1274.

Karmiloff-Smith, A., Aschersleben, G., de Schonen, T., Elsabbagh, M., Hohenberger, A. & Serres, J. (2010). Constraints on the timing of infant cognitive change: domain-specific or domain-general? *European Journal of Developmental Science, 4*, 31–45.

Karmiloff-Smith, A., D'Souza, D., Dekker, T. M., Van Herwegen, J., Xu, F., Rodic, M. & Ansari, D. (2012a). Genetic and environmental vulnerabilities in children with neurodevelopmental disorders. *Proceedings of the National Academy of Sciences of the United States of America, 109*, 17261–17265.

Karmiloff-Smith, A., Broadbent, H., Farran, E. K., Longhi, E., D'Souza, D., Metcalfe, K. & Sansbury, F. (2012b). Social cognition in Williams syndrome: Genotype/phenotype insights from partial deletion patients. *Frontiers in Developmental Psychology, 3, 168*, 1–8.

Kesslak, J. P., Nagata, S. F., Lott, I. & Nalcioglu, O. (1994). Magnetic resonance imaging analysis of age-related changes in the brains of individuals with Down's syndrome. *Neurology, 44*, 1039–1045.

Krakow, J. B. & Kopp, C. B. (1982). Sustained attention in young Down syndrome children. *Topics in Early Childhood Special Education, 2*, 32–42.

Lipton, J. S. & Spelke, E. S. (2003). Origins of number sense: large-number discrimination in human infants. *Psychological Science, 14*, 396–401.

Liston, C., McEwen, B. S. & Casey, B. J. (2009). Psychosocial stress reversibly disrupts prefrontal processing and attentional control. *Proceedings of the National Academy of Sciences, 106*, 912–917.

Meaney, M. J. & Szyf, M. (2005). Environmental programming of stress responses through DNA methylation: life at the interface between a dynamic environment and a fixed genome. *Dialogues in Clinical Neuroscience, 7*, 103–123.

Mervis, C. B., Morris, C. A., Bertrand, J. & Robinson, B. F. (1999). Williams syndrome: findings from an integrated program of research. In H. Tager-Flusberg (ed.), *Neurodevelopmental Disorders: Contributions to a New Framework from the Cognitive Neurosciences* (pp. 65–110). Cambridge, MA: MIT Press.

Mills, D. L., Coffy-Corins, S. & Neville, H. (1997). Language comprehension and cerebral specialisation from 13–20 months. *Developmental Neuropsychology, 13*, 397–445.

Mills, D. L., Alvarez, T. D., St. George, M., Appelbaum, L. G., Bellugi, U. & Neville, H. (2000). Electrophysiological studies of face processing in Williams syndrome. *Journal of Cognitive Neuroscience, 12*, 47–64.

Minagawa-Kawai, Y., Mori, K., Naoi, N. & Kojima, S. (2007). Neural attunement processes in infants during the acquisition of a language-specific phonemic contrast. *Journal of Neuroscience, 27*, 315–321.

Nadel, L. (1986). Down syndrome in neurobiological perspective. In C. J. Epstein (ed.), *The Neurobiology of Down Syndrome* (pp. 197–221). New York, NY: Raven Press.

Neville, H. J., Mills, D. L. & Bellugi, U. (1994). Effects of altered auditory sensitivity and age of language acquisition on the development of language-relevant neural systems: preliminary studies of Williams syndrome. In S. Broman & J. Grafman (eds), *Atypical*

Cognitive Deficits in Developmental Disorders: Implications for Brain Function (pp. 67–83). Hillsdale, NJ: Lawrence Erlbaum.

Paterson S. J., Brown J. H., Gsödl M. K., Johnson, M. H. & Karmiloff-Smith, A. (1999). Cognitive modularity and genetic disorders. *Science, 286,* 2355–2358.

Pennington, B. F., Moon, J., Edgin, J., Stedron, J. & Nadel, L. (2003). The neuropsychology of Down syndrome: evidence for hippocampal dysfunction. *Child Development, 74,* 75–93.

Pinter, J. D., Brown, W. E., Eliez, S., Schmitt, J. E., Capone, G. T. & Reiss, A. L. (2001). Amygdala and hippocampal volumes in children with Down syndrome: A high-resolution MRI study. *Neurology, 56,* 972–974.

Rast, M. & Meltzoff, A. N. (1995). Memory and representation in young children with Down syndrome: exploring deferred imitation and object permanence. *Development and Psychopathology, 7,* 393–407.

Raz, N., Torres, I. J., Briggs, S. D. & Spencer, W. D. (1995). Selective neuroanatomic abnormalities in Down's syndrome and their cognitive correlates: Evidence from MRI morphometry. *Neurology, 45,* 356–366.

Riby, D. M. & Hancock, P. J. B. (2008). Viewing it differently: Social scene perception in Williams syndrome and Autism. *Neuropsychologia, 46,* 2855–2860.

Scerif, G. & Karmiloff-Smith, A. (2005). The dawn of cognitive genetics? Crucial developmental caveats. *Trends in Cognitive Sciences, 9,* 126–135.

Siegler, R. S. & Svetina, M. (2002). A microgenetic/cross-sectional study of matrix completion: comparing short-term and long-term change. *Child Development, 73,* 793–809.

Simon, T. J. (1997). Reconceptualizing the origins of number knowledge: a 'non numerical' account. *Cognitive Development, 12,* 349–372.

Steele, A., Brown, J. & Scerif, G. (2012). Integrating domain-general and domain-specific developmental processes: cross-syndrome, cross-domain dynamics. In E. K. Farran & A. Karmiloff-Smith (eds), *Neurodevelopmental Disorders Across the Lifespan: A Neuroconstructivist Approach* (pp. 339–362). Oxford, UK: Oxford University Press.

Tassabehji, M., Metcalfe, K., Karmiloff-Smith, A., Carette, M. J., Grant, J., Dennis, N., ... Donnai, D. (1999). Williams syndrome: use of chromosomal microdeletions as a tool to dissect cognitive and physical phenotypes. *The American Journal of Human Genetics, 64,* 118–125.

Tassabehji, M., Hammond, P., Karmiloff-Smith, A., Thompson, P., Thorgeirsson, S. S., Durkin, M. E., ... Donnai, D. (2005). GTF2IRD1 in craniofacial development of humans and mice. *Science, 310,* 1184–1187.

Thomas, M. S. C., Annaz, D., Ansari, D., Scerif, G., Jarrold, C. & Karmiloff-Smith, A. (2009). Using developmental trajectories to understand developmental disorders. *Journal of Speech, Language, and Hearing Research, 52,* 336–358.

Tobii (2003). *Tobii User Manual* (2nd ed.). Stockholm, Sweden: Tobii.

Tomalski, P., Moore, D. G., Ribeiro, H., Axelsson, E. L., Murphy, E., Karmiloff-Smith, A., ... Kushnerenko, E. (2013). Socioeconomic status and functional brain development – associations in early infancy. *Developmental Science, 16,* 676–687.

Tottenham, N., Hare, T. A., Quinn, B. T., McCarry, T. W., Nurse, M., Gilhooly, T., ... Casey, B. J. (2010). Prolonged institutional rearing is associated with atypically large amygdala volume and difficulties in emotion regulation. *Developmental Science, 13,* 46–61.

Tottenham, N., Hare, T. A., Millner, A., Gilhooly, T., Zevin, J. D. & Casey, B. J. (2011). Elevated amygdala response to faces following early deprivation. *Developmental Science, 14*, 190–204.

Tyler, L. K., Shafto, M. A., Randall, B., Wright, P., Marslen-Wilson, W. D. & Stamatakis, E. A. (2009). Preserving syntactic processing across the adult life span: the modulation of the frontotemporal language system in the context of age-related atrophy. *Cerebral Cortex, 20*, 352–364.

Van Herwegen, J., Ansari, D., Xu, F. & Karmiloff-Smith, A. (2008). Small and large number processing in infants and toddlers with Williams syndrome. *Developmental Science, 11*, 637–643.

Vicari, S., Bellucci, S. & Carlesimo, G. A. (2000). Implicit and explicit memory: a functional dissociation in persons with Down syndrome. *Neuropsychologia, 38*, 240–251.

Wilson, B. A., Greenfield, E., Clare, L., Baddeley, A., Cockburn, J., Watson, P., ... Crawford, J. (2008). *The Rivermead Behavioural Memory Test – Third Edition.* London, UK: Pearson Assessment.

Xu, F. (2003). Numerosity discrimination in infants: evidence for two systems of representations. *Cognition, 89*, B15–B25.

Xu, F. & Arriaga, R. I. (2007). Number discrimination in 10-month-old infants. *British Journal of Developmental Psychology, 25*, 103–108.

3

MAKING USE OF BRAIN–BEHAVIOR LINKS

Brian W. Haas

3.1 Introduction

A primary goal of research exploring neurodevelopmental disorders is to produce results that translate to improved syndrome- and symptom-specific diagnostic and intervention techniques. Understanding the biological basis of abnormal cognitive and behavioral functioning in neurodevelopmental disorders creates new opportunities to target biological systems during intervention. Additionally, the inclusion of biological diagnostic criteria for neurodevelopmental disorders improves diagnosis accuracy and facilitates access to more effective treatment options. Recent progress in brain-imaging technologies provides an unprecedented opportunity to explore the neural basis of atypical cognitive and behavioral functioning in neurodevelopmental disorders.

In this chapter, we will describe the value of making brain–behavior links in neurodevelopmental disorders. We will survey several brain-imaging modalities and identify *how* each modality is an effective tool to elucidate brain–behavior linkage in neurodevelopmental disorders. Next, we provide *empirical examples* of how brain imaging has elucidated complex brain–behavioral linkage in specific disorder groups. Lastly, we will discuss current challenges and provide suggestions for future research endeavors.

3.2 Brain-imaging modalities

3.2.1 Structural neuroimaging

Magnetic Resonance Imaging (MRI) is a technique that provides a relatively high-resolution perspective onto the anatomical characteristics of the brain. Specifically, MRI works by passing a strong magnetic pulse through a medium (in this case the brain), and quantifying how the characteristics of the magnetic pulse are altered (Logothetis, 2008). A basic principle of MRI is that different tissue types within the brain (e.g. gray matter, white matter, skull, and cerebral spinal fluid) affect how a magnetic pulse travels in a consistent and specific way. By measuring alterations in the magnetic pulse passed through many areas of the brain, a three-dimensional image can be constructed. This image shows the location of specific tissue types within the living human brain (Figure 3.1A).

Here is an analogy for the way that MRI works. Think of shining a flashlight through a glass of water and measuring the characteristics of the light on the other end of the glass. Next, think of comparing this to the characteristics of light that pass through a glass filled with a different type of liquid, say juice. Clearly, you would expect that there would be differences in the characteristics of the light that reaches the other end of the glass based on the contents within the glass (water versus juice). The same logic applies to MRI: the characteristics of the magnetic pulse that reach the other end of the brain differ according to the contents (tissue type) within the brain.

How can MRI be used to understand the biological basis of abnormal cognitive and behavioral functioning in neurodevelopmental disorders? MRI can be used to rule out the existence of large-scale brain anomalies that affect the presence or severity of psychological symptoms. For example, MRI can be used to identify the presence of tumors, cerebral swelling, hemorrhaging and/or lesions. Having access to this information can help to guide a clinician when making a diagnosis.

MRI can be used to identify how the size of specific brain regions is different in a neurodevelopmental disorder compared to healthy controls. Based on standardized neuroanatomical atlases, trained researchers can manually delineate brain regions.

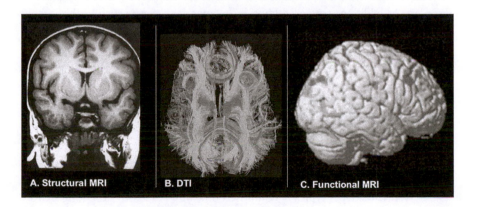

FIGURE 3.1   Examples of data acquired from three different types of brain-imaging modalities. Panel A shows a coronal slice of the brain using structural Magnetic Resonance Imaging (MRI). Panel B shows a color-coded directional map of the brain using Diffusion Tensor Imaging (DTI). Panel C shows a three-dimensional render of brain activation found using functional Magnetic Resonance Imaging (fMRI).

For example, sets of rules are used to guide where the boundary exists between two brain regions. After a given brain region is delineated in a sample diagnosed with a neurodevelopmental disorder and a sample of healthy controls, between-group comparisons can be made. The results of such an approach can help to identify what parts of the brain are, on average, abnormal in size in a disorder, and what parts of the brain are not abnormal.

Another method to compare structural characteristics of brain regions between two samples is to use an approach called voxel based morphometry (VBM) (Ashburner & Friston, 2000). MR images are comprised of many small three-dimensional boxes termed voxels. Pixels are two-dimensional squares and voxels are three-dimensional boxes. Once a MR image has been constructed, each voxel has a particular value (i.e. intensity) that corresponds to a likelihood of being a particular tissue type (e.g. gray matter). By comparing the values within voxels, between sample groups, results can be obtained that represent alterations in tissue type (i.e. intensity) or size (i.e. volume). VBM is a particularly valuable analysis approach to search the entire brain for structural abnormalities (Ashburner & Friston, 2001).

Many analytical methods have been developed to quantify subtle anatomical characteristics of the brain. For example, there currently exists several different ways to measure cortical complexity (Dale, Fischl & Sereno, 1999; Fischl, Sereno & Dale, 1999; Van Essen et al., 2001). Cortical complexity is a measure of the spatial frequency of pumps (gyri) and grooves (sulci and fissures) over the surface of the brain. Greater cortical complexity is generally considered to be advantageous. More folding along the surface of the brain places neurons in closer proximity to one another and is believed to result in more efficient communication (Zilles, Palomero-Gallagher & Amunts, 2013). Measuring cortical complexity in neurodevelopmental disorders can elucidate the structural organization of the brain in neurodevelopmental disorders. In addition, cortical folding is an important step occurring throughout development. Thus, measuring cortical complexity can help to support hypotheses that involve aberrations in brain development in neurodevelopmental disorders.

Diffusion Tensor Imaging (DTI) is a technique also used to measure structural characteristics within the brain. DTI data is typically collected from a MRI machine. However, the way that DTI data are produced and analyzed works in a very different way than MRI. DTI works by measuring the extent and direction of the movement (i.e. diffusion) of water molecules in response to a magnetic pulse. Data representative of the diffusion of water molecules can help to identify very small and subtle structural characteristics within the brain (Figure 3.1B). DTI is particularly well suited to detect if a particular brain region is comprised of white matter. White matter is typically comprised of axons. An axon is the long narrow shaft of a neuron, in which action potentials propagate and travel along. Typically, a fatty substance called myelin surrounds axons. The movement of water molecules that are within or near myelinated axons tends to be restricted. Therefore, when a location within the brain is found to be characterized by a large proportion of linear (as compared to random or circular) movement, the likelihood of that region being comprised by axon is greater.

Here is an analogy for how DTI works. Think of measuring the way that a water molecule within a celery stock/stalk/stick is able to move. Then think of the way that a water molecule is able to move if it were within a large bucket. You would expect that the movement of the water molecule within the celery stock would be in a more linear pattern relative to the water molecule in the large bucket. The same basic principle applies to DTI: linear movement of water molecules is associated with being restricted by the linear (tube-like) attributes of the axon.

How can DTI be used to understand the biological basis of abnormal cognitive and behavioral functioning in neurodevelopmental disorders? The major advantage of DTI is being able to detect white matter abnormalities. Thus, DTI is an effective tool to identify if neurodevelopmental disorders are characterized by structural alterations within white matter (Cascio, Gerig & Piven, 2007). The structure of white matter undergoes many important changes throughout development, including differentiation and pruning. DT imaging provides a unique window on how developmental trajectories within the brain may go awry in neurodevelopmental disorders.

Many approaches to analyzing DTI data are designed to quantify and compare diffusion metrics within white matter tracts between groups. Fractional anisotropy (FA) is a commonly used DTI metric representative of the proportion of linear diffusion (i.e. movement) relative to total diffusion (i.e. movement) (Basser, Mattiello & LeBihan, 1994). FA values range between 0 and 1, where high FA values typically correspond to the presence of white matter or greater "white matter integrity." FA values can be calculated and averaged across an entire tract or calculated and compared on a single voxel basis. Recently, automated atlas-based approaches have been developed to segment DTI data into specific white matter tracts within the brain (Oishi et al., 2009). DTI metrics such as FA can be used to examine the association between white matter integrity and cognitive behavioral abnormalities in neurodevelopmental disorders.

3.2.2 Functional neuroimaging

Electroencephalography (EEG) is a noninvasive recording technique designed to measure changes in electrical potential over the scalp. EEG is principled on the fact that neurons function by propagating action potentials. Action potentials are short-lasting events in which the electrical membrane potential of a neuron rapidly rises and falls. If a sufficient amount of action potentials occur, changes in electrical signal travel through the brain, cerebral spinal fluid, skull and skin. Thus, EEG measures a summation of many action potentials that have occurred close to the surface of the cerebral cortex. The measurement of neuronal activity using EEG paired with the presentation of a stimulus is called an event-related potential (ERP). EEG is characterized by having relatively good temporal resolution and relatively poor spatial resolution (for further discussion see Chapter 4).

EEG and ERPs can be used to discover brain–behavior links in neuro-developmental disorders. EEG is an optimal tool to quantify fluctuations in brain activity (i.e. neuronal oscillations) over time. For example, EEG is often used to diagnose conditions such as epilepsy, as epileptic patients exhibit specific patterns of neuronal oscillations (Jerrett & Corsak, 1988). In addition, EEG is often used to measure changes in sleep patterns. Each stage of sleep is associated with a specific pattern of neuronal oscillations (e.g. delta, theta, alpha, beta, and gamma). Thus, EEG can be used to characterize how certain neurodevelopmental conditions are associated with abnormalities in sleep. Lastly, EEG is an effective tool to differentiate neurodevelopmental conditions from conditions such as encephalopathy or delirium.

Using ERPs is an effective method to study the temporal dynamics of neuronal responses during the processing of specific types of information in neurodevelopmental disorders. In typical ERP experiments research participants are presented with a visual, cognitive or motor stimulus. The research can then measure the change in electrical signal paired with each specific stimulus. Thus, ERPs can elucidate subtle differences in the timing of neuronal activity when responding to a particular stimulus. This provides researchers with the opportunity to investigate specific psychological processes. For example, dissociable patterns of neuronal activity could be evaluated as related to cognitive versus emotional processing. These findings can help to clarify what neural processes are affected and what neuronal processes are spared in a specific neurodevelopmental disorder. ERPs are also an effective way to characterize the order in which an individual processes a series of cognitive steps during psychological processing. Thus, ERPs can help identify the basis for abnormal decision-making or processing speed in neurodevelopmental disorders.

Functional Magnetic Resonance Imaging (fMRI) is a noninvasive brain-imaging technique that measures changes in the quantity of oxygenated blood within the brain (Figure 3.1C). As with structural MRI, fMRI works by sending a magnetic pulse through the brain. However, with fMRI, the primary focus is on the amount of oxygen within the blood. Therefore, during fMRI data collection, a magnetic resonance machine is tuned to be sensitive to changes in oxygen. The basic principle of fMRI is that the characteristics of a magnetic pulse are altered in a specific and measurable way according to the amount of oxygenated blood that exists in the tissue that the magnetic pulse passes through. Thus, researchers have the opportunity to quantify changes in levels in oxygen within the brain associated with particular psychological processes.

Measuring changes in oxygenated blood provides an indirect metric of neuronal activity. Neuronal activity is a metabolic process that uses oxygen. It is assumed that active neurons utilize more oxygen than inactive neurons and that the brain will compensate by sending additional oxygenated blood to recently active neurons. Thus, fMRI sheds light onto the functioning brain. fMRI is characterized by relatively good spatial resolution and relatively poor temporal resolution. For example, fMRI can identify if a brain region as small as the amygdala, which is about the size of an almond, is active during a task or not. On the other hand, it typically takes a magnetic resonance machine about two seconds to acquire a whole brain image. This means that a researcher is limited to characterizing the temporal dynamics of brain function on a scale of approximately two seconds.

fMRI is a very useful tool to study brain and behavior links in neurodevelopmental disorders (but see Chapter 4 for a discussion about the difficulties when using fMRI and MRI in neurodevelopmental disorders). By using fMRI, researchers can identify how specific brain regions function during many different types of psychological processes. Increases in anatomical specificity can help to elucidate what parts of the brain are affected and what parts of the brain are spared in neurodevelopmental disorders. In addition, many fMRI experiments are designed to include a behavioral response from the participant. Typically, behavioral responses are collected through a button box that participants have on their laps during fMRI scanning. By collecting behavioral responses, researchers can characterize brain function associated with accuracy or reaction time. Together, this information improves the understanding of how abnormal brain function may impact day-to-day cognitive or social behavior in neurodevelopmental disorders.

3.3 Brain and behavior links in neurodevelopmental disorders

The advancement of neuroscientific techniques improves the understanding of brain–behavior linkages. Improving the understanding of brain–behavior linkages is valuable because it opens the door to new treatment approaches for individuals with neurodevelopmental disorders. With greater understanding of brain–behavior links, clinicians are more likely to consider biologically based interventions. Improving the understanding of brain–behavior linkages is also valuable because it provides a more detailed description of a disorder and will thus improve the accuracy of diagnoses. With greater understanding of brain–behavior links, those making diagnoses are more likely to include biological metrics to diagnose neurodevelopmental disorders. In the following section we will provide empirical examples of how brain imaging has elucidated complex brain–behavioral linkages in specific neurodevelopmental disorders.

Autism Spectrum Disorder (ASD) is a neurodevelopmental disorder characterized by impaired social interaction and verbal and non-verbal communication, and by restricted, repetitive behavior. Many brain-imaging studies have sought to identify the neural correlates of impaired social processing. Two brain regions that are particularly important to processing social information are the fusiform gyrus and the amygdala. The fusiform gyrus is located on the inferior medial surface of the temporal lobe and contains the fusiform face area (FFA). The FFA is a highly specialized brain region involved in face recognition (Kanwisher, McDermott & Chun, 1997). Many functional neuroimaging studies demonstrate that activation within the FFA is associated with the ability to perceive faces (Grill-Spector, Knouf & Kanwisher, 2004; Kanwisher & Yovel, 2006). In addition, damage to the FFA often results in impairments in face processing such as in prosopagnosia (Barton, Press, Keenan & O'Connor, 2002).

Brain-imaging studies show that individuals with ASD exhibit reduced amount of activity within the FFA relative to healthy controls (Jiang et al., 2013). In addition, the structure of the fusiform gyrus is abnormal in ASD as compared to healthy controls (Waiter et al., 2004). Lastly, recent evidence indicates that connections to and from the FFA are affected in ASD (Deshpande, Libero, Sreenivasan, Deshpande & Kana, 2013). Together, these studies demonstrate that brain regions involved in recognizing complex features of human faces are abnormal. These abnormalities likely impact observed impairments in social communication typically associated with ASD (for a further discussion of social abilities in ASD see Chapters 7 and 12).

The amygdala is located within the medial temporal lobe of the brain and is involved in assessing the emotional salience of information. Activation of the amygdala is often observed when processing highly arousing facial expressions or scenes (Costafreda, Brammer, David & Fu, 2007). In addition, damage to the amygdala often results in deficits in emotional recognition (Adolphs, Baron-Cohen & Tranel, 2002) and memory (Adolphs, Cahill, Schul & Babinsky, 1997). fMRI studies demonstrate that individuals with ASD exhibit aberrations in amygdala response to emotional stimuli as compared to healthy controls (Kleinhans et al., 2011; Weng et al., 2011). Additionally, individuals with ASD exhibit reduced volume of the amygdala relative to healthy controls (Nacewicz et al., 2006). Recent studies using DTI also show structural abnormalities in the white matter fibers that connect with the amygdala in ASD (Conturo et al., 2008; Jou et al., 2011). Combined, this research shows that abnormal structure and function of the amygdala in ASD may in part impact deficits in emotion processing in this condition.

Fragile X syndrome (FXS) is a neurodevelopmental disorder caused by a trinucleotide repeat (CGG) mutation of the fragile X mental retardation 1 (FMR1) gene on chromosome Xq27.3. Individuals with FXS often exhibit a psychological phenotype characterized by delays in cognitive function, deficits in inhibitory control, and a particularly high prevalence of autistic behavior (Reiss & Dant, 2003; Reiss & Hall, 2007; for a further discussion of FXS see Chapter 10). Several brain-imaging studies show that FXS is associated with abnormal structure and function of key brain regions involved in both cognitive and social processing.

One of the most pronounced behaviors within the FXS phenotype is reduced inhibitory control. The frontostriatal network is an important brain system subserving the ability to exhibit effective cognitive and motor control (Robbins, 2007). Accordingly, fMRI studies show reduced activation with the frontostriatal pathway in FXS as compared to healthy controls (Menon, Leroux, White & Reiss, 2004; Mobbs et al., 2007). Furthermore, DTI research shows that individuals with FXS exhibit white matter alterations within the frontostriatal pathway (Barnea-Goraly et al., 2003). White matter alterations within the frontostriatal pathway in FXS have been found in children as young as three years of age (Haas et al., 2009a). Additionally, the caudate nucleus is an important brain region involved in inhibitory control. Structural MRI studies show that individuals with FXS exhibit an abnormally enlarged volume of the caudate nucleus as compared to healthy controls and this abnormal volume of the caudate nucleus is associated with the severity of symptoms in children with FXS (Peng et al., 2013).

Individuals with FXS tend to exhibit increased social anxiety as compared to healthy controls (Hagerman & Sobesky, 1989). In particular, direct eye contact often results in abnormally increased anxiety in FXS. Some brain-imaging studies have explored the brain basis of increased social anxiety in FXS. Garrett, Menon, MacKenzie and Reiss (2004) used fMRI and an experimental paradigm comprised of photographs of faces with either direct or averted gaze. The results of this study demonstrated that individuals with FXS exhibited increased insula activation during direct gaze as compared to healthy controls. The insula is an important brain region involved in monitoring emotional states and in particular anxiety (Canteras, Resstel, Bertoglio, Carobrez Ade & Guimaraes, 2010). This finding provides a neural correlate to the tendency of individuals with FXS to experience heightened anxiety during direct gaze processing.

Williams syndrome (WS) is a neurodevelopmental condition that effects approximately 1 in every 8–10,000 individuals and is caused by a deletion of ~26–28 genes on chromosome 7q11.23. The WS phenotype is characterized by a distinctive pattern of social behavior and emotion processing. Individuals with WS are often described as being hypersocial, overtly social and socially uninhibited (Bellugi et al., 2007; Haas & Reiss, 2012) (see also Chapter 12 for a detailed discussion of WS). Accordingly, brain-imaging research has sought to investigate the neural correlates of abnormal social and emotional processing in WS.

Structural and functional MRI studies show that WS is associated with abnormal structure and function within brain regions important for face processing such as the fusiform gyrus and FFA. Thompson and colleagues (2005) used a 3D cortical surface modeling approach and demonstrated that adults with WS exhibit greater cortical gray matter thickness of the fusiform gyrus relative to healthy controls. Campbell and colleagues (2009) used VBM to show regionally specific increases and decreases of gray matter volume within the fusiform gyrus in WS relative to healthy controls. Together, these studies indicate that, like ASD, WS is associated with abnormal structure of the fusiform gyrus.

fMRI has been used to investigate characteristics of the FFA in WS. Mobbs et al. (2004) used fMRI to demonstrate that individuals with WS exhibit greater activation within the FFA when responding to faces relative to healthy controls. In addition, while individuals with WS exhibit a reduced total volume of the fusiform gyrus (structurally defined), the FFA (functionally defined) is larger in WS as compared to healthy controls (Golarai et al., 2010). Together, these findings indicate that an increase in neural resources allotted to face processing within the fusiform gyrus may be an important neural substrate related to increased attentional bias towards facial expressions in WS.

Brain-imaging research has also shown that WS is associated with abnormal structure and function within brain regions important for social-emotional processing. Structural MRI studies have shown that the volume of the amygdala is greater in WS relative to healthy controls (Martens, Wilson, Dudgeon & Reutens, 2009). Furthermore, the volume of the amygdala is correlated with approachability ratings of emotional facial expressions in WS. Recently, the results of surface-based modeling analysis showed that individuals with WS exhibit localized increased volume of the bilateral posterior cortical nucleus, lateral nucleus, and the central nucleus of the amygdala (Haas, Sheau, Kelley, Thompson & Reiss, 2014). Together, these findings indicate that one neural mechanism underlying emotional processing abnormalities in WS may be an enlarged volume of the amygdala.

WS is associated with abnormal amygdala response to social-emotional stimuli. fMRI studies showed that adults with WS exhibit a reduced, or blunted, amygdala response to fearful facial expressions as compared to healthy controls (Haas et al., 2009b). Additionally, the tendency to approach strangers is correlated with the amount of amygdala response to fearful facial expressions in WS (Haas et al., 2009c). Interestingly, in contrast to the pattern of amygdala response to fearful facial expressions, individuals with WS exhibit greater amygdala response to happy facial expressions relative to controls (Haas et al., 2009b). Combined, these findings suggest that reduced amygdala response to fearful facial expressions may be a neural substrate related to the tendency to uninhibitedly (or "fearlessly") approach strangers in WS, while increased amygdala response to happy facial expressions may be a neural substrate related to the tendency to be more driven to approach others in general in WS.

WS is associated with abnormal anatomical and functional connectivity between brain regions important for face and emotional processing. Individuals with WS exhibit less functional connectivity between the FFA and amygdala relative to healthy controls (Sarpal et al., 2008). DTI shows that individuals with WS exhibit an increase in the volume, fractional anisotropy and fiber density index of white matter fibers related to the fusiform gyrus in WS relative to controls (Haas et al., 2012). Additionally, recent DTI research shows that diffusion tensor metrics within the fusiform gyrus are associated with behavioral measures of social cognition in WS (Figure 3.2) (Haas et

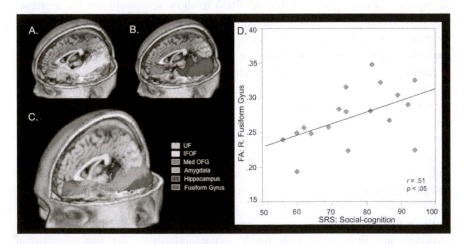

FIGURE 3.2   Diffusion tensor imaging research in Williams syndrome. Panels A, B and C display white matter tracts and mixed tissue matter regions of interest in this study. Panel C displays all white matter tracts and mixed tissue matter regions. Panel D displays the association between a DTI metric (fractional anisotropy) and social cognition in children with Williams syndrome (adapted from Haas et al., 2013., *Cerebral Cortex*).

al., 2013). These studies indicate that the neural circuitry connecting brain regions important for social-emotional processing is abnormal in WS.

3.4 Conclusions

Brain-imaging research has provided tremendous insight into the brain basis of abnormal behavior in neurodevelopmental disorders. These findings have improved diagnostics and the efficacy of treatment approaches for many of these conditions. A major goal of many current research endeavors is to design more targeted treatment approaches. Brain-imaging research has the potential to greatly advance the design of symptom- and syndrome-specific intervention techniques. For example, results of a brain-imaging assessment during diagnosis may identify certain biological substrates that are spared versus affected in a patient. This information could then be used to administer a targeted treatment approach tailored to that individual patient.

Many limitations in brain-imaging research of neurodevelopmental disorders lie in the physical constraints of many imaging modalities. This is profoundly evident in the case of MRI. Many individuals with neurodevelopmental disorders exhibit increased anxiety and heightened sensitivity to loud sounds. Being in a MRI machine can sometimes cause claustrophobia and can be extremely loud.

One way to alleviate anxiety in research participants with neurodevelopmental disorders is to use a series of measures prior to the MRI scan. For example, asking participants and their families or guardians to: 1) view, at least twice, a professionally prepared videotape containing all of the experiences, sights and sounds of structural and functional imaging; 2) listen to a 20-minute narrated audio clip that contains a collection of MRI sounds; 3) review extensively illustrated written materials that include instructions for learning "games" that reduce head motion; 4) if the participant has access to the internet, practice simple "games" on a special web page we have designed for potential research subjects. Furthermore, it is often important that each participant undergoes a "practice scan" in a simulated scanner environment (several if necessary). MRI simulators are full replicas of a MRI scanner and include speakers for simulating sounds, a motorized table, and a head coil with a mounted LCD screen for showing video images of fMRI tasks.

Because of the physical constraints associated with many brain-imaging modalities, it can be difficult to generalize observed effects to more "real-life" situations. Thus, in the future it will be important to design data collection approaches and experimental tasks that are highly ecologically valid. Such advancements will facilitate how results of brain-imaging research can be translated to improving outcomes for people diagnosed with neurodevelopmental disorders and related conditions.

Lastly, it is extremely challenging to interpret the specificity of the relationship between observed behaviors and observed characteristics in the brain. The majority of brain–behavior research is observational and thus there are no experimental manipulations. It is therefore very difficult to determine the directionality of causation. Are behavioral abnormalities present because of abnormalities within the brain or are abnormalities within the brain present because of behavioral abnormalities? Clearly, this is an extremely complex theoretical and empirical issue. Insight into the answer to this question will be achieved by continued progress in neuroscientific techniques, analysis approaches and innovative thinking.

Practical tips

1. Collecting neuroimaging data from participants with neurodevelopmental disorders requires patience and great attention and sensitivity to the comfort level of each participant.
2. Data collected over multiple time points provides improved insight into the development of the brain and behavior in neurodevelopmental disorders.
3. It is important to be aware of the limitations of correlational research; correlation does not imply causation.

References

Adolphs, R., Cahill, L., Schul, R. & Babinsky, R. (1997). Impaired declarative memory for emotional material following bilateral amygdala damage in humans. *Learning & Memory, 4*, 291–300.

Adolphs, R., Baron-Cohen, S. & Tranel, D. (2002). Impaired recognition of social emotions following amygdala damage. *Journal of Cognitive Neuroscience, 14*, 1264–1274.

Ashburner, J. & Friston, K. J. (2000). Voxel-based morphometry – the methods. *Neuroimage, 11*, 805–821.

——(2001). Why voxel-based morphometry should be used. *Neuroimage, 14*, 1238–1243.

Barnea-Goraly, N., Eliez, S., Hedeus, M., Menon, V., White, C. D., Moseley, M. & Reiss, A. L. (2003). White matter tract alterations in fragile X syndrome: preliminary evidence from diffusion tensor imaging. *American Journal of Medical Genetics Part B Neuropsychiatric Genetics, 118*, 81–88.

Barton, J. J., Press, D. Z., Keenan, J. P. & O'Connor, M. (2002). Lesions of the fusiform face area impair perception of facial configuration in prosopagnosia. *Neurology, 58*, 71–78.

Basser, P. J., Mattiello, J. & LeBihan, D. (1994). MR diffusion tensor spectroscopy and imaging. *Biophysical Journal, 66*, 259–267.

Bellugi, U., Jarvinen-Pasley, A., Doyle, T. F., Reilly, J., Reiss, A. L. & Korenberg, J. (2007). Affect, social behavior, and the brain in Williams syndrome. *Current Directions in Psychological Science, 16*, 99–101.

Campbell, L. E., Daly, E., Toal, F., Stevens, A., Azuma, R., Karmiloff-Smith, A., Murphy, D. G. & Murphy, K. C. (2009). Brain structural differences associated with the behavioural phenotype in children with Williams syndrome. *Brain Research, 1258*, 96–107.

Canteras, N. S., Resstel, L. B., Bertoglio, L. J., Carobrez Ade, P. & Guimaraes, F. S. (2010). Neuroanatomy of anxiety. *Current Topics in Behavioral Neuroscience, 2*, 77–96.

Cascio, C. J., Gerig, G. & Piven, J. (2007). Diffusion tensor imaging: Application to the study of the developing brain. *Journal of American Academy of Child and Adolescent Psychiatry, 46*, 213–223.

Conturo, T. E., Williams, D. L., Smith, C. D., Gultepe, E., Akbudak, E. & Minshew, N. J. (2008). Neuronal fiber pathway abnormalities in autism: an initial MRI diffusion tensor tracking study of hippocampo-fusiform and amygdalo-fusiform pathways. *Journal of the International Neuropsychololgy Society, 14*, 933–946.

Costafreda, S. G., Brammer, M. J., David, A. S. & Fu, C. H. (2007). Predictors of amygdala activation during the processing of emotional stimuli: A meta-analysis of 385 PET and fMRI studies. *Brain Research Review, 58*(1), 57–70.

Dale, A. M., Fischl, B. & Sereno, M. I. (1999). Cortical surface-based analysis: I. Segmentation and surface reconstruction. *Neuroimage, 9*, 179–194.

Deshpande, G., Libero, L. E., Sreenivasan, K. R., Deshpande, H. D. & Kana, R. K. (2013). Identification of neural connectivity signatures of autism using machine learning. *Frontiers in Human Neuroscience, 7*, 670.

Fischl, B., Sereno, M. I. & Dale, A. M. (1999). Cortical surface-based analysis: II: Inflation, flattening, and a surface-based coordinate system. *Neuroimage, 9*, 195–207.

Garrett, A. S., Menon, V., MacKenzie, K. & Reiss, A. L. (2004). Here's looking at you, kid: neural systems underlying face and gaze processing in fragile X syndrome. *Archives of General Psychiatry, 61*, 281–288.

Golarai, G., Hong, S., Haas, B. W., Galaburda, A. M., Mills, D. L., Bellugi, U., Grill-Spector, K. & Reiss, A. L. (2010). The fusiform face area is enlarged in Williams syndrome. *The Journal of Neuroscience, 30*, 6700–6712.

Grill-Spector, K., Knouf, N. & Kanwisher, N. (2004). The fusiform face area subserves face perception, not generic within-category identification. *Nature Neuroscience, 7*, 555–562.

Haas, B. W. & Reiss, A. L. (2012). Social brain development in Williams syndrome: the current status and directions for future research. *Frontiers in Psychology, 3*, 186–228.

Haas, B. W., Barnea-Goraly, N., Lightbody, A. A., Patnaik, S. S., Hoeft, F., Hazlett, H., Piven, J. & Reiss, A. L. (2009a). Early white-matter abnormalities of the ventral frontostriatal pathway in fragile X syndrome. *Developmental Medicine and Child Neurology, 51*, 593–599.

Haas, B. W., Mills, D., Yam, A., Hoeft, F., Bellugi, U. & Reiss, A. (2009b). Genetic influences on sociability: heightened amygdala reactivity and event-related responses to positive social stimuli in Williams syndrome. *Journal of Neuroscience, 29*, 1132–1139.

Haas, B. W., Hoeft, F., Searcy, Y. M., Mills, D., Bellugi, U. & Reiss, A. (2009c). Individual differences in social behavior predict amygdala response to fearful facial expressions in Williams syndrome. *Neuropsychologia, 48*, 1283–1288.

Haas, B. W., Hoeft, F., Barnea-Goraly, N., Golarai, G., Bellugi, U. & Reiss, A. L. (2012). Preliminary evidence of abnormal white matter related to the fusiform gyrus in Williams syndrome: a diffusion tensor imaging tractography study. *Genes, Brain and Behavior, 11*, 62–68.

Haas, B. W., Barnea-Goraly, N., Sheau, K. E., Yamagata, B., Ullas, S. & Reiss, A. L. (2013). Altered microstructure within social-cognitive brain networks. *Cerebral Cortex*. doi: 10.1093/cercor/bht135

Haas, B. W., Sheau, K., Kelley, R. G., Thompson, P. M. & Reiss, A. L. (2014). Regionally specific increased volume of the amygdala in Williams syndrome: evidence from surface-based modeling. *Human Brain Mapping, 35*, 866–874.

Hagerman, R. J. & Sobesky, W. E. (1989). Psychopathology in fragile X syndrome. *American Journal of Orthopsychiatry, 59*, 142–152.

Jerrett, S. A. & Corsak, J. (1988). Clinical utility of topographic EEG brain mapping. *Clinical EEG and Neuroscience, 19*, 134–143.

Jiang, X., Bollich, A., Cox, P., Hyder, E., James, J., Gowani, S. A., … Riesenhuber, M. (2013). A quantitative link between face discrimination deficits and neuronal selectivity for faces in autism. *Neuroimage Clinical, 2,* 320–331.

Jou, R. J., Jackowski, A. P., Papademetris, X., Rajeevan, N., Staib, L. H. & Volkmar, F. R. (2011). Diffusion tensor imaging in autism spectrum disorders: preliminary evidence of abnormal neural connectivity. *Australian and New Zealand Journal of Psychiatry, 45,* 153–162.

Kanwisher, N. & Yovel, G. (2006). The fusiform face area: a cortical region specialized for the perception of faces. *Philosophical Transactions of the Royal Society of London B: Biological Science, 361,* 2109–2128.

Kanwisher, N., McDermott, J. & Chun, M. M. (1997). The fusiform face area: a module in human extrastriate cortex specialized for face perception. *Journal of Neuroscience, 17,* 4302–4311.

Kleinhans, N. M., Richards, T., Johnson, L. C., Weaver, K. E., Greenson, J., Dawson, G. & Aylward, E. (2011). fMRI evidence of neural abnormalities in the subcortical face processing system in ASD. *Neuroimage, 54,* 697–704.

Logothetis, N. K. (2008). What we can do and what we cannot do with fMRI. *Nature, 453,* 869–878.

Martens, M. A., Wilson, S. J., Dudgeon, P. & Reutens, D. C. (2009). Approachability and the amygdala: insights from Williams syndrome. *Neuropsychologia, 47,* 2446–2453.

Menon, V., Leroux, J., White, C. D. & Reiss, A. L. (2004). Frontostriatal deficits in fragile X syndrome: relation to FMR1 gene expression. *Proceedings of the National Academy of Sciences USA, 101,* 3615–3620.

Mobbs, D., Garrett, A. S., Menon, V., Rose, F. E., Bellugi, U. & Reiss, A. L. (2004). Anomalous brain activation during face and gaze processing in Williams syndrome. *Neurology, 62,* 2070–2076.

Mobbs, D., Eckert, M. A., Mills, D., Korenberg, J., Bellugi, U., Galaburda, A. M. & Reiss, A. L. (2007). Frontostriatal dysfunction during response inhibition in Williams syndrome. *Biological Psychiatry, 62,* 256–261.

Nacewicz, B. M., Dalton, K. M., Johnstone, T., Long, M. T., McAuliff, E. M., Oakes, T. R., Alexander, A. L. & Davidson, R. J. (2006). Amygdala volume and nonverbal social impairment in adolescent and adult males with autism. *Archives of General Psychiatry, 63,* 1417–1428.

Oishi, K., Faria, A., Jiang, H., Li, X., Akhter, K., Zhang, J., … Mori, S. (2009). Atlas-based whole brain white matter analysis using large deformation diffeomorphic metric mapping: application to normal elderly and Alzheimer's disease participants. *Neuroimage, 46,* 486–499.

Peng, D. X., Kelley, R. G., Quintin, E. M., Raman, M., Thompson, P. M. & Reiss, A. L. (2013). Cognitive and behavioral correlates of caudate subregion shape variation in fragile X syndrome. *Human Brain Mapping, 35*(6), 2861–2868.

Reiss, A. L. & Dant, C. C. (2003). The behavioral neurogenetics of fragile X syndrome: analyzing gene-brain-behavior relationships in child developmental psychopathologies. *Developmental Psychopathology, 15,* 927–968.

Reiss, A. L. & Hall, S. S. (2007). Fragile X syndrome: assessment and treatment implications. *Child and Adolescent Psychiatric Clinics of North America, 16,* 663–675.

Robbins, T. W. (2007). Shifting and stopping: fronto-striatal substrates, neurochemical modulation and clinical implications. *Philosophical Transactions of the Royal Society London B: Biological Science, 362,* 917–932.

Sarpal, D., Buchsbaum, B. R., Kohn, P. D., Kippenhan, J. S., Mervis, C. B., Morris, C. A., Meyer-Lindenberg, A. & Berman, K. F. (2008). A genetic model for understanding higher order visual processing: functional interactions of the ventral visual stream in Williams syndrome. *Cerebral Cortex, 18*, 2402–2409.

Thompson, P. M., Lee, A. D., Dutton, R. A., Geaga, J. A., Hayashi, K. M., Eckert, M. A., … Reiss, A. L. (2005). Abnormal cortical complexity and thickness profiles mapped in Williams syndrome. *Journal of Neuroscience, 25*, 4146–4158.

Van Essen, D. C., Drury, H. A., Dickson, J., Harwell, J., Hanlon, D. & Anderson, C. H. (2001). An integrated software suite for surface-based analyses of cerebral cortex. *Journal of the American Medical Informatics Association, 8*, 443–459.

Waiter, G. D., Williams, J. H., Murray, A. D., Gilchrist, A., Perrett, D. I. & Whiten, A. (2004). A voxel-based investigation of brain structure in male adolescents with autistic spectrum disorder. *Neuroimage, 22*, 619–625.

Weng, S. J., Carrasco, M., Swartz, J. R., Wiggins, J. L., Kurapati, N., Liberzon, I., … Monk, C. S. (2011). Neural activation to emotional faces in adolescents with autism spectrum disorders. *Journal of Child Psychology and Psychiatry, 52*, 296–305.

Zilles, K., Palomero-Gallagher, N. & Amunts, K. (2013). Development of cortical folding during evolution and ontogeny. *Trends in Neurosciences, 36*(5), 275–284.

4

RESEARCHING THE BRAIN IN NEURODEVELOPMENTAL DISORDERS

Sarah Lloyd-Fox

4.1 Why do we use brain imaging, and what do we hope to find?

The development of non-invasive brain-imaging techniques over the last 20 years has led to an exponential growth in our understanding of brain function and structure. Over the last decade, advances in neuroimaging technology and software have opened a new avenue for research of the developing human brain, allowing us to investigate questions that until recently would have seemed impossible with existing behavioural methods. Importantly, neuroimaging methods do not rely on an overt signal from the participant (such as a point or verbal information), which may be both difficult to elicit in certain populations and influenced by a number of factors such as motivation, social inhibition and temperament. Furthermore, children and infants often understand more than they are able to produce, and measuring the brain can side step this issue. Moreover, brain-imaging measurements are not susceptible to subjective decisions from the experimenter, and provide a dependent measure that can be used across a wide range of populations, cultures and settings. Advances in neuroimaging research have allowed us to further understand the development of typical cognition and brain function. Critically, this knowledge has allowed a recent shift in the use of neuroimaging towards the study of the developing brain in situations where this development may be compromised in some way. These may include the impact of acute brain injury in early infancy, chronic conditions (such as cerebral palsy), the impact of environmental factors (such as poverty and nutrition), and genetically related conditions or developmental disorders (such as Williams syndrome, Down syndrome, Autism Spectrum Disorders or ADHD). In particular, objective measures of brain function within the first few months and years of life could be used to assess how the timing and nature of developmental disorders impact on cognitive development, and to inform and evaluate interventional strategies (see Chapter 2 for a detailed discussion).

This chapter will overview the primary methods for studying the brain during development, then focus on the relatively new technique of functional Near Infrared Spectroscopy (fNIRS) outlining why it is used increasingly in developmental research. Then, I will highlight some of the practical challenges involved with studying infants and children and overview the key developmental psychopathology findings with fNIRS.

4.2 Measuring brain function and anatomy

Neuroimaging methods either detect the direct activation related to electrical activity of the brain (e.g. electroencephalography: EEG; magnetoelectro-encephalography: MEG) or the consequent haemodynamic response (e.g. positron emission tomography: PET; functional magnetic resonance imaging: fMRI; functional near infrared spectroscopy: fNIRS – see Figure 4.1). Chapter 3 discussed the traditional brain-imaging techniques such as MRI, fMRI, DTI and EEG in detail. Understanding the conceptual, methodological and statistical challenges that these technologies pose for the study of the developing brain will allow researchers to direct the appropriate method to the developmental disorder under consideration (Peterson, 2003).

A major limitation for developmental brain-imaging research is methodological. Many of these techniques, which are well established in adults, have limiting factors restricting or preventing their use in infants and young children including those with neurodevelopmental disorders (see Figure 4.2). PET requires the use of radioisotopes, whilst fMRI and MEG require the participant to remain very still, usually swaddled or restrained. There has been some infant research published using these techniques (Blasi et al., 2011; Dehaene-Lambertz et al., 2010; Dehaene-Lambertz, Dehaene & Hertz-Pannier, 2002; Huotilainen et al., 2003; Imada et al., 2006; Tzourio-Mazoyer et al., 2002). However, this work has generally been restricted to the study of sleeping or sedated infants or children over the age of five. Studies are rarely undertaken with PET on infants and children unless there is a clinical need (Chugani, Phelps & Mazziotta, 1987; Tzourio-Mazoyer et al., 2002) as the use of radioisotopes in healthy developing populations is not encouraged or generally approved by ethical committees.

One other technique increasingly used with developmental populations is MEG (for a review see Hari & Salmelin, 2012). MEG has very fine temporal resolution and potentially finer spatial resolution (Dick, Lloyd-Fox, Blasi, Elwell & Mills, 2013). Typically, participants sit in a seat with a MEG scanner placed around their head and must remain relatively motionless. For these reasons MEG has largely been restricted to the study of older children and adults rather than with early developmental populations, though recent advances and pioneering work suggests this technique may become more and more suitable (Draganova et al., 2005; Imada et al., 2006; Travis et al., 2011).

To study brain function in infants and young children (including those with, or at risk of, a developmental disorder), the most frequently used methods are EEG

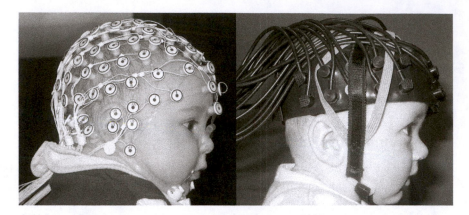

FIGURE 4.1 Left: An infant wearing a Hydrocel Geodesic Sensor Net (http://www. egi.com). Right: An infant wearing the BBK-NIRS headgear (photos with permission from S. Lloyd-Fox, Birkbeck).

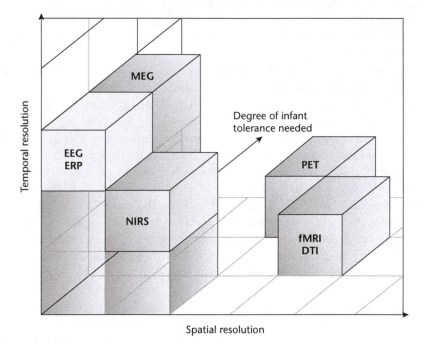

FIGURE 4.2 The relative degree of tolerance needed from the infant for each method, ranging from light grey (low) to dark grey (high), and the spatial and temporal resolution of NIRS compared with other infant functional neuroimaging methods: EEG, electroencephalography; ERP, event-related potential; MEG, magnetoencephalography; NIRS, near infrared spectroscopy; fMRI, functional magnetic resonance imaging; DTI, diffusion tensor imaging; PET, positron emission tomography. Reprinted from Lloyd-Fox, Blasi and Elwell, *Neuroscience and Biobehavioural Reviews*, 34. Copyright 2010, with permission from Elsevier.

and fNIRS (described below). They both use a similar experimental setting, are non-invasive and easy to administer with this age range. MRI has been used extensively with older children (over the age of five years) for studies of brain function and structure, and more frequently for the study of brain anatomy in younger children and infants. Given that all these techniques are non-invasive, the ability to take repeated measurements within the same individuals facilitates longitudinal, developmental and intervention studies. Yet, below, we will discuss the advantages and disadvantages of these non-invasive measures for use in infants, young children and those with neurodevelopmental disorders.

4.3 functional Near Infrared Spectroscopy (fNIRS)

The use of near infrared light to monitor intact organs began as a discovery at a dinner table with the passage of light being observed through a steak bone at a family supper in the 1970s (Jöbsis-vanderVliet, 1999). In 1993 the first reports were published of the use of NIRS to detect the haemodynamic response to cortical activation. Since then, the technology has been used to investigate cortical function in a range of age groups including adults (Ferrari & Quaresima, 2012) and children (Nagamitsu, Yamashita, Tanaka & Matsuishi, 2012). It is relatively recently that researchers have realized the potential of NIRS as an assay of infants' neuronal activity and brain organization (Lloyd-Fox, Blasi & Elwell, 2010). There is a range of commercially produced as well as 'in-house' manufactured NIRS systems available. The choice of which system to use is often driven by the cost and availability of infant- or child-appropriate arrays and headgear (for more detailed reviews of available systems and their application in infancy research, see Lloyd-Fox et al., 2010; Wolf, Ferrari & Quaresima, 2007).

When neurons fire, their metabolic demands change, provoking a complex set of changes in oxygen and glucose consumption, local cerebral blood flow and blood volume (Buxton, 2009). To a first approximation, a typical haemodynamic response to cortical neuronal activation in adults drives an increase in local blood flow that is disproportionate to the local oxygen demand, thus leading to an increase in oxyhaemoglobin (HbO_2) and a (smaller) decrease in deoxyhaemoglobin (HHb) as it is displaced from the veins, and hence an increase in total haemoglobin (HbT) (Villringer & Chance, 1997; for a complete treatment, see Buxton, 2009). Haemoglobin is the protein in red blood cells that transports oxygen and contains iron. This change in local haemoglobin concentrations is the basis of NIRS. Biological tissue is relatively transparent to light in the near infrared part of the spectrum, allowing several centimetres of tissue to be illuminated. This fortuitous 'optical window' coincides with the favourable differential absorption spectra of oxy- and deoxy- haemoglobin, thus allowing near-infrared absorption spectroscopy methods to provide a non-invasive measure of tissue oxygenation and haemodynamics.

With this optical technique, the light migrates from sources to detectors located on the head, by travelling through the skin, skull and underlying brain tissue

(Jöbsis, 1977; Villringer & Chance, 1997). In infants the majority of the light, measured by the detector in each channel (source–detector pair), has interrogated cortex approximately midway between source and detector and half this distance in depth from the scalp surface (Fukui, Ajichi & Okada, 2003). The attenuation (or loss) of this light (in the wavelength range 650–1000nm) is due to both absorption and scattering effects within these tissues, which will differ according to the age of the participant. Blood oxyhaemoglobin (HbO_2) and deoxyhaemoglobin (HHb) chromophores have different absorption properties of near infrared light enabling blood oxygenation to be measured. If scattering is assumed to be constant, the measured changes in the attenuation of the near infrared light can therefore be used to calculate the changes in blood oxyhaemoglobin (HbO_2), deoxyhaemoglobin (HHb) and total haemoglobin ($HbT = HbO_2 + HHb$) in the illuminated tissue. The changes in concentration of these chromophores can be used as surrogate markers of brain blood oxygen level, and hence provide a means of investigating brain function.

Stimulus onset and neuronal activation induces an increase in the concentration of HbO_2, which is usually accompanied by a lesser decrease in HHb concentration. This activation-induced vascular response is known as the haemodynamic response function (HRF). The shape of the HRF may vary according to the evoking stimuli (i.e. differences in amplitude are observed between brief and prolonged stimulus presentation) as well as the underlying neural activity. Furthermore, the light transport properties of tissue, and the thickness of the tissue and skull, differ over development and as a consequence light travels further, and will interrogate more of the brain, in younger infants (Duncan et al., 1996; Fukui et al., 2003). In pre-term infants and neonates – if measurement channels are placed over the whole head (optical tomography) – it is possible to interrogate both cortical and subcortical brain regions. However, beyond this age when the head size exceeds approximately 11cm diameter, this is no longer possible. The majority of studies with infants use arrays of channels over targeted brain regions (optical topography), and measure cortical brain regions only, with regions such as the fusiform face gyrus or insula being out of reach.

Due to the relatively transparent properties of the neonate head, initial work with infants took place within a clinical setting investigating cerebral oxygenation in neonates. Work particularly focused on sick and/or premature babies to study infants at risk for subsequent neurodevelopmental abnormalities (Brazy, Lewis, Mitnick & Jöbsis vander Vliet, 1985; Nicklin, Hassan, Wickramasinghe & Spencer, 2003; Wyatt, Cope, Delpy, Wray & Reynolds, 1986). Later, developmental researchers began to apply NIRS to the investigation of functional cortical activation: the first study to be published in infants was undertaken by Meek and colleagues in 1998 (Meek et al., 1998). In a basic NIRS experiment, the onset of a stimulus (for instance a flashing checkerboard) triggers neuronal activation, which thereby induces an increase in the concentration of HbO_2 and a lesser decrease in HHb concentration. The particular amplitude and timing of this activation-induced vascular response is known as the haemodynamic response function

(HRF). The shape of the signal may vary according to the evoking stimuli (i.e. differences in amplitude are observed between brief and prolonged stimulus presentation) as well as the underlying neural activity.

Further refinement and application of fNIRS over the next ten years will contribute significantly to the advancement of our understanding of the developing brain, particularly during infancy. Recent work in various research labs has already led to major progress in these areas. For example, the development of multiple source-detector distance arrays to investigate depth discrimination of the haemodynamic response; an ever-increasing number of channels allowing for a wider coverage of the head; and advances in the design of the headgear providing improved quality of the optical signals and flexibility of testing environment (for review see Lloyd-Fox et al., 2010). Indeed, evidence of the flexibility of this technology is provided by our recent work using fNIRS to conduct the first functional neuroimaging study in Africa (Lloyd-Fox et al., 2014). Strikingly, from the time of arrival at the rural field-station we were able to set up the equipment, train a local field worker and run our first fNIRS infant participant within two and a half hours of arrival. This recent research highlights the flexibility of this technology and potential future applications. Future innovations on the horizon include the development of wireless fNIRS systems which will enable research to be even more ecologically valid with testing done at clinics or even in the home, and the capacity for recordings while the infant or child is fully mobile (i.e. crawling, walking).

The number of research laboratories that have recently acquired, or are in the process of acquiring, a system for fNIRS is increasing rapidly. The use of NIRS to study functional brain activation in infants is a rapidly increasing research area (Cristia et al., 2013; Gervain et al., 2011; Lloyd-Fox et al., 2010). Whereas in early fNIRS studies the main aim was typically to detect the neural response to basic stimuli in primary cortical areas, such as response to acoustic tones in the auditory cortex (Sakatani, Chen, Lichty, Zuo & Wang, 1999) or stroboscopic flashing light in the visual cortex (Hoshi et al., 2000; Zaramella et al., 2001), as with EEG, more recently researchers have focussed on more complex questions about the brain and cognition such as the processing of object permanence and identity (Baird et al., 2002; Wilcox, Hirshkowitz, Hawkins & Boas, 2013), social communication (Grossmann, Parise & Friederici, 2010; Minagawa-Kawai et al., 2009), speech and voice perception (Gervain et al., 2011; Lloyd-Fox, Blasi, Mercure, Elwell & Johnson, 2012), and human actions (Ichikawa, Kanazawa, Yamaguchi & Kakigi, 2010; Lloyd-Fox, Wu, Richards, Elwell & Johnson, 2013b). Furthermore, recently the technique has been applied to the study of functional connectivity across infancy (Homae et al., 2010; Watanabe, Homae & Taga, 2010). Since the first in 1998, the number of published fNIRS infant studies has increased dramatically and now exceeds 100. In a recent attempt to document these studies, researchers have developed a database repository for fNIRS developmental researchers to update new publications so that the community can stay up to date on new findings (Cristia et al., 2013). fNIRS has also been used extensively in studies of child development, particularly by researchers in Japan who have historically had longstanding collaborations with the commercial suppliers of NIRS systems and therefore are one of the countries with the most prolific publication rate (e.g. Moriguchi & Hiraki, 2009, 2011).

A recent shift in the use of fNIRS has been towards the study of the infant brain on an individual level (Lloyd-Fox et al., 2013b; Wilcox et al., 2013). This advance in the application of fNIRS is important as the identification of significant haemodynamic responses within individuals allows us to look at the relationship between brain function and other variables such as age, demographics and behavioural data. For example, we have recently discovered a relationship between individual infant's patterns of brain activation to the perception of other's actions and the development of the infant's own fine motor skills (Lloyd-Fox et al., 2013b). Further, combining neural markers with behavioural assessments allowed us to rule out effects of age, gender and general cognitive development. It is essential, if we are to move forward with the use of fNIRS as a measure of individual differences, that we first identify the factors influencing reliability in the measures. In recent work, we investigated the replicability of obtaining similar haemodynamic responses across a longitudinal study (Blasi, Lloyd-Fox, Johnson & Elwell, 2014) at the group and individual level. While group test–re-test analyses showed a high degree of correlation in the magnitude and spatial distribution of the response across the two measurements (8.5 months apart: at 4–8 and 12–16 months), the individual reliability showed greater variability. The latter variability was acceptable, and within the range of individual reliability for fMRI data (Bennett & Miller, 2010). However, these findings highlight the importance of using standardized and reliable data acquisition parameters.

4.4 fNIRS compared to other neuroimaging techniques

The relative attributes of EEG, fMRI and fNIRS are outlined in Table 4.1 (see also Chapter 3 for a discussion). The major advantage of fNIRS compared with EEG is that it is less susceptible to data corruption by movement artefacts and offers a more highly spatially resolved image of activation allowing the localization of brain responses to specific cortical regions. The temporal resolution of EEG is highest: the precision of which can reach up to a thousand hertz (Luck, 2005). In comparison with fMRI, fNIRS has high temporal resolution, is silent allowing easy presentation of auditory stimuli, and can measure both oxy- and deoxy-haemoglobin providing a more complete measure of the haemodynamic response. Furthermore, both fNIRS and EEG are far less invasive, cost less in terms of both the equipment and session running costs, and are more ecologically valid and easier to administer in relation to fMRI, particularly in infants. fNIRS and EEG can both be: 1) undertaken while the participants are sitting on a chair or their parent's lap, rather than lying down within a MRI scanner; 2) can accommodate some degree of movement, in contrast to MRI which requires the participant to remain motionless; and 3) often involve shorter lengths of assessment (EEG/NIRS: 5–10 minutes vs fMRI: 30–60 minutes), compared to fMRI. This is important as it has been found that there is often considerably more motion artefact in the data from developmental populations compared with adult populations (Kotsoni, Byrd & Casey, 2006) and due to the length of fMRI studies participants may not complete the study (i.e. infants can wake up before the study has finished or children can get bored and inattentive). Furthermore, in fMRI differences in the extent of head movement between different ages can introduce confounds into the experimental design and analysis (Power, Barnes, Snyder, Schlaggar & Petersen, 2012).

When undertaking research with infants, fNIRS headgear can be placed on the head and a study is ready to begin within 30 seconds. For EEG when using the saline electrodes (as in Figure 4.1) administration time is relatively short and the study can begin within approximately one minute. However, the gel electrodes can take considerably longer (ten to fifteen minutes) to prepare and so in developmental populations can have a significant impact on compliance (although the recordings generally have better signal to noise ratio). It is recommended with both methods that two experimenters run the study so that one can entertain the participant while the headgear is prepared. For MRI, depending on the age of the population under study, the administration and preparation time can be considerable. If studying infants, usually one must wait for them to fall asleep (sedation is generally not used in healthy populations), and then they are carefully swaddled, and ear protection is administered before they enter the scanner room (Figure 4.1). For older children, as well as ear protection, some time is required to desensitize them to the method beforehand, either with information pamphlets and/or a mock scanner session where they can see the set-up and hear the sound of the scanner before the actual testing session. A meta-analysis (Leroux, Lubin, Houdé & Lanoë, 2013) of fMRI studies of children and adolescents (which included 4,000 individuals) found that coaching preparation (rather than a mock scanner) and paradigm choice had the most significant effect on data inclusion and quality. Despite these efforts, sometimes the study will not work with children as they will find the environment too claustrophobic or clinical, will continue to find the noise level aversive, or may not be eligible for scanning if they have metal in their body, i.e. orthodontic devices.

Though fMRI and fNIRS measure the same haemodynamic response, generally MRI techniques have an intrinsically limited acquisition rate usually at a minimum of one hertz (Huettel, Song & McCarthy, 2008; Weishaupt, 2006), whereas NIRS can acquire data rapidly, up to hundreds of hertz, thus providing a more complete temporal picture (Huppert, Hoge, Diamond, Franceschini & Boas, 2006). MRI is the best technique for measuring precise spatial anatomy and precisely localized functional responses (mms). In contrast, the depth resolution of fNIRS is dependent on the age of the infant or child and the optical properties of the tissue (Fukui et al., 2003), and the spatial resolution is limited by the source-detector configuration (0.5mm upwards). For both fNIRS and EEG there is no capacity for measuring brain structure for anatomical reference, therefore MRI will always be the primary choice for obtaining structural information.

TABLE 4.1 The relative attributes of the three popular infant neuroimaging techniques

Technique	fNIRS	EEG	fMRI
Type of response measured	Changes in HbO_2 and HHb concentration	Neuronal excitation	Changes in BOLD (mainly HHb concentration)
Spatial localization of response	Good	Relatively poor	Very good
Time locking of response	Good	Very good	Relatively poor
Acquisition of signal	Milliseconds	Milliseconds	Seconds
Timing of signal	Seconds	Milliseconds	Seconds
Participant state	Awake/asleep	Awake/asleep	Asleep/immobile
Experimental setting	Infant on parent's lap or seated next to parent	Infant on parent's lap or seated next to parent	Infant wrapped up on bed in MRI scanner
Freedom of movement of participant	Relatively high	Relatively high (but preferably not)	None
Freedom of movement of equipment	Yes	For certain systems	No
Length of preparation of participant	Short	Short/Medium	Long
Length of experiment	Short	Short	Long
Instrumentation noise	None	None	High – ear protection needed
Cost of study	Fairly low	Fairly low	Relatively high

Researchers have begun to try to optimize fNIRS data by using information from structural age-appropriate MRI templates. Alternatively, structural infant MRIs measured during one session could be used in combination with NIRS functional data measured during a second session, to localize responses. This technique is often used in transcranial magnetic stimulation (TMS) studies with adults with the use of MRI templates and provides a more accurate alternative to scalp anatomical landmarks (such as aligning data based on the position of the nasion, inion and pre-auricular points), which can only provide a general understanding of the underlying brain regions. For developmental work, it is largely impractical to obtain structural MRI scans for each participant, which is why age-appropriate templates are an essential tool. In recent work we have investigated the reliability of co-registration of individual MRI-NIRS vs MRI templates (Lloyd-Fox et al., 2014). We co-registered NIRS channels to MRIs from the same infants aged four to seven months, and found reliable estimates of frontal and temporal cortical regions across this age range with the individual MRI data, which was largely confirmed during analyses using age-appropriate MRI templates. A standardized scalp surface map was generated of fNIRS channel locators to reliably locate cortical regions for NIRS developmental researchers, when individual MRI scans are unavailable. Current work is underway to co-register ten to twenty coordinates and EEG electrodes with underlying anatomy to provide a standardized map of scalp locations for the whole head (Richards, in preparation). These tools will be of great benefit to developmental researchers studying infancy, and could be extended across the first years of life.

Finally, research is underway to provide optimized measurements of brain activation by combining the advantages of these neuroimaging methods. This practice has been successfully implemented in research with adult participants, providing simultaneous measurements from two techniques, e.g. combined fNIRS and EEG (Moosmann et al., 2003), fNIRS and MRI (Steinbrink et al., 2006), and fMRI and EEG (Dale & Halgren, 2001; Eichele et al., 2005). Recently, researchers have also implemented multimodal measures for the study of infants (Cooper et al., 2009; Telkemeyer et al., 2009). In the first of these (Telkemeyer et al., 2009), newborn infants (3.32 ± 1.27 days) were presented with tonal auditory stimuli that varied in temporal structure and length (12, 25, 160 and 300 ms). Analysis of the auditory evoked potentials (AEPs) revealed a focussed response in the frontal and central electrodes. However, the EEG measures did not reveal any significant differences between the four conditions (12, 25, 160, and 300ms segments). In contrast, the haemodynamic measures (fNIRS) revealed a significant effect for the 25ms condition in the inferior and posterior temporal regions, and a significant effect of hemisphere in the temporoparietal region. These effects are of great importance as the integration of 25–50ms variations are essential for the perception of speech, and these findings suggest newborns are sensitive to such stimuli from the first days of life. This study highlights the importance of multimodal investigation, as the concurrent measures allowed the significant EEG effect to be investigated in further detail with the fNIRS. This multimodality approach has the potential to improve neurodevelopmental research through the study and/or clinical neuro-monitoring of infants at risk of compromised development due to, for example, a developmental disorder or in pre-term and term infants with acute brain injury (Toet & Lemmers, 2009).

4.5 Studying developmental disorders with fNIRS

As outlined above, several advantages of fNIRS (i.e. tolerance of movement, use in ecologically valid settings, easy set-up and administration) make it a highly suitable method for the study of individuals with psychiatric or developmental disorders. Indeed, the number of fNIRS studies that have been directed towards psychiatric research questions has increased significantly in recent years, totaling over 100 in late 2013 (Ehlis, Schneider, Dresler & Fallgatter, 2014). In adults and children these include studies on schizophrenia, eating disorders, affective syndromes, personality disorders, anxiety, and developmental disorders such as

Attention Deficit Hyperactivity Disorder (ADHD) (Ehlis et al., 2014). The majority of fNIRS studies on developmental disorders in childhood (after two years of age) have so far focussed on ADHD (see Chapter 9 for a detailed discussion of ADHD). These studies have consistently found altered haemodynamic responses (during tasks such as the Stroop test, Go/No-Go or working memory paradigms) in the frontal cortex (Jourdan Moser, Cutini, Weber & Schroeter, 2009; Negoro et al., 2010; Schecklmann et al., 2010; Xiao et al., 2012). fNIRS has also been increasingly used in the study of infants and children who may be at risk of compromised development. This form of research is particularly important in prospective longitudinal studies of infants at risk as it enables the identification of biomarkers of compromised development prior to the typical onset of observable behavioural markers, which usually become apparent in the second year of life or later. The assessment of individual differences in infants' responses is necessary for the discovery of early warning markers in infants at risk for compromised neurodevelopment (Elsabbagh & Johnson, 2010) and consequently for the development of prodromal interventions (see further discussion in Chapter 2 and Chapter 7). Importantly, we can also contrast patterns of brain activity in those infants at risk who do not go on to develop a developmental disorder with those without increased risk to assess whether some infants also develop compensatory mechanisms or display other patterns of responses. Whilst behavioural measures have been unable to distinguish between infants with low and high risk of developing Autism Spectrum Disorders (ASD) defined by a familial diagnosis before the first year of life, several recent EEG and fNIRS studies have identified differences in brain function in younger infants (Elsabbagh et al., 2009; Elsabbagh et al., 2012; Fox, Wagner, Shrock, Tager-Flusberg & Nelson, 2013; Guiraud et al., 2011; Lloyd-Fox et al., 2013a; Luyster, Wagner, Vogel-Farley, Tager-Flusberg & Nelson, 2011; McCleery, Akshoomoff, Dobkins & Carver, 2009). For example, Lloyd-Fox and colleagues (Lloyd-Fox et al., 2013a) used a social visual and auditory paradigm to investigate functional brain responses in infants with a familial risk of developing ASD. Infants were presented with social human movements (i.e. 'Peek-a-boo') and non-human static images (i.e. cars, helicopters, trains) while listening to vocal (i.e. laughter, crying, yawning) and non-vocal sounds (i.e. water running, rattles and bells).

We found evidence of diminished activation in response to both the visual and auditory social cues in infants at high risk of developing ASD when compared with age-matched low-risk infants (Figure 4.3). The observed differences were seen as early as four to six months of age and, in the absence of early behavioural markers. These findings are in line with EEG and fMRI research in older children finding atypical patterns of brain activation to the perception of social human actions (Pelphrey & Carter, 2008) and auditory stimuli (Čeponienė et al., 2003; Eyler, Pierce & Courchesne, 2012).

Adopting a similar approach, a fNIRS study by Fox and colleagues (Fox et al., 2013) with seven-month-olds who viewed videos of their mother or a stranger, found differences in the spatial distribution, timing and magnitude of the

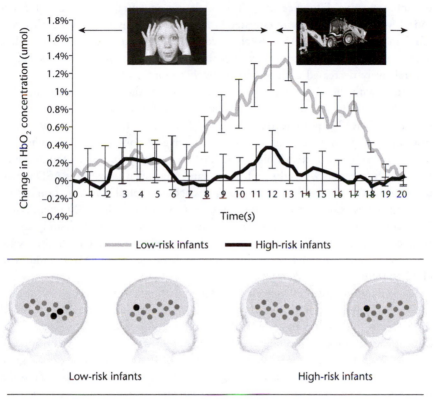

FIGURE 4.3   Visual and auditory social selective responses during a fNIRS study in infants with and without a familial risk of Autism Spectrum Disorders. Statistically significant haemodynamic responses to social > non-social visual stimuli (upper right panel) and vocal > non-vocal auditory stimuli (lower panel) are shown for the channel-by-channel t-test analysis in low- (grey) and high- (black) risk infants. The time course on the left shows the haemodymanic response to the visual social stimuli for these infants in the highlighted channel. This figure is adapted from a figure which appears in Lloyd–Fox et al. (2013a), Reduced neural sensitivity to social stimuli in infants at risk of autism, *Proceedings of the Royal Society, B, 280,* 1758, published by the Royal Society under the terms of the Creative Commons Attribution License.

haemodynamic response in high-risk ASD infants compared to low-risk infants, possibly reflecting differences in neurovasculature or neural architecture. Further fNIRS work by this group investigated functional connectivity across the first year of life in infants at risk for ASD (Keehn, Wagner, Tager-Flusberg & Nelson, 2013). They reported increased connectivity at three months relative to low-risk infants and relatively decreased connectivity at twelve months of age. These results are consistent with the view that atypical functioning of the brain may be manifest from the first few months of life in infants at risk for a later diagnosis of ASD. However, it is also possible that we have detected early manifestations of the broader ASD phenotype, trait activity or adaptive responses in infants who will later go on to be unaffected (Kaiser et al., 2010). It will therefore be of importance to revisit these results when the high-risk infants have been assessed for ASD at two to three years of age, to allow us to ascertain whether atypical brain function during early infancy is associated with later outcome (ASD or broader ASD phenotype). Interestingly, in support of this work in infancy, a recent fNIRS study found reduced interhemispheric connectivity in eight- to eleven-year-old children with ASD in bilateral temporal cortices, in line with other recent fMRI findings in children (Dinstein et al., 2011).

Recently, new research has been undertaken with infants with Down syndrome (DS) (see Chapter 11 for a detailed discussion of DS). In this study, they measured spontaneous fluctuations in cerebral blood oxygenation with fNIRS (Imai et al., 2014) to assess functional connectivity in infants who were born pre-term, at term, or with DS, while they were sleeping. While the early pre-term (gestational age of 23–34 weeks), late pre-term, and term (gestational age of 34–40 weeks) infants did not reveal any differences in connectivity, differences in functional connectivity and local haemodynamics were found in the infants with DS. These analyses suggested that the infants with DS had decreased functional connectivity relative to the other infants. However, it should be noted that while the early pre-term and late pre-term groups contained sample sizes of twelve to fifteen infants, the group with DS consisted of five infants. Therefore, individual differences in connectivity and/or signal variability may have had a far greater impact on the group data in the latter compared with the former participant groups. Continued research will help to elucidate these findings further.

fNIRS has recently been used as a prospective measure for risk markers of developmental psychopathology (Fekete, Beacher, Cha, Rubin & Mujica-Parodi, 2014). In previous research it has been shown that effortful control (EC) has been associated with the development of anxiety, depression and Attention Deficit Hyperactivity Disorder (ADHD). In this study they investigated small-world network properties (that is the degree to which functional demands for integration and segregation in networks are balanced) of the prefrontal cortex (known to be involved in EC) while children watched naturalistic videos. They found that children who exhibited lower effortful control on a behavioural task showed compromised small-world properties of the prefrontal cortex during the fNIRS study. The authors highlight the importance of future longitudinal studies to monitor such associations and to assess how these early indicators of risk link to later developmental psychopathology.

These findings highlight the sensitivity of fNIRS as a tool to provide an early biomarker of atypical development and to identify the physiological mechanisms behind atypical brain function.

4.6 Practical guidelines for measuring brain function in populations with neurodevelopmental disorders

There is an ever-increasing number of studies published using neuroimaging techniques to study developmental disorders in infants and children, many of which are discussed in greater detail elsewhere in this book (see Chapter 3). Developmental functional and structural imaging studies increasingly help to define the typically developing brain and assist in generating hypotheses about atypical function and target brain structures for research in developmental psychopathology (Bush, Valera & Seidman, 2005).

However, as outlined earlier, there are many practical considerations of brain imaging, which are specific to the study of infants and children. These may be amplified with some developmental psychopathological populations and should be given careful consideration during the preparation for new studies. Firstly, children may have a lower tolerance or higher anxiety in novel situations and so practice sessions with the neuroimaging equipment may become essential. Increased levels of anxiety have been reported across many developmental disorders, including Williams syndrome (Dykens, 2003).

For the EEG studies that form part of our longitudinal study on infants at risk for ASD at the Centre for Brain and Cognitive Development, Birkbeck University of London when the participants become older (one to two years of age) we practise putting EEG caps on teddies, the parents and the experimenters in the friendly reception area before moving to the testing session. A soft hat is placed on top of the EEG net to prevent infants from reaching and pulling on the elastic connectors, which could hurt them and damage the cap. Kylliäinen and colleagues use MEG to study children with ASD and run mock MEG scanning sessions as well as sending information videos and pamphlets to the families before the testing session (Kylliäinen, Braeutigam, Hietanen, Swithenby & Bailey, 2006). Some individuals may also have lower motivation to take part in the study (i.e. Down syndrome; Wishart, 1995), which may be more pronounced with the higher level of tolerance that neuroimaging techniques can require.

Secondly, with some populations it may be important to restrict the social interactions and number of new people that the infants and toddlers meet, which would be true for both behavioural and neuroimaging studies. In our work with infants at risk for ASD the team of experimenters consist of two people who remain constant across the visit, with one particularly focussed on interacting with the participant while the other communicates with the parent. This is standard practice across many labs working with developmental populations with ASD. Furthermore, in other developmental populations, such as Williams syndrome, it may also be important to restrict the number of experimenters as individuals with this developmental disorder are often highly sociable and so having too many people to interact with may distract them or expend their resources on activities other than the experimental paradigms of interest.

Thirdly, inattentiveness and/or motor restlessness has been reported across many developmental disorders such as ADHD and Williams syndrome (Dykens & Rosner, 1999). This can be a major confound for brain-imaging studies, particularly fMRI, where the children are required to remain still and concentrate for significant periods of time. In contrast, this is where fNIRS has a firm advantage over other techniques. In less restrictive neuroimaging studies such as NIRS or EEG, it may help to allow children with ADHD to stand up and stretch and have several breaks during a ten- to twenty-minute study. Monitoring attention during the task by either videotaping the participant or measuring heart rate or body movements with actigraphy is extremely useful to either remove segments in which the participant was inattentive or to study the effect of attentional states on other brain processes.

Fourthly, some individuals may need physical support which may affect the range of neuroimaging studies that they are able to participate in and/or affect the experimental paradigms under investigation. For example, infants and some young children may need to sit on their parent's lap while taking part in an EEG or NIRS study but depending on the experimental paradigm (i.e. physical arousal), parent's touch may need to be carefully monitored. For the majority of developmental disorders, individuals do not conform to a rigid set of diagnosed cognitive and physical abilities but rather sit on a spectrum. Those with more severe physical impairments may need further support when undergoing brain-imaging studies, such as adapted chairs or equipment.

Finally, it is important to be aware of a number of conceptual issues that come with the study of atypical development (Vanderwert & Nelson, 2014). Firstly, as Vanderwert and Nelson (2014) emphasize, there is a substantial need for careful phenotyping of the population in question and without this it may prove very difficult to identify why one group differs from another. Secondly, as highlighted in the study on DS above, many of these studies are conducted with small sample sizes. Therefore, there is a great need for larger-scale longitudinal research to be undertaken, particularly as there can be such a high degree of individual variability in some developmental disorders (see Chapter 7 for a discussion). Indeed, it is possible that atypical group responses in small samples could simply reflect atypical responses in the general population. Finally, most studies that have investigated developmental disorders with fNIRS thus far have simply reported group differences in the haemodynamic response. Although this is important, such findings do not address the deeper issue of why such differences have arisen, whether there is a difference in neural circuitry, whether particular effects differ across disorders, or whether they are present at birth or arise through infancy and childhood (Vanderwert & Nelson, 2014).

4.7 Conclusions

We anticipate that further refinement and application of fNIRS over the next ten years will contribute significantly to the advancement of our understanding of the developing brain. Recent work in various research labs has already led to major progress in these areas. For example, the development of multiple source-detector distance arrays to investigate depth discrimination of the haemodynamic response; an ever-increasing number of channels allowing for a wider coverage of the head; and advances in the design of the headgear providing improved quality of the optical signals (for review see Lloyd-Fox et al., 2010). Furthermore, the number of research laboratories that have recently acquired, or are in the process of acquiring, a system for fNIRS is increasing rapidly. A growing proportion of these are applying fNIRS to the study of neurodevelopmental disorders, and I estimate we will see a substantial number of publications on innovative work in this area over the next few years. Future innovations on the horizon include the development of wireless fNIRS systems that will enable research to be even more ecologically valid with testing done at clinics or even in the home, and the capacity for recordings while the infant or child is fully mobile (i.e. crawling, walking); combined EEG-fNIRS systems for enhanced data collection of both temporal and spatial information; and the development of more appropriate headgear for testing a wider range of participants such as during toddlerhood (i.e. can measure around hair while still being comfortable and lightweight). In recent work at the Central European University in Budapest we have also conducted studies with two infants wearing fNIRS headgear simultaneously to investigate responses in a communicative context with a third person (adult actor) and assess the influence of the presence of each other (Lloyd-Fox, Széplaki-Köllőd, Yin, J & Csibra, under review). This approach could have a wide application across research designed to evoke an ecologically valid setting.

Over the last two decades, functional and structural imaging has allowed great advances in our understanding of the neural networks and brain regions that evidence atypical function in developmental disorders. A major component of this work has been to look at the common behavioural markers associated with developmental psychopathologies, and to investigate the regions of the brain known to be involved in these processes during typical brain function. Strong emphasis has been placed on conducting larger-scale studies, which refine neuroanatomical focus, integrate paradigms which interrogate multiple developmental disorders (given the overlapping diagnosis of disorders, i.e. ADHD/ASD in so many individuals; see discussion in Chapter 9), combine brain-imaging work with measures of behaviour and environment, and interface with genetic studies (Bush et al., 2005; Karmiloff-Smith et al., 2012; Karmiloff-Smith, 1998; for further discussion see Chapters 1 and 2). Furthermore, the way in which we measure developmental disorders should be given careful consideration as recruitment criteria, success rates, analytical procedures of imaging data and age at test could constrain the interpretation of different populations. Finally, careful thought should always be given to why we choose to study developmental disorders with brain-imaging techniques, and the relevance of the measures that are undertaken for the questions asked.

Practical tips

1. Careful thought should be given when choosing to study developmental disorders with brain-imaging techniques, i.e. what is the relevance of the measure that you want to use, and how can your chosen technique help advance our understanding of developmental disorder X?
2. With fNIRS, the most successful studies, particularly with awake infants, rely on well-designed headgear. Most commercial NIRS systems do not provide infant headgear and the design of this is largely left for the researcher to solve. Therefore, remember that the better the fit of the headgear, the lower the likelihood of creating artefact in the signal during movement of the infant, and the higher the signal to noise ratio.
3. fNIRS is highly suitable for studies with infants, both awake and asleep, where the intention is to localize responses to the surface of the cortex. However, remember that fNIRS can only measure to a certain depth into the head, and that this depth decreases from birth to adulthood, therefore measurement of subcortical regions is largely beyond the scope of this technique.

References

Baird, A. A., Kagan, J., Gaudette, T., Walz, K. A., Hershlag, N. & Boas, D. A. (2002). Frontal lobe activation during object permanence: Data from near-infrared spectroscopy. *NeuroImage, 16*(4), 1120–1126.

Bennett, C. M. & Miller, M. B. (2010). How reliable are the results from functional magnetic resonance imaging? *Annals of the New York Academy of Sciences, 1191*(1), 133–155.

Blasi, A., Mercure, E., Lloyd-Fox, S., Thomson, A., Brammer, M., Sauter, D., … Murphy, D. G. (2011). Early specialization for voice and emotion processing in the infant brain. *Current Biology, 21*, 1220–1224.

Blasi, A., Lloyd-Fox, S., Johnson, M. H. & Elwell, C. E. (2014). Test-retest reliability of fNIRS in infants. *Neurophotonics*, 1(2), 025005.

Brazy, J. E., Lewis, D. V., Mitnick, M. H. & Jöbsis vander Vliet, F. F. (1985). Noninvasive monitoring of cerebral oxygenation in preterm infants: preliminary observations. *Pediatrics, 75*(2), 217–225.

Bush, G., Valera, E. M. & Seidman, L. J. (2005). Functional neuroimaging of attention-deficit/hyperactivity disorder: A review and suggested future directions. *Biological Psychiatry, 57*(11), 1273–1284.

Buxton, R. (2009). *Introduction to Functional Magnetic Resonance Imaging: Principles and Techniques* (2nd ed.). Cambridge, UK: Cambridge University Press.

Čeponienė, R., Lepistö, T., Shestakova, A., Vanhala, R., Alku, P., Näätänen, R. & Yaguchi, K. (2003). Speech–sound-selective auditory impairment in children with autism: They can perceive but do not attend. *Proceedings of the National Academy of Sciences of the United States of America, 100*(9), 5567–5572.

Chugani, H. T., Phelps, M. E. & Mazziotta, J. C. (1987). Positron emission tomography study of human brain functional development. *Annals of Neurology, 22*(4), 487–497.

Cooper, R. J., Everdell, N. L., Enfield, L. C., Gibson, A. P., Worley, A. & Hebden, J. C. (2009). Design and evaluation of a probe for simultaneous EEG and near-infrared imaging of cortical activation. *Physics in Medicine and Biology, 54*(7), 2093–2102.

Cristia, A., Dupoux, E., Hakuno, Y., Lloyd-Fox, S., Schuetze, M., Kivits, J., … Minagawa-Kawai, Y. (2013). An online database of infant functional near infrared spectroscopy studies: A community-augmented systematic review. *PLoS ONE, 8*(3), e58906.

Dale, A. M. & Halgren, E. (2001). Spatiotemporal mapping of brain activity by integration of multiple imaging modalities. *Current Opinion in Neurobiology, 11*(2), 202–208.

Dehaene-Lambertz, G., Dehaene, S. & Hertz-Pannier, L. (2002). Functional neuroimaging of speech perception in infants. *Science, 298*(5600), 2013–2015.

Dehaene-Lambertz, G., Montavont, A., Jobert, A., Allirol, L., Dubois, J., Hertz-Pannier, L. & Dehaene, S. (2010). Language or music, mother or Mozart? Structural and environmental influences on infants' language networks. *Brain and Language, 114*(2), 53–65.

Dick, F., Lloyd-Fox, S., Blasi, A., Elwell, C. E. & Mills, D. (2013). Neuroimaging methods. In D. Mareschal, B. Butterworth & A. Tolmie (eds), *Educational Neuroscience* (pp. 13–45). Chichester: John Wiley & Sons.

Dinstein, I., Pierce, K., Eyler, L., Solso, S., Malach, R., Behrmann, M. & Courchesne, E. (2011). Disrupted neural synchronization in toddlers with autism. *Neuron, 70*(6), 1218–1225.

Draganova, R., Eswaran, H., Murphy, P., Huotilainen, M., Lowery, C. & Preissl, H. (2005). Sound frequency change detection in fetuses and newborns, a magneto-encephalographic study. *NeuroImage, 28*(2), 354–361.

Duncan, A., Meek, J. H., Clemence, M., Elwell, C. E., Fallon, P., Tyszczuk, L., … Delpy, D. T. (1996). Measurement of cranial optical path length as a function of age using phase resolved near infrared spectroscopy. *Pediatric Research, 39*(5), 889–894.

Dykens, E. M. (2003). Anxiety, fears, and phobias in persons with Williams syndrome. *Developmental Neuropsychology, 23*(1–2), 291–316.

Dykens, E. M. & Rosner, B. A. (1999). Refining behavioral phenotypes: Personality–motivation in Williams and Prader-Willi syndromes. *American Journal of Mental Retardation, 104*(2), 158–169.

Ehlis, A.-C., Schneider, S., Dresler, T. & Fallgatter, A. J. (2014). Application of functional near-infrared spectroscopy in psychiatry. *NeuroImage, 85*, 478–488.

Eichele, T., Specht, K., Moosmann, M., Jongsma, M. L. A., Quiroga, R. Q., Nordby, H. & Hugdahl, K. (2005). Assessing the spatiotemporal evolution of neuronal activation with single-trial event-related potentials and functional MRI. *Proceedings of the National Academy of Sciences of the United States of America, 102*(49), 17798–17803.

Elsabbagh, M. & Johnson, M. H. (2010). Getting answers from babies about autism. *Trends in Cognitive Sciences, 14*(2), 81–87.

Elsabbagh, M., Volein, A., Csibra, G., Holmboe, K., Garwood, H., Tucker, L., … Charman, T. (2009). Neural correlates of eye gaze processing in the infant broader autism phenotype. *Biological Psychiatry, 65*(1), 31–38.

Elsabbagh, M., Mercure, E., Hudry, K., Chandler, S., Pasco, G., Charman, T., … Johnson, M. H. (2012). Infant neural sensitivity to dynamic eye gaze is associated with later emerging autism. *Current Biology, 22*(4), 338–342.

Eyler, L. T., Pierce, K. & Courchesne, E. (2012). A failure of left temporal cortex to specialize for language is an early emerging and fundamental property of autism. *Brain,* *135*(3), 949–960.

Fekete, T., Beacher, F. D. C. C., Cha, J., Rubin, D. & Mujica-Parodi, L. R. (2014). Small-world network properties in prefrontal cortex correlate with predictors of psychopathology risk in young children: A NIRS study. *NeuroImage, 85,* 345–353.

Ferrari, M. & Quaresima, V. (2012). A brief review on the history of human functional near-infrared spectroscopy (fNIRS) development and fields of application. *NeuroImage,* *63*(2), 921–935.

Fox, S. E., Wagner, J. B., Shrock, C. L., Tager-Flusberg, H. & Nelson, C. A. (2013). Neural processing of facial identity and emotion in infants at high risk for Autism Spectrum Disorders. *Frontiers in Human Neuroscience, 7*(89), 1–18.

Fukui, Y., Ajichi, Y. & Okada, E. (2003). Monte Carlo prediction of near-infrared light propagation in realistic adult and neonatal head models. *Applied Optics, 42*(16), 2881–2887.

Gervain, J., Mehler, J., Werker, J. F., Nelson, C. A., Csibra, G., Lloyd-Fox, S., … Aslin, R. A. (2011). Near-infrared spectroscopy: A report from the McDonnell infant methodology consortium. *Developmental Cognitive Neuroscience, 1*(1), 22–46.

Grossmann, T., Parise, E. & Friederici, A. D. (2010). The detection of communicative signals directed at the self in infant prefrontal cortex. *Frontiers in Human Neuroscience, 4,* 201–218.

Guiraud, J. A., Kushnerenko, E., Tomalski, P., Davies, K., Ribeiro, H., Johnson, M. H. & others (2011). Differential habituation to repeated sounds in infants at high risk for autism. *Neuroreport, 22*(16), 845.

Hari, R. & Salmelin, R. (2012). Magnetoencephalography: From SQUIDs to neuroscience. *NeuroImage, 61*(2), 386–396.

Homae, F., Watanabe, H., Otobe, T., Nakano, T., Go, T., Konishi, Y. & Taga, G. (2010). Development of global cortical networks in early infancy. *Journal of Neuroscience, 30*(14), 4877–4882.

Hoshi, Y., Kohri, S., Matsumoto, Y., Kazutoshi, C., Matsuda, T., Okajima, S. & Fujimoto, S. (2000). Haemodynamic responses to photic stimulation in neonates. *Pediatric Neurology,* 23, 323–327.

Huettel, S., Song, A. W. & McCarthy, G. (2008). *Functional Magnetic Resonance Imaging* (2nd ed.). Sunderland, MA: Sinauer Associates.

Huotilainen, M., Kujala, A., Hotakainen, M., Shestakova, A., Kushnerenko, E., Parkkonen, L., … Näätänen, R. (2003). Auditory magnetic responses of healthy newborns. *Neuroreport, 14*(14), 1871–1875.

Huppert, T. J., Hoge, R. D., Diamond, S. G., Franceschini, M. A. & Boas, D. A. (2006). A temporal comparison of BOLD, ASL, and NIRS hemodynamic responses to motor stimuli in adult humans. *Neuroimage, 29*(2), 368–382.

Ichikawa, H., Kanazawa, S., Yamaguchi, M. K. & Kakigi, R. (2010). Infant brain activity while viewing facial movement of point-light displays as measured by near-infrared spectroscopy (NIRS). *Neuroscience Letters, 482*(2), 90–94.

Imada, T., Zhang, Y., Cheour, M., Taulu, S., Ahonen, A. & Kuhl, P. K. (2006). Infant speech perception activates Broca's area: a developmental magnetoencephalography study. *Neuroreport, 17*(10), 957–962.

Imai, M., Watanabe, H., Yasui, K., Kimura, Y., Shitara, Y., Tsuchida, S., … Taga, G. (2014). Functional connectivity of the cortex of term and preterm infants and infants with Down's syndrome. *NeuroImage, 85,* 272–278.

Jöbsis, F. F. (1977). Noninvasive, infrared monitoring of cerebral and myocardial oxygen sufficiency and circulatory parameters. *Science, 198*(4323), 1264–1267.

Jöbsis-vanderVliet, F. F. (1999). Discovery of the near-infrared window into the body and the early development of near-infrared spectroscopy. *Journal of Biomedical Optics, 4,* 392–396.

Jourdan Moser, S., Cutini, S., Weber, P. & Schroeter, M. L. (2009). Right prefrontal brain activation due to Stroop interference is altered in attention-deficit hyperactivity disorder – A functional near-infrared spectroscopy study. *Psychiatry Research, 173*(3), 190–195.

Kaiser, M. D., Hudac, C. M., Shultz, S., Lee, S. M., Cheung, C., Berken, A. M., … Pelphrey, K. A. (2010). Neural signatures of autism. *Proceedings of the National Academy of Sciences, 107*(49), 21223–21228.

Karmiloff-Smith, A. (1998). Development itself is the key to understanding developmental disorders. *Trends in Cognitive Sciences, 2*(10), 389–398.

Karmiloff-Smith, A., D'Souza, D., Dekker, T. M., Van Herwegen, J., Xu, F., Rodic, M. & Ansari, D. (2012). Genetic and environmental vulnerabilities in children with neurodevelopmental disorders. *Proceedings of the National Academy of Sciences, 109*(Supplement 2), 17261–17265.

Keehn, B., Wagner, J. B., Tager-Flusberg, H. & Nelson, C. A. (2013). Functional connectivity in the first year of life in infants at-risk for autism: a preliminary near-infrared spectroscopy study. *Frontiers in Human Neuroscience, 7,* 444–469.

Kotsoni, E., Byrd, D. & Casey, B. J. (2006). Special considerations for functional magnetic resonance imaging of pediatric populations. *Journal of Magnetic Resonance Imaging, 23*(6), 877–886.

Kylliäinen, A., Braeutigam, S., Hietanen, J. K., Swithenby, S. J. & Bailey, A. J. (2006). Face- and gaze-sensitive neural responses in children with autism: A magneto-encephalographic study. *The European Journal of Neuroscience, 24,* 2679–2690.

Leroux, G. I., Lubin, A., Houdé, O. & Lanoë, C. I. (2013). How to best train children and adolescents for fMRI? Meta-analysis of the training methods in developmental neuroimaging. *Neuroeducation, 2,* 44–70.

Lloyd-Fox, S., Blasi, A. & Elwell, C. E. (2010). Illuminating the developing brain: the past, present and future of functional near infrared spectroscopy. *Neuroscience and Biobehavioral Reviews, 34,* 269–284.

Lloyd-Fox, S., Blasi, A., Mercure, E., Elwell, C. E. & Johnson, M. H. (2012). The emergence of cerebral specialization for the human voice over the first months of life. *Social Neuroscience, 7,* 317–330.

Lloyd-Fox, S., Blasi, A., Elwell, C. E., Charman, T., Murphy, D. & Johnson, M. H. (2013a). Reduced neural sensitivity to social stimuli in infants at risk for autism. *Proceedings of the Royal Society B: Biological Sciences, 280*(1758), 20123026. doi: 10.1098/rspb.2012.3026

Lloyd-Fox, S., Wu, R., Richards, J. E., Elwell, C. E. & Johnson, M. H. (2013b). Cortical activation to action perception is associated with action production abilities in young infants. *Cerebral Cortex.* doi: 10.1093/cercor/bht207.

Lloyd-Fox, S., Papademetriou, M., Darboe, M. K., Everdell, N. L., Wegmuller, R., Prentice, A. M., … Elwell, C. E. (2014). Functional near infrared spectroscopy (fNIRS) to assess cognitive function in infants in rural Africa. *Scientific Reports, 4*. doi: 10.1038/srep04740.

Lloyd-Fox, S., Széplaki-Köllőd, B., Yin, J. & Csibra, G. (under review) Are you talking to me? Neural activations in 6-month-old infants in response to being addressed during natural interactions.

Lloyd-Fox, S., Richards, J. E., Blasi, A., Murphy, D. G. M., Elwell, C. E. & Johnson, M. H. (2014). Co-registering NIRS with underlying cortical areas in infants. *Neurophotonics*, 1(2), 025006.

Luck, S. J. (2005). Ten simple rules for designing and interpreting erp experiments. In T. C. Handy (ed.), *Event-Related Potentials: A Methods Handbook* (pp. 17–32). Massachusetts: MIT Press.

Luyster, R. J., Wagner, J. B., Vogel-Farley, V., Tager-Flusberg, H. & Nelson, C. A. (2011). Neural correlates of familiar and unfamiliar face processing in infants at risk for Autism Spectrum Disorders. *Brain Topography, 24*(3–4), 220–228.

McCleery, J. P., Akshoomoff, N., Dobkins, K. R. & Carver, L. J. (2009). Atypical face versus object processing and hemispheric asymmetries in 10-month-old infants at risk for autism. *Biological Psychiatry, 66*, 950–957.

Meek, J. H., Firbank, M., Elwell, C. E., Atkinson, J., Braddick, O. & Wyatt, J. S. (1998). Regional hemodynamic responses to visual stimulation in awake infants. *Pediatric Research, 43*, 840–843.

Minagawa-Kawai, Y., Matsuoka, S., Dan, I., Naoi, N., Nakamura, K. & Kojima, S. (2009). Prefrontal activation associated with social attachment: facial-emotion recognition in mothers and infants. *Cerebral Cortex, 19*, 284–292.

Moosmann, M., Ritter, P., Krastel, I., Brink, A., Thees, S., Blankenburg, F., … Villringer, A. (2003). Correlates of alpha rhythm in functional magnetic resonance imaging and near infrared spectroscopy. *NeuroImage, 20*(1), 145–158.

Moriguchi, Y. & Hiraki, K. (2009). Neural origin of cognitive shifting in young children. *Proceedings of the National Academy of Sciences of the United States of America, 106*(14), 6017–6021.

——(2011). Longitudinal development of prefrontal function during early childhood. *Developmental Cognitive Neuroscience, 1*(2), 153–162.

Nagamitsu, S., Yamashita, Y., Tanaka, H. & Matsuishi, T. (2012). Functional near-infrared spectroscopy studies in children. *BioPsychoSocial Medicine, 6*(1), 7.

Negoro, H., Sawada, M., Iida, J., Ota, T., Tanaka, S. & Kishimoto, T. (2010). Prefrontal dysfunction in attention-deficit/hyperactivity disorder as measured by near-infrared spectroscopy. *Child Psychiatry and Human Development, 41*(2), 193–203.

Nicklin, S., Hassan, I., Wickramasinghe, Y. & Spencer, S. (2003). The light still shines, but not that brightly? The current status of perinatal near infrared spectroscopy. *Archives of Disease in Childhood Fetal and Neonatal Edition, 88*(4), F263–F268.

Pelphrey, K. A. & Carter, E. J. (2008). Charting the typical and atypical development of the social brain. *Development and Psychopathology, 20*(4), 1081–1102.

Peterson, B. S. (2003). Conceptual, methodological, and statistical challenges in brain imaging studies of developmentally based psychopathologies. *Development and Psychopathology, 15*(3), 811–832.

Power, J. D., Barnes, K. A., Snyder, A. Z., Schlaggar, B. L. & Petersen, S. E. (2012). Spurious but systematic correlations in functional connectivity MRI networks arise from subject motion. *NeuroImage, 59*(3), 2142–2154.

Richards, J. E. (in preparation). Scalp surface locations and underlying cortical areas in infants.

Sakatani, K., Chen, S., Lichty, W., Zuo, H. & Wang, Y. (1999). Cerebral blood oxygenation changes induced by auditory stimulation in newborn infants measured by near infrared spectroscopy. *Early Human Development, 55,* 229–236.

Schecklmann, M., Romanos, M., Bretscher, F., Plichta, M. M., Warnke, A. & Fallgatter, A. J. (2010). Prefrontal oxygenation during working memory in ADHD. *Journal of Psychiatric Research, 44*(10), 621–628.

Steinbrink, J., Villringer, A., Kempf, F., Haux, D., Boden, S. & Obrig, H. (2006). Illuminating the BOLD signal: combined fMRI-fNIRS studies. *Magnetic Resonance Imaging, 24*(4), 495–505.

Telkemeyer, S., Rossi, S., Koch, S. P., Nierhaus, T., Steinbrink, J., Poeppel, D., … Wartenburger, I. (2009). Sensitivity of newborn auditory cortex to the temporal structure of sounds. *Journal of Neuroscience, 29*(47), 14726.

Toet, M. C. & Lemmers, P. M. A. (2009). Brain monitoring in neonates. *Early Human Development, 85*(2), 77–84.

Travis, K. E., Leonard, M. K., Brown, T. T., Hagler, D. J., Curran, M., Dale, A. M., … Halgren, E. (2011). Spatiotemporal neural dynamics of word understanding in 12- to 18-month-old-infants. *Cerebral Cortex, 21*(8), 1832–1839.

Tzourio-Mazoyer, N., De Schonen, S., Crivello, F., Reutter, B., Aujard, Y. & Mazoyer, B. (2002). Neural correlates of woman face processing by 2-month-old infants. *NeuroImage, 15*(2), 454–461.

Vanderwert, R. E. & Nelson, C. A. (2014). The use of near-infrared spectroscopy in the study of typical and atypical development. *NeuroImage, 85,* 264–271.

Villringer, A. & Chance, B. (1997). Non-invasive optical spectroscopy and imaging of human brain function. *Trends in Neurosciences, 20*(10), 435–442.

Watanabe, H., Homae, F. & Taga, G. (2010). General to specific development of functional activation in the cerebral cortexes of 2- to 3-month-old infants. *NeuroImage, 50*(4), 1536–1544.

Weishaupt, D. (2006). *How Does MRI Work?: An Introduction to the Physics and Function of Magnetic Resonance Imaging* (2nd ed.). Berlin: Springer.

Wilcox, T., Hirshkowitz, A., Hawkins, L. & Boas, D. A. (2013). The effect of color priming on infant brain and behavior. *NeuroImage, 15,* 302–313.

Wishart, J. G. (1995). Cognitive abilities in children with Down syndrome: developmental instability and motivational deficits. In C. Epstein, T. Hassold, I. T. Lott, L. Nadel & D. Patterson (eds), *Etiology and Pathogenesis of Down Syndrome* (pp. 57–92). New York: Wiley-Liss.

Wolf, M., Ferrari, M. & Quaresima, V. (2007). Progress of near-infrared spectroscopy and topography for brain and muscle clinical applications. *Journal of Biomedical Optics, 12*(6), 062104.

Wyatt, J. S., Cope, M., Delpy, D. T., Wray, S. & Reynolds, E. O. (1986). Quantification of cerebral oxygenation and haemodynamics in sick newborn infants by near infrared spectrophotometry. *Lancet, 2*(8515), 1063–1066.

Xiao, T., Xiao, Z., Ke, X., Hong, S., Yang, H., Su, Y., … Liu, Y. (2012). Response inhibition impairment in high functioning autism and attention deficit hyperactivity disorder: evidence from near-infrared spectroscopy data. *PloS One, 7*(10), e46569.

Zaramella, P., Freato, F., Amigoni, A., Salvadori, S., Marangoni, P., Suppjei, A., Schiavo, B. & Chiandetti, L. (2001). Brain auditory activation measured by near-infrared spectroscopy (NIRS) in neonates. *Pediatric Research, 49,* 213–220.

5

CAUSAL MODELLING OF DEVELOPMENTAL DISORDERS

Insights from animal and computational models of Specific Language Impairment

Themis Karaminis

5.1 Introduction

In this chapter we discuss the use of model systems to gain a better understanding of causes of developmental disorders. We focus on two types of model systems: animal and computational models. Animal models are based on manipulations of the genetic make-up of non-human species; computational models are based on computer simulations of development in atypical learning systems. Both approaches provide a framework for the causal modelling of developmental disorders. This framework allows us to implement possible causes of disorders and suggest plausible links between deficits observed within different scales or levels of description. For example, animal models can suggest how disruptions in the function of a given gene, which encodes a protein involved in some aspects of neurodevelopment, lead to atypicalities in brain regions that underlie certain aspects of the animal's cognitive profile. Computational models can show that a given type of computational deficit, applied to a learning system that interacts with a cognitive environment (e.g. a learning system acquiring a linguistic domain–verb morphology), simulates atypical development (e.g. error patterns symptomatic of language impairments). Animal and computational models complement aetiological theories of atypical development with mechanistic explanations, which consider causal relationships between atypicalities within different levels of description. More generally, animal and computational models address the challenge to specify observed associations between different levels of discourse, for example, between given gene variants and individual variability in behaviour.

We review the main characteristics, assumptions, strengths and limitations of the animal and the computational modelling approaches focussing on their application to the study of language acquisition and Specific Language Impairment (SLI). SLI is a neurodevelopmental disorder diagnosed in children presenting pronounced difficulties in language learning and use – either in comprehension or in production or in both. For a more comprehensive review of SLI and subtypes of Language Impairment, see Chapter 8. The causes of SLI are unknown, and cognitive theories suggest different types of underlying deficit. SLI also has a strong genetic component. A number of studies have identified several genes that contribute to the phenotype of the impairment, most likely via *endophenotypes* of speech and language impairment, shared between SLI and comorbid developmental disorders (e.g. Autism Spectrum Disorders, ASD; see Chapter 7, and Attention Deficit Hyperactivity Disorder, ADHD; see Chapter 9). The mechanism under which genes give rise to language impairments involves dynamic interactions between multiple genetic and environmental factors and remains unknown. In this chapter, we aim to demonstrate the use of model systems to understand aspects of this mechanism.

We also consider the animal and computational modelling approaches in relation to three idiosyncratic characteristics of language as a research theme. The first characteristic is that language is a uniquely human behaviour. The use of animals to study impairments in its acquisition seems counterintuitive. We will refer to the major assumptions that allow the study of language acquisition within an animal–modelling framework and allude to links between these assumptions and evolutionary theories. The second idiosyncratic characteristic of language concerns the fascinating ability of children to acquire linguistic knowledge aptly and at a very young age. A school of thought in the field of language acquisition has explained this phenomenon in terms of an innate predisposition of the human species for language acquisition (e.g. Chomsky, 1965, 1981, 1986, 1995, 1998; Pinker, 1994, 1999). Extrapolating this explanation, some theories of SLI have suggested that the impairment stems from disruptions in genes specifically involved in the learning of particular aspects of language (e.g. 'grammar genes'; Pinker, 1994). It is now, however, believed that genetic effects on cognition are much more complex and indirect (Karmiloff-Smith, Scerif & Thomas, 2002; Marcus & Fisher, 2003). Here, we will refer to computational modelling approaches offering a level of description in which phenomena in typical and atypical language acquisition are explained without the need for postulating pre-specified linguistic knowledge or impairments of it. Finally, a third idiosyncratic characteristic of the domain of language concerns cross-linguistic variation. Cross-linguistic variation challenges theories of atypical language development to suggest causal explanations that are general across languages. We will consider this challenge within the computational modelling framework.

5.2 Specific Language Impairment

SLI is a neurodevelopmental disorder with a prevalence of about 7 per cent in children (one to two children in every classroom; Tomblin et al., 1997). SLI is diagnosed when children fail to develop age-appropriate language and this occurs in the absence of factors that are usually concomitant with language learning problems, such as hearing impairments, frank neurological damage or low non-verbal intelligence scores (Leonard, 1998).

Children with SLI present weaknesses in all areas of language (phonology, morphology, grammar, syntax, semantics), in both comprehension and production (for reviews, see Bishop, 1997; Bishop & Leonard, 2000; Leonard, 1998). Some of these weaknesses, such as difficulties in non-word repetition tasks (Gathercole & Baddeley, 1990), sentence repetition tasks (McGregor & Leonard, 1994), and tasks involving the production of past-tense forms or third person singular of the present tense (Rice, Wexler & Cleave, 1995; van der Lely & Ullman, 2001), are present in the language of most children with SLI and persist across development. Such weaknesses are considered to be behavioural markers of the impairment (Conti-Ramsden, Botting & Faragher, 2001; Gardner, Froud, McClelland & van der Lely, 2006). However, the profile of SLI across different areas of language is uneven and SLI is described as a significantly heterogeneous impairment (Leonard, 1998; for subtypes within SLI see Rapin & Allen, 1987; Wilson & Risucci, 1986).

5.3 Theoretical accounts of SLI

What could cause a cognitive impairment that particularly impacts the linguistic domain? Is there some particular problem with part or parts of the language system? Or is there a more widespread problem in some property on which language processing relies? There are two distinct theoretical proposals to explain the underlying deficit of SLI based on the language-specific profile of the impairment. They differ in their perspective on the nature and the representation of linguistic knowledge.

The first proposal, often referred to as language-specific accounts of SLI, attributes the language-specific profile of the impairment to deficits in brain systems that underlie the processing of language. These accounts (e.g. Gopnik, 1990; Gopnik & Crago, 1991; Hadley & Short, 2005; Rice et al., 1995; van der Lely & Stollwerck, 1997; Wexler, 2003) suggest that certain linguistic features or operations are either absent or have not developed in the language of children with SLI. For example, the Extended Optional Infinitive account (Rice et al., 1995) posits that children with SLI present a protraction of an early developmental stage (the Optional Infinitive stage) in which children produce unmarked forms in contexts that require morphological marking (Yesterday, I *eat* a cake).

Others posit that the underlying deficits in SLI are not localised to the linguistic system (non-language-specific theories). For example, general processing limitations or slower processing (e.g. Bishop, 1994; Kail, 1994; Leonard, Bortolini, Caselli, McGregor & Sabbadini, 1992; Leonard et al., 2007) might lead to language impairments. A slightly different view suggests that SLI is due to deficit in speech perception (Tallal & Piercy, 1973a, 1973b) or in phonological working memory (Gathercole & Baddeley, 1990; Gathercole, 2006; Falcaro et al., 2008). These deficits are peripheral to the language system, in the sense that they are not localised to grammar.

Language-specific accounts of SLI are typically stated in linguistic terms (a deficit in linguistic rule X), thus they are predicated upon the so-called symbolic theories of language (e.g. Chomsky, 1965, 1998; Pinker, 1994, 1999). One of the main tenets of symbolic theories of language acquisition is that humans have an innate (and unique across species) ability to learn language. This ability is also encapsulated in the notion of Universal Grammar (Chomsky, 1965, 1995, 1998), a theoretical construct including a minimal set of properties (mainly in the form of abstract linguistic rules, the so-called symbolic rules) that all human languages share. Universal Grammar also refers to the genetic endowment constraining human ability to develop language, as well as to the properties/areas of the human brain that support this ability. Some language-specific descriptions of SLI suggest that the impairment stems from disruptions in the function of genes specific to the learning of grammar (e.g. Pinker, 1994, 1999; see Karmiloff-Smith, Scerif & Thomas, 2002 for more examples and a discussion). These causal explanations of SLI represent a trend of overly simplified analyses of the links between genotypes and phenotypes in accounting for language impairments. They postulate '*direct, specific, one-to-one* mappings between genes and cognition' (Karmiloff-Smith et al., 2002, p. 312). The relationship between genotypes and phenotypes, however, is far less direct and involves many-to-many mappings between genes and lower-level mechanisms, rather than linguistic features (Karmiloff-Smith et al., 2002).

Non-language specific explanations of SLI fall closer to the so-called connectionist accounts of language acquisition (e.g. Plunkett & Marchmann, 1991, 1993; Rumelhart & McClelland, 1986). These accounts do not rely upon the assumption of innate linguistic knowledge. Connectionist accounts believe linguistic behaviour is the outcome of a developmental process in which a learning system, with no pre-specified linguistic knowledge, extracts regularities from the linguistic environment which it is exposed to. The computational modelling approach to the causal modelling of SLI discussed later in this chapter refers to connectionist explanations. One of the strengths of non-language-specific accounts of SLI relative to language-specific accounts is the focus on developmental processes. Language-specific accounts propose a more static view of the language system, where certain grammatical features are absent from the start.

More recent theoretical proposals for SLI include characteristics of both language-specific and non-language-specific explanations. For example, the Procedural Deficit Hypothesis (PDH; Ullman & Pierpont, 2005, see also Tomblin, Mainela-Arnold & Zhang, 2007) suggests that SLI is due to a deficit in the Procedural Memory System, a general brain system supporting a range of functions, both linguistic and non-linguistic, with a 'procedural' character. Deficits in the Procedural System should lead to impairments of rule-based aspects of language in SLI. In a similar vein, Evans, Saffran and Robe-Torres (2009), as well as Hsu and Bishop (2011) suggest that impairments in statistical and implicit learning bias the language learning system towards rote learning and cause weaknesses in rule-based aspects of language.

Rice's (2012, 2013) Growth Signal Disruption hypothesis is another example of a theory that combines specific and general learning difficulties to explain SLI, whilst also emphasising the importance of development. The hypothesis posits that children with SLI present atypical growth patterns in their linguistic abilities. A general pattern is that language in children with SLI onsets later, but presents a growth trajectory similar to those of typically developing children. A deceleration of language growth however, is observed in early adolescence in SLI. The Growth Signal Disruption hypothesis suggests that the underlying deficit of SLI involves impairments in the timing of genetic mechanisms regulating language onset and growth. The Growth Signal Disruption hypothesis also highlights the need to document language growth patterns in SLI with evidence from genetic studies.

5.4 Genetics of language impairments

SLI has a strong genetic component, as evidenced by studies that assessed its heritability. For a review of behavioural genetics studies on SLI, see Stromswold (1998, 2001; see also Bishop & Hayiou-Thomas, 2008, for evidence that heritability estimates depend on sample selection methods).

Like many developmental disorders, SLI is a complex disorder, i.e. it involves combinations of multiple alleles (variants of genes), which also interact with environmental factors. Genetic studies on SLI have identified several genes or regions of the genome that contribute to the impairment. Studies employing so-called linkage analysis search through the genome of family members for chromosome regions that present inheritance patterns that can be linked to behavioural traits of language impairment.[1] Linkage studies have found linkage regions on chromosomes 16 (SLIC, 2002, 2004; Falcaro et al., 2008), 19 (SLIC, 2002, 2004; Falcaro et al., 2008), 13 (Bartlett et al., 2002, 2004) and 7 (Villanueva et al., 2011). Studies employing association analysis look for direct correlations between variants of genes and behavioural traits in the general population.[2] Newbury et al. (2009), who employed a variant of association analysis focussing on family members, identified ATP2C2 and CMIP, two genes on chromosome 16, associated with SLI. Vernes et al. (2008) found associations between the CNTNAP2 gene of chromosome 7 and SLI. For a review of genetic analysis studies on SLI see Newbury, Fisher and Monaco (2010).

There is an interesting exception to language impairments with a complex inheritance pattern. This is the case of a speech and language disorder with a Mendelian inheritance pattern,[3] identified in the late 1980s through a pedigree known as the 'KE family' (Hurst, Baraitser, Auger, Graham & Norell, 1990). The Mendelian inheritance pattern was suggestive of the disorder being due to a single gene (monogenic). The phenotype of the KE family presented deficits in many areas of receptive and expressive language, as well as a condition involving difficulties in controlling orofacial muscles to produce fluent intelligible speech, referred to as developmental verbal dyspraxia (Vargha-Khadem, Watkins, Alcock, Fletcher & Passingham, 1995). Neuroimaging studies on the KE family have found structural and functional atypicalities, for example, differences in grey matter density and atypical patterns of activation in areas involved in speech and language processing (Liégeois et al., 2003; Vargha-Khadem et al., 1998).

Gene mapping studies in the KE family and an unrelated individual with a similar form of language disorder identified a single mutation in the FOXP2 gene of chromosome 7 (Lai, Fisher, Hurst, Vargha-Khadem & Monaco, 2001). The discovery of the FOXP2 gene is considered as a window to molecular pathways of language impairments (Fisher & Scharff, 2009). FOXP2 itself does not contribute to SLI (Newbury et al., 2002). However, it regulates the function of numerous other genes that are important for neurodevelopment (Vernes et al., 2011). The discovery of associations between the CNTNAP2 gene and language impairment (Vernes et al., 2008; discussed above) was based on the identification of this gene in the network of genes regulated by FOXP2. As CNTNAP2 is also implicated in other language-related disorders, such as ASD and Tourette's syndrome (Arking et al., 2008), it is likely that interactions between FOXP2 and CNTNAP2 underlie endophenotypes of language impairment, shared between different disorders.

The discovery of FOXP2 also initiated a series of animal models. These were designed to study the function of the gene and its effects on the developing brain in detail.

5.5 Animal models of language impairments

5.5.1 Methods

Animal models of developmental disorders are based on technologies for engineered modifications in animal genetic make-up. These models aim to delineate the function of the human gene of interest, which presents a counterpart (homologous gene) in the species used for the particular animal model. The human version of a gene is usually denoted with capital letters (e.g. FOXP2), while the animal homologue is denoted with lower-case letters (e.g. Foxp2). These models of developmental disorders exploit animals in which the function of the given gene is disrupted. They aim to identify the effects of such disruptions on the animal's anatomy, structural and functional characteristics of the brain, and behaviour. Animal modelling studies employ methodologies and procedures that may cause lethality or a level of harm that would not be considered ethical to inflict on humans. An experimental advantage is that certain species (e.g. rodents) are easy to breed, as they reproduce often and quickly.

A key assumption of the animal-modelling framework is that the human and the animal versions of the genes are similar. This assumption relates to the notion of evolutionary conservation. For example, FOXP2 is highly conserved across species. The human and the mouse version of this gene differ only by three bases (~99.5 per cent similarity; Enard et al., 2002), while the human and the zebra finch (a bird species) version differ by eight bases (~99.5 per cent similarity; Enard et al., 2002). This is an important reason why animal models of FOXP2 are all based on rodents or birds.

Another important assumption, on which the animal models rely, is that the function of homologous genes is similar across the human and animal species. Gene expression data are used to support this assumption. For example, the mouse and the human version of FOPX2 present similar spatiotemporal patterns of expression, and their expression is more pronounced in brain circuits that are fundamental for motor control and sensorimotor integration (Fisher, 2006; Lai, Gerrelli, Monaco, Fisher & Copp, 2003).

The final modelling assumption concerns the behavioural traits on which animal species might be compared to humans. The development of animal models for language impairments poses particular challenges with regards to this issue. For example, mouse-modelling studies of FOXP2 have assumed that ultrasonic vocalisations (USVs) produced by pups when separated from their mothers may serve as an analogue of human speech and communication. This assumption has been debated by other studies, on the basis of core features of communication that are absent from USVs (e.g. voluntary control, auditory feedback) and evidence that innate and learnt vocalisations utilise different pathways (Gaub, Groszer, Fisher & Ehret, 2010; Jürgens, 2009). Other mouse models of FOXP2 have considered data from motor-skill learning tasks. Those models were consistent with evidence for the expression of the gene in related brain regions. This assumption also implies that human communication is based on a range of sensorimotor abilities that evolved over time to support language (Fisher & Marcus, 2006).

For the purposes of this chapter, we will focus on mouse models of FOXP2. We shall note, however, that the bird homologue of FOXP2 has been found in birds that learn their song from their parents. Foxp2 in birds presents strong expression patterns in brain areas supporting songbirds' learning (Haesler et al., 2004), while its inactivation results in incomplete and inaccurate imitation of tutor songs. For Haesler et al. (2007), songbirds provide a genuine model for the study of vocal learning and speech development. Others argue that a relationship between Foxp2 and recurrent pattern learning does not necessarily imply a relationship between the same gene and language learning. For a more comprehensive presentation of animal models of language impairments, see Vernes and Fisher (2013).

5.5.2 Representative mouse models of SLI

Shu et al. (2005) have generated a knockout mouse model of FOXP2. In knockout animal models, the function of a whole gene is blocked. Knockout animals can be homozygous, when both copies of the target gene are disrupted, and heterozygous, when only one copy of the gene is disrupted. Shu et al. (2005) considered USVs as a proxy for human language. They compared their frequency in homozygous knockouts, heterozygous knockouts and wild-type pups when separated from their mothers. Homozygous knockouts showed complete lack of USVs. They also presented severe motor impairments and premature death. Heterozygous knockouts showed a modest developmental delay and normal learning and memory in a water-maze task.[4] However, they presented significantly lower rates of USV in response to separation. Both homozygous and heterozygous mice showed abnormalities in Purkinje cells, consistent with previous findings for the expression of FOXP2/Foxp2 (Lai et al., 2003). Shu et al. (2005) concluded that these findings suggested an involvement of FOXP2 in the development of social communication.

Fujita et al. (2008) examined USVs using the knockin mouse line Foxp2-R552H. The knockin mice are engineered to carry particular variants of a given gene. Knockin mice models consider more subtle manipulations of the genetic make-up than those in knockout models and therefore provide more refined models of disorders. The Foxp2-R552H mouse line, in particular, implemented mutations akin to those found in FOXP2 alleles of the KE family. Similar to the complete knockout model of Shu et al. (2005), homozygous knockin mice showed severe impairments in USVs and premature death. Unlike Shu et al. (2005), the heterozygous knockin mice did not differ from their wild-type peers in the rate of USVs, although some differences were identified in qualitative characteristics of USVs. In particular, vocalisations of heterozygous mice could be categorised into three main types, whistle-type, short-length and click-type vocalisations; vocalisations of wild-type pups were mainly whistle-type USVs (Fujita et al., 2008). Both homozygous and heterozygous knockouts presented neurological abnormalities, the most dominant being immature arbors in Purkinje cells.

Groszer et al. (2008) and Gaub et al. (2010) used mouse lines Foxp2-R552H (also used in Fujita et al. 2008) and Foxp2-S321X. Mouse line Foxp2-S321X carries point mutations akin to those in the FOXP2 gene in an individual with developmental verbal dyspraxia (MacDermot et al., 2005). Homozygous mice from both lines showed severe developmental delay and reduced viability, i.e. similar to Shu et al. (2005) and Fujita et al. (2008). Heterozygous mice showed no delay or reduced viability. Behavioural measures examined by Groszer et al. (2008) included USVs and the performance in motor skill learning tasks. Heterozygous Foxp2-R552H mice pups presented no differences in the frequency of USVs or their acoustic properties compared to wild-type littermates. Heterozygous mice, however, did demonstrate impairments in a range of tasks that involved motor skill learning. At the neural circuitry level, heterozygous mice presented different properties in synaptic plasticity. In particular, they presented reduced long-term depression in striatal neurons and cerebellar Purkinje cells, known to be involved in the learning of motor skills. Disruptions were greater in the heterozygotes of the R552H line than the S321X line. Groszer et al. (2008) and Gaub et al. (2010) suggested that their data support the involvement of circuits underpinning motor skills in language and cognition.

In summary, the knockout model of FOXP2 by Shu et al. (2005) has shown impairments in USVs, and was used to suggest a pathway between disruptions in the function of Foxp2 and deficits in social communication. The knockin mouse models of Fujita et al. (2008) and Groszer et al. (2008), which implemented precise mutations similar to those found in human alleles of the gene, did not find differences in the rates of USVs between heterozygous knockins and wild-type mice. Groszer et al. (2008) and Gaub et al. (2010) have shown that heterozygous knockin models presented deficits related to motor skill learning rather than USVs. These results suggest a causal pathway between disruptions in the function of FOXP2 and language impairment, possibly mediated by deficits in brain systems supporting the learning or rapid movement sequences.

The discrepancies between findings from different mouse modelling studies reflect methodological differences within the animal-modelling framework. For example, studies using heterozygous knockin mice, i.e. mouse models of language impairment with fine-grained manipulations in their genetic make-up, did not support findings from the earlier knockout model of Shu et al. (2005) for deficits in USV. By suggesting that deficits in motor skill learning demonstrate causal pathways between FOXP2 and language impairments mediated by sensorimotor brain systems (i.e. systems subserving lower-level functions in both linguistic and non-linguistic species), mouse models of language impairments also present interesting similarities to non-language specific accounts of SLI. Of course, the inability of animal models to address language acquisition in a direct way is an inherent limitation of the framework. To address this limitation, animal models need to be complemented with other modelling or empirical methodologies.

5.6 Computational modelling approaches

5.6.1 Methods

We now turn to causal modelling approaches to developmental language impairments based on computational simulation. Similar to animal models, computational models manipulate factors to establish causal relations between deficits observed within different levels of description. Unlike animal models, computational models also include a simulated linguistic environment. This allows computational models to focus on human language acquisition (rather than an analogue animal behaviour). It also allows studying the interplay between environmental and intrinsic variation in language impairments.

The particular type of computational models on which we will focus are connectionist models, also referred to as parallel distributed processing (PDP) or artificial neural network models. This class of models accounts for causes of developmental impairments within the neurocomputational level. The neurocomputational level corresponds to an intermediate level of description falling between low-level anatomical characteristics or computational properties of the brain, and cognition. It refers to details and parameters of an implemented learning system, presenting loose similarities to the anatomy of the brain (e.g. an artificial neural network processing architecture) and incorporating general principles of neural computation (e.g. an analogue of synaptic plasticity). The learning system interacts with a structured cognitive environment, and this enables connectionist systems to simulate cognitive phenomena in a target domain, generating data that are comparable to human data (e.g. accuracy rates in a psycholinguistic task). Connectionist models offer mechanistic explanations of cognitive phenomena in atypical development by suggesting ways in which an underlying deficit could affect the computational properties of the learning system and its interaction with the environment across the developmental process. More generally, connectionist models are implemented cognitive models conforming to the major theoretical commitments of the neuroconstructivist framework (Mareschal, Johnson, Sirois, Thomas & Westermann, 2007; Mareschal, Sirois, Westermann & Johnson, 2007; Thomas & Karmiloff-Smith, 2003), such as the idea that theories of cognitive development should be consistent with theories of functional brain development; that development is an emergent phenomenon involving the interaction of experience-dependent learning systems with structured physical and social environments; that this process is multiply constrained; and that the causes of developmental disorders can be better understood when studying atypicalities within a developing rather than a static system.

From a practical point of view, connectionist models implement architectures of processing units (artificial neurons) interconnected via weighted connections (synapses). The weighted connections transfer input and output activation signals to and from each unit. The output activation signal of a given unit is determined by the weighted sum of its input activation signals, i.e. from the units specified by the processing architecture. Effectively, the network of artificial neurons processes activation patterns in a parallel and distributed fashion. Information about stimuli is presented to the architecture in the form of input activation patterns, fed to a special set of units referred to as the input layer of the network. The output activation signal of another special set of units (output layer) is taken to be the response of the architecture to the stimuli. Experience-dependent learning is implemented in connectionist models as the architecture is repeatedly exposed to stimuli sets (training sets) representing the target domain of the model. Throughout the stimuli presentation, a learning algorithm modifies the strength of the weighted connections. A common type of learning algorithm implements so-called supervised learning (e.g. back-propagation of error, Rumelhart, Hinton & Williams, 1986). In supervised learning, the target domain is represented as mappings between input and target patterns (the latter produced in the output layer of the network). The learning algorithm modifies the connection weights appropriately, so that the network gradually acquires the associations between the input and target patterns. On each learning trial, the weights are modified so that the next time that the same input is presented the output will be closer to the target (other things being equal).

The research strand within the connectionist modelling framework addressing the acquisition of linguistic domains (e.g. morphology, syntax) is also referred to as connectionist psycholinguistics. Connectionist models of language acquisition typically consider cognitive architectures where different groups of units within the input and the output layer are dedicated to the encoding of different types of linguistic information relevant to the target domain. For example, in architectures for the learning of the English past tense (e.g. talk/talked) a group of input units encodes the phonological structure of the bare form (/tɔk/), another group of input units represents the meaning ('to talk'), while the output units encode the phonological structure of the past tense forms (/tɔkt/). The stimuli comprising the training set can correspond to real or artificial languages. Artificial languages are model versions of real languages, focussing on properties that are more relevant to the target domain of the model (e.g. the frequencies of different sentence types rather than the richness of the vocabulary, in a model of syntactic processing). The use of artificial languages presents advantages for experimental control, but real languages are important for verifying the psycholinguistic plausibility of the models. In any case, the modelling assumptions on the composition of the training set are an integral part of the model. This is because connectionist models are not simply challenged to learn associations between input and output patterns in the training set. They aim to also acquire these in a psycholinguistically plausible manner, i.e. similar to typically developing children. Both questions (language learnability and psycholinguistic plausibility) are addressed in the connectionist-modelling framework by considering a language-learning mechanism that extracts statistical regularities in the linguistic environment. Pre-specification of linguistic knowledge, for example, explicitly defined morphological or syntactic rules, is not necessary – contra symbolic explanations of language acquisition (e.g. Chomsky, 1986; Pinker, 1994, 1999). Rule-based behaviour emerges through the repeated exposure of the cognitive architecture to the linguistic environment, due to the processing of different stimuli in a similar manner within the PDP learning system (e.g. Plunkett & Marchman, 1991, 1993; Rumelhart & McClelland, 1986).

Connectionist studies of developmental language impairments presuppose a connectionist model of typical language development. Having established that a given architecture acquires its target domain in a psycholinguistically plausible manner, connectionist approaches to language impairments typically consider conditions of an underlying deficit for the learning mechanism and examine whether these affect language learning in the model similar to patterns in atypical development. Deficits are defined within the neurocomputational level of description, and are assumed to constraint the computational properties of the system. Importantly, the simulated deficits need to be theoretically grounded. For example, to assess aetiological explanations of SLI positing that a phonological/perceptual deficit underlies the impairment, connectionist models might consider the addition of noise or the pruning of connections in parts of the architecture related to the processing of phonological information.

5.6.2 Earlier connectionist studies of SLI

Earlier connectionist studies on SLI have addressed the viability of individual aetiological accounts for the impairment exploring the difficulties of children with SLI in particular subdomains of language. For example, Hoeffner and McClelland (1993), as well as Joanisse (2004) have shown that a phonological/perceptual deficit could simulate weaknesses in the acquisition of verbal morphology. Hoeffner and McClelland (1993) considered a system acquiring multiple verb inflections (base forms, progressive, third person singular of the present, past tense and past participle) and implemented a perceptual deficit for SLI via a scheme of weaker phonological representations than those in the version of the model for typical development. The perceptual deficit was particularly pronounced in word-final phonemes (Leonard, Sabbadini, Leonard & Volterra, 1987; Tallal & Piercy, 1973a, 1973b) and generated patterns of performance symptomatic of SLI, such as pronounced impairments in the past tense and the third person singular and increases in the rates of omission errors. Joanisse (2004) simulated a phonological deficit with the addition of random noise in the phonological representations in a system learning English past-tense mappings, and demonstrated that this deficit could simulate pronounced deficits in regular past tenses and rule-based inflection of novel items, as well as less severe difficulties in irregular past tenses (van der Lely & Ullman, 2001). Joanisse and Seidenberg (2003) considered a phonological/perceptual deficit in an architecture exposed to sentences of an artificial grammar. These authors demonstrated that this type of deficit could account for patterns of performance of children with SLI with regards to anaphoric resolution (e.g. identifying the pronoun reference noun in *Mary said Elaine mocked her\herself*, target data from van der Lely & Stollwerck, 1997), suggesting that a perceptual deficit or limitations in phonological working memory might underlie the difficulties of children with SLI in syntactic comprehension. Thomas and Redington (2004), however, have simulated difficulties of children with SLI in complex sentence interpretation (e.g. in assigning agent and patient roles to the nouns of object-cleft sentences: *It is the cat that the dog chases*, data from Dick, Wulfeck, Krupa-Kwiatkowski & Bates, 2004) with a different type of deficit, which was more compatible with general processing limitations rather than phonological working memory limitation accounts of SLI. The neurocomputational deficit in Thomas and Redington (2004) was the use of fewer units in the so-called hidden layer of the architecture, an intermediate layer of units between the input and the output layer thought to be the processing capacity of the network.

Unlike the above studies, which focussed on a single type of deficit for simulating SLI, Thomas (2005) compared a range of possible deficits in a neural network acquiring the English past tense (see also Thomas & Karmiloff-Smith, 2003). Thomas (2005) discussed implications of these simulations for the main tenets of the Procedural Deficit Hypothesis (PDH; Ullman & Pierpont, 2005) for SLI. The atypical condition that better captured the profile of SLI in past tense (e.g. more pronounced difficulties in regular than irregular inflection, van der Lely & Ullman, 2001) was the use of a lower temperature value. Temperature is a neurocomputational parameter modulating the sensitivity of individual units to changes in the incoming activation patterns. At a network level, temperature is thought to relate to the sensitivity of the network to regularities in the training set. An implication of simulations in Thomas (2005) was that the patterns of impairments in past tense morphology of children with SLI were produced within the same processing mechanism, suggesting that the claims of the Procedural Deficit Hypothesis for a deficit in a brain system dedicated to the processing of regulars needed to be better specified.

In summary, Hoeffner and McClelland (1993), Joanisse (2004), Joanisse and Seidenberg (2003) and Thomas and Redington (2004) provided evidence for the viability of individual accounts of SLI in accounting for the profile of the impairment in individual areas of language. Thomas (2005), as well as Thomas and Karmiloff-Smith (2003) compared a range of implementations for SLI in the past tense and examined its relevance to the Procedural Deficit Hypothesis. Thomas and Karmiloff-Smith (2003) have considered a modelling framework for the comparison of multiple theories for the atypical acquisition of the English past tense through implementation.

5.6.3 A systematic modelling approach to SLI

Karaminis (2012), as well as Karaminis and Thomas (2010), combined features of many previous connectionist models of typical development and SLI to develop a research programme for the systematic exploration of causes of SLI in multiple areas of language and with a cross-linguistic perspective. This research programme is presented in Figure 5.1. It involved the development of models for the acquisition of three core areas of language, namely inflectional morphology, syntactic comprehension and syntactic production. Acquiring inflectional morphology was seen as learning to modify the phonological form of nouns, verbs and adjectives appropriately according to grammatical context (e.g. Yesterday, I *ate* a sandwich).

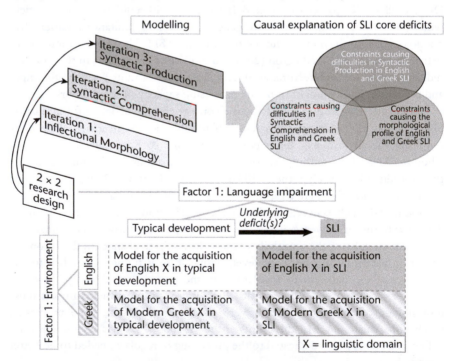

FIGURE 5.1 Research design for the causal modelling of SLI in English and Greek.

Acquiring syntactic comprehension was seen as learning to associate words in sentences with thematic roles (e.g. The dog chases the cat; 'The dog' is the agent of the action denoted by the verb 'to chase', i.e. similar to Thomas and Redington, 2004). Finally, acquiring syntactic production was assumed to require learning mappings between sentence meanings and particular linguistic forms (e.g. mapping the same agent–action–patient meaning to an active or passive sentence: The dog chases the cat vs. The cat is chased by the dog).

A key novelty in the modelling approach of Karaminis (2012) and Karaminis and Thomas (2010) was the use of a core 2×2 research design in all three models of language acquisition (lower part of Figure 5.1). The 2×2 design challenged models to account for interactions between a learning system and an environment in typical development and SLI in two different languages, English and Greek. With regards to the modelling of possible causes of SLI, the 2×2 research design implied that the model for the acquisition of linguistic domain X compared different types of deficit on the ability to capture the profile of SLI in X in both languages. The iterative application of the core 2×2 design in the three language areas could point to a unified explanation of SLI, addressing the heterogeneity of difficulties in many language areas.

The cross-linguistic paradigm of English and Modern Greek exploited the contrast between two language typologies. English is a language with a fairly simple morphological system, wide use of morphologically unmarked words, and inflections that are either fully regular (e.g. third person singular) or can be described in terms of a dichotomy between regular and irregular (e.g. past tense). The great majority of English sentences present a subject–verb–object (SVO) word order. Modern Greek presents an especially complex system of morphology, where multiple morphemes may be fused in single word forms to mark multiple grammatical categories (e.g. verb: number, person, tense, aspect, mood/voice; Stephany, 1997). Multiple conjugational classes for the realisation of different grammatical features are combined, resulting in an especially rich morphological system, which could not be described in terms of a dichotomy between regular and irregular inflection. Word order in sentences can be flexible, to reflect topic and focus.

Models for the acquisition of English and Greek should target markedly different patterns of acquisition. For example, as Greek does not employ unmarked forms, omission errors are not possible. Studies on typical language acquisition in Greek have suggested that early developmental error patterns include the overuse of certain grammatical forms of high frequency (e.g. the nominative singular of nouns) in place of their lower-frequency counterparts (e.g. genitive of nouns). This could correspond to an analogue of the optional infinitive stage, explained as a prototype effect of high-frequency forms (see Matthews & Theakston, 2006). Importantly, and unlike English, those high-frequency forms yielding prototype effects are different across word classes.

The three models developed in Karaminis (2012), as well as Karaminis and Thomas (2010), considered different architectures and training sets, appropriate for their target domains. Two principles, however, were common across models. First, the architecture of the three models had a common form, which included multiple types of information or cues presented to the input layer of the network (e.g. inflectional morphology: phonology, semantics, grammatical class and inflection). This entailed that the acquisition of the target domains involved learning to integrate these cues in a flexible manner, i.e. deciding which of these were more or less relevant to the acquisition of different types of mappings. Second, training sets corresponded to artificial languages with psycholinguistically motivated frequency structures. These structures were based on estimates for the distribution of phonological, morphological and syntactic characteristics of English and Modern Greek, derived from child-directed or adult language corpora.[5]

Interactions between the distributional characteristics of the input and the learning mechanism accounted for a wide range of empirical phenomena in the acquisition of morphology and syntax comprehension/production in the two languages. For example, the model of inflectional morphology simulated omission errors in English, and prototype effects particular to world classes that were consistent with empirical data for the acquisition of Greek (Stephany, 1997). The model suggested that differences between early error patterns in the acquisition of English and Modern Greek morphology were superficial. The emergence of both error types could be accounted for by interactions between the same learning mechanism, allowing prototype effects of high-frequency forms to happen, and two different patterns of statistical regularities in the linguistic environment. Importantly, the same type of deficit altered the behaviour of the model for typical development in a way that was consistent with differences in the linguistic performance of children with SLI and TD children in English and Greek. The SLI version of the English model of inflectional morphology simulated an increase in the rates of omission errors, while the SLI version of the Greek model simulated increased rates of overuse of high-frequency forms within each grammatical class.

Simulations with the three models suggested three different conditions of deficit that accounted for the profile of the impairment in their target domains. In the model of inflectional morphology, the best fit to the empirical data was provided by a combination of deficits. In particular the use of fewer hidden units in the hidden layer (as in Thomas & Redington, 2004) and weaker phonological representations (similar to Hoeffner and McClelland, 1993). In the model of syntactic comprehension, SLI was captured by attenuating a so-called recurrency parameter, reducing the strength of information about the internal states of the system during the course of processing of given sentences. In the model of syntactic production, SLI was simulated using a lower temperature value (akin to Thomas, 2005). The conditions simulating SLI were not identical in the three models, suggesting no specific type of underlying deficit to account for SLI across language areas. However, all conditions shared correspondence to general-processing-limitations accounts of the impairment. The model of inflectional morphology in particular, suggested the mechanistic validity of a double-hit theory. A combination of deficits was required to capture the full range of target empirical phenomena in morphology (deficits considered in isolation did not suffice).

Another finding with important implications for theories of SLI was the ability of the model of syntactic comprehension to simulate increases in SLI in the rates of sentences such as *Which cat does the cat chases someone?*. Van der Lely and Battell (2003) have argued that this type of response would not be predicted by general-processing-limitations accounts of SLI, as these would suggest omission of constituents rather than commission errors (e.g. marking person twice in sentence). The model of syntactic production challenged this claim.

The model of syntactic comprehension addressed an interesting dissociation between English and Greek with regards to the comprehension of passive voices, as empirical data suggested that children with SLI presented deficits in the interpretation of passives in Greek but not in English (Dick et al., 2004; Stavrakaki, 2006). The model accounted for this dissociation considering the greater involvement of morphological cues in sentence interpretation in Greek, and by showing that the deficit implement SLI affected the cues used for sentence disambiguation differentially in the two languages.

Modelling results also included testable predictions for the acquisition of Greek. For example, the model of syntactic comprehension predicted patterns of impairments in the comprehension of different sentence types, depending on the saliency of morphological cues. Another example, the model of inflectional morphology predicted particular types of responses that should be produced in past tense production tasks including multiple persons and numbers.

In summary, a systematic investigation of language acquisition in SLI under the connectionist framework suggested that general processing limitations is viable as an explanation of the cognitive profile of the impairment in different areas of language and different languages. This general modelling approach addressed similarities and dissociations between the profile of the impairment across languages and generated testable predictions.

5.7 Conclusions

We have discussed the usefulness of animal and computational modelling approaches in explaining causal links of developmental disorders described within different levels of description. We have focussed on language acquisition and SLI, and reviewed recent mouse models of the FOXP2 gene and connectionist models of SLI.

Mouse models of Foxp2 have delineated details of the function of this gene and its role on the development of the mouse brain. They identified causal pathways between disruptions in the function of Foxp2 and impaired motor skill learning. Findings of mouse modelling studies of the FOXP2 suggest evolutionary links between neural circuits underlying motor skill learning/sensorimotor integration and language/cognition. They also suggest causal pathways to FOXP2-related language phenotypes, mediated by deficits in the neural circuits underpinning the processing of rapid movement sequences.

We also discussed advances within a causal modelling framework based on computational simulations of development. Connectionist models occlude many of the details of the genetic level of description to focus on the interactions between a neurocomputational learning system and a structured cognitive environment. This class of models allows for direct comparison between simulation results and human data. Connectionist models of developmental disorders suggest causal links between underlying deficits in the learning system and cognitive deficits. Recent connectionist models of SLI have suggested the viability of general processing limitations as an explanation that addresses cross-linguistic patterns of deficits in different language areas. We believe that model systems are a valuable tool for understanding, testing and advancing theories of developmental disorders.

Practical tips

1. Models must be general. Consider both environmental variability (e.g. cross-cultural differences, differences related to socio-economic status) and intrinsic variability (e.g. different developmental disorders).
2. Use models to generate novel predictions. Testable predictions are essential to validate the models and improve our understanding of causal theories of developmental disorders. Both animal and computational models should be used to specify the empirical investigation of testable predictions in humans.
3. Aim to make models accessible to users with different levels of expertise in modelling. Facilitate access, replication and extension of models. Develop resources that explain the implementation. Supply documentation or develop user interfaces that explain the operation of the model and the effects of parameter manipulations. See Addyman and French (2012) for suggested practices to make models more accessible (but see also Cooper and Guest, 2014).

Notes

1 Linkage-based analyses typically report results in the Logarithm of Odds (LOD) scores, which express the likelihood that given chromosome regions are close to ('linked to') a gene variant assumed present in a high proportion of affected individuals (Newbury & Monaco, 2008). The method assumes that the probability that two regions from the same chromosome are inherited together in an individual is proportional to the physical distance between them.
2 Association analyses typically report p values of the probability that a given gene allele is more frequent in individuals with a disorder than in controls. Significance thresholds must be corrected for multiple testing as many genetic markers are examined. For example, in the so-called Genome-wide association studies (GWAS) significance thresholds are in the order of 10^{-7} or 10^{-8}.
3 Traits with a Mendelian inheritance pattern involve a single gene and no environmental effect. These can be dominant or recessive. In dominant inheritance patterns, such as FOXP2, individuals who carry at least one copy of a mutant allele (responsible for the disorder) are affected by the disorder. In recessive inheritance patterns, only individuals carrying two copies of a mutant allele are affected by the disorder.

4 Water-maze tasks (e.g. Morris, 1984) are thought to tap spatial memory and learning abilities of animals. In a typical water-maze task a round pool is filled with opaque water. Rats or mice should find a hidden escape platform, located just below the surface of the water. Rodents learn to do so using extra-maze visual cues.

5 For example, in the English model of Inflectional Morphology the tagged Brown corpus (Francis & Kučera, 1982) was used to measure the frequencies of different grammatical categories (e.g. verbs), inflections (e.g. past tense), or allomorphic suffixes within certain inflections (e.g. -/t/,/d/, and -/^d/ past tenses). These counts were used to constrain frequencies in the artificial language training set.

References

Addyman, C. & French, R. M. (2012). Computational modeling in cognitive science: A manifesto for change. *Topics in Cognitive Science, 4*, 332–341.

Arking, D. E., Cutler, D. J., Brune, C. W., Teslovich, T. M., West, K., ... Chakravarti, A. (2008). A common genetic variant in the neurexin superfamily member CNTNAP2 increases familial risk of autism. *American Journal of Human Genetics, 82*(1), 160–164.

Bartlett, C. W., Flax, J. F., Logue, M. W., Vieland, V. J., Bassett, A. S., Tallal, P. & Brzustowicz, L. M. (2002). A major susceptibility locus for specific language impairment is located on 13q21. *American Journal of Human Genetics, 71*(1), 45–55.

Bartlett, C. W., Flax, J. F., Logue, M. W., Smith, B. J., Vieland, V. J., Tallal, P. & Brzustowicz, L. M. (2004). Examination of potential overlap in autism and language loci on chromosomes 2, 7, and 13 in two independent samples ascertained for specific language impairment. *Human Heredity, 57*(1), 10–20.

Bishop, D. V. M. (1994). Grammatical errors in specific language impairment: Competence or performance limitations? *Applied Psycholinguistics, 15*, 507–550.

——(1997). *Uncommon Understanding: Development and Disorders of Language Comprehension in Children.* Hove, UK: Psychology Press.

Bishop, D. V. M. & Hayiou-Thomas, M. E. (2008). Heritability of specific language impairment depends on diagnostic criteria. *Genes, Brain and Behaviour, 7*, 365–372.

Bishop, D. V. M. & Leonard, L. B. (eds) (2000). *Speech and Language Impairments in Children: Causes, Characteristics, Intervention and Outcome.* Hove, UK: Psychology Press.

Chomsky, N. (1965). *Aspects of the Theory of Syntax.* Cambridge, MA: MIT Press.

——(1981). *Lectures on Government and Binding.* Dordrecht: Foris.

——(1986). *Knowledge of Language: Its Nature, Origin and Use.* New York, NY: Praeger.

——(1995). *The Minimalist Program.* Cambridge, MA: MIT Press.

——(1998). *Minimalist Iniquities: The Framework.* Cambridge, MA: MIT Press.

Conti-Ramsden, G., Botting, N. & Faragher, B. (2001). Psycholinguistic markers for specific language impairment (SLI). *The Journal of Child Psychology and Psychiatry and Allied Disciplines, 42*(6), 741–748.

Cooper, R. P. & Guest, O. (2014). Implementations are not specifications: Specification, replication and experimentation in computational cognitive modeling. *Cognitive Systems Research*, 27, 42–49.

Dick, F., Wulfeck, B., Krupa-Kwiatkowski, M. & Bates, E. (2004). The development of complex sentence interpretation in typically developing children compared with children with specific language impairments or early unilateral focal lesions. *Developmental Science, 7*(3), 360–377.

Enard, W., Przeworski, M., Fisher, S. E., Lai, C. S., Wiebe, V., ... Pääbo, S. (2002). Molecular evolution of FOXP2, a gene involved in speech and language. *Nature, 418*(6900), 869–872.

Evans, J. L., Saffran, J. R. & Robe-Torres, K. (2009). Statistical learning in children with Specific Language Impairment. *Journal of Speech, Language, and Hearing Research, 52*, 321–335.

Falcaro, M., Pickles, A., Newbury, D. F., Addis, L., Banfield, E., ... SLI Consortium (2008). Genetic and phenotypic effects of phonological short-term memory and grammatical morphology in specific language impairment. *Genes, Brain, and Behaviour, 7*(4), 393–402.

Fisher, S. E. (2006). How can animal studies help to uncover the roles of genes implicated in human speech and language disorders? In G. S. Fisch & J. Flint (eds), *Transgenic and Knockout Models of Neuropsychiatric Disorders* (pp. 127–149). Totowa, NJ: Humana Press.

Fisher, S. E. & Marcus, G. F. (2006). The eloquent ape: genes, brains and the evolution of language. *Nature Reviews Genetics, 7*, 9–20.

Fisher, S. E. & Scharff, C. (2009). FOXP2 as a molecular window into speech and language. *Trends in Genetics, 25*(4), 166–177.

Francis, W. & Kučera, H. (1982). *Frequency Analysis of English Usage.* Boston, MA: Houghton Mifflin.

Fujita, E., Tanabe, Y., Shiota, A., Ueda, M., Suwa, K., Mariko, Y. M. & Momoi, T. (2008). Ultrasonic vocalization impairment of Foxp2 (R552H) knockin mice related to speech-language disorder and abnormality of Purkinje cells. *Proceedings of the National Academy of Sciences USA, 105*(8), 3117–3122.

Gardner, H., Froud, K., McClelland, A. & van der Lely, H. (2006). The development of the Grammar and Phonology Screening (GAPS) test to assess key markers of specific language difficulties in young children. *International Journal of Language & Communication Disorders, 41*(5), 513–540.

Gathercole, S. E. (2006). Nonword repetition and word learning: The nature of the relationship. *Applied Psycholinguistics, 27*, 513–543.

Gathercole, S. E. & Baddeley, A. D. (1990). Phonological memory deficits in language disordered children: Is there a causal connection? *Journal of Memory and Language, 29*, 336–360.

Gaub, S., Groszer, M., Fisher, S. E. & Ehret, G. (2010). The structure of innate vocalizations in Foxp2-deficient mouse pups. *Genes, Brain, and Behaviour, 9*(4), 390–401.

Gopnik, M. (1990). Feature blind grammar and dysphasia. *Nature, 344*(62–68), 715.

Gopnik, M. & Crago, M. (1991). Familial aggregation of the developmental language disorders. *Cognition, 39*, 1–50.

Groszer, M., Keays, D. A., Deacon, R. M., de Bono, J. P., Prasad-Mulcare, S., ... Fisher, S. E. (2008). Impaired synaptic plasticity and motor learning in mice with a point mutation implicated in human speech deficits. *Current Biology, 18*(5), 354–362.

Hadley, P. & Short, H. (2005). The onset of tense marking in children at-risk for SLI. *Journal of Speech, Language, and Hearing Research, 48*, 1344–1362.

Haesler, S., Wada, K., Nshdejan, A., Morrisey, E. E., Lints, T., Jarvis, E. D. & Scharff, C. (2004). FoxP2 expression in avian vocal learners and non-learners. *Journal of Neuroscience, 24*(13), 3164–3175.

Haesler, S., Rochefort, C., Georgi, B., Licznerski, P., Osten, P. & Scharff, C. (2007). Incomplete and inaccurate vocal imitation after knockdown of FoxP2 in songbird basal ganglia nucleus Area X. *PLoS Biol, 5*:e321.

Hoeffner, J. H. & McClelland, J. L. (1993). Can a perceptual processing deficit explain the impairment of inflectional morphology in developmental dysphasia? A computational investigation. In E. V. Clark (ed.), *Proceedings of the 25th Child Language Research Forum* (pp. 38–49). Cambridge, UK: Cambridge University Press.

Hsu, H. & Bishop, D. (2011). Grammatical difficulties in children with Specific Language Impairment: Is learning deficient? *Human Development, 53*(5), 264–277.

Hurst, J. A., Baraitser, M., Auger, E., Graham, F. & Norell, S. (1990). An extended family with a dominantly inherited speech disorder. *Developmental Medicine and Child Neurology, 32*(4), 352–355.

Joanisse, M. F. (2004). Specific language impairments in children: Phonology, semantics, and the English past tense. *Current Directions in Psychological Science, 13*(4), 156–160.

Joanisse, M. F. & Seidenberg, M. S. (2003). Phonology and syntax in specific language impairment: Evidence from a connectionist model. *Brain and Language, 86*, 40–56.

Jürgens, U. (2009). The neural control of vocalization in mammals: A review. *Journal of Voice, 23*(1), 1–10.

Kail, R. (1994). A method for studying the generalized slowing hypothesis in children with specific language impairment. *Journal of Speech and Hearing Research, 37*, 418–421.

Karaminis, T. (2012). *Connectionist Modelling of Morphosyntax in Typical and Atypical Development for English and Modern Greek*. Unpublished doctoral dissertation, University of London.

Karaminis, T. N. & Thomas, M. S. C. (2010). A cross-linguistic model of the acquisition of inflectional morphology in English and Modern Greek. In S. Ohlsson & R. Catrambone (eds), *Proceedings of the 32nd Annual Conference of the Cognitive Science Society* (pp. 730–735). Austin, TX: Cognitive Science Society.

Karmiloff-Smith, A., Scerif, G. & Thomas, M. S. C. (2002). Different approaches to relating genotype to phenotype in developmental disorders. *Developmental Psychobiology, 40*, 311–322.

Lai, C. S., Fisher, S. E., Hurst, J. A., Vargha-Khadem, F. & Monaco, A. P. (2001). A forkhead-domain gene is mutated in a severe speech and language disorder. *Nature, 413*(6855), 519–523.

Lai, C. S. L., Gerrelli, D., Monaco, A. P., Fisher, S. E. & Copp, A. J. (2003). FOXP2 expression during brain development coincides with adult sites of pathology in a severe speech and language disorder. *Brain, 126*(11), 2455–2462.

Leonard, L., Ellis-Weismer, S., Miller, C., Francis, D., Tomblin, J. & Kail, R. (2007). Speed of processing, working memory, and language impairment in children. *Journal of Speech, Language, and Hearing Research, 50*(2), 408–428.

Leonard, L., Sabbadini, L., Leonard, J. & Volterra, V. (1987). Specific language impairment in children: A crosslinguistic study. *Brain and Language, 32*, 233–252.

Leonard, L. B. (1998). *Children with Specific Language Impairment*. Cambridge, MA: MIT Press.

Leonard, L. B., Bortolini, U., Caselli, M. C., McGregor, K. K. & Sabbadini, L. (1992). Morphological deficits in children with specific language impairment: The status of features in the underlying grammar. *Language Acquisition, 2*, 151–179.

Liégeois, F., Baldeweg, T., Connelly, A., Gadian, D. G., Mishkin, M. & Vargha-Khadem, F. (2003). Language fMRI abnormalities associated with FOXP2 gene mutation. *Nature Neuroscience, 6*(11), 1230–1237.

MacDermot, K. D., Bonora, E., Sykes, N., Coupe, A. M., Lai, C. S., Vernes, S. C., ... Fisher, S. E. (2005). Identification of FOXP2 truncation as a novel cause of developmental speech and language deficits. *American Journal of Human Genetics, 76*(6), 1074–1080.

McGregor, K. K. & Leonard, L. B. (1994). Subject pronoun and article omissions in the speech of children with specific language impairment: A phonological interpretation. *Journal of Speech and Hearing Research, 37*, 171–181.

Marcus, G. F. & Fisher, S. E. (2003). FOXP2 in focus: What can genes tell us about speech and language? *Trends in Cognitive Sciences, 7*, 257–262.

Mareschal, D., Johnson, M. H., Sirois, S., Thomas, M.S.C. & Westermann, G. (eds) (2007). *Neuroconstructivism, Vol. 1: How the Brain Constructs Cognition.* Oxford, UK: Oxford University Press.

Mareschal, D., Sirois, S., Westermann, G. & Johnson, M. H. (eds) (2007). *Neuroconstructivism, Vol. 2: Perspectives and Prospects.* Oxford, UK: Oxford University Press.

Matthews, D. E. & Theakston, A. L. (2006). Errors of omission in English-speaking children's production of plurals and the past tense: The effects of frequency, phonology, and competition. *Cognitive Science, 30*, 1027–1052.

Morris, R. (1984). Developments of a water-maze procedure for studying spatial learning in the rat. *Journal of Neuroscience Methods, 11*, 47–60.

Newbury, D. F. & Monaco, A. P. (2008). The application of molecular genetics to the study of language impairments. In C. F. Norbury, J. B. Tomblin & D. V. M. Bishop (eds), *Understanding Developmental Language Disorders: From Theory to Practice* (pp. 79–92). Hove, UK: Psychology Press.

Newbury, D. F., Bonora, E., Lamb, J. A., Fisher, S. E., Lai, C.S.L., ... the International Molecular Genetic Study of Autism Consortium (2002). FOXP2 is not a major susceptibility gene for autism or Specific Language Impairment. *American Journal of Human Genetics, 70*, 1318–1327.

Newbury, D. F., Fisher, S. E. & Monaco, A. P. (2010). Recent advances in the genetics of language impairment. *Genome Medicine, 2*, 6–14.

Newbury, D. F., Winchester, L., Addis, L., Paracchini, S., Buckingham, L. L., ... Monaco A. P. (2009). CMIP and ATP2C2 modulate phonological short-term memory in language impairment. *American Journal of Human Genetics, 85*, 264–272.

Pinker, S. (1994). *The Language Instinct.* New York: Penguin.

——(1999). *Words and Rules.* London: Weidenfeld & Nicolson.

Plunkett, K. & Marchman, V. (1991). U-shaped learning and frequency effects in a multi-layered perceptron: Implications for child language acquisition. *Cognition, 38*(1), 43–102.

——(1993). From rote learning to system building: Acquiring verb morphology in children and connectionist nets. *Cognition, 48*(1), 21–69.

Rapin, I. & Allen, D. A. (1987). Developmental dysphasia and autism in preschool children: Characteristics and subtypes. *Proceedings of the First International Symposium on Specific Speech and Language Disorders in Children* (pp. 20–35). London, UK: Association of All Speech Impaired Children.

Rice, M. L. (2012). Toward epigenetic and gene regulation models of specific language impairment: Looking for links among growth, genes, and impairments. *Journal of Neurodevelopmental Disorders, 4*, 27–41.

——(2013). Language growth and genetics of specific language impairment. *International Journal of Speech-Language Pathology, 15*(3), 223–233.

Rice, M. L., Wexler, K. & Cleave, P. (1995). Specific Language Impairment as a period of extended optional infinitive. *Journal of Speech and Hearing Research, 38*, 850–863.

Rumelhart, D. E. & McClelland, J. L. (1986). On learning the past tenses of English verbs. In J. L. McClelland & D. E. Rumelhart (eds), *Parallel Distributed Processing: Explorations in the Microstructure of Cognition* (Vol. 2: Psychological and Biological Models, pp. 216–271). Cambridge, MA: MIT Press.

Rumelhart, D. E., Hinton, G. & Williams, R. (1986). Learning internal representations by error propagation. In D. E. Rumelhart, J. L. McClelland & the PDP Group (eds), *Parallel Distributed Processing: Explorations in the Microstructure of Cognition* (Vol. 1: Foundations, pp. 318–362). Cambridge, MA: MIT Press.

Shu, W., Cho, J. Y., Jiang, Y., Zhang, M., Weisz, D., … Buxbaum, J. D. (2005). Altered ultrasonic vocalization in mice with a disruption in the Foxp2 gene. *Proceedings of the National Academy of Sciences USA, 102*(27), 9643–9648.

SLI consortium (SLIC) (2002). A genome-wide scan identifies two novel loci involved in specific language impairment. *American Journal of Human Genetics, 70*(2), 384–398.

——(2004). Highly significant linkage to the SLI1 locus in an expanded sample of individuals affected by specific language impairment. *American Journal of Human Genetics, 74*(6), 122512–122538.

Stavrakaki, S. (2006). Developmental perspectives on Specific Language Impairment: Evidence from the production of wh-questions by Greek SLI children over time. *Advances in Speech-Language Pathology, 8*(4), 384–396.

Stephany, U. (1997). The acquisition of Greek. In D. I. Slobin (ed.), *The Crosslinguistic Study of Language Acquisition* (Vol. 4) (Chapter 3: pp. 183–334). Hillsdale, NJ: Erlbaum.

Stromswold, K. (1998). Genetics of spoken language disorders. *Human Biology, 70*(2), 297–324.

——(2001). The heritability of language: A review and metaanalysis of twin, adoption and linkage studies. *Language, 77*(4), 647–723.

Tallal, P. & Piercy, M. (1973a). Defects of non-verbal auditory perception in children with developmental aphasia. *Nature, 241*, 468–469.

——(1973b). Developmental aphasia: Impaired rate of nonverbal processing as a function of sensory modality. *Neuropsychologia, 11*, 389–398.

Thomas, M. S. C. (2005). Characterising compensation. *Cortex, 41*(3), 434–442.

Thomas, M. S. C. & Karmiloff-Smith, A. (2003). Modelling language acquisition in atypical phenotypes. *Psychological Review, 110*(4), 647–682.

Thomas, M. S. C. & Redington, M. (2004). Modelling atypical syntax processing. In W. G. Sakas (ed.), *COLING 2004, Psycho-Computational Models of Human Language Acquisition* (pp. 87–94). Geneva, Switzerland: COLING.

Tomblin, J. B., Mainela-Arnold, E. & Zhang, X. (2007). Procedural learning in adolescents with and without specific language impairment. *Language Learning and Development, 3*, 269–293.

Tomblin, J. B., Records, N. L., Buckwalter, P., Zhang, X., Smith, E. & O'Brien, M. (1997). The prevalence of specific language impairment in kindergarten children. *Journal of Speech and Hearing Research, 40*, 1245–1260.

Ullman, M. & Pierpont, E. (2005). Specific Language Impairment is not specific to language: The Procedural Deficit hypothesis. *Cortex, 41*(3), 399–433.

van der Lely, H. K. J. & Battell, J. (2003). Wh-movement in children with grammatical SLI: A test of the RDDR hypothesis. *Language, 79*, 153–181.

van der Lely, H. K. J. & Stollwerck, L. (1997). Binding theory and specifically language impaired children. *Cognition, 62*, 245–290.

van der Lely, H. K. J. & Ullman, M. (2001). Past tense morphology in specifically language impaired children and normally developing children. *Language and Cognitive Processes, 16*, 177–217.

Vargha-Khadem, F., Watkins, K., Alcock, K., Fletcher, P. & Passingham, R. (1995). Praxic and nonverbal cognitive deficits in a large family with a genetically transmitted speech and language disorder. *PNAS USA, 92*(3), 930–933.

Vargha-Khadem, F., Watkins, K. E., Price, C. J., Ashburner, J., Alcock, K.J., ... Passingham, R. E. (1998). Neural basis of an inherited speech and language disorder. *PNAS USA, 95*(21), 12695–12700.

Vernes, S. C. & Fisher, S. E. (2013). Genetic pathways implicated in speech and language. In S. Helekar (ed.), *Animal Models of Speech and Language Disorders* (pp. 13–40). New York: Springer.

Vernes, S. C., Newbury, D. F., Abrahams, B. S., Winchester, L., Nicod, J., ... Fisher, S. E. (2008). A functional genetic link between distinct developmental language disorders. *New England Journal of Medicine, 359*(22), 2337–2345.

Vernes, S. C., Oliver, P. L., Spiteri, E., Lockstone, H. E., Puliyadi, R., ... Fisher S. E. (2011). Foxp2 regulates gene networks implicated in neurite outgrowth in the developing brain. *PLoS Genetics, 7*(7): e1002145.

Villanueva, P., Newbury, D. F., Jara, L., De Barbieri, Z., Mirza, G., ... Palomino, H. (2011). Genome-wide analysis of genetic susceptibility to language impairment in an isolated Chilean population. *European Journal of Human Genetics, 19*(6), 687–695.

Wexler, K. (2003). Lenneberg's dream: Learning, normal language development and specific language impairment. In Y. Levy & J. Schaeer (eds), *Language Competence Across Populations: Towards a Definition of Specific Language Impairment* (pp. 11–61). Mahwah, NJ: Erlbaum.

Wilson, B. & Risucci, D. (1986). A model for the clinical quantitative classification: Generation-application to language disordered preschool children. *Brain and Language, 27*, 281–309.

6

ACORNS

A tool for visual modelling of causes and outcomes in neurodevelopmental disorders

Derek G. Moore and Rachel George

6.1 Introduction

Visualisation and notation systems are widely used in science to provide a tool with which to map, compare and debate models and theories. Visualisation aids understanding by representing, specifying and simplifying what is complex or unseen. This in turn can make conceptual frameworks easier to understand and may bring new rigour to a discipline by ensuring a greater level of precision in theoretical debate. Furthermore, an engaging and accessible form of visualisation can help disciplines communicate complexity to a wider public audience in an engaging and accessible way. One well-known example of a *visualisation* tool is the ball-and-stick model used in chemistry. This provides a universal framework for representing bonds between atoms and modelling the physical structure of molecules. This system is not simply descriptive, but provides a theory-neutral tool to map, compare and propose a range of structures, starting positions and outcomes of reactions under a variety of different conditions. It is hard to imagine how chemistry could function without this universal visualisation system, and how limited scientific and pedagogical understanding would be if chemists did not have this tool. *Notation* is the use of icons, symbols, letters and numbers as a means of providing additional information over multiple dimensions, linked with the other components of the visualisation. Notation is used in chemistry but is most widely encountered in music, which uses a score to represent time and pitch; variations in the form of a musical note (open, block, tailed) to indicate different numbers of beats, clusters of notes to represent chords, and linked letters and symbols to indicate dimensions such as volume or attack.

While visualisations of child development are often included in textbooks these are usually metaphorical or descriptive and do not offer the visual and notational precision of ball-and-stick models or musical scores. A common example is Waddington's visualisation of the 'epigenetic landscape', which is a metaphorical illustration of how aspects of development become more channelled with time. Another common textbook visualisation is Bronfenbrenner's (1979) illustration of the many layers of social influence as a systemic framework of concentric rings. While an elegant illustration, this does not show precise relationships between factors over time. Developmental science draws on evidence across many sub-disciplines (developmental psychology, neuroscience, biology, genetics, etc.), with an ever-increasing focus on complex hypotheses of cause-and-effect and more and more temporal precision. It combines data about individual-level factors with those of wider social and environmental factors (linking with the disciplines of education, epidemiology, sociology, public health, etc.). The complexity of development, and the many potential causal factors involved, over many layers of influence over developmental time, makes it difficult to simultaneously represent all existing data. This explains the need to generate a precise and universal visualisation and notation tool of development.

While visual models created by researchers provide some attempt to make links between data and theory, and sometimes these appear in journal articles, these are often limited in scope. They are often ad-hoc, box-and-arrow diagrams which represent a narrow set of abilities, and are made without a universally understood set of rules and layout and without any clear notation. Consequently, models are created which do not fully account for changing influences over time, and that give few precise indications of relative rates of development and variance of outcomes. Furthermore, because models are created ad hoc, with each researcher laying out their models differently, they are harder to understand and cannot easily be linked together with other theoretical models of different capacities that may occur earlier or later in development, or at different levels of explanation.

Without a universal and comprehensive system we may be limiting our horizons and making it more difficult to see where gaps arise in theory and data and generate new theory. We propose that to make broader links between data and theory there is a need to create a new way to visualise complex developmental models. Developmental science may benefit by creating shared visualisation and notation tools that will allow more theoretical clarity and facilitate communication of theory within and between disciplines. This may lead to clearer understanding and more complete theory. We propose that there is a need for a comprehensive, shared visual modelling system that is able to represent the full range of normative and atypical development. Such a system would need to be able to illustrate the full range of possible causal models, and illustrate developmental outcomes in a way that is temporally precise and in a way that can facilitate links between different researchers.

Importantly, the models they create should be able to be understood as stand-alone diagrams, without the need for extensive explanatory text, as is the case for ball-and-stick models, and musical scores. If a diagram requires extensive explanatory text then it is likely that the visualisation and notation system contains inherent ambiguity, which reduces precision and diminishes its use for the development of comprehensive theories. We argue here and previously (Moore & George, 2011), along with others (Morton, 2004), that the lack of a common visualisation and notation framework may be inhibiting developmental science and be contributing to miscommunication within and between sub-disciplines about the relevance of different levels of explanation and the understanding of the process of 'development itself' (Karmiloff-Smith, 1998). This in turn may be contributing to a form of theoretical ghettoisation, where researchers tend to provide models, accounts and debate within an overly narrow range of explanation; for example, restricting accounts to cognitive or biological factors, within relatively constrained periods of development; which in turn may lead to the marginalisation of accounts from sub-disciplines with which these theoreticians are less familiar.

Furthermore, the absence of a clear way of representing and linking together the full breadth of development, across all levels of functioning, and over the full range of developmental time, may be encouraging theoreticians in sub-disciplines to create theories with cause–outcome explanations that are overly focussed on statistical associations between a restricted number of factors within small time periods, that lend themselves to simple and 'static' models of cause; and that do not focus on plausible developmental accounts over longer periods of time. This may also lead to a tendency to apply perspectives from adult neuropsychology, rather than construct full developmental perspectives (Karmiloff-Smith, 1997) and to see the infant brain in terms of adult neurological domains rather than as an emerging system (Karmiloff-Smith, 2009).

In sum we have proposed that there is a need for an expansive and common system for modelling hypothetical associations over long developmental periods, across the many levels of explanation. We propose that this may be critical for improving our ability to clearly and precisely:

1. provide theoretical accounts of the influence of a full range of factors across all levels of explanation;
2. represent the dynamic cascade of developmental processes over time;
3. provide clear and comprehendible accounts of transactional processes;
4. synthesise and combine known statistical data and hypothetical models across sub-disciplines;
5. identify genuine gaps in our knowledge;
6. identify key areas of agreement and key strengths and weaknesses in existing theoretical models;
7. create new, more comprehensive, interdisciplinary, theoretical accounts.

A visualisation system that could provide these utilities will be beneficial in informing future debate, the direction of future research, and ensuring that findings from across the many sub-disciplines are synthesised into comprehensive models that can have impact on theory, practice and policy. A universal visualisation for developmental science would be of particular help to better represent atypical developmental processes, with implications for future clinical practice and interventions.

Currently the use of ad-hoc visualisations, each created to suit a specific theory or set of data, does not facilitate wider debate about the developmental nature of syndromes. Restricted 'static' models of developmental syndromes, that focus on a small range of abilities, within limited levels of explanation, narrow developmental periods, and where change over time is not made explicit, tend to hide rather than highlight the importance of developmental accounts in theories of neuro-developmental populations. Creating a more expansive and comprehensive universal modelling system will allow the creation of far more comprehensive 'meta-theories' of developmental difficulties. A universal system that brings together complex interdisciplinary multi-level data in a precise yet accessible way will also make it far easier to explain developmental causes and provide clearer and more precise rationales for interventions. A universal notation will also allow theoreticians from many disciplines to use a universal language to communicate to students, clinicians and policy makers from outside of their disciplines.

A good visualisation will more clearly identify syndrome-specific versus general processes of development and provide more meaningful accounts of between- and within-group variance for cohorts with developmental difficulties. This in turn will give clinicians better guidance on where and when it could be effective to intervene at a group and individual level. This is also important to allow researchers and clinicians to communicate a clear rationale to policy makers and funders about how and when to target interventions. Engaging and accessible visualisations of complex 'big data' is having more and more influence on policy in the fields of health economics (see Rosling, 2007), and we need to ensure developmental science has an equal influence.

6.2 ACORNS: an accessible cause–outcome representation and notation system

In a recent paper for clinicians and researchers working in the area of intellectual difficulties (Moore & George, 2011) we described a visualisation system we have called ACORNS (an Accessible, Cause–Outcome Representation and Notation System). Here we present an updated account of the application of this system for a broader audience. ACORNS is designed to be used across disciplines to allow for greater precision in theory, and allow researchers across sub-disciplines to use a shared lingua franca to combine and bridge between data, across levels of explanation, and over developmental periods.

We have created this system to facilitate our understanding of developmental difficulties and link together sub-disciplines to facilitate theoretical debate. ACORNS specifies a set of rules on how to represent causal relationships with arrows; and includes notation designed to clearly indicate atypical changes in relative degree, rate and variance in functioning across time. The system was designed to build on and improve on previous attempts to create a causal modelling system (see Developmental Causal Modelling, DCM, Morton & Frith, 1995; Morton, 2004), and to explicitly facilitate the creation of representations of 'development itself' (Karmiloff-Smith, 1998).

6.2.1 The frame

The visualisation is built upon a 'frame'. This frame facilitates the depiction of causal factors and outcomes over time, with horizontal lines demarking boundaries between different conceptual levels of explanation. The frame shows developmental time progressing from left to right across the page. The addition of an explicit time dimension facilitates the sequential representation of changing trajectories of effects across development across levels. Similar to a musical score, the frame can be extended over as many pages as necessary to illustrate the long-term nature of development.

Simple models that researchers create which depict unidirectional causal relationships, between behaviour and cognition, and environmental and social influences, at one 'snapshot' in time, give an incomplete representation of the process of development. However, models that try to indicate developmental influences using double-headed arrows to illustrate bi-directional influence between a potential cause and a longer-term causal outcome are also problematic. Bi-directional arrows in effect 'disappear' the developmental dimension from theory. This is because they do not show the sequence and order in which these bi-directional influences occur over time. By making the time dimension explicit ACORNS not only can serve a useful function for visualisation, but also challenge theoreticians to provide fuller developmental accounts which show how development unfolds across the temporal dimension and not brush development under the carpet.

The ACORNS frame depicts six levels of explanation separated by horizontal lines. Three levels, biology, cognition and behaviour, were illustrated in Morton's DCM (2004); we have added to this by depicting affect and cognition as two sub-levels, separated by a dashed line to reflect the fact that some factors link across the interface of cognitive and social–affective levels (see Figure 6.1). Also, for the full depiction of development and causal pathways, we have added a physical- and a social–environmental level, one above and one below these three levels (see Moore & George, 2011 for a fuller account of the difference between ACORNS and Morton's DCM approach to environmental influences). These two levels in combination with the time dimension not included in DCM, help depict the way that the environment acts upon the individual. This can be either through direct physical and biological processes such as the impact of stress or recreational drugs in utero, or through the impact of social processes such as parenting, peer interactions, schooling and community influences.

The depiction of the changing influence of the environment over time is important to facilitate the representation of theories that propose transactional processes. Transactional accounts (see Sameroff, 2009) describe bi-directional processes in which individual characteristics and those of the environment mutually affect each other over time, while the characteristics and environment are themselves also changed and changing. These transactions are central to a number of causal theories, and we need a visualisation system that can clearly illustrate these dynamic processes.

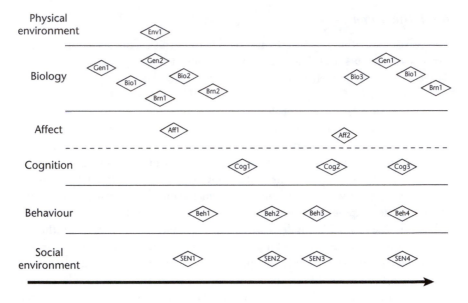

FIGURE 6.1 Showing the ACORNS frame and the mapping of factors over different points in time using diamond-shaped boxes.

6.2.2 Mapping and plotting

ACORNS mapping requires the identification of the key points along developmental trajectories over a number of domains, and the systematic placing of boxes showing these key points in development within a time frame. Each box may be a point along a linear, or non-linear developmental trajectory (see Thomas, 2005; Thomas et al., 2009).

Figure 6.1 shows the ACORNS frame and gives an illustration of how to undertake a hypothetical *mapping* of key factors within this context. As one objective of creating ACORNS is to provide a clear visualisation which can aid understanding, we have used diamond-shaped boxes for mapping of factors, so that when factors within the same conceptual level (for example within the biological or cognitive levels) are linked using arrows, this creates the illusion that these factors are laid out within a single three-dimensional plane.

We use the term *mapping* to refer to the process in which these diamond-shaped boxes are used to depict a sequence of changing rates and levels of functioning over many domains within and across levels within the time frame. Mapping is not to be confused with *plotting* which refers to the extrapolation of developmental trajectories within a single domain of functioning based on actual data (see Thomas et al., 2009). Mapping adds to plotting by outlining the full picture of developmental change, giving a representation of the complete range of delayed, atypical and also relatively spared or typical outcomes for a population.

Information from plotting is essential to provide the profile of change needed to undertake wider mapping and modelling;[1] but *mapping* includes the representation of known data as well as hypothetical causes and outcomes; and extends the idea of plotting by allowing the direct contrast of outcomes across a full range of domains relevant for understanding the specific difficulties of a population. The idea is to give a full picture of population characteristics to show both the difficulties and specific characteristics of a population, and also to show contrasts in typical and atypical aspects of functioning across populations, illustrating unique profiles of relative delay, sparing or difference.[2]

It would be better if there were an agreed, full and comprehensive picture of the key points in development for each population of developmental difficulty (e.g. Autism, Down syndrome, Williams syndrome, Fragile X, etc.), but one difficulty for our field is that these points are not always agreed upon between theoreticians. Currently, different theories place different importance on specific clusters of abilities with the range of abilities and time periods varying from theory to theory. One of the benefits of using a common modelling system is to facilitate debate about these critical points, to ensure that theories account for all the key developmental processes (see Section 6.5, Discussion). It is also important for theoreticians to recognise and differentiate between key measurement points (points in development that are commonly assessed) versus theoretically critical points (points where causal effects begin to operate).

In many cases there is a common accepted age for the measurement of abilities, which may be dictated by a child's ability to cope with task demands, or common educational practices. This point of measurement will often occur later in development than the initial point of emergence of an ability, at the point at which an ability is consolidated enough to assess meaningful individual differences. For theoretical purposes it will be necessary to place a box both at the point at which reliable measurement is taken, and also at the hypothesised point of initial emergence of any ability. This will allow a model to depict the causal factors that constrain or facilitate the emergence of abilities, as well as showing the point of reliable measurement of these abilities, and the factors that might constrain performance. It may also be important to show intermediate points (nodes) along the trajectory where other factors may have begun to have an influence on the emergence of the ability (see Figure 6.1: Cog1 and Cog2; Beh1, Beh2, Beh3; and SEN1, SEN2, SEN3).

To summarise, the creation of agreed key points along trajectories, and the creation of comprehensive mappings of abilities over different populations of children with developmental difficulties is itself an important endeavour, which requires considerable shared effort. This requires the precise mapping of a number of nodes that illustrate: 1) the point in time at which it might be theoretically assumed any critical ability first emerges in typical populations; 2) the point (if different to 1) where there can be reliable measurement of this functioning; 3) the point where there is evidence of atypical outcomes in functioning, rate of development or variance in functioning; and 4) the points along a developmental trajectory where factors causally influence each other. Mapping is an essential starting point for the creation of models of development. Once mapping is complete it is possible to overlay theoretical accounts of cause using arrows.

6.2.3 Modelling

Modelling is the process of representing hypothesised causal pathways between the functions and capacities that have been mapped, using arrows to indicate the direction of cause. Figure 6.2 shows how to add a number of linking arrows to the mapping depicted in Figure 6.1 to depict hypothetical causal pathways that could be proposed to depict hypothetical influences acting in and/between levels between a set of factors.

To differentiate between causal pathways acting within and between levels, and over time, we use specific rules on how and when to use three different orientations of arrows.

Horizontal arrows are used for linking a series of points over time in the development of a single aspect of functioning (e.g. now linking Cog1 and Cog2; Beh1, Beh2, Beh3; and SEN1, SEN2, SEN3). This is analogous to a linked series of snapshots along a developmental trajectory depicting the initial point of emergence, points of common measurement and points where causal factors begin to affect outcomes (see later).

Diagonal arrows are used to depict causal links between different aspects of functioning from within a single level of description, at a particular point in time.

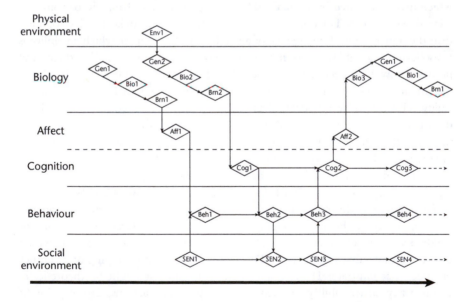

FIGURE 6.2   Illustrating how arrows are used to depict points along trajectories within a domain of functioning (linked by horizontal arrows) causal pathways within levels of functioning (linked by diagonal arrows), and effects between levels of functioning (linked by vertical arrows).

So for example, they may be used to link two boxes within the cognitive level and to show how two different cognitive functions are causally related.

Vertical arrows are used on the other hand to show causal links between factors acting across levels, for example an environmental factor impacting on a biological process. In ACORNS these arrows can be used to show causal chains moving both up and down, depicting transactional effects between levels. It should be noted that neither up nor down is given any causal precedence in this system as any level may influence any other in either direction, top to bottom and vice-versa. Of important note is that we argue that only vertical arrows should be used to depict *causal* chains between factors from different levels. The reason for this restriction is to ensure that theoreticians provide fully articulated developmental accounts of causal sequences as they emerge over specific time frames.

While a factor may have been found to have a statistical relationship with a different factor at a different level at a later point in development, depicting this as a direct causal link using a diagonal arrow is likely to be misleading. A longitudinal statistical relationship depicted by a simple box-and-arrow diagram, showing an arrow leading from a factor at one level at time 1 (e.g. a biological process in early infancy) to one at time 2 at another level (e.g. a social behaviour in childhood), may not depict the full causal sequence by which one factor came to cause the other. While it is tempting to represent a longitudinal statistical association as a causal pathway in this way, this is potentially a form of conceptual shortcut.

A restriction on the use of diagonal arrows with this system, in addition to improving the visualisation of within- and between-level influences, prevents theoreticians from ignoring potential intermediate developmental sequences acting between levels of explanation, by simply drawing an arrow linking two factors over time, and failing to specify the point in time when the cause in one level (i.e. a biological process) *began* to effect a process in another level (i.e. cognitive functioning). Of course the effect may have continued over time, and this can easily be illustrated as a sequence of continuing links between levels over time. The strength of restricting arrows in the way we propose is to challenge theoreticians to provide a full and explicit account of a hypothesised chain of plausible mediating and moderating factors across and within levels. Theorists need to add the links of the full causal chain or to say why no intermediate processes are needed, but nevertheless to commit to a hypothesis about when a factor begins to affect the other in time.

To aid the overall visualisation of developmental sequences, when a causal chain is hypothesised to cascade between levels from top to bottom, or bottom to top, we recommend (where possible) illustrating the temporal element of the sequence by offsetting boxes to the right as causal sequences proceed. Specifically, with top to bottom causal chains, we recommend that arrows emerge from the right-hand or bottom corner of a diamond and link vertically downwards to a left-hand or top corner of the factor below. Correspondingly, where a causal chain is moving in the other direction from a level at the bottom upwards, then arrows emerge from a right-hand or top corner of a diamond and link vertically upwards to a left-hand or bottom corner of the factor above (again see Figure 6.2).

Figure 6.2 shows how these modifications and conventions can be applied to a simple set of hypothetical factors. The model shows a developmental cascade in which an initial environmental effect might influence gene expression, leading to differences in behaviour which influence the social environment, which in turn has reciprocal effects on behaviour leading to effects on cognitive and biological levels. This is a relatively simple model with a direct link from a genetic cause to brain and cognitive outcomes, but also showing the temporal sequence and the subsequent transactional processes where social influences then act back on biological. Real development is likely to be even more complex and to require greatly extended models.

6.2.4 Notation

The visualisation already outlined can be used to outline a sequence of causal links, but does not provide a visualisation of the differential range of causes or effects. This becomes particularly important when trying to create and illustrate models of development for populations or individuals who show unique and subtle differences or delays in development over many factors. One of our key motives for creating ACORNS was to be able to create a visualisation system that can be used to compare and contrast similar and different developmental pathways across populations of children with developmental difficulties, and to provide more nuanced and fuller accounts of their development.

To facilitate clear, comprehensive and systematic mapping and modelling of individual differences and developmental difficulties, visualisation needs to show not only temporal causal links and sequences, but also to illustrate differential and relative degrees of functioning, relative timing of emergence and differences in variance of outcomes in functioning over points in time across different domains; and thereby show the relative degrees of difference in processes across each developing domain.

Figure 6.3 illustrates two symbols that can be added to boxes and arrows to show a range of differential relative outcomes in developmental models. These have been designed to tap into common iconography, are intuitive and easy to read, and can add clarity to basic box-and-arrow models; and are designed to be grouped with boxes (like clusters of acorns) and used to illustrate, at different points of development, these differential rates of relative functioning and timing of abilities across time. These indicators require theoreticians not only to be explicit about 'causal assumptions' but also to be explicit and more precise about their 'outcome assumptions' and give a clear and accessible representation of the unfolding dynamic nature of typical and atypical development. The two indicators are a cylinder and a clock face.

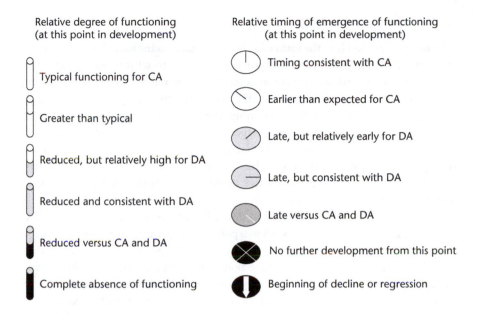

Relative degree of functioning
(at this point in development)

Typical functioning for CA

Greater than typical

Reduced, but relatively high for DA

Reduced and consistent with DA

Reduced versus CA and DA

Complete absence of functioning

Relative timing of emergence of functioning
(at this point in development)

Timing consistent with CA

Earlier than expected for CA

Late, but relatively early for DA

Late, but consistent with DA

Late versus CA and DA

No further development from this point

Beginning of decline or regression

FIGURE 6.3   Indicators of relative degree of functioning and relative timing of emergence.

6.2.5 Relative degree of functioning (shaded cylinder)

The first indicator is a vertical cylinder used to depict six possible relative degrees of functioning. Here 'liquid' in the cylinder is depicted as full and clear to indicate typical functioning; and fills up with darker liquid to show decreasing degrees of functioning. These are depicted relative first to what would be expected in the typical case relative to chronological age (CA); and then relative to what would be expected given the overall developmental age (DA), as averaged over all areas of functioning (in the cognitive domain this is referred to as mental age). The use of shading in these indicators is a particular aid to visualisation, so that when viewed as part of a complex model it is easier to get a sense of emerging areas of difficulty and to see the whole picture.

The six relative settings of degree of functioning that we recommend are:

1. a 'full' white cylinder indicating a degree of functioning that is *typical*;
2. a white cylinder with an additional white ring on top indicating a *heightened* degree of functioning relative to CA;[3]
3. a half-and-half, white and grey cylinder indicating a degree of functioning that is less than expected for CA but *relatively spared* compared to DA;
4. a simple all-grey cylinder indicating a degree of functioning that is *DA-equivalent*, i.e. that which would be consistent with overall DA;
5. a half-and-half, grey and black cylinder indicating a degree of functioning that is *relatively impaired* compared to DA; and finally
6. an all-black cylinder indicating a deficit or *absence* of an ability.

Relative timing (clock face)

The second notation is in the form of a clock face used to indicate the *relative timing of development* at the point selected. Again this is relative to what would be expected in the typical case relative to chronological age, or relative to what would be expected in terms of point 1 (above). In the case of a particular aspect of functioning, at any point in time a level of functioning may be higher than that expected for developmental age, but timing of emergence could be later or earlier than other aspects of functioning for developmental age – hence the need to disambiguate timing from level of functioning. When combined with the cylinder, the clock face allows us to depict both the relative degree of functioning at a point in time, and the relative timing of development.

In our previous paper we referred to this as *rate* of development, but as rate, by definition, is an extrapolation between two points in time, the term 'timing' is perhaps more precise in specifying development at a specific point in time. Given that ACORNS is depicting snapshots in time along trajectories, it is more consistent with this approach to talk about relative timing at the point depicted, rather than rates of development between points, although of course these are intrinsically linked.

There are seven[4] ordinal clock-face settings for the timing of development where the clock points to timing consistent with typical development (on the hour); with earlier timing of development, or later timing of development, the clock becomes more shaded and shows later points on the dial the later an area of function occurs relative to chronological age (CA), and then developmental age (DA). The indicator can also be used to show the point in time when development ceased; or to mark the starting point for a decline or regression in functioning.

The seven settings are:

1. a white clock face set at noon, indicating the timing is *typical* for CA;
2. a white clock face set at 'five-to', indicating when the timing of a process is early relative to chronological age;
3. a grey clock face showing 'five-past', indicating the timing is late relative to CA but *relatively early* compared to their general developmental age (DA);
4. a grey clock face showing 'quarter-past', indicating that timing is equivalent to that of general DA;
5. a dark grey clock face showing 'twenty-past'; indicating that timing is later compared to DA.

We also include two clock faces to depict the absence of change and the beginning of a reverse in developmental trajectories:

6. a black clock face with crossed hands indicating that development has ceased beyond this point;
7. a black clock with a downward-pointing arrow indicating the point where a decline or regression in functioning may have begun.

In Figure 6.4 we present three hypothetical developmental trajectories taken from Thomas et al. (2009). These illustrate different hypothetical courses of development within three single domains of functioning compared to typical development. The trajectories produced by Thomas et al. represent continuous assessment of these abilities over the course of development. Alongside these we show how these trajectories might be represented with a corresponding ACORNS sequence of indicators. This shows each of the trajectories as a progression or a sequence of linked boxes, depicting key points in time. The two ACORNS indicators indicate the relative degree of functioning and relative timing in functioning.

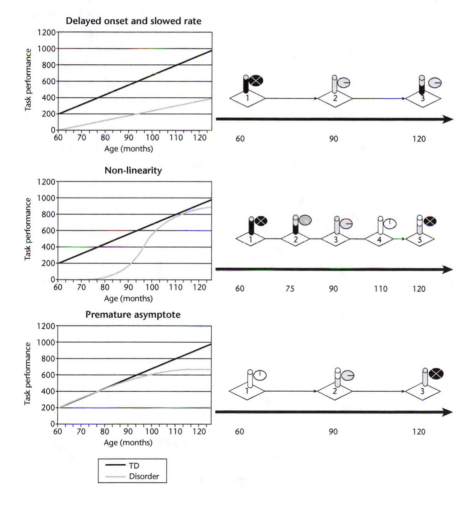

FIGURE 6.4   Using ACORNS indicators to show change in development at key points along trajectories (based on Thomas et al., 2009).

6.2.6 Using visualisation and notation to illustrate multiple causal pathways and individual differences

Notating relative variance in functioning

Although often unmentioned in theoretical accounts of development, providing detailed accounts of differences in variation of functioning may be critical for developing complete causal theories. In order to facilitate and encourage these fuller accounts, we propose using a third indicator, which is a double-arrowed box representing different patterns of variance over areas of functioning.

The indicator has a central line indicating the mean, and two additional lines indicating spread or standard deviation (similar to a boxplot). Figure 6.5 shows the depiction of typical variance along with five common forms of atypical variance relative to normal depicted using the indicator. The five atypical forms are: *increased* variance indicated by grey whiskers; *reduced* variance indicated by a reduced central shaded area; *skewed* variance, indicated by an off-centre shaded area; a *bimodal* distribution indicated by two shaded areas at each end with no central mean line; and *uniformity* or no variance indicated by an empty black indicator. Note that in terms of visualisation we have not made these atypical variances differ significantly in extent of shading, as it is not always clear whether a particular atypical variance represents a poorer or more positive outcome. We here show variance relative to typical, in effect relative to what would be expected on a similar task for a normal population. This may be adapted using additional shading and colour, where there is a need to compare relative variance between different atypical populations.

This element of development is rarely the focus of theoretical accounts, but we contend that the use of this indicator, when used in tandem with other ACORNS indicators, is important for presenting a full picture of outcomes. Theories of developmental difficulties rarely focus on pattern of variance as an important

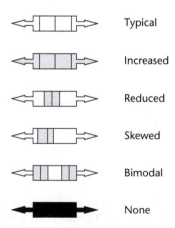

FIGURE 6.5 ACORNS indicators of patterns of variance.

outcome in its own right, tending to focus on mean levels of performance. However, for some syndromes this is likely to be a very important indicator of differences in causal pathways and may help define the syndrome. Where there is increased variance this needs to be explained, and may suggest a greater number of causal factors at work that lead to increased variance. Correspondingly, where reduced variance is encountered this might (although not necessarily) indicate a single and unique causal process. For example, there is far greater variance in early cognitive performance in children with Down syndrome (DS) than TD children (Wishart, 1993). This may be key to understanding their development. This variability in functioning from session to session may not just reflect instability in cognitive functioning but variation in aspects of 'mastery motivation'. This, in turn, may have a number of origins, including differences in the sense of agency in children with DS that may have origins in early mother–infant interactions (see Cebula, Moore & Wishart, 2010).

Figure 6.6 shows the effect of adding the indicators to the box-and-arrow diagram presented in Figure 6.2. Note how the shading of the notation gives an immediate and accessible representation of outcomes and difficulties as they unfold over time. An animated version of this model is also included on our web page to further illustrate how ACORNS can be used to depict the dynamic sequence of cascading developmental effects (see http://www.uel.ac.uk/ircd/projects/acorns/).

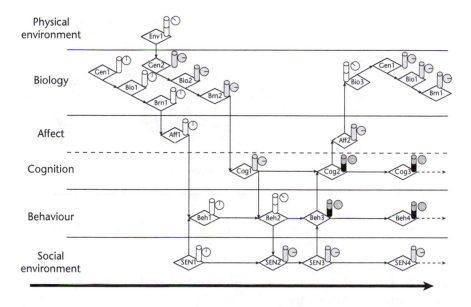

FIGURE 6.6   Combining two main indicators: arrows depicting causal pathways and trajectories and adding other pictorial elements to aid ease of understanding.

6.3 Causal versus statistical models

A final area that ACORNS can aid in clarifying is the specification of the difference between those sets of constructs for which there are known and reliable statistical relationships, and additional constructs that may have yet to be reliably assessed but which may form important elements of theoretical causal pathways. In Figure 6.7 we show how to represent variables that have been determined and the statistical links between these (dotted arrows) alongside hypothetical causal pathways. Note that here diagonal lines are allowed, as in this case these show *statistical* relationships between measures taken at different points in time, and not the theoretical causal processes that act within and across levels. This approach is important as it can illustrate both the statistical relationships that have been assessed using a potentially limited range of measures alongside more complete causal models that include these measures as well as the many hypothesised factors and causal pathways that may underlie these known statistical relationships and which are theoretically plausible but that have yet to be determined.

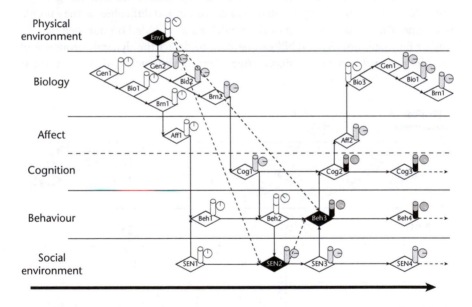

FIGURE 6.7   Model with overlaid statistical associations (dotted arrows) between measured factors.

6.4 Using ACORNS to map common and discrete pathways for developmental difficulties

One of our reasons for developing ACORNS is to ensure that the development of populations with developmental difficulties is presented in terms of the full multi-layered range of causal pathways. There has been a tendency for theoreticians to focus on a limited cluster of causes and outcomes to 'explain' developmental difficulties, and to apply similar approaches to developing children and infants as used in adult neuropsychology, which concentrates on static and relatively fixed double-dissociations, comparing so-called 'intact' versus 'spared' abilities within and between domains. Correspondingly many theories have focussed on so-called core behavioural, cognitive and/or genetic origins to explain the cause of developmental difficulties implying that the primary purpose is to disentangle biological processes. These approaches correspondingly have tended to put less emphasis on more complex accounts of how core abilities may *become* domain-specific, through a process of interactive specialisation (see Johnson, 2011), and the role of a range of social and environmental influences. Correspondingly many past accounts have also been less concerned with, and paid little attention to, explaining individual differences within populations with developmental difficulties, preferring to focus on commonalities rather than variance. This in turn has done little to help clinicians in addressing the unique profiles of individual cases presented to them.

While biological processes are critical to understanding developmental difficulties, it is becoming clear from the study of epigenetics, that even the most fundamental genetic processes are subject to environmental influence: a genuinely developmental account must be able to offer explanations of the emergence of profiles of common outcomes for a group of individuals with a shared diagnosis, *and* also be able to account for how within-group individual differences emerge. Such accounts need to consider within-group variation not only, for example, in terms of variance in gene expression, but in terms of differential transactional processes, and the relative influence on individuals of multiple causal pathways which, depending on their relative influence, may lead to differential outcomes in subsequent areas of functioning.

As outlined in Moore and George (2011) ACORNS is designed to facilitate a more nuanced and visually accessible picture of a syndrome than is possible using ad-hoc box-and-arrow diagrams; and to convey a clear picture of causal assumptions. Of particular importance is the ability of ACORNS to convey in a systematic way developmental change as it unfolds over time. ACORNS is able to show multiple transactional influences operating over all levels from biological to social-environmental levels. In turn this allows the illustration of how effects may cascade over many 'parallel' causal pathways: showing the influence of the physical environment, molecular biological process, brain function and structure, affective responses, cognitive process, behaviours and social interactions. The intention is that ACORNS can show a range of common causal effects for populations with developmental difficulties, but also be useful to clinicians in illustrating how differential effects may be operating for individuals within a population, that may lead to subtly different outcomes. ACORNS can be used not only to show developmental population profiles but also to depict the development of individuals and serve a useful clinical as well as theoretical function.

To illustrate how ACORNS can be used to illustrate causal processes underpinning a particular developmental difficulty, Figure 6.8 outlines some of the cognitive and social causal pathways that may operate in the early development of

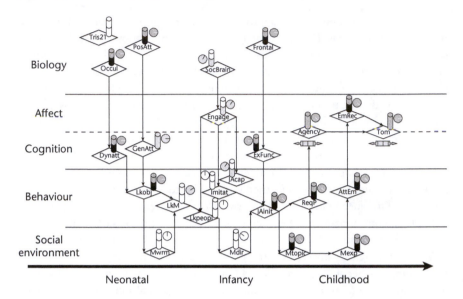

FIGURE 6.8 Causal model of early Down syndrome from Moore and George (2011), including indicators of variance.

infants with Down syndrome. This model represents a route by which neuro-cognitive difficulties (in ocular control and posterior attention) may lead to different patterns of behaviour in social interactions, which in turn lead to a different style of behaviour in mothers, which in turn may impact on cognitive and social development (see Moore & George, 2011; and Cebula, Moore & Wishart, 2010, for a full account of this transactional model). It is our intention in subsequent papers to use ACORNS to facilitate better and clearer accounts and facilitate cross-syndrome comparisons. It is important that we do not simply see different syndromes in terms of mirrors of preserved versus impaired abilities, but are able to illustrate and understand the similar and different developmental pathways that populations (and individuals within syndromes) follow to achieve similar developmental outcomes.

6.5 Discussion

We have presented the arguments for the need for the common use of a precise and clear form of visual representation for causal modelling of developmental difficulties in the developing interdisciplinary field of developmental science. We have presented the necessary structural and notational components of such a visualisation in the form of ACORNS, an Accessible Cause–Outcome, Representation and Notation System; and used ACORNS to represent the complex multiple causal influences which it is necessary to include in full accounts of developmental difficulties. We have, by way of example, added to our previous paper and used the notation to begin to link ACORNS with trajectory analysis and show how it can be used to illustrate different pathways and link these to statistical data.

Our aim has been to create a shared system that challenges and facilitates researchers to create far more comprehensive, joined-up and subtle accounts of developmental difficulties, that do not oversimplify the complexity of development, do not focus on one restricted developmental period, and do not give causal theoretical precedence to any one level of explanation over others, in what is likely to be a complex transactional process across levels over developmental periods.

Different theories place different importance on specific clusters of abilities; the benefit of using a common mapping and modelling system is to facilitate debate about these critical points, to ensure that theories account for all the key developmental processes, and distinguish between points in time key for reliable measurement versus points in developmental time that are of causal significance. The use of ACORNS to map within a clear temporal framework over a number of developmental difficulties should facilitate detailed debate between researchers across disciplines; allow direct comparisons to be made across syndromes to identify common and unique developmental processes; and can be used by clinicians to begin to identify theoretically clear rationale for intervention and to link group accounts with individual pathways using the same system.

These aims are important, as this is a truly interdisciplinary area, which needs to find a common language that can accommodate a range of perspectives from different fields of biological and social sciences. To develop comprehensive, multi-level theories we need to have a universal and commonly accepted modelling approach that can bring together theoreticians from across these disciplines and overcome the tendency of each to consider a restricted range of causal factors within one or two levels of explanation. The strength of ACORNS is to provide a graphical form of notation able to represent a large number of different sources of existing data alongside hypothetical causal pathways. Using the ACORNS mapping, modelling and notation process, the models can illustrate the emerging impact of causal processes in determining relative strengths and weaknesses within populations over a range of levels of explanations; and can do so in an immediately accessible visual form. What is not so apparent on the page of a journal is how engaging and useful it is to see these models as animations, depicting the unfolding influences of factors as development unfolds from left to right across the page. Note that all models are available on the ACORNS website to download and adapt for use.

Note that one key demonstration of the benefit of any tool is not just in how it can reformulate what is already known but also how it can highlight and reveal areas of uncertainty and new theory. There are still large gaps in knowledge between observed adult outcomes and potential biological and genetic 'causes'. To progress these fields we need to be able to give far more detailed and temporally specified accounts of developmental processes and what is also apparent is that even with the best reviews of evidence, there remain many ambiguities in how researchers specify the relative versus absolute nature of timing and levels of functioning across levels and areas of functioning. The ACORNS notation and models will hopefully facilitate a more rigorous approach in this respect with the system illustrating the importance of collecting comprehensive longitudinal data. We need to ensure we have multiple snapshots along trajectories of development in order to assess the relative changes and timings of functioning, and better specify potential causal cascading effects.

In summary, we hope that researchers will begin to adopt a more universal approach to the representation of their causal assumptions using the ACORNS systems, so that it is possible to engage in more efficient and nuanced debates about the complexity of the development of populations and individuals with developmental difficulties, rather than arguing within highly constrained perspectives. It is of more and more importance for our field that we begin to develop and communicate agreed models of development that do not simplify the causal processes, but make explicit their complexity, while also making the understanding of this complexity easier and more accessible to policy makers, clinicians and students. We believe ACORNS is an important step in this direction.

Practical tips

1. Before you begin modelling make sure you have a clear idea of the specific nature of each aspect of functioning. In particular make a clear distinction between behavioural and cognitive factors. For example in your model, digit span (the behaviour) may be a causal product of verbal working memory (a cognitive function). Start with a large piece of paper.
2. Once you have sketched out a model and want to make a publishable model you can download Word templates from the website: http://www.uel.ac.uk/ircd/projects/acorns/. These files include the indicators. This is free to use so long as you are happy for us to show your model on our website once it is published.
3. Do not try to map too long a period of development on a single A4 page. When mapping infant development, you may need to set the scale to as little as one month (or less) a page to allow you to map out the temporal order of all the factors in the level of detail required.

Notes

1   This approach highlights the importance of trying to develop tasks that can assess a capacity across individuals in phenotypes across as wide an age range as possible, so that the development of a particular capacity itself can be explored without this being confounded with differing task demands (see Thomas et al., 2009).
2   Morton (2004) proposed that mapping should be restricted only to those outcomes that are critical in defining a specific developmental difficulty or syndrome, and that for parsimony one should avoid 'redundant' pathways that show non-specific 'general' delays, concentrating on showing outcomes that are unique. We contend that to gain insight it is not always just a matter of mapping those behaviours that define a syndrome but also those that appear relatively spared or show contrasts with other populations. Of course mapping can never be complete because research data is always expanding. Indeed

one of the main activities of experimental developmental psychology is to create new experimental tasks that elicit behaviour to reveal even more subtle differences between populations; and the creation of tasks that can be used to plot developmental trajectories over wider age ranges promises to produce more detailed developmental data that can then be mapped.

3 Note that while a heightened degree of functioning could be positive for typical children it may be an important indicator of difference in atypical populations, such as calendrical calculation in ASD, or the over-expression of Hsa21 genes in Down syndrome.

4 Note that in the original ACORNS notation there were six indicators but in order to allow full models of atypical development we have added this extra indicator to indicate where there may be the beginnings of regression.

References

Bronfenbrenner, U. (1979). *The Ecology of Human Development: Experiments by Nature and Design*. Cambridge, MA: Harvard University Press.

Cebula, K., Moore, D. G. & Wishart, J. (2010) Social cognition in children with Down's syndrome: challenges to research and theory building. Invited Review. *Journal of Intellectual Disability Research, 54*, 113–134.

Johnson, M. H. (2011). Interactive specialization: a domain-general framework for human functional brain development? *Developmental Cognitive Neuroscience, 1*(1), 7–21.

Karmiloff-Smith, A. (1997). Crucial differences between developmental cognitive neuroscience and adult neuropsychology. *Developmental Neuropsychology, 13*(4), 513–524.

——(1998). Development itself is the key to understanding developmental disorders. *Trends in Cognitive Sciences, 2*(10), 389–398.

——(2009). Nativism versus neuroconstructivism: Rethinking the study of developmental disorders. *Developmental Psychology, 45* (1), 56–63.

Moore, D. G. & George, R. (2011). ACORNS: a tool for the visualisation and modelling of atypical development. *Journal of Intellectual Disability Research, 55*(10), 956–972.

Morton, J. (2004) *Understanding Developmental Disorders: A Causal Modelling Approach*. Oxford: Blackwell.

Morton, J. & Frith, U. (1995) Causal modelling: structural approaches to developmental psychopathology. In D. Cicchetti & D. Cohen (eds), *Developmental Psychopathology* (pp. 357–390). New York: Wiley.

Rosling, H. (2007). Visual technology unveils the beauty of statistics and swaps policy from dissemination to access. *Journal of the International Association for Official Statistics, 24*(1–2), 103–104.

Sameroff, A. J. (ed.) (2009). *The Transactional Model of Development: How Children and Contexts Shape Each Other*. Washington, DC: American Psychological Association.

Thomas, M. S. C. (2005). Plotting the causes of developmental disorders. *Trends in Cognitive Sciences, 9*(10), 465–466.

Thomas, M. S. C., Annaz, D., Ansari, D., Serif, G., Jarrold, C. & Karmiloff-Smith, A. (2009). Using developmental trajectories to understand developmental disorders. *Journal of Speech, Language, and Hearing Research, 52*, 336–358.

Wishart, J. G. (1993). The development of learning difficulties in children with Down's syndrome. *Journal of Intellectual Disability Research, 37*, 389–403.

PART II

Neurodevelopmental disorders and their challenges for researchers

7

VARIABILITY IN NEURO-DEVELOPMENTAL DISORDERS

Evidence from Autism Spectrum Disorders

Tony Charman

7.1 Introduction

Autism has been one of the most widely studied neurodevelopmental disorders since it was first described in the 1940s by Leo Kanner (1943) and Hans Asperger (1944). Indeed, it has been highlighted that relative to its prevalence (and more arguably its impact on the individual) autism both receives more research funding, and generates more research publications than many other neurodevelopmental disorders that are also very impairing for individuals, their families and those who care for them (Bishop, 2010). The positives of this is that the disorder is now much better understood; notwithstanding the fundamental conundrums and uncertainties that still exist about what causes the disorder, in particular at the level of the individual (Lai, Lombardo & Baron-Cohen, 2013). One touchstone for researchers and clinicians in the field over the past decade and more is that autism is very heterogeneous or variable. This variability includes both aetiology and phenotypic presentation – both in terms of the range and characteristics of individuals who meet the diagnostic criteria for the disorder and in terms of individual variability and outcome over the course of development. To clinicians and researchers, this heterogeneity presents both challenges and opportunities. In the present chapter we outline recent work on variability in Autism Spectrum Disorders (ASD). We emphasise the impact this has on our understanding of its prevalence, causes, diagnosis, cognitive and behavioural profile, and in particular, its developmental trajectory across the lifespan.

7.2 Definitions and diagnosis

A clear sign of how heterogeneity in autism is being embraced is reflected in the changes to its classification and diagnosis in the recent revision of the DSM.

Previous DSM-IV-TR (APA, 2000) and ICD-10 (WHO, 1993) definitions included 'core autism' ('autistic disorder' in DSM-IV; 'childhood autism' in ICD-10) and a number of other putative subtypes of 'pervasive developmental disorder', including Asperger syndrome, but DSM-5 has been changed to a unified diagnosis of Autism Spectrum Disorder (ASD) (DSM-5; APA, 2013). This was based on a number of research findings; not least the evidence that even amongst expert groups the use of the sub-classifications in DSM-IV was unreliable (Lord et al., 2012). Foremost amongst the changes to the diagnostic classification are the replacement of the ASD triad with an ASD dyad, comprising social communication and restricted repetitive behaviour (RRB) domains, and the inclusion of hypo- or hyper-reactivity to sensory stimuli as a core diagnostic criterion within the RRB domain.

Like the majority of neuropsychiatric disorders, ASD is defined as a behavioural syndrome, such that a specific cluster of signs and symptoms are assumed to signify a latent disease entity (Kendell & Jablensky, 2003). The term ASD is now used to describe a range of neurodevelopmental conditions that demonstrate considerable phenotypic heterogeneity; both in terms of presentation at any one age and across development and which are likely to differ in underlying aetiology. This heterogeneity has prompted biological scientists to coin the term 'the autisms' (Geschwind & Levitt, 2007), which serves as a helpful reminder that we are not dealing with a unitary 'disease condition'. However, all individuals with ASD share what some consider a primary impairment in social relatedness and reciprocity, alongside impairments in the use of language for communication and an 'insistence on sameness', which is in keeping with Kanner's (1943) original description of classically 'autistic' children. The presence of social and communication abnormalities, in combination with limited imagination and generativity, was previously characterised as the 'triad of impairments' by Wing and Gould (1979).

The change in the diagnostic system has provoked much debate, ranging from a concern about some individuals who met DSM-IV criteria for a pervasive developmental disorder (in particular of pervasive developmental disorder – not otherwise specified) not meeting DSM-5 criteria for ASD (and thus potentially being barred from access to services) to advocates with a diagnosis of Asperger syndrome/disorder expressing concern that it amounted to them having their diagnosis removed (Happé, 2011; Kulage, Smaldone & Cohn, 2014). Another change that was introduced in DSM-5 was the inclusion of language level, intellectual ability, onset, comorbid or co-occurring disorders and medical conditions to be listed alongside a diagnosis of ASD as 'clinical specifiers'. One view is that this may provide an opportunity to identify subtypes in ASD, which in some ways has become the 'Holy Grail' now that heterogeneity is widely recognised, if not yet embraced (Grzadzinski, Huerta & Lord, 2013; see Figure 7.1). However, to date, putative subtypes have proved elusive despite the claims of those keen to touch this great prize (Charman et al., 2011a).

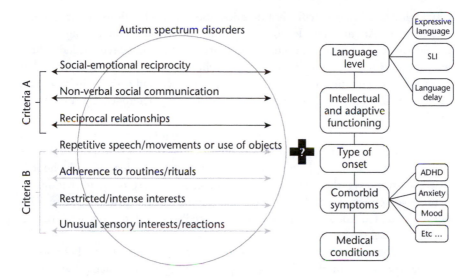

FIGURE 7.1 DSM-5 criteria for Autism Spectrum Disorders (reproduced from Grzadzinski et al., (2013) *Molecular Autism*, with permission).

Another change in DSM-5 is that the presence of a diagnosis of Attention Deficit Hyperactivity Disorder (ADHD; see Chapter 9 for a discussion) is no longer an exclusionary criteria for ASD. This follows the wide recognition over the past decade that co-occurrence ('comorbidity') between ASD and ADHD is common. This co-occurrence between individuals who meet the behavioural diagnostic criteria for ASD and the behavioural diagnostic criteria for another neuropsychiatric disorder is not restricted to ADHD. In the population-based Special Needs and Autism cohort (SNAP), 70 per cent of eleven- to twelve-year-old children with ASD met criteria for at least one additional psychiatric disorder and 40 per cent had two or more additional disorders (Simonoff et al., 2008). The most common psychiatric disorders in this age group were anxiety disorders (in aggregate 42 per cent); oppositional defiant disorder: ODD (30 per cent), and ADHD (28 per cent). These findings are in line with other studies, although the age range examined varies and, in particular, mood disorders may rise with increasing age (Hofvander et al., 2009).

However, this additional source of variability is not unique to ASD; it is part of a much broader revolution in psychiatry. With the imminent arrival of DSM-5 the USA National Institute of Mental Health launched the 'Research Domain Criteria' (RDoC) initiative (Insel et al., 2010). The motivation of this initiative is the recognition that whilst the DSM and ICD classification systems have clinical utility as descriptions (or a dictionary) of clinical symptoms that commonly co-occur – with the hope of providing some *reliability* of how mental health and neurodevelopmental disorders are described – they lack biological *validity*. That is, the mapping between genetic, neural or other neurobiological or neurocognitive aetiological factors and specific disorders described in the classification system is not one-to-one. At multiple levels (symptoms, behaviours, underlying neuro-development and function, genetics) similar atypicalities can be seen in individuals who meet diagnostic criteria for different psychiatric disorders while, on the other hand, these atypicalities are not necessarily seen in each and every individual who meets the diagnostic criteria for a particular disorder – heterogeneity rules (so to speak)!

The RDoC is a framework or approach that attempts to link behaviour and cognitive systems to underlying neurobiological systems and genetic predispositions in a way that cuts across the currently described diagnostic categories. The hope is that this may pave the way to novel treatments that act on perturbations to neurodevelopment, rather than treating the symptoms or the 'disorder' per se. This personalised medicine approach has been described as 'stratified psychiatry' (Kapur, Phillips & Insel, 2012).

In addition to recognition of the heterogeneous aetiology and behavioural phenotype of ASD, another challenge to perceiving ASD as a unitary disorder has come from 'fractionation' of the autistic 'triad' of symptom domains, namely social impairments, communication impairments and rigid and repetitive behaviours (Happé, Ronald & Plomin, 2006). Ronald and colleagues' work on a large UK general population twin sample found that correlations between continuous measures of social, communication and repetitive behaviour were lower than expected. Further, whilst each aspect of the triad was highly heritable, the genetic influences on each of these domains of behaviour were largely non-overlapping (Ronald, Happé & Plomin, 2005; Ronald et al., 2006). Happé and Ronald (2008) went on to review the evidence for 'fractionation' at the behavioural and cognitive level in diagnosed cases and found broadly supportive evidence (see also Brunsdon & Happé, 2014).

Another important aspect of understanding heterogeneity and variability comes from the recognition that these difficulties, once considered a particular characteristic of rare individuals, are now seen as a broad dimension of individual difference that is widely distributed in the general population (Constantino & Todd, 2003). In a behavioural genetic analysis of a large twin sample Robinson and colleagues (Robinson et al., 2011) found both moderate to high heritability of autistic traits across the general population, and a similarly high heritability in extreme-scoring groups (the top 5 per cent, 2 per cent and 1 per cent of scorers). A continuous liability shift toward autistic trait affectedness was seen in the co-twins of individuals scoring in the top 1 per cent, suggesting shared aetiology between extreme scores and normal variation. This is the strongest evidence to date that ASD can be conceptualised as the quantitative extreme of a neurodevelopmental continuum.

7.3 Causes and prevalence

It is well established that ASD are highly heritable, although recent findings suggest that environmental factors that act prenatally might play a larger role than previously thought (Hallmayer et al., 2011; Lyall, Schmidt & Hertz-Picciotto, 2014). The genetic mechanisms involved in ASD are complex and include rare chromosomal anomalies, several individual genes of major effect and numerous common variants of small effect (Jeste & Geschwind, 2014). Although there is no proven primary explanatory pathway for how these various aetiological factors combine and interact over development in order to produce the recognisable behavioural phenotype, it is assumed that they act on various synaptic neural developmental processes that disrupt brain development and function that underlies the emergent behavioural phenotype (Gliga, Jones, Charman & Johnson, under review).

ASD are more common than was previously recognised, affecting approximately 1 in 100 children and adolescents (Baird et al., 2006; Baron-Cohen et al., 2009; CDC, 2012), although one recent study reported prevalence as high as 2 per cent (Kim et al., 2011). Despite the challenges in conducting adult epidemiological studies for a childhood onset neurodevelopmental disorder, a recent study has also reported a similar prevalence of ~1 per cent in an adult population-representative sample (Brugha et al., 2011). There are a number of factors that likely explain this rise in measured prevalence, including the broadening of the diagnostic concept, better identification of ASD in individuals with average intelligence, and recognition and application of the diagnosis of ASD in individuals with sensory impairments and known genetic conditions (Charman et al., 2009). However, a true rise in prevalence cannot be ruled out. What is clear is that variability of phenotypic or behavioural presentation has had a significant impact on our understanding of how common ASD are and has been one of the drivers of the change from the historical figure of 4 to 5 per 10,000 children having classic 'Kanner autism' (Lotter, 1966) or even the 20 per 10,000 children who met Wing and Gould's (1979) criteria for the 'triad of impairments'.

In our prevalence study the broadest clinical best estimate for all ASD was 1.16 per cent (Baird et al., 2006). However, we also applied a criterion for what we called 'narrow autism': cases meeting ICD-10 childhood autism criteria and the autism thresholds on the most widely used parent report (Autism Diagnostic Interview-Revised: ADI-R; Lord, Rutter & LeCouteur, 1994) and observational schedule (Autism Diagnostic Observation Schedule-Generic: ADOS-G; Lord et al., 2000). Using this more restrictive definition the prevalence of 'narrow autism' was 0.25 per cent (Baird et al., 2006; Charman et al., 2009). Thus, within the same study, which is perhaps more secure than comparing across different epidemiological studies with different samples, methods and designs, the prevalence estimates vary by a factor of 4 depending on whether one uses the broadest or the narrowest threshold for who one counts as a 'case'. This might provoke uncertainty or disquiet in many readers but in the absence of a unitary biological marker, and hence reliance on clinical application of behavioural diagnostic criteria, variability in the presentation of ASD has a significant impact on how common we understand the disorder to be.

7.4 Stability of diagnosis

Another critical way in which variability exists in ASD is not the variability *between* individuals who meet the diagnostic criteria for the disorder but variability *within* individuals over time. The increasing use of the term 'neurodevelopmental disorder' to describe conditions such as ASD and the others covered in this volume, reflects both the fact that our understanding of these conditions has a brain basis (notwithstanding the biological and environmental factors that influence development for any individual), but also that their presentation changes with development. One clinical challenge that arises from the recognition that variability is to be expected within, as well as between, individuals with ASD is the extent to which the diagnosis should be considered stable over time. In part, this is a philosophical debate since different positions can be taken as to whether this should be considered a 'lifetime diagnosis' – that is if someone has at some point in development met the diagnostic criteria for ASD they should be considered 'autistic' even if the symptoms remit and abilities improve such that at a later point they no longer fulfil the criteria (see later section on outcomes). However, with particular respect to young children it is a real clinical question and one that many parents ask clinicians when they are given the diagnosis about their young child.

Over the past fifteen years many research groups have prospectively studied cohorts of children who had been given the diagnosis at a relatively young age of two to three years (Charman & Baird, 2002). These teams followed the children up into middle childhood and examined the extent to which diagnosis remained stable (see Rondeau et al., 2011 for a review). What emerged from this work were some clear messages (ASD can be accurately diagnosed in two-year-olds) but also some areas of uncertainty that will take continued study to resolve (in some cases diagnosis appears less stable).

The first such studies (Cox et al., 1999; Lord, 1995; Moore & Goodson, 2003; Stone et al., 1999) all showed high stability of diagnosis from two to three years to age four to five years, particularly for 'core' autism, with somewhat lower stability for broader ASD and pervasive developmental disorder not otherwise specified (PDD-NOS). Several studies also found that restricted and repetitive behaviours, activities and interests were less evident at two years of age than at three to five years of age (Cox et al., 1999; Moore & Goodson, 2003; Stone et al., 1999). More recent studies differ from the earlier ones in a number of features, most notably considerably larger sample sizes (N = 172 Lord, Risi, DiLavore, Shulman, Thurm & Pickles, 2006; N = 77 Kleinman et al., 2008) and follow-up periods that extend to age seven years (Charman et al., 2005) and age nine years (Lord et al., 2006; Turner, Stone, Pozdol & Coonard, 2006). These studies confirmed that the diagnosis of ASD is highly stable in these samples but that of broader ASD is less so. In some studies there was greater movement from having an ASD diagnosis at age two years to a non-spectrum diagnosis at age four years (Kleinman et al., 2008; Turner & Stone, 2007), with higher IQ and better language competency being associated with this pattern. Overall, the general pattern is of relatively high stability of diagnosis, replicating the earlier pioneering longitudinal work of Marian Sigman and colleagues who found high stability of diagnosis of children from four years of age through to middle childhood (thirteen years) and young adulthood (nineteen years) (McGovern & Sigman, 2005; Sigman & Ruskin, 1999). Long-term adult outcomes will be discussed further later on in this chapter.

Two recent studies have reported findings that speak to the issue of whether ASD should be considered a 'lifetime diagnosis', and the issue of diagnostic stability. Fein and colleagues (Fein et al., 2013) reported on a sample of children and young adults (eight to thirteen years) who had previously been given an ASD diagnosis (and had language delay) before the age of five years but who had what they term 'optimal outcome'. Optimal outcome was defined as: not meeting ASD criteria on the Autism Diagnostic Observation Schedule (ADOS; Lord et al., 2000) confirmed by expert clinical review; a full scale IQ greater than 77 (1.5 SD from the average of 100); Vineland Adaptive Behavior Scale (VABS; Sparrow, Balla & Cichetti, 1995) communication and socialisation domain scores greater than 77; and inclusion in regular education classrooms with no specific or individual support for ASD. The optimal outcome group had language scores on the Clinical Evaluation of Language Fundamentals (CELF-IV; Semel, Wiig & Secord, 2003) in the average range and higher than a group of individuals with 'high functioning autism' (HFA) – that is, individuals with ASD with average IQ. Fein et al. (2013) speculated about what factors, including receipt of early intervention, might be associated with such an outcome but the retrospective nature of their design limits their ability to demonstrate such effects. A prospective study of children followed from two years to nineteen years of age also identified a small group (N = 8) who were described as having 'very positive outcome' and no longer met the diagnostic criteria at age nineteen years (Anderson, Liang & Lord, 2014). At the initial two- and three-year visits this group differed from others with IQ > 70 who did still meet diagnostic criteria for ASD at nineteen years, by showing a reduction (compared to an increase) in repetitive and restricted behaviour between two and three years, in their levels of hyperactivity at age three years and in terms of increased access to treatment by age three years. What is not known is what proportion of individuals with ASD will have such positive outcomes but these two reports have engendered much interest and debate, both about what it means to have an 'optimal' outcome and what factors, including access to, type and intensity of treatment, may promote such gains.

However, the real-world clinical issue of stability of diagnosis is a reminder both of the variability that exists in individuals with ASD and of the sometimes-fragile clinical certainty that exists when one is dealing with a behaviourally defined disorder. The threshold that is set for determining if sufficient symptoms are present in number and severity (and impact) to warrant the diagnosis – remembering the four-fold difference in prevalence depending on the narrowness or broadness of the criterion employed in the Baird et al. (2006) study – and the limits to the accuracy and reliability of measurement of a complex behavioural phenotype cut across the notion of 'diagnostic stability', although in the clinical world may not fatally undermine it in the absence of an alternative.

7.5 Cognitive and behavioural profiles

The long-established view of intellectual abilities in ASD was that up to 75 per cent of individuals had an intellectual disability (previously referred to as 'mental retardation'), defined by an IQ < 70 alongside accompanying impairment in everyday adaptive functioning (Tsatsanis, 2005). One additional change in DSM-5 is that intellectual disability has a secondary descriptive name ('intellectual developmental disorder') to indicate that the deficits in cognitive capacity begin early in the developmental period. Since the original description by Lockyer and Rutter (1970), it has been a widespread clinical view that Performance IQ (PIQ) is typically higher than Verbal IQ (VIQ). In addition there is evidence at a subtest level (e.g. on Wechsler intelligence tests) of a characteristic profile of strengths (or 'peaks') on subtests such as Block Design and weaknesses (or 'troughs') on subtests such as Comprehension (Happé, 1995; Mayes & Calhoun, 2003). However, some of these widely held views about the intelligence of children with ASD were first formed several decades ago when conceptualisation of ASD was very different from today. It may be the case that historical data do not apply to children who currently receive an ASD diagnosis (Charman et al., 2009; Fombonne, 2009), particularly since the evolving diagnostic criteria have widened to include a more heterogeneous population of individuals, especially those at the more able end of the intellectual spectrum.

Reflecting this, recent epidemiological studies have found that 50 per cent of children with an ASD have intellectual disability (Bertrand et al., 2001; Chakrabarti & Fombonne, 2005; Charman et al., 2011b). Furthermore, in their epidemiological sample Charman et al. (2011a) found only weak support for a distinctive PIQ-VIQ profile: at a group mean level PIQ was higher than VIQ (but only by a few points) and when examined at the level of clinically meaningful PIQ-VIQ discrepancies the most common profile was for PIQ to be similar to VIQ. There was some support for a distinctive profile at the WISC subtest level but it was only partly consistent with the previous literature. In line with other studies, performance on the Vocabulary and Comprehension subtests was poor compared to other abilities (Charman et al., 2011b). However, neither Block Design nor Object Assembly was a significant strength as has been reported previously (Happé, 1995; Lincoln, Allen & Kilman, 1995; Mayes & Calhoun, 2003; Caron, Mottron, Berthiaume & Dawson, 2006). Picture Completion and Picture Arrangement, which both heavily rely on visual materials, were areas of strength ('peaks') in the total ASD sample and in the subgroup with IQ > 70. Variability is also apparent in terms of attainments such as reading and mathematics abilities, where individuals with ASD are more likely than others to show 'peaks' (particularly in numerical abilities) and 'troughs' (particularly in reading comprehension) than others (Jones et al., 2009a). In a secondary analysis of the factors associated with poor reading comprehension

Ricketts, Jones, Happé and Charman (2013) found that both aspects of structural language skills and social behaviour and social cognition (theory of mind) were involved, indicating the factors that influence this variability.

7.6 Language and communication development

Delayed language milestones are common in many preschool children with ASD. However, whilst it is not uncommon for two- and three-year-olds with ASD to be non-verbal, language and non-verbal communication abilities typically do begin to develop throughout the preschool period as children enter kindergarten and school (Charman, Drew, Baird & Baird, 2003; Luyster, Lopez & Lord, 2007). Previously, the prognosis in terms of the proportion of children with ASD who go on to develop functional language was considered poor, with papers from the 1970s and 1980s suggesting that perhaps only 50 per cent of children develop functional speech (De Myer et al., 1973; Freeman, Ritvo, Needleman & Yokota, 1985) – a reflection of the severely autistic and intellectually delayed cohorts who were first studied longitudinally.

More recently it has become clear that language onset and outcomes are very variable, but generally more positive, for children with ASD. For example, in the large clinical cohort described by Hus and colleagues (N = 983; mean age 8 years, SD 5 years, range 4 to 52 years; Hus, Pickles, Cook, Risi & Lord, 2007) only 10 per cent had no single words, 41 per cent had delay in single word onset (> 24 months) but single words when assessed, and half were not delayed in single word onset. For phrase speech, the comparable figures were 24 per cent of individuals with no phrase speech when assessed, 51 per cent with delayed phrase speech onset (> 33 months) but phrased speech when assessed, and 25 per cent were not delayed in phrase speech (Hus et al., 2007). A large study (N = 535) of children with ASD who were at least eight years of age and who did not acquire phrase speech before the age of four years found that 70 per cent had attained phrase speech at the time of assessment (Wodka, Mathy & Kalb, 2013). Higher non-verbal IQ and less social impairment were both independently associated with the acquisition of phrase and fluent speech, as well as earlier age at acquisition. This study highlights that many severely language-delayed children with ASD attained phrase or fluent speech at or after age four years.

A longitudinal study which measured language ability at age two, three, five and nine years used growth curve modelling to plot the trajectory of language development through the preschool years into middle childhood (Anderson et al., 2007). At a group level, the trajectory of growth in language abilities was slower for the children with a diagnosis of ASD than for the children with PDD-NOS or a non-spectrum developmental disorder. However, within each diagnostic group language growth and outcomes were very variable – and this variability increased over time – with some children in each group making such good progress that their language abilities were at the expected level at age nine years, whereas other children in each group, in particular a subset of the children with 'core' autism, made very little progress at all. Symptom severity at age two, non-verbal cognitive abilities and joint attention skills were significant predictors of language outcomes at age nine years.

Within the domain of language and communication, there is also variability between receptive and expressive abilities, in particular as language is emerging. There is increasing recognition that whilst expressive language competencies might be the most evident delay for some preschool children with ASD, receptive abilities can be relatively more delayed (Charman et al., 2003; Hudry et al., 2010; Luyster et al., 2007). This is clinically important but requires sensitive handling to explain that what parents sometimes take as 'understanding' is often understanding of familiar routines and contextual cues rather than language comprehension per se. However, this finding is important as it related to the appropriate focus for social communication approaches to intervention for preschool children with ASD where one critical focus is on communication *understanding,* as opposed to production or outcome (Charman, 2010).

7.7 Developmental trajectories

One advance in the past decade follows both from the increasing study of cohorts of children and young people with ASD longitudinally and also a more sophisticated approach to statistical analysis where groups are using a variety of novel statistical modelling approaches (e.g. hierarchical linear modelling, generalised estimating equations, latent class growth models) to investigate trajectories of development over time. Gotham, Pickles and Lord (2012) studied a cohort of 345 children from two to fifteen years of age looking at ASD symptom severity as measured by the ADOS, Verbal IQ (VIQ) and adaptive behaviour as measured by the Vineland. They found four classes of trajectory described (with percentage of their sample) as 'persistent high' (46 per cent), 'persistent moderate' (38 per cent), 'worsening' (9 per cent) and 'improving' (7 per cent). Whilst all classes showed a general increase in VIQ over time this was most marked in the small 'improving' group. For adaptive behaviour as measured by the Vineland with the exception of the 'improving' class all other classes showed a marked decline. This reflects the well-established fact that everyday adaptive behaviour falls behind intellectual ability and potential as measured on a formal IQ test, even for more able individuals (Charman et al., 2011b; Saulnier & Klin, 2007). This suggests that aspects of the ASD phenotype such as poor social skills, limitations in communication and rigid and repetitive ways of thinking and behaving mean that individuals with ASD face significant challenges in a 'neurotypical' world. Fountain, Winter and Bearman (2012) examined trajectories of social, communication and repetitive behaviour in a very large sample (> 6,000) of children between two and fourteen years of age. They also found a relatively small (~10 per cent) group of 'bloomers' whose social abilities improved over time (see Figure 7.2).

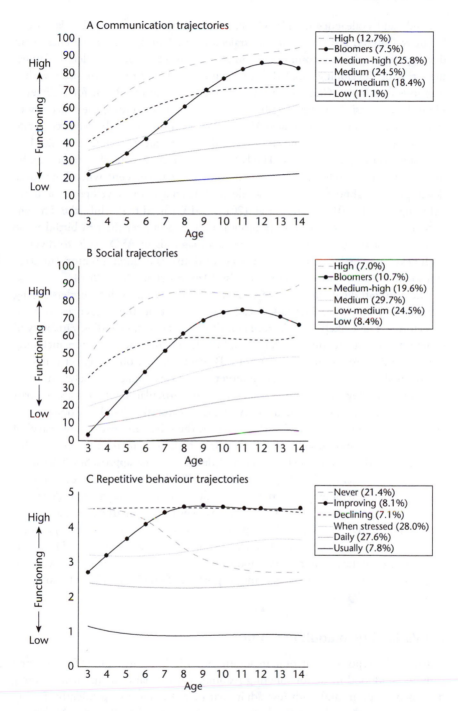

FIGURE 7.2 Modelled (A) communication, (B) social and (C) repetitive behaviour symptom trajectories based on CDER scores by age (reproduced from Fountain et al. (2012) *Pediatrics*, with permission).

Landa and colleagues (Landa, Gross, Stuart & Bauman, 2012; Landa, Gross, Stuart & Faherty, 2013) used similar trajectory modelling to examine changes in development and social communication abilities in infants and toddlers at familial high risk of developing ASD due to having an older brother or sister with a diagnosis (see Jones, Gliga, Bedford, Charman & Johnson, 2014, for a review). Here the emphasis is on tracking from a young age (six months) the trajectory of at-risk siblings who go on to have ASD at 36 months of age – the recurrence rate in such studies has been found to be around 20 per cent (Ozonoff et al., 2011) – compared to those who do not. The latter group in these 'babysibs' studies can be divided into those who are 'unaffected' and the ~20 per cent who show some developmental abnormality such as delayed language or developmental delay (Messinger et al., 2013). Landa et al. (2012, 2013) found that whilst the different outcome groups look similar at six months of age soon after the first birthday the trajectories of those who go on to receive a diagnosis of ASD begin to diverge, with developmental slowing across a range of domains including motor, language and social communication abilities (see also Ozonoff et al., 2010, 2014).

These longitudinal studies have provided a new window into understanding variability in outcome. The task ahead is to understand the influences on such trajectories. These likely include both constitutional factors, including variability in genetic and brain structure and function, but also environmental factors including but not limited to specific interventions. Recent reviews on the effectiveness of behavioural and developmental interventions vary quite widely in how optimistically they read the evidence-base for particular interventions, in part reflecting the poor quality and quantity of the research that had been done in the area until recently (Charman, 2011). However, there has emerged a 'new wave' of better-designed randomised controlled trials and there is increasing evidence for interventions that employ behavioural and developmental approaches (Charman, 2014; Dawson et al., 2010; Dawson & Bernier, 2013). The Fountain et al. (2012) study found that demographic variables, including ethnicity and parental education, also affected the trajectory of ASD symptoms over time. In part these studies raise optimism because we know it is possible, in at least some cases, to 'shift' developmental trajectories to influence a more favourable outcome. However, they are also salutary as not every child responds well to a particular intervention (e.g. Kasari, 2014) and for a significant proportion of children with ASD outcome is poor.

7.8 Variability in adult outcome

Initial studies reporting outcome in adulthood of individuals with ASD diagnosed early in childhood made for sobering reading, with social outcome being largely described as 'poor' and with few adults with ASD living independently, having gainful employment, close friendships or intimate relationships (Howlin, Mawhood & Rutter, 2000; Howlin, Savage, Moss, Tempier & Rutter 2014). A number of cohorts have now been followed into adulthood and even middle age and the picture that emerges is more variable (for a review, see Magiati, Tay & Howlin, 2014). Howlin and colleagues (Howlin, Moss, Savage & Rutter, 2013) recently reported on a sample followed into their 40s and found that whilst diagnosis remained stable symptoms gradually improved over time. However, few were living independently or were in work and many had considerable care needs and limited opportunities for societal engagement. In the same sample a small minority of individuals who had had IQs greater than 70 in childhood had very poor outcomes, and were not able to complete IQ assessments in middle adulthood. This group had severe behavioural difficulties and half had epilepsy, demonstrating how neurodevelopmental factors, including brain development and function, can affect outcome. Smith, Maenner and Seltzer (2012) also report that some adults with ASD reach a plateau in terms of their everyday adaptive skills after an increase in these during adolescence and early adulthood. The extent to which this is due to the removal of the supportive environment provided by school and college is not known. However, it does highlight the need for ongoing community services for individuals with ASD into adulthood. Another factor that may influence outcome, and one that parents of adults with ASD report high levels of concern about, is the ongoing mental health, emotional and behavioural difficulties experienced by the majority of adults on the autism spectrum (e.g. Eaves & Ho, 2008; Gray et al., 2012). Just as the commonly co-occurring mental health difficulties need to be assessed as part of the diagnostic process in children and young people, they need to be routinely considered in the management and care planning for adults with ASD (NICE, 2012).

Other studies of adult outcome offer a more positive picture. Farley et al. (2009) reported that half of their small sample of 41 adults had 'good or very good' outcomes. Several features might explain this, ranging from the fact that in childhood this sample was relatively 'high functioning' in that their IQ was 84 to the fact that they were members of the Church of Jesus Christ of the Latter Day Saints in Salt Lake City, a community that provides substantial support in education, occupation and societal participation.

Overall, variability in these adult outcome studies is very high. In many studies childhood IQ, language skills and social abilities are all positively associated with better adult outcomes (Magiati et al., 2014). In several more recent studies outcomes are reported to be better than in initial reports but a significant majority of individuals with ASD require substantial support as adults and a minority show some deterioration in function and ability. It would be hoped that in future studies the earlier identification and better intervention and educational support that have become more widely available in many communities will lead to better outcomes. However, as with our understanding of the effectiveness of early intervention, our current understanding of the factors that promote 'better' outcome in adulthood in this lifelong neurodevelopmental condition is still very partial.

7.9 Searching for subtypes on the autism spectrum

The realisation that the clinical syndrome of ASD is heterogeneous in aetiology and presentation poses significant scientific challenges. The search for genetic or brain structure/function abnormalities might be more efficient if 'true' subgroups within ASD could be identified for study, rather than the heterogeneous whole. One approach to subgrouping is to study biological syndromes of known aetiology that are frequently associated with ASD, such as Fragile X syndrome (Belmonte & Bourgeron, 2006) or tuberous sclerosis (de Vries, 2010). However, it might not be the case that biological subtypes will be associated with 'neat' cognitive or behavioural phenotypes; even in biologically based syndromes where ASD shows raised prevalence there exists considerable behavioural and cognitive (e.g. IQ) heterogeneity (Chonchaiya, Schneider & Hagerman, 2009; Prather & de Vries, 2004).

Conversely, there is some (though as yet, fairly weak) evidence that constraining the *behavioural* phenotype to a narrower subgroup within ASD might help identify the genetic underpinnings. Some studies have found increased linkage when studying samples characterised or subgrouped on the basis of social responsiveness (Duvall et al., 2007), language delay (Alarcon et al., 2002) or 'insistence on sameness' (Shao et al., 2003). There is currently much work ongoing that aims to identify behavioural subtypes of ASD that might provide insights or even breakthroughs into understanding their aetiology (e.g. Ingram, Takahashi & Miles, 2008; Lane, Molloy & Bishop, 2014; Munson et al., 2008). To date, however, few distinct behavioural subtypes have been identified and none have yet been well replicated.

The existence of *cognitive* subgroups might have considerable practical implications for intervention. Identifying subgroups of individuals with ASD who have atypicalities in a particular cognitive domain would give scope for carefully targeted interventions, focussed on improving areas of weakness through practice or providing alternative pathways to task performance and learning. Further, if cognitive strengths exist in an identifiable subgroup of individuals with ASD, then not only could positive outcomes be gained by developing and nurturing areas of ability, but it might be possible to utilise these 'talents' to overcome or 'bootstrap' areas of weakness. For example, Scheuffgen, Happé, Anderson and Frith (2000) showed that inspection time (a marker of processing speed and efficiency) was far better in ASD than would be expected from measured IQ (e.g. on Wechsler scales), and suggested that non-social routes to learning might maximise this potential.

Jones et al. (2009b) examined auditory discrimination abilities (frequency, intensity, duration) in 79 adolescents with ASD and found that as a group they were not different to controls. However, they found enhanced frequency discrimination was present in around one in five individuals with ASD in the frequency domain. In this putative subgroup they identified a profile of average or above average IQ but a history of delayed language milestones. There was also an a priori motivation to examine this developmental profile as it has been suggested that an over-focus on perceptual cues, particularly pitch, during speech negatively impacts upon linguistic processing (Järvinen-Pasley, Pasley & Heaton, 2008).

Bonnel and colleagues have since replicated this finding using a similar paradigm (Bonnel et al., 2010). This provides some, but modest, evidence of a putative ASD cognitive subtype.

Another approach has been to compare cognitive profiles across individuals with ASD and those with ADHD to look at the specificity of cognitive profiles. Van der Meer and colleagues (van der Meer et al., 2012) compared cognitive profiles of motor speed and variability, executive functioning, attention, emotion recognition, and detail-focussed processing style across children with ASD, those with ADHD, and those with comorbid ASD + ADHD. They found some specificity with response variability being specifically associated with ADHD and not ASD; and impaired social cognition being specific to ASD. Those with comorbid ASD and ADHD showed the cognitive profile characteristic of each disorder but in many domains at a more severe level than seen in individuals with isolated ASD or ADHD, broadly consistent with an additive model (see also Johnson, Gliga, Jones & Charman, in press). The potential value of such studies is that if 'true' cognitive subtypes of ASD exist they could be used to guide education and intervention, such that interventions could be targeted at specific areas of difficulty or strength and could be used to bootstrap or circumvent areas of weakness.

7.10 Heterogeneity as 'nuisance' or 'noise'

Most of the experimental work on cognition in ASD adopts the between-group experimental paradigm, where task performance is compared between a group of individuals with ASD and a control, or comparison group. However, the reporting of these findings (in terms of the group with ASD being 'impaired' or 'advanced', depending on the direction of group differences) de-emphasises variability within the group with ASDs and the overlap in scores between the groups. Furthermore, there is often greater heterogeneity in the ASD group than in the comparison group (SD tend to be larger). Investigators have begun to tackle this issue head on, identifying subgroups with impaired/intact performance and demonstrating the spread of scores of the ASD and the control group, paying attention to overlap and to outliers, as well as to mean group differences (see Milne et al., 2006; Pellicano, 2010; White, Hill, Happé & Frith, 2009, for some of the best examples of this approach). The fact that there is nearly always overlap in performance between the ASD group and the comparison group serves as a reminder that we are investigating the degree to which cognitive systems are differently 'set' or 'tuned' compared to typically developing individuals and not the absolute presence or absence of an all-or-none cognitive function/ability. Alternatively, tasks might be tapping into an end point of development, with compensation and other factors causing variation in outcome on tests even when all members of the group have shared an initial impairment (Karmiloff-Smith et al., 2012).

Another significant challenge presented by recognition of the heterogeneity in ASD is the tradition in the field of studying small sample sizes. This was traditionally the only practical route to study ASD, given the rarity of the diagnosis in the 1970s and 1980s. In addition, most researchers are interested in findings of large effect size, given the dramatic nature of the difference between ASD and controls in so many domains. However, multiple studies reporting on small samples increase the chance of spurious findings entering the literature (Ioannidis, 2005). This has begun to change in the past few years and researchers are recruiting increasingly larger samples. In the behavioural field, complex modelling approaches are used with ASD sample sizes in the hundreds (Munson et al., 2008) and thousands (Frazier et al., 2010; Ingram et al., 2008), although it is rare to have sample sizes above 100 in the cognitive field (Charman et al., 2011a). Large sample sizes are required particularly if one of the primary aims of a study is to identify subgroups or subtypes of ASD (that might or might not be associated with particular behavioural or biological subtype). A number of national and international consortia have evolved that aim to recruit samples of hundreds and thousands of participants for behavioural, cognitive and brain studies specifically to attempt to address these issues, e.g. IBIS (http://www.ibis-network.org/); BASIS (http://www.basisnetwork.org/); EU-AIMS (http://www.eu-aims.eu/home/).

7.11 Conclusions

Heterogeneity in ASD is here to stay! A personal observation would be that it has taken the field some while to feel comfortable with this wide variability and move on from seeing it as a nuisance, almost as if it got in the way of studying 'proper' or 'pure' ASD. However, a new generation of studies and scientists are now working towards using this heterogeneity to advance our understanding of ASD in a wide range of areas from genetics, to brain development, to understanding the influences on developmental trajectory and outcome, to developing and testing developmentally based models of intervention. There are considerable challenges ahead but to see the field fully embracing the variability seen in individuals on the autism spectrum is a sign that we are at least on the way.

Practical tips

1. Understand where your sample lies on the dimension between a narrowly defined subgroup on the autism spectrum that may be limited in generalisability and a broader all-inclusive sample where you will want to systematically consider the effects of factors such as age, IQ, language abilities, co-occurring psychiatric disorders on your variables of interest.
2. Because heterogeneity is the norm and not the exception, detailed behavioural phenotyping, whilst being resource and time intensive, often produces more secure and clinically meaningful findings.
3. Longitudinal studies are essential to better understand the interplay between influences on development over time. When setting up a study consider at the outset what you would have wished to have measured at the initial assessment

if you were to take a longitudinal approach to your question of interest. You can never go back and collect measures retrospectively!

References

Alarcon, M., Cantor, R. M., Liu, J. J., Gilliam, T. C., Geschwind, D. H. & Autism Genetic Resource Exchange, C. (2002). Evidence for a language quantitative trait locus on chromosome 7q in multiplex autism families. *American Journal of Human Genetics, 70,* 60–71.

American Psychiatric Association (APA) (2000). *Diagnostic and Statistical Manual of Mental Disorders 4th Edn. – Text Revision (DSM-IV-TR).* Washington, DC: American Psychiatric Association.

——(2013). *Diagnostic and Statistical Manual of Mental Disorders 5th Edn. (DSM-5).* Washington, DC: American Psychiatric Association.

Anderson, D. K., Lord, C., Risi, S., Shulman, C., Welch, K., DiLavore, P. S., ... Pickles, A. (2007). Patterns of growth in verbal abilities among children with autism spectrum disorder. *Journal of Consulting and Clinical Psychology, 75*(4), 594–604.

Anderson, D. K., Liang, J. W. & Lord, C. (2014). Predicting young adult outcome among more and less cognitively able individuals with autism spectrum disorders. *Journal of Child Psychology and Psychiatry, 55,* 485–494.

Asperger, H. (1944). '"Die Autistischen Psychopathen" im Kindesalter [Autistic psychopaths in childhood]'. *Archiv für Psychiatrie und Nervenkrankheiten* (in German), *117,* 76–136.

Baird, G., Simonoff, E., Pickles, A., Chandler, S., Loucas, T., Meldrum, D. & Charman, T. (2006). Prevalence of disorders of the autism spectrum in a population cohort of children in South Thames: The Special Needs and Autism Project (SNAP). *Lancet, 368*(9531), 210–215.

Baron-Cohen, S., Scott, F. J., Allison, C., Williams, J., Bolton, P., Matthews, F. E. & Brayne, C. (2009). Prevalence of autism-spectrum conditions: UK school-based population study. *British Journal of Psychiatry, 194*(6), 500–509.

Belmonte, M. K. & Bourgeron, T. (2006). Fragile X syndrome and autism at the intersection of genetic and neural networks. *Nature Neuroscience, 9*(10), 1221–1225.

Bertrand, J., Mars, A., Boyle, C., Bove, F., Yeargin-Allsopp, M. & Decoufle, P. (2001). Prevalence of autism in a United States population: The Brick Township, New Jersey, investigation. *Pediatrics, 108*(5), 1155–1161.

Bishop, D. V. M. (2010). Which neurodevelopmental disorders get researched and why? *Plos One, 5*(11), e15112.

Bonnel, A., McAdams, S., Smith, B., Berthiaume, C., Bertone, A., Ciocca, V., ... Mottron, L. (2010). Enhanced pure-tone pitch discrimination among persons with autism but not Asperger syndrome. *Neuropsychologia, 48*(9), 2465–2475.

Brugha, T. S., McManus, S., Bankart, J., Scott, F., Purdon, S., ... Meltzer, H. (2011). Epidemiology of autism spectrum disorders in adults in the community in England. *Archives of General Psychiatry, 68(5),* 459–465.

Brunsdon, V. E. A. & Happé, F. (2014). Exploring the 'fractionation' of autism at the cognitive level. *Autism, 18*(1), 17–30.

Caron, M. J., Mottron, L., Berthiaume, C. & Dawson, M. (2006). Cognitive mechanisms, specificity and neural underpinnings of visuospatial peaks in autism. *Brain, 129,* 1789–1802.

CDC (Centre for Disease Control and Intervention) (2012). http://www.cdc.gov/media/releases/2012/p0329_autism_disorder.html

Chakrabarti, S. & Fombonne, E. (2005). Pervasive developmental disorders in preschool children: Confirmation of high prevalence. *American Journal of Psychiatry, 162*(6), 1133–1141.

Charman, T. (2010). Developmental approaches to understanding and treating autism. *Folia Phoniatrica et Logopaedica, 62*(4), 166–177.

——(2011). Glass half full or half empty? Testing social communication interventions for young children with autism (Invited Commentary). *Journal of Child Psychology and Psychiatry, 52*, 22–23.

——(2014). Early identification and intervention in autism spectrum disorders: Some progress but not as much as we hoped. *International Journal of Speech-Language Pathology, 16*(1), 15–18.

Charman, T. & Baird, G. (2002). Practitioner review: Diagnosis of autism spectrum disorder in 2- and 3-year-old children. *Journal of Child Psychology and Psychiatry, 43*(3), 289–305.

Charman, T., Drew, A., Baird, C. & Baird, G. (2003). Measuring early language development in preschool children with autism spectrum disorder using the MacArthur Communicative Development Inventory (Infant Form). *Journal of Child Language, 30*(1), 213–236.

Charman, T., Taylor, E., Drew, A., Cockerill, H., Brown, J. A. & Baird, G. (2005). Outcome at 7 years of children diagnosed with autism at age 2: Predictive validity of assessments conducted at 2 and 3 years of age and pattern of symptom change over time. *Journal of Child Psychology and Psychiatry, 46*(5), 500–513.

Charman, T., Pickles, A., Chandler, S., Wing, L., Bryson, S., Simonoff, E., ... Baird, G. (2009). Commentary: Effects of diagnostic thresholds and research vs service and administrative diagnosis on autism prevalence. *International Journal of Epidemiology, 38*(5), 1234–1238.

Charman, T., Jones, C. R. G., Pickles, A., Simonoff, E., Baird, G. & Happé, F. (2011a). Defining the cognitive phenotype of autism. *Brain Research, 1380*, 10–21.

Charman, T., Pickles, A., Simonoff, E., Chandler, S., Loucas, T. & Baird, G. (2011b). IQ in children with autism spectrum disorders: Data from the Special Needs and Autism Project (SNAP). *Psychological Medicine, 41*(3), 619–627.

Chonchaiya, W., Schneider, A. & Hagerman, R. J. (2009). Fragile X: A family of disorders. *Advances in Pediatrics, 56*(1), 165–186.

Constantino, J. N. & Todd, R. D. (2003). Autistic traits in the general population – A twin study. *Archives of General Psychiatry, 60*(5), 524–530.

Cox, A., Klein, K., Charman, T., Baird, G., Baron-Cohen, S., Swettenham, J., ... Wheelwright, S. (1999). Autism spectrum disorders at 20 and 42 months of age: Stability of clinical and ADI-R diagnosis. *Journal of Child Psychology and Psychiatry, 40*(5), 719–732.

Dawson, G. & Bernier, R. (2013). A quarter century of progress on the early detection and treatment of autism spectrum disorder. *Development and Psychopathology, 25*(4), 1455–1472.

Dawson, G., Rogers, S., Munson, J., Smith, M., Winter, J., Greenson, J., ... Varley, J. (2010). Randomized, controlled trial of an intervention for toddlers with autism: The Early Start Denver Model. *Pediatrics, 125*(1), E17–E23.

De Myer, M. K., Barton, S., Demyer, W. E., Norton, J. A., Allen, J. & Steele, R. (1973). Prognosis in autism – Follow-up study. *Journal of Autism and Childhood Schizophrenia, 3*(3), 199–246.

de Vries, P. J. (2010). Targeted treatments for cognitive and neurodevelopmental disorders in tuberous sclerosis complex. *Neurotherapeutics, 7*(3), 275–282.

Duvall, J. A., Lu, A., Cantor, R. M., Todd, R. D., Constantino, J. N. & Geschwind, D. H. (2007). A quantitative trait locus analysis of social responsiveness in multiplex autism families. *American Journal of Psychiatry, 164*(4), 656–662.

Eaves, L. C. & Ho, H. H. (2008). Young adult outcome of autism spectrum disorders. *Journal of Autism and Developmental Disorders, 38*(4), 739–747.

Farley, M. A., McMahon, W. M., Fombonne, E., Jenson, W. R., Miller, J., Gardner, M., … Coon, H. (2009). Twenty-year outcome for individuals with autism and average or near-average cognitive abilities. *Autism Research, 2*(2), 109–118.

Fein, D., Barton, M., Eigsti, I. M., Kelley, E., Naigles, L., Schultz, R. T., … Tyson, K. (2013). Optimal outcome in individuals with a history of autism. *Journal of Child Psychology and Psychiatry, 54*(2), 195–205.

Fombonne, E. (2009). Epidemiology of pervasive developmental disorders. *Pediatric Research, 65*(6), 591–598.

Fountain, C., Winter, A. S. & Bearman, P. S. (2012). Six developmental trajectories characterize children with autism. *Pediatrics, 129*(5), E1112–E1120.

Frazier, T. W., Youngstrom, E. A., Sinclair, L., Kubu, C. S., Law, P., Rezai, A., … Eng, C. (2010). Autism spectrum disorders as a qualitatively distinct category from typical behavior in a large, clinically ascertained sample. *Assessment, 17*(3), 308–320.

Freeman, B. J., Ritvo, E. R., Needleman, R. & Yokota, A. (1985). The stability of cognitive and linguistic parameters in autism – a 5-year prospective-study. *Journal of the American Academy of Child and Adolescent Psychiatry, 24*(4), 459–464.

Geschwind, D. H. & Levitt, P. (2007). Autism spectrum disorders: developmental disconnection syndromes. *Current Opinion in Neurobiology, 17*(1), 103–111.

Gliga, T., Jones, E., Charman, T. & Johnson, M. H. (under review). Early endophenotypes for autism.

Gotham, K., Pickles, A. & Lord, C. (2012). Trajectories of autism severity in children using standardized ADOS scores. *Pediatrics, 130*(5), E1278–E1284.

Gray, K. M., Keating, C., Taffe, J. R., Brereton, A. V., Einfeld, S. L. & Tonge, B. J. (2012). Trajectory of behavior and emotional problems in autism. *American Journal on Intellectual and Developmental Disabilities, 117*, 121–133.

Grzadzinski, R., Huerta, M. & Lord, C. (2013). DSM-5 and autism spectrum disorders (ASDs): An opportunity for identifying ASD subtypes. *Molecular Autism, 4*(1), 12–18.

Hallmayer, J., Cleveland, S., Torres, A., Phillips, J., Cohen, B., Torigoe, T., … Risch, N. (2011). Genetic heritability and shared environmental factors among twin pairs with autism. *Archives of General Psychiatry, 68*(11), 1095–1102.

Happé, F. G. E. (1995). The role of age and verbal ability in the theory of mind task performance of subjects with autism. *Child Development 66*, 843–855.

——(2011). Criteria, categories, and continua: Autism and related disorders in DSM-5. *Journal of the American Academy of Child and Adolescent Psychiatry, 50*(6), 540–542.

Happé, F. & Ronald, A. (2008). The 'fractionable autism triad': A review of evidence from behavioural, genetic, cognitive and neural research. *Neuropsychology Review, 18*(4), 287–304.

Happé, F., Ronald, A. & Plomin, R. (2006). Time to give up on a single explanation for autism. *Nature Neuroscience, 9*(10), 1218–1220.

Hofvander, B., Delorme, R., Chaste, P., Nyden, A., Wentz, E., Stahlberg, O., … Leboyer, M. (2009). Psychiatric and psychosocial problems in adults with normal-intelligence autism spectrum disorders. *BMC Psychiatry, 9*, 35–44.

Howlin, P., Mawhood, L. & Rutter, M. (2000). Autism and developmental receptive language disorder – A follow-up comparison in early adult life. II: Social, behavioural, and psychiatric outcomes. *Journal of Child Psychology and Psychiatry and Allied Disciplines, 41*(5), 561–578.

Howlin, P., Moss, P., Savage, S. & Rutter, M. (2013). Social outcomes in mid- to later adulthood among individuals diagnosed with autism and average nonverbal IQ as children. *Journal of the American Academy of Child and Adolescent Psychiatry, 52*(6), 572–581.

Howlin, P., Savage, S., Moss, P., Tempier, A. & Rutter, M. (2014). Cognitive and language skills in adults with autism: A 40-year follow-up. *Journal of Child Psychology and Psychiatry, 55*(1), 49–58.

Hudry, K., Leadbitter, K., Temple, K., Slonims, V., McConachie, H., Aldred, C., … Pact Consortium (2010). Preschoolers with autism show greater impairment in receptive compared with expressive language abilities. *International Journal of Language & Communication Disorders, 45*(6), 681–690.

Hus, V., Pickles, A., Cook, E. H., Risi, S. & Lord, C. (2007). Using the autism diagnostic interview-revised to increase phenotypic homogeneity in genetic studies of autism. *Biological Psychiatry, 61*(4), 438–448.

Ingram, D. G., Takahashi, T. N. & Miles, J. H. (2008). Defining autism subgroups: A taxometric solution. *Journal of Autism and Developmental Disorders, 38*(5), 950–960.

Insel, T., Cuthbert, B., Garvey, M., Heinssen, R., Pine, D. S., Quinn, K., … Wang, P. (2010). Research Domain Criteria (RDoC): Toward a new classification framework for research on mental disorders. *American Journal of Psychiatry, 167*(7), 748–751.

Ioannidis, J. P. A. (2005). Why most published research findings are false. *Plos Medicine, 2*(8), 696–701.

Järvinen-Pasley, A., Pasley, J. & Heaton, P. (2008). Is the linguistic content of speech less salient than its perceptual features in autism? *Journal of Autism and Developmental Disorders, 38*(2), 239–248.

Jeste, S. S. & Geschwind, D. H. (2014). Disentangling the heterogeneity of autism spectrum disorder through genetic findings. *Nature Reviews Neurology, 10*(2), 74–81.

Johnson, M. H., Gliga, T., Jones, E. J. H. & Charman, T. (in press). Infant development, Autism and ADHD: Early pathways to emerging disorders. *Journal of Child Psychology and Psychiatry*.

Jones, C. R. G., Happé, F., Baird, G., Simonoff, E., Marsden, A. J. S., Tregay, J., … Charman, T. (2009a). Auditory discrimination and auditory sensory behaviours in autism spectrum disorders. *Neuropsychologia, 47*(13), 2850–2858.

Jones, C. R. G., Happé, F., Golden, H., Marsden, A. J. S., Tregay, J., Simonoff, E., … Charman, T. (2009b). Reading and arithmetic in adolescents with autism spectrum disorders: Peaks and dips in attainment. *Neuropsychology, 23*(6), 718–728.

Jones, E., Gliga, T., Bedford, R., Charman, T. & Johnson, M. H. (2014). Developmental pathways to autism: A review of prospective studies of infants at risk. *Neuroscience and Biobehavioral Reviews, 39*, 1–33.

Kanner, L. (1943). Autistic disturbances of affective contact. *Nervous Child, 2*, 217–250.

Kapur, S., Phillips, A. G. & Insel, T. R. (2012). Why has it taken so long for biological psychiatry to develop clinical tests and what to do about it? *Molecular Psychiatry, 17*(12), 1174–1179.

Karmiloff-Smith, A., D'Souza, D., Dekker, T. M., Van Herwegen, J., Xu, F., Rodic, M. & Ansari, D. (2012). Genetic and environmental vulnerabilities in children with neurodevelopmental disorders. *Proceedings of the National Academy of Sciences of the United States of America, 109*, 17261–17265.

Kasari, C. (2014). Are we there yet? The state of early prediction and intervention in autism spectrum disorder. *Journal of the American Academy of Child and Adolescent Psychiatry, 53*(2), 133–134.

Kendell, R. & Jablensky, A. (2003). Distinguishing between the validity and utility of psychiatric diagnoses. *American Journal of Psychiatry, 160*(1), 4–12.

Kim, Y. S., Leventhal, B. L., Koh, Y. J., Fombonne, E., Laska, E., Lim, E. C., … Grinker, R. R. (2011). Prevalence of autism spectrum disorders in a total population sample. *American Journal of Psychiatry, 168*(9), 904–912.

Kleinman, J. M., Ventola, P. E., Pandey, J., Verbalis, A. D., Barton, M., Hodgson, S., … Fein, D. (2008). Diagnostic stability in very young children with autism spectrum disorders. *Journal of Autism and Developmental Disorders, 38*(4), 606–615.

Kulage, K. M., Smaldone, A. M. & Cohn, E. G. (2014). How will DSM-5 affect autism diagnosis? A systematic literature review and meta-analysis. *Journal of Autism and Developmental Disorders, 44*(8), 1918–1932.

Lai, M. C., Lombardo, M. V. & Baron-Cohen, S. (2013). Autism. *Lancet, 6736*(13), 61539–61541.

Landa, R. J., Gross, A. L., Stuart, E. A. & Bauman, M. (2012). Latent class analysis of early developmental trajectory in baby siblings of children with autism. *Journal of Child Psychology and Psychiatry, 53*(9), 986–996.

Landa, R. J., Gross, A. L., Stuart, E. A. & Faherty, A. (2013). Developmental trajectories in children with and without autism spectrum disorders: The first 3 years. *Child Development, 84*(2), 429–442.

Lane, A. E., Molloy, C. A. & Bishop, S. L. (2014). Classification of children with autism spectrum disorder by sensory subtype: A case for sensory-based phenotypes. *Autism Research*. doi: 10.1002/aur.1368 [epub ahead of print].

Lincoln, A. J., Allen, M. H. & Kilman, A. (1995). The assessment and interpretation of intellectual abilities in people with autism. In E. Schopler & G. B. Mesibov (eds), *Learning and Cognition in Autism* (pp. 89–117). New York: Plenum.

Lockyer, L. & Rutter, M. (1970). A 5- to 15-year follow-up study of infantile psychosis: 4 patterns of cognitive ability. *British Journal of Social and Clinical Psychology, 9*(2), 152–163.

Lord, C. (1995). Follow-up of two-year-olds referred for possible autism. *Journal of Child Psychology and Psychiatry and Allied Disciplines, 36*(8), 1365–1382.

Lord, C., Rutter, M. L. & LeCouteur, A. (1994). The Autism Diagnostic Interview-Revised: A revised version of a diagnostic interview for caregivers of individuals with possible pervasive developmental disorders. *Journal of Autism and Developmental Disorders, 24*, 659–685.

Lord, C., Risi, S., Lambrecht, L., Cook, E. H., Jr., Leventhal, B. L., … Rutter, M. (2000). The Autism Diagnostic Observation Schedule-Generic: A standard measure of social and communication deficits associated with the spectrum of autism. *Journal of Autism and Developmental Disorders, 30*, 205–223.

Lord, C., Risi, S., DiLavore, P. S., Shulman, C., Thurm, A. & Pickles, A. (2006). Autism from 2 to 9 years of age. *Archives of General Psychiatry, 63*(6), 694–701.

Lord, C., Petkova, E., Hus, V., Gan, W. J., Lu, F. H., Martin, D. M., … Risi, S. (2012). A multisite study of the clinical diagnosis of different autism spectrum disorders. *Archives of General Psychiatry, 69*(3), 306–313.

Lotter, V. (1966). Epidemiology of autistic conditions in young children. *Social Psychiatry, 1,* 124–137.

Luyster, R., Lopez, K. & Lord, C. (2007). Characterizing communicative development in children referred for autism spectrum disorders using the MacArthur-Bates Communicative Development Inventory (CDI). *Journal of Child Language, 34*(3), 623–654.

Lyall, K., Schmidt, R. J. & Hertz-Picciotto, I. (2014). Maternal lifestyle and environmental risk factors for autism spectrum disorders. *International Journal of Epidemiology, 43(2)*, 443–464.

Magiati, I., Tay, X. W. & Howlin, P. (2014). Cognitive, language, social and behavioural outcomes in adults with autism spectrum disorders: A systematic review of longitudinal follow-up studies in adulthood. *Clinical Psychology Review, 34*(1), 73–86.

Mayes, S. D. & Calhoun, S. L. (2003). Analysis of WISC-III, Stanford-Binet-IV, and academic achievement test scores in children with autism. *Journal of Autism and Developmental Disorders, 33*(3), 329–341.

McGovern, C. W. & Sigman, M. (2005). Continuity and change from early childhood to adolescence in autism. *Journal of Child Psychology and Psychiatry, 46*(4), 401–408.

Messinger, D., Young, G. S., Ozonoff, S., Dobkins, K., Carter, A., Zwaigenbaum, L., … Sigman, M. (2013). Beyond autism: A Baby Siblings Research Consortium study of high-risk children at three years of age. *Journal of the American Academy of Child and Adolescent Psychiatry, 52*(3), 300–308.

Milne, E., White, S., Campbell, R., Swettenham, J., Hansen, P. & Ramus, F. (2006). Motion and form coherence detection in autistic spectrum disorder: Relationship to motor control and 2:4 digit ratio. *Journal of Autism and Developmental Disorders, 36*(2), 225–237.

Moore, V. & Goodson, S. (2003). How well does early diagnosis of autism stand the test of time? Follow-up study of children assessed for autism at age 2 and development of an early diagnostic service. *Autism, 7*(1), 47–63.

Munson, J., Dawson, G., Sterling, L., Beauchaine, T., Zhou, A., Koehler, E., … Abbott, R. (2008). Evidence for latent classes of IQ in young children with autism spectrum disorder. *American Journal on Mental Retardation, 113*(6), 439–452.

National Institute for Health and Clinical Excellence (NICE) (2012). *Autism: Recognition, Referral, Diagnosis and Management of Adults on the Autism Spectrum (CG: 142).* London: NHS Evidence.

Ozonoff, S., Iosif, A. M., Baguio, F., Cook, I. C., Hill, M. M., Hutman, T., … Young, G. S. (2010). A prospective study of the emergence of early behavioral signs of autism. *Journal of the American Academy of Child and Adolescent Psychiatry, 49*(3), 256–266.

Ozonoff, S., Young, G. S., Carter, A., Messinger, D., Yirmiya, N., Zwaigenbaum, L., … Stone, W. L. (2011). Recurrence risk for autism spectrum disorders: A Baby Siblings Research Consortium study. *Pediatrics, 128*(3), E488–E495.

Ozonoff, S., Young, G. S., Belding, A., Hill, M., Hill, A., … Iosif, A. M. (2014). The broader autism phenotype in infancy: When does it emerge? *Journal of the American Academy of Child and Adolescent Psychiatry, 53(4)*, 398–407.

Pellicano, E. (2010). The development of core cognitive skills in autism: A 3-year prospective study. *Child Development, 81*(5), 1400–1416.

Prather, P. & de Vries, P. J. (2004). Behavioral and cognitive aspects of tuberous sclerosis complex. *Journal of Child Neurology, 19*(9), 666–674.

Ricketts, J., Jones, C. R. G., Happé, F. & Charman, T. (2013). Reading comprehension in autism spectrum disorders: The role of oral language and social functioning. *Journal of Autism and Developmental Disorders, 43*(4), 807–816.

Robinson, E. B., Koenen, K. C., McCormick, M. C., Munir, K., Hallett, V., Happé, F., … Ronald, A. (2011). Evidence that autistic traits show the same etiology in the general population and at the quantitative extremes (5%, 2.5%, and 1%). *Archives of General Psychiatry, 68*(11), 1113–1121.

Ronald, A., Happé, F. & Plomin, R. (2005). The genetic relationship between individual differences in social and nonsocial behaviours characteristic of autism. *Developmental Science, 8*(5), 444–458.

Ronald, A., Happé, F., Bolton, P., Butcher, L. M., Price, T. S., Wheelwright, S., … Plomin, R. (2006). Genetic heterogeneity between the three components of the autism spectrum: A twin study. *Journal of the American Academy of Child and Adolescent Psychiatry, 45*(6), 691–699.

Rondeau, E., Klein, L. S., Masse, A., Bodeau, N., Cohen, D. & Guile, J. M. (2011). Is pervasive developmental disorder not otherwise specified less stable than autistic disorder? A meta-analysis. *Journal of Autism and Developmental Disorders, 41*(9), 1267–1276.

Saulnier, C. A. & Klin, A. (2007). Brief report: Social and communication abilities and disabilities in higher functioning individuals with autism and Asperger syndrome. *Journal of Autism and Developmental Disorders, 37*(4), 788–793.

Scheuffgen, K., Happé, F., Anderson, M. & Frith, U. (2000). High 'intelligence', low 'IQ'? Speed of processing and measured IQ in children with autism. *Development and Psychopathology, 12*(1), 83–90.

Semel, E., Wiig, E. H. & Secord, W. (2003). *Clinical Evaluation of Language Fundamentals – Fourth Edition UK (CELF-4 UK)*. San Antonio, TX: The Psychological Corporation.

Shao, Y. J., Cuccaro, M. L., Hauser, E. R., Raiford, K. L., Menold, M. M., Wolpert, C. M., … Pericak-Vance, M. A. (2003). Fine mapping of autistic disorder to chromosome 15q11-q13 by use of phenotypic subtypes. *American Journal of Human Genetics, 72*(3), 539–548.

Sigman, M. & Ruskin, E. (1999). Continuity and change in the social competence of children with autism, Down syndrome, and developmental delays. *Monographs of the Society for Research in Child Development, 64*(1), 1–114.

Simonoff, E., Pickles, A., Charman, T., Chandler, S., Loucas, T. & Baird, G. (2008). Psychiatric disorders in children with autism spectrum disorders: Prevalence, comorbidity, and associated factors in a population-derived sample. *Journal of the American Academy of Child and Adolescent Psychiatry, 47*(8), 921–929.

Smith, L. E., Maenner, M. J. & Seltzer, M. M. (2012). Developmental trajectories in adolescents and adults with autism: The case of daily living skills. *Journal of the American Academy of Child and Adolescent Psychiatry, 51*(6), 622–631.

Sparrow, S., Balla, D. & Cichetti, D. (1995). *Vineland Adaptive Behaviour Scales – 2nd Edn.* Circle Pines, Minnesota: American Guidance Services.

Stone, W. L., Lee, E. B., Ashford, L., Brissie, J., Hepburn, S. L., Coonrod, E. E. & Weiss, B. H. (1999). Can autism be diagnosed accurately in children under 3 years? *Journal of Child Psychology and Psychiatry and Allied Disciplines, 40*(2), 219–226.

Tsatsanis, K., D. (2005) Neuropsychological characteristics in autism and related conditions. In F. R. Volkmar, R. Paul, A. Klin & D. Cohen (eds), *Handbook of Autism and Pervasive Developmental Disorders* (3rd ed.), (pp. 365–381). New Jersey: Wiley.

Turner, L. M. & Stone, W. L. (2007). Variability in outcome for children with an ASD diagnosis at age 2. *Journal of Child Psychology and Psychiatry, 48*(8), 793–802.

Turner, L. M., Stone, W. L., Pozdol, S. L. & Coonard, E. E. (2006). Follow-up of children with autism spectrum disorders from age 2 to age 9. *Autism, 10*(3), 243–265.

van der Meer, J. M. J., Oerlemans, A. M., van Steijn, D. J., Lappenschaar, M. G. A., de Sonneville, L. M. J., Buitelaar, J. K. & Rommelse, N. N. J. (2012). Are autism spectrum disorder and Attention-Deficit/Hyperactivity Disorder different manifestations of one overarching disorder? Cognitive and symptom evidence from a clinical and population-based sample. *Journal of the American Academy of Child and Adolescent Psychiatry, 51*(11), 1160–1172.

White, S., Hill, E., Happé, F. & Frith, U. (2009). Revisiting the strange stories: Revealing mentalizing impairments in autism. *Child Development, 80*(4), 1097–1117.

Wing, L. & Gould, J. (1979). Severe impairments of social-interaction and associated abnormalities in children: Epidemiology and classification. *Journal of Autism and Developmental Disorders, 9*(1), 11–29.

Wodka, E. L., Mathy, P. & Kalb, L. (2013). Predictors of phrase and fluent speech in children with autism and severe language delay. *Pediatrics, 131*(4), E1128–E1134.

World Health Organization (WHO) (1993). *Mental Disorders: A Glossary and Guide to their Classification in Accordance with the 10th Revision of the International Classification of Diseases: Research Diagnostic Criteria (ICD-10)*. Geneva: WHO.

8

DIFFERENT PROFILES OF DEVELOPMENT

Evidence from children with primary language impairment

Victoria Knowland and Nicola Botting

8.1 Introduction: developmental language impairment

In a volume about research issues in developmental disorders, language impairment can act as an informative case study on the challenges and importance of specificity, heterogeneity and change over time. Language development is clearly of considerable clinical import and the impact of atypicality in this domain can be severe. The aim of this chapter is to describe some of the theoretical challenges faced by researchers and clinicians in the field of language impairment and make some practical suggestions for how those challenges could begin to be tackled.

Language impairments are associated with many developmental disorders (e.g. Finestack, Richmond & Abbeduto, 2009; Martin, Klusek, Estigarribia & Roberts, 2009) but language can also be the primary domain of neurodevelopmental deficit in the case of, what is often termed, 'Specific Language Impairment' (SLI; refer back to Chapter 5 for further discussion). Children with SLI are diagnostically defined as showing a deficit in one or more aspects of the acquisition and use of oral language which is not explained by sensory or neurological issues, low non-verbal IQ or insufficient opportunity to learn. Deficits may be seen across any or all sub-domains of language, be it structural (phonology, syntax/morphology, semantics) or functional (pragmatics). SLI has an estimated prevalence of 7 per cent in school-aged children (Tomblin, Records, Buckwalter, Zhang & Smith, 1997). The impact of language impairments on children's lives is increasingly being recognised, as are the long-term effects through adolescence and adulthood in areas such as educational attainment, occupational status (Johnson, Beitchman & Brownlie, 2010) and mental health (Arkkila, Rasanen, Roine & Vilkman, 2008; Beitchman et al., 2001; Conti-Ramsden & Botting, 2008).

To receive a diagnosis of SLI a child must show a performance disparity between standardised tests of language ability and non-verbal IQ. Depending on the classification system adopted, non-verbal IQ must either be within the normal range (*Diagnostic and Statistical Manual*; American Psychiatric Association, 2013) or show a disparity of at least one standard deviation with language ability (International Classification of Diseases; World Health Organization, 2008). Since not only the diagnostic criteria but also the standardised assessments used vary between countries, regions, clinics, and even individual assessors, the extent to which verbal and non-verbal ability may be dissociated varies. This means that the children receiving diagnoses and intervention show a wide range in profiles, as do those included in research studies, which has implications for how the disorder is understood and defined. Furthermore, even when children meet criteria on standardised tests, cognitive function measured by other means may be lower than for typically developing controls (Farrell & Phelps, 2000), and children with clinical referrals for language difficulties may score below the typical range on standardised tests of non-verbal IQ (Stark & Tallal, 1981). Here we will use the term 'Primary Language Impairment' (Primary LI) to reflect this variability. Terms used in the papers cited in this chapter range from SLI to language impairment through to language-related learning problems.

The key clinical features of Primary LI are much debated but often include a marked impairment in syntax/morphology (Conti-Ramsden, Botting & Faragher, 2001a; Paul, 2001; Rice, Tomblin, Hoffman, Richman & Marquis, 2004) and phonological processing including phonological memory (Bishop, North & Donlan, 1996; Botting & Conti-Ramsden, 2001; Dollaghan & Campbell, 1998; Gathercole & Baddeley, 1990) and phonological awareness (Briscoe, Bishop & Norbury, 2001). Tense marking (Rice, Wexler & Cleave, 1995) and phonological short-term memory (Gathercole & Baddeley, 1990) as measured by non-word and sentence repetition performance (Bishop et al., 1996; Conti-Ramsden et al., 2001a), have been proposed as the most reliable single indicators of persistent impairment (Bishop et al., 1996; Conti-Ramsden et al., 2001a; Rice et al., 1995). Risk factors for Primary LI include a family history of language impairment (Barry, Yasin & Bishop, 2007; Tomblin, 1997), low socio-economic status (Stanton-Chapman, Chapman, Bainbridge & Scott, 2002), perinatal insult and low birth weight (Stanton-Chapman et al., 2002). The aetiology of the disorder is not well understood, partly due to some of the issues we will discuss here. Broadly, there are two competing theories of Primary LI: one is that an underlying deficit specific to the language system is responsible (see Rice, 2000), the other posits a more general limitation in information processing such as slow speed of processing (Miller, Kail, Leonard & Tomblin, 2001) or a deficit in procedural memory (Ullman & Pierpoint, 2005).

We will structure this chapter around four central questions. Firstly, to what extent is the deficit in Primary LI restricted to the language domain? Secondly, within language, how do children with the same broad diagnosis of Primary LI cluster; that is, are there subgroups? Specificity in developmental disorders is important to the clinician who needs to understand the child's full profile in order to intervene accordingly (see discussion in Chapters 1 and 14); the experimental researcher who needs to either recruit children with common underlying conditions or embrace heterogeneity (linking to Chapter 7); and the theoretician, for whom patterns of development across domains of cognition may support or refute developmental modularity of mind (see Chapter 2). Thirdly, we will ask how profiles change over childhood; how stable is cognitive development in Primary LI and what does that mean clinically and theoretically? Fourthly and finally, we will ask how the environment interacts with child-internal factors in the manifestation of language impairment. To conclude, we will draw out those questions which we consider to be most pressing in the field at this time.

8.2 How 'specific' is language impairment?

As we have seen, the official diagnostic criteria for language impairment require that the child shows a deficit in the domain of language, which is not explained by a deficit in non-verbal IQ, in other words that the deficit is *specific* to language development. However, measurement of abilities beyond the domain of language in a sample of children with a diagnosed language impairment will quickly reveal additional and wide-ranging areas of difficulty. Such heterogeneity raises some difficult questions clinically but may also be informative as to the underlying nature of this disorder which manifests, at least most saliently, in the language domain.

Motor development is one area which has been relatively well-described in children with Primary LI. Difficulties in this area have been found to range from inaccurate tapping to a beat (Corriveau & Goswami, 2009) and slow peg moving skills (e.g. Owen & McKinlay, 1997; Powell & Bishop, 1992) to the delayed development of unaided walking (Haynes & Naidoo, 1991). In a comprehensive review paper, Hill (2001) draws out patterns of the most consistently seen motor deficits. She shows that on experimental tasks of motor control, children with Primary LI are more likely to show impairments on tasks of speed than accuracy; with respect to gross motor behaviour, the domain of balance is most likely to be impaired; a further area of weakness is symbolic or representational gesture, be it transitive or intransitive (e.g. Hill, 1998; Hill, Bishop & Nimmo-Smith, 1998; Dewey, Roy, Square-Storer & Hayden, 1988; Dewey & Wall, 1997). Finally, sequences of movements are more likely to be impaired than single movements or postures (e.g. Dewey et al., 1988). Informatively, certain motor deficits may be more tightly correlated with certain aspects of language difficulty. For example, in seven- to thirteen-year-old children with Primary LI, tapping skills demonstrate shared genetic influence with speech production accuracy (Bishop, 2002). This relationship is further supported by the finding that inconsistent phonological errors and verbal dyspraxia show an association with peg moving and motor accuracy tasks (Bradford & Dodd, 1994, 1996). This evidence suggests that motor immaturity may be most closely linked to phonological output deficits.

In the domain of mathematical development, Donlan, Cowan, Newton and Lloyd (2007) found seven- to nine-year-old children with Primary LI to be as competent as their age-matched peers at understanding logical arithmetic principles, but to show considerable procedural difficulties. Difficulties included basic counting, with 40 per cent of the language impaired group failing to count to twenty compared to 4 per cent of their age-matched peers. Counting, in turn, influenced calculation abilities. Performance on mathematical tasks may also be directly hampered by language limitations. While age-matched peers facilitate their numerical problem solving using verbal counting, a group of three- to five-year-old children with Primary LI, when prompted to use this strategy by Arvedson (2002), showed a 50 per cent decline in accuracy.

One area of particular importance for academic attainment is executive function, which may be subdivided into complex working memory, switching, and inhibition components (Henry, Messer & Nash, 2012). Marton (2008) compared five- to six-year-old children with Primary LI to typical controls on complex working memory tasks in language and visuo-spatial domains and found deficits across the board. Henry and colleagues (2012) also compared children with Primary LI (aged eight to fourteen years) to typical controls and children with general cognitive delay, on a range of verbal and non-verbal tasks tapping executive function. When controlling for age, non-verbal IQ and verbal IQ the Primary LI group differed from the typical group on five out of ten measures, but did not differ from the group with general delay. At an individual level, children with Primary LI varied between performing zero out of ten tasks more than one standard deviation below the control group up to eight out of ten tasks below the normal range. Tasks that require increased attention control and executive function therefore seem to be unusually challenging for children with a language difficulty, especially when working memory demands are high (Alloway & Archibald, 2008), although the high individual variability in this area is notable.

Not only do children with a diagnosis of Primary LI show difficulties outside the domain of language, but often frank comorbidity, or co-occurrence, with other behaviourally defined developmental disorders is seen. Cohen and colleagues (Cohen, Barwick, Horodezky, Vallance & Im, 1998) found that 63.6 per cent of children between seven and fourteen years who presented at paediatric psychiatric clinics could be diagnosed as language impaired, with Attention Deficit Hyperactivity Disorder (ADHD; see Chapter 9 for a discussion) being the most common primary psychiatric diagnosis in this group. The relationship here is difficult to untangle though as attention difficulties could co-occur with language problems or could influence language development or performance on language assessments, or indeed language problems could impact upon attention. Williams and colleagues (Williams, Stott, Goodyer & Sahakian, 2000) explored groups of children with and without Primary LI and hyperactivity, and found that having a primary diagnosis of language disorder revealed more differences on cognitive function regardless of hyperactivity than vice versa. On the other hand, the fact that comprehension seems to be the most affected subdomain of language in children with attention difficulties (Bruce, Thernlund & Nettebladt, 2006) arguably points to the influence of attention on language acquisition.

Given the difficulties in motor development discussed above it is unsurprising that Developmental Coordination Disorder (DCD) is also highly co-comorbid with Primary LI. DCD, as diagnosed using a comprehensive movement battery such as the Movement ABC (Henderson & Sugden, 1992), has a prevalence rate between 40 per cent (Cermak, Ward & Ward, 1986) and 90 per cent (Robinson, 1991) in children with a primary diagnosis of language disorder, compared to the 6 per cent prevalence rate in the general child population (APA, 1994).

There has been some discussion in the literature about the appropriate diagnostic breadth of Primary LI; in particular whether developmental dyslexia and Autism Spectrum Disorders (ASD; see Chapter 7 for a discussion) should be thought of as existing on the same continuum (e.g. Bishop & Snowling, 2004; Williams, Botting & Boucher, 2008). Thus far, the evidence points to separate but overlapping disorders. In the case of dyslexia, Catts and colleagues (Catts, Adolf, Hogan & Weismer, 2005) screened a large sample of children (N = 527) for oral language ability in kindergarten and reading ability in fourth grade. Using a criterion which demanded a full scale IQ discrepancy and low achievement in fourth grade, base rate prevalence of dyslexia was 8.6 per cent, while in the group who met diagnostic criteria for Primary LI in kindergarten this rate was significantly higher at 17 per cent. Some estimates of the percentage of children with Primary LI who show literacy difficulties severe enough to be classed as dyslexic in the school years vary substantially, with some in excess of 50 per cent. For example, Conti-Ramsden and colleagues found that 77 per cent of their sample of children with Primary LI performed below minus one standard deviation on single word reading (Conti-Ramsden, Botting, Simkin & Knox, 2001b). This pattern of relatively unaffected literacy ability in a substantial proportion of children with spoken language difficulties (see also Botting, 2007) suggests at least a degree of dissociation between oral and written language development in children with developmental difficulties. Although, to our knowledge, no work has yet explored brain activation in good and poor readers with a background of oral language impairment, it is possible that behavioural performance masks atypical but compensated routes to reading in the brain.

Language impairment in children with ASD is a slightly different issue as children with this diagnosis cannot additionally be diagnosed with Primary LI. However, structural language is affected in ASD. For example Rapin and Dunn (2003) found that 63 per cent of a large sample of preschool children with ASD had a mixed expressive/receptive language deficit. Conti-Ramsden and colleagues also showed that a higher proportion of children diagnosed with SLI at age seven (3.9 per cent) develop significant symptoms associated with ASD later in life (Conti-Ramsden, Simkin & Botting, 2006). It seems though that structural language problems in those with ASD tend to show quite different patterns than in children with Primary LI. For example, children with ASD show fewer errors of third person singular tense marking (Cantwell, Baker & Rutter, 1978) and are less likely to have articulatory (Kjelgaard & Tager-Flusberg, 2001) or purely expressive (Rapin & Dunn, 2003) problems (see Williams, Botting & Boucher, 2008, for a full discussion of the relationship between ASD and language).

A fascinating aspect of research into the specificity of language disorders is untangling co-occurrence from inter-dependence. Are children with a deficit in one domain more likely to show deficits elsewhere because of some third causal factor, such as slow processing speed, or do these patterns of impairment result from domains of cognition being inter-dependent over development? Models of development are increasingly moving toward the idea that information processing cannot be modular through infancy and childhood, but rather that atypical processing anywhere in the system will influence processing in all other interacting domains (but see Botting & Marshall, in press, for a discussion about the complexities of this). Furthermore, the likelihood is slim that perinatal impairments in information processing, at the start of developmental pathways, will be limited to only one type of stimulus in one modality given that those impairments will most likely relate to fundamental aspects of neuron development (see Karmiloff-Smith, 1998, for an overview of this position).

It seems likely that different diagnoses overlap with language impairments for different reasons, and show developmental interactions to greater or lesser extents. For example, in the motor domain, fine motor control could be more developmentally relevant to the acquisition of speech than gait development is. In other domains, such as mathematical ability, progress may be additionally hampered by problems being couched in quite complex verbal terms. A working ontology of how developmental disorders overlap (which disorders are most likely to co-occur and which deficits are more tightly correlated across domains) does not yet exist (but see Chapter 6). With regard to language, the indication thus far is simply that the more severe the language impairment, the more likely another diagnosis will be evident (see Westerlund, Bergkvist, Lagerberg & Sundelin, 2002), with pure phonological disorder being the least likely to have additional comorbid diagnoses (Beitchman et al., 1996). The bottom line is that current classification systems seem to impose a parsimony which is unlikely to adequately reflect the underlying developmental mechanisms responsible for deficits in language acquisition.

8.3 Do subgroups of language impairment exist?

Although at one level of description children with language impairments are grouped together, the heterogeneity of this group has long been acknowledged. The critical question is whether this heterogeneity arises due to distinct and meaningful subgrouping defined by multiple continuous variables, or whether all language impairments have a common underlying aetiology with varying symptoms due to interaction with other factors. This is an important question as the aetiology of any disorder necessarily suggests potential intervention or prevention.

Language is a complex behaviour and as such there are many ways in which development could be constrained. In 1992 Bishop set out six hypotheses to account for atypical language acquisition ranging from a deficit in language-specific mechanisms such as the use of morpho-syntactic knowledge, to inadequacy of auditory perception, to general cognitive mechanisms like limited speed and capacity of information processing. There have been multiple studies which have used large groups of children with Primary LI to statistically dissociate subgroups, with the aim of understanding different routes to impairment. The first such study was published in 1983 by Rapin and Allen, who set out three classes of language disorder: 1) receptive/expressive developmental language disorder, including children with receptive and expressive deficits in phonology and syntax; 2) expressive developmental language disorder syndromes, covering developmental verbal dyspraxia and phonologic programming deficits; and 3) higher order processing disorders, including word finding deficits and pragmatic language impairment. Apart from controversy over whether verbal dyspraxia and pragmatic language impairment should be classified under specific disorders of language, these broad subgroups have held fairly well (Conti-Ramsden, Crutchley & Botting, 1997). However, the fact that the statistically defined subgroups do not adequately describe all children diagnosed with Primary LI (e.g. Conti-Ramsden, St.Clair, Pickles & Durkin, 2012) and that categories are not stable over time (e.g. Van Weerdenburg, Verhoeven & van Balkam, 2006; Conti-Ramsden & Botting, 1999; and see below) suggests that this classification only goes some way to describing individual variability.

A more pure form of the subgroup notion has been suggested under the term Grammatical Specific Language Impairment (van der Lely, 1997), which describes children who have a difficulty representing the dependent relationships between syntactic elements of a sentence. The extent to which these children show isolated syntactic deficits has, however, been questioned. Bishop, Bright, James, Bishop and van der Lely (2000) found a small sample of children who could be described by this profile, but more usually grammatical impairments were accompanied by non-verbal deficits or linguistics deficits beyond syntax. As outlined above, theoretical notions about the interactive nature of cognitive development would strongly argue against the possibility of an isolated deficit in syntactic formulation (Karmiloff-Smith, 1998; Thomas & Karmiloff-Smith, 2002).

In clinical practice, the terms expressive language disorder (production), receptive language disorder (comprehension) and mixed expressive-language disorder are enduring sub-classifications and this is reflected in some diagnostic schedules (e.g. ICD-10). Because it is difficult to argue that a child can have intact expressive language impairment in the context of impaired comprehension, the 'receptive language disorder' label is rarely used and in DSM-5 only the first and last of these subgroups is represented. Social communication disorder has also been added to reflect a body of literature which argues for the existence of children with pragmatic language impairments but without the restricted interests and obsessions seen in ASD (Botting & Conti-Ramsden, 1999; Bishop, 1989; Bishop, Chan, Adams, Hartley & Weir, 2000).

A parallel stream of research in the mission to classify and understand developmental language impairments is the search for specific, low-level deficits which might, over developmental time, result in different categories of language impairment. There are many recorded perceptual deficits which have been linked to Primary LI. These include judging auditory rise-time and sound duration (Corriveau, Pasquini & Goswami, 2007); and attentional difficulties filtering out irrelevant auditory signals

(Stevens, Sanders & Neville, 2006). Auditory processing has been under investigation as a possible cause of language disorders since the 1980s (e.g. Tallal, 1980) when children with Primary LI were found to have a particular difficulty reporting the temporal order of rapid auditory stimuli (see Chapter 5 for further discussion of underlying mechanisms). Now, it seems that while auditory processing is impaired in at least some individuals with Primary LI (Rosen, Adlard & van der Lely, 2009; van der Lely, Rosen & Adlard, 2004; Wright et al., 1997), group differences tend to be driven by a subset of the language impaired group, and for those who do show impairments, these impairments are not limited to rapid processing as was originally put forward (see Rosen, 2003, for a review). If auditory processing problems were sufficient to cause language disorders then one would expect a strong relationship between auditory skills and language, which is not seen (see Rosen, 2003). Also children with mild hearing loss who have impaired auditory processing, but for different reasons do not show the same degree of difficulty on language tasks (Briscoe et al., 2001). However, deficits in auditory processing may yet be implicated in certain language behaviours. For example, frequency discrimination has been linked to non-word repetition (McArthur & Bishop, 2004). Therefore, the degree of variability seen in auditory processing in Primary LI, which once looked so promising as a causal factor (Hill, Hogben & Bishop, 2005), demonstrates instead the importance of mapping the multiple developmental pathways which may lead to language deficits (see Chapter 2 for a discussion). Notably, this needs to happen at both behavioural and brain levels that Bishop and McArthur (2004) found atypical ERP responses to an auditory processing task in participants with Primary LI who showed behavioural responses within the normal range. This dissociation between behavioural and brain level data suggests that alternative routes to information processing may develop.

The current lack of clear developmental pathways which lead to different profiles of language ability causes researchers to adopt a broad sweep approach to recruitment. Though useful in terms of understanding the behavioural abilities of children with Primary LI, this circumstance is not conducive to unpicking underlying processing problems. Given that group level results where children with Primary LI differ from their typically developing peers tend to be driven by a sub-sample of children, researchers in the field should make it normal practice to report individual differences rather than just group level effects. Embracing variability like this would mean that the heterogeneity which has come to be a hallmark of language impairment could be seen as the key to understanding causality rather than a barrier to it.

8.4 How does language impairment change over developmental time?

When discussing any human behaviour it would be lacking to talk about diagnoses or domains of cognition as static: development is synonymous with change (the hallmarks of Chapter 2 of this text). The variability and change within the domain of language is evidenced by how difficult it is to predict trajectories. In a sample of children identified as being at risk for language delay at age two, based on parental reports of communicative competence, over 50 per cent showed resolved language by age four (Dale, Price, Bishop & Plomin, 2003); the authors reported a 60 to 70 per cent chance of predicting group membership based on two-year-old language profiles. This same pattern of rapid resolution to within the normal range over the ages of around three to six has been repeatedly shown (Bishop, 2005; Bishop & Edmundson, 1987; Paul, 1996; Rescorla, Dahlsgaard & Roberts, 2000; Whitehurst & Fischel, 1994). This pattern of change, especially over the pre-school years, has important clinical implications. Given the high caseload and time constraints in speech and language therapy clinics, it would not be feasible to intervene with all children presenting with problems at age three. Since early intervention is thought to have the greatest impact in the case of developmental delay or disorder (Ward, 1999), it would be highly beneficial to be able to identify those children likely to show persisting language deficits early. One promising finding is that using trajectories of change to predict later language ability is more effective than a single measurement at any given point on that trajectory (Rowe, Raudenbush & Goldin-Meadow, 2012).

By the age of around seven, children identified as having a language impairment are less likely to show a resolving trajectory, but even so their profiles of ability are not stable over time. The Manchester Language Study has followed 242 children diagnosed with language impairment from the age of seven through, most recently, to age seventeen and has been particularly informative about the process of developmental change. At age seven subgroups were identified using a combination of clustering based on standardised scores plus teacher ratings to give six groups, closely aligned to Rapin & Allen's (Conti-Ramsden et al., 1997). At age eight, although cluster means remained stable, 45 per cent of individual children had moved clusters (Conti-Ramsden & Botting, 1999). Analysis of the children's assessment scores suggested that movement between clusters represented clinical change in profiles, with changes in phonology and vocabulary being particularly apparent, and with children who had the most severe impairments showing most stability. This work emphasises that language impairments are behaviourally defined and, as discussed above, behavioural subgroups do not necessarily represent stable or deterministic neurophysiological pathways. It may also suggest an intriguing possibility that the subgroups themselves are stable but that individual children develop through different stages of language impairment. However, more investigation is needed to examine this idea further.

Not only do profiles within the language domain change over time, so does the extent to which children with Primary LI show a discrepancy between verbal and non-verbal ability. Declines in non-verbal IQ over time in children with a diagnosis of Primary LI has been repeatedly reported in the literature (Botting, 2005; Conti-Ramsden et al., 2001b; Krassowski & Plante, 1997; Mawhood, Howlin & Rutter, 2000; Paul & Cohen 1984; Tomblin, Freese & Records, 1992). The verbal and non-verbal trajectories of the Manchester Language Study sample have been tracked from age seven to seventeen (Conti-Ramsden et al., 2012). Language development in this group remained reasonably steady, except for a period of accelerated growth in receptive language at age seven to eight. However, performance IQ trajectories were more variable, with 32 per cent of the sample showing deceleration. This meant that one-third of the group would not have met clinical criteria for a diagnosis of Primary LI by late childhood/adolescence despite showing considerable continued difficulty in the language domain. Longitudinal data therefore suggest that older and younger children selected for research projects on the same criteria of disparity are likely to have quite different profiles when taking age into account: if the younger children in cross-sectional studies were followed up in later childhood, they may well look different to children recruited as having Primary LI at an older age. Perhaps then, using a disparity measure in clinical diagnosis is at best only useful in younger children. Botting (2005) found that better language outcome at fourteen years was associated with stable IQ profiles between seven and fourteen years; a finding which argues for the inter-dependence of verbal and non-verbal development. The role of language in non-verbal cognitive development is arguably particularly important given the performance demands of many activities and assessments, and the extent to which language is necessary to access new information in educational settings. If this is the case, then those children who are more in need of support for their language difficulties are less likely to get a diagnosis of language impairment as they may well show additional difficulties in non-verbal assessments. This lack of stability in non-verbal skills, as well as the broad picture of difficulties, has led many researchers to call for a change in the term *specific* language impairment (see Bishop, 2014; Reilly et al., 2014).

8.5 What is the impact of the environment on language impairment?

Finally, we turn to the important and complex question of how environmental input interacts with child-internal factors to impact on language development. We know that multiple aspects of parental behaviour (Alston & St. James-Roberts, 2005; Hart & Risley, 1995; Hoff & Naigles, 2002; Tamis-LeMonda, Bornstein & Baumwell, 2001) and the home environment (Bishop et al., 1999) can have a substantial impact on language acquisition, and that by the first year of school socio-economic status (SES) explains over 30 per cent of the variance observed in language ability (Noble, McCandliss & Farah, 2007). Law and colleagues also found a significantly raised percentage of disadvantaged children meeting criteria for Primary LI (Law et al., 2012). This socio-economic imbalance is represented in early referrals to speech and language therapy clinics (Tomblin et al., 1997). Yet, compared to the increased risk of language impairment evident in children from low SES backgrounds, this group is still under-referred to clinical services. A key question then is whether the language deficits seen in children from disadvantaged backgrounds share the same features, prognosis and potential for intervention as do congenital or inherited disorders (if such a clear distinction can be made at all). This is important both for researchers trying to understand the reason for variability in language development and for clinicians who are overwhelmed, under-resourced, and need to be able to tell not only which children are likely to have persisting problems, but also who will respond to what kind of intervention.

Currently there are no known diagnostic markers for language impairments with different origins. That is, there are no tests which are able to predict the primary limitation on language acquisition for individual children with an acceptable level of specificity and sensitivity. Having said that, groups-level differences are beginning to be established. For example, children from low SES backgrounds do not show the same deficits in tense marking that children with Primary LI do (Pruitt & Oetting, 2009) and some recent work into Dynamic Assessment (scaffolding and training paradigms) suggests that this is a promising tool for discriminating those with persistent Primary LI regardless of background (Camilleri & Botting, 2013; Hasson, Dodd & Botting, 2012). An interesting potential distinction has also been drawn using the event-related potential (ERP) method. Stevens and colleagues measured neuromodulation by auditory attention in children with SLI (Stevens et al., 2006) and separately in children from low SES backgrounds (Stevens, Lauinger & Neville, 2009), both at age three to eight years. They found that neuromodulation was substantially reduced in both groups compared to typically developing or higher SES children, so both groups of children found it difficult or impossible to ignore distracting auditory stimuli. However, while for the language impaired children this deficit arose from an inability to enhance the task-relevant signal, children from low SES backgrounds were less able to suppress the task-irrelevant distractor signal. Although the low SES children involved in this work did not show language deficits as a group, the work points to potential mechanistic differences for language deficits which may present as quite similar behaviourally. The developmental pathways relating to this finding have yet to be investigated.

The potential for different underlying causes of language impairments has recently been supported through the use of computational modelling (Thomas & Knowland, 2014). In a population of networks (children) learning the English past tense, multiple parameters were varied, both internal to the networks (e.g. network size), and external (the quantity of input available). A subset of networks showed a delay in task acquisition, but, crucially, this delay could occur for one of two reasons. The first group showed reduced *capacity,* that is, they were poor at learning the task no matter how much input they received. The other delay group showed poor *plasticity*, that is, they changed slowly in response to input, but given enough input (equivalent to a rich language environment) this group was able to achieve a good final level of performance. Although this model has not been prospectively tested, a re-analysis of available data from Bishop (2005) has supported the idea that SES (represented in the model by quantity of input) might only impact on language acquisition for a subgroup of children. According to the model, those with resilient language systems, and those with poor language due to low capacity, should not show an interaction with SES, while those with low plasticity should.

The reality of how environmental and genetic factors interact over the course of language acquisition will, of course, be extremely complex (for a detailed description of current understanding of genetic and environmental factors see Bishop, 2001). It is likely that SES effects go beyond a lack of informational richness in the environment, to influences on the language system through nutritional status, which is known to affect brain development (Tanner & Finn-Stevenson, 2002), level of home chaos (Chen, Cohen & Miller, 2010), plus the potential confound of inherited disorder. In the language of the Thomas and Knowland model (2014), SES may not just interact with system plasticity but might also be causally related to level of plasticity and capacity.

The flip side of the question of environmental impact on language acquisition is the extent to which environmental modifications can be effective in the remediation of language impairments. We know that behavioural interventions can be, at least moderately, effective for expressive language impairments (Law et al., 2012). Intervention may entail targeting specific linguistic problems with a speech and language therapist (e.g. Ebbels, 2007) or training parents in supportive interaction techniques (Roberts & Kaiser, 2011). To our knowledge, no intervention techniques have yet been compared directly across high and low SES groups, nor do we understand if programmes which aim to enrich language input are more effective for children showing certain behavioural profiles at the onset of intervention. The capacity/plasticity model offers the possibility to identify those children who are likely to benefit from language enrichment programmes, which could be cost-effectively run in educational settings.

Studying the influence of the environment is likely to be highly informative as to the primary constraints of language development for different children. Such patterns may be seen across other developmental disorders where SES effects are seen in the domain of impairment, including dyslexia (Molfese, Modglin & Molfese, 2003), dyscalculia, and ADHD (Gross-Tsur, Manor & Shalev, 1996).

8.6 Conclusions

This chapter set out to present the profiles of development seen in children with primary deficits in the language domain. We conclude here by briefly answering the questions we posed in each section, and suggesting the most pressing research questions relating to each issue.

8.6.1. How 'specific' is language impairment?

The answer: not very. The extent of impairment across different areas of cognition in children with a diagnosis of Primary LI is not yet clear, but as far as we are aware deficits have been found in every area so far studied. The continued use of the term *specific* language impairment therefore seems to be a misnomer, and may in itself be an obstacle to clinical and empirical investigation of the extent of problems experienced. A thorough ontology of how different behaviourally defined developmental disorders overlap would be useful both clinically and for research purposes to help uncover possible directions of influence and key areas for assessment. Cross-domain deficits could be taken to suggest a non-specific neurophysiological correlate. One possibility put forward to explain developmental language disorders is that small malformations in the development of the neocortex, including abnormal neuronal migration, around key structures such as the Sylvian Fissure may disrupt normal language processing (de Vasconcelos et al., 2006; Galaburda, LoTurco, Ramus, Fitch & Rosen, 2006; Galaburda, Sherman, Rosen, Aboitz & Geschwind, 1985; Guerreiro et al., 2002). The appeal of this hypothesis is its flexibility, and consequently its potential to explain both varying severity and co-occurring deficits across widely disparate domains. However, the prevalence of such neocortical abnormalities is not known and the large, longitudinal studies needed to test such a hypothesis may have to wait for neuroimaging equipment with finer resolution.

8.6.2. Do subgroups of language impairment exist?

The answer here is that certainly they do behaviourally, but it is not yet clear what the implications of that are in terms of causality or intervention. There is important work to be done here in the form of large, prospective studies of language profiles from birth, which also measure profiles in an in-depth and comprehensive way. Can different behavioural subgroups be traced back to different early impairments in, for example, auditory processing or attention? If reliable pathways can be identified then the right intervention at the right point early in development is the best chance for preventing long-term and potentially devastating language deficits. This is likely to be a highly complex picture with multiple genetic and environmental influences contributing to subtly different paths to impairment (Bishop, 2001). A first achievable step to these ends would be for language researchers to routinely consider not just group profiles but individual differences in studies of the sensory and cognitive abilities of children with language impairments.

8.6.3. How does language impairment change over developmental time?

The most parsimonious answer here is: substantially but unpredictably. This is a particularly important issue in both the clinic and the lab, partly because it is often neglected. The fact that profiles are dynamic means that: behaviourally defined diagnoses will become more or less applicable over time; some children will resolve their difficulties without additional input; areas of primary weakness will change; and children recruited to research at different ages may not be directly comparable. In research the difficulty of dynamic profiles creates a financial dilemma: it's expensive to track development over time. However, understanding the factors that predict change and how different domains of cognition impact on one another over development is crucial if intervention and knowledge of the disorder is to be optimised.

8.6.4. What is the impact of the environment on language impairment?

This is probably the most difficult question to answer, as so far the research is most limited here. It seems that the environment has a huge influence on the variability seen in language development in general. What is not known is just how different children who have clinically low language for environmental reasons are to children who have inherited a language disorder. The key questions are as follows: Are there any reliable markers that differentiate these groups? Are some behavioural subgroups seen more often in children from disadvantaged backgrounds? Are there certain types of intervention which are more effective for children from disadvantaged backgrounds? At what level does disadvantage act? Upon the quality and/or quantity of linguistic information available or upon the child's ability to use that information? These questions are ripe for investigation and the effects of disadvantage on language development is potentially an area where researchers, clinicians and teachers together can make a meaningful and lasting impact on children's lives.

Practical tips

1. Variability: analysing individual differences between children with language impairment, rather than focusing on group effects, will help establish the different routes to impairment.
2. Change over time: the changing profiles of individuals with language impairment throughout childhood mean that different diagnostic criteria might be appropriate at different ages.
3. The environment: the extent to which social deprivation might impact on language acquisition will be vital to both explaining and optimally treating impairment.

References

Alloway, T. P. & Archibald, L. (2008). Working memory and learning in children with developmental coordination disorder and specific language impairment. *Journal of Learning and Disability, 41*, 251–262.

Alston, E. & St James-Roberts, I. (2005). Home environments of 10-month-old infants selected by the WILSTAAR screen for pre-language difficulties. *International Journal of Language and Communication Disorders, 40*(2), 123–136.

American Psychiatric Association (1994). *Diagnostic and Statistical Manual of Mental Disorders, 4th edition. (DSM-IV).* Washington, DC: American Psychiatric Association.

——(2013). *Diagnostic and Statistical Manual of Mental Disorders, 5th edition. (DSM-5).* Arlington, VA: American Psychiatric Publishing.

Arkkila, E., Rasanen, P., Roine, R. P. & Vilkman, E. (2008). Specific language impairment in childhood is associated with impaired mental health and social well-being in adulthood. *Logopedics Phoniatrics Vocology, 33*(4), 179–189.

Arvedson, P. J. (2002). Young children with specific language impairment and their numerical reasoning. *Journal of Speech, Language, and Hearing Research, 45*(5), 970–982.

Barry, J. G., Yasin, I. & Bishop, D. V. M. (2007). Heritable risk factors associated with language impairments. *Genes Brain and Behaviour, 6*(1), 66–76.

Beitchman, J. H., Brownlie, E. B., Inglis, A., Wild, J., Ferguson, B., Schachter, D., … Mathews, R. (1996). Seven-year follow-up of speech/language impaired and control children: Psychiatric outcome. *Journal of Child Psychology and Psychiatry, 37*, 961–970.

Beitchman, J. H., Wilson, B., Johnson, C. J., Atkinson, L., Young, A., Adlaf, E., … Douglas, L. (2001). Fourteen-year follow-up of speech/language impaired and control children: Psychiatric outcome. *Journal of the American Academy of Child and Adolescent Psychiatry, 40*(1), 75–82.

Bishop, D. V. M. (1989). Autism, Asperger's syndrome and semantic-pragmatic disorder: Where are the boundaries? *The British Journal of Disorders of Communication, 24*(2), 107–121.

——(2001). Genetic and environmental risks for specific language impairment in children. *Philosophical Transactions of the Royal Society of London, B, 356*, 369–380.

——(2002). Motor immaturity and specific speech and language impairment: Evidence for a common genetic basis. *American Journal for Medical Genetics (Neuropsychiatric Genetics), 114*, 56–63.

——(2005). DeFries-Fulker analysis of twin data with skewed distributions: Cautions and recommendations from a study of children's use of verb inflections. *Behavior Genetics, 35*(4), 479–490.

——(2014; in press). Ten questions about terminology for children with unexplained language problems. *International Journal of Language and Communication Disorders.*

Bishop, D. V. M. & Edmundson, A. (1987). Language-impaired four-year-olds: Distinguishing transient from persistent impairment. *Journal of Speech and Hearing Disorders, 52*, 156–173.

Bishop, D. V. M. & McArthur, G. M. (2004). Immature cortical responses to auditory stimuli in specific language impairment: Evidence from ERPs to rapid tone sequences. *Developmental Science, 7*, F11–F18.

Bishop, D.V.M. & Snowling, M. J. (2004). Developmental Dyslexia and Specific Language Impairment: Same or different? *Psychological Bulletin, 130*(6), 858–886.

Bishop, D. V. M., North, T. & Donlan, C. (1996). Nonword repetition as a behavioural marker for inherited language impairment: Evidence from a twin study. *Journal of Child Psychology and Psychiatry, 37*(4), 391–403.

Bishop, D. V. M., Bishop, S. J., Bright, P., James, C., Delaney, T. & Tallal, P. (1999). Different origin of auditory and phonological processing problems in children with language impairment: Evidence from a twin study. *Journal of Speech, Language, and Hearing Research, 42*, 155–168.

Bishop, D. V. M., Bright, P., James, C., Bishop, S. & van der Lely, H. K. (2000). Grammatical SLI: A distinct subtype of developmental language impairment? *Applied Psycholinguistics, 21*, 159–181.

Bishop, D. V. M., Chan, J., Adams, C., Hartley, J. & Weir, F. (2000). Conversational responsiveness in specific language impairment: Evidence of disproportionate pragmatic difficulties in a subset of children. *Developmental Psychopathology, 12*(2), 177–199.

Botting, N. (2005). Non-verbal cognitive development and language impairment. *Journal of Child Psychology and Psychiatry, 46*(3), 317–326.

——(2007). The relationship between reading skill and descriptive picture narratives in late-primary age children with a history of language impairment. *Educational and Child Psychology, 24*(4), 31–43.

Botting, N. & Conti-Ramsden, G. (1999) Pragmatic language impairment without autism: The children in question. *Autism* 3(4), 371–396.

——(2001). Non-word repetition and language development in children with specific language impairment (SLI). *International Journal of Language and Communication Disorders, 36*(4), 421–432.

Botting, N. & Marshall, C. (in press). Domain-specific and domain-general approaches to developmental disorders: The example of Specific Language Impairment. In D. Williams & L. Centifanti (eds), *Handbook of Developmental Psychpathology*. Oxford: Wiley-Blackwell.

Bradford, A. & Dodd, B. (1994). The motor planning abilities of phonologically disordered children. *European Journal of Disorders of Communication, 29*, 349–369.

——(1996). Do all speech-disordered children have motor deficits? *Clinical Linguistics and Phonetics, 10*, 77–101.

Briscoe, J., Bishop, D. V. M. & Norbury, C. F. (2001). Phonological processing, language and literacy: A comparison of children with mild to moderate sensori-neural hearing loss and those with specific language impairment. *Journal of Child Psychology and Psychiatry, 42*, 329–340.

Bruce, B., Thernlund, G. & Nettebladt, U. (2006). ADHD and language impairment: A study of the parent questionnaire FTF (Five to Fifteen). *European Child and Adolescent Psychiatry, 15*, 52–60.

Camilleri, B. & Botting, N. (2013). Beyond static assessment of children's receptive vocabulary: A dynamic assessment of word learning ability. *International Journal of Language and Communication Disorders, 48*(5), 565–581.

Cantwell, D., Baker. L. & Rutter, M. (1978). Comparative study of infantile autism and specific developmental receptive language disorder 4: Analysis of syntax and language function. *Journal of Child Psychology and Psychiatry, 19*(4), 351–362.

Catts, H. W., Adolf, S. M., Hogan, T. & Weismer, S. E. (2005). Are specific language impairment and dyslexia distinct disorders? *Journal of Speech, Language, and Hearing Research, 48*(6), 1378–1396.

Cermak, S. A., Ward, E. A. & Ward, L. M. (1986). The relationship between articulation disorders and motor coordination in children. *American Journal of Occupational Therapy, 40*, 546–550.

Chen, E., Cohen, S. & Miller, G. E. (2010). How low socioeconomic status affects 2-year hormonal trajectories in children. *Psychological Science, 21*(1), 31–37.

Cohen, N. J., Barwick, M. A., Horodezky, N. B., Vallance, D. D. & Im, N. (1998). Language, achievement, and cognitive processing in psychiatrically disturbed children with previously identified and unsuspected language impairments. *Journal of Child Psychology and Psychiatry, 39*(6), 865–877.

Conti-Ramsden, G. & Botting, N. (1999). Classification of children with specific language impairment: Longitudinal considerations. *Journal of Speech, Language, and Hearing Research, 42*, 1195–1204.

——(2008). Emotional health in adolescents with and without a history of specific language impairment (SLI). *Journal of Child Psychology and Psychiatry, 49*(5), 516–525.

Conti-Ramsden, G., Crutchley, A. & Botting, N. (1997). The extent to which psychometric tests differentiate subgroups of children with SLI. *Journal of Speech, Language, and Hearing Research, 40*, 765–777.

Conti-Ramsden, G., Botting, N. & Faragher, B. (2001a). Psycholinguistic markers of Specific Language Impairment (SLI). *Journal of Child Psychology and Psychiatry, 42*(6), 741–748.

Conti-Ramsden, G., Botting, N., Simkin, Z. & Knox, E. (2001b). Follow-up of children attending infant language units: Outcomes at 11 years of age. *International Journal of Language and Communication Disorders, 36*, 207–219.

Conti-Ramsden, G., Simkin, Z. & Botting, N. (2006). The prevalence of autism spectrum disorders in adolescents with a history of specific language impairment (SLI). *Journal of Child Psychology and Psychiatry, 47*(6), 621–628.

Conti-Ramsden, G., St.Clair, M., Pickles, A. & Durkin, K. (2012). Developmental trajectories of verbal and non-verbal skills in individuals with a history of specific language impairment: From childhood to adolescence. *Journal of Speech, Language and Hearing Research, 55*, 1716–1735.

Corriveau, K. & Goswami, U. (2009). Rhythmic motor entrainment in children with speech and language impairments: Tapping to the beat. *Cognition, 45*, 119–130.

Corriveau, K., Pasquini, E. & Goswami, U. (2007). Basic auditory processing skills and Specific Language Impairment: A new look at an old hypothesis. *Journal of Speech, Language, and Hearing Research, 50*, 647–666.

Dale, P. S., Price, T. S., Bishop, D. V. M. & Plomin, R. (2003). Outcomes of early language delay: I. Predicting persistent and transient language difficulties at 3 and 4 years. *Journal of Speech, Language, and Hearing Research, 46*, 544–560.

de Vasconcelos Hage, S. R., Cendes, F., Montenegro, M. A., Abramides, D. V., Guimaraes, C. A. & Guerreiro, M. M. (2006). Specific language impairment: Linguistic and neurobiological aspects. *Arq Neuropsiquiatr, 64*(2A), 173–180.

Dewey, D. & Wall, K. (1997). Praxis and memory deficits in language-impaired children. *Developmental Neuropsychology, 13*, 507–512.

Dewey, D., Roy, E. A., Square-Storer, P. A. & Hayden, D. (1988). Limb and oral praxic abilities of children with verbal sequencing deficits. *Developmental Medicine and Child Neurology, 30*, 743–751.

Dollaghan, C. & Campbell, T. F. (1998). Nonword repetition and child language impairment. *Journal of Speech, Language, and Hearing Research, 41*, 1136–1146.

Donlan, C., Cowan, R., Newton, E. J. & Lloyd, D. (2007). The role of language in mathematical development: Evidence from children with Specific Language Impairments. *Cognition, 103*(1), 23–33.

Ebbels, S. (2007). Teaching grammar to school-aged children with specific language impairment using shape coding. *Child Language Teaching and Therapy, 23*, 67–93.

Farrell, M. & Phelps, L. (2000). The use of the Leiter-R and UNIT in the assessment of children with language impairments. *Journal of Psychoeducational Assessment, 18*, 268–274.

Finestack, L. H., Richmond, E. K. & Abbeduto, L. (2009). Language development in individuals with Fragile-X Syndrome. *Topics in Language Disorders, 29*(2), 133–148.

Galaburda, A. M., Sherman, G. F., Rosen, G. D., Aboitz, F. & Geschwind, N. (1985). Developmental dyslexia: Four consecutive patients with cortical abnormalities. *Annals of Neurology, 18*(2), 222–233.

Galaburda, A. M., LoTurco, J., Ramus, F., Fitch, R. H. & Rosen, G. D. (2006). From genes to behaviour in developmental dyslexia. *Nature Neuroscience, 9*, 1213–1217.

Gathercole, S. E. & Baddeley, A. D. (1990). Phonological memory deficits in language disordered children: Is there a causal connection? *Journal of Memory & Language, 29*, 336–360.

Gross-Tsur, V., Manor, O. & Shalev, R. S. (1996). Developmental dyscalculia: Prevalence and demographic features. *Developmental Medicine and Child Neurology, 38*(1), 25–33.

Guerreiro, M. M., Hage, S. R., Guimaraes, C. A., Abramides, D. V., Fernandes, W., Pacheco, P. S., ... Cendes, F. (2002). Developmental language disorder associated with polymicrogyria. *Neurology, 59*(2), 245–250.

Hart, B. & Risley, T. R. (1995). *Meaningful Differences in the Everyday Experience of Young American Children*. Baltimore, MD: Paul H. Brookes Publishing Co.

Hasson, N., Dodd, B. & Botting, N. (2012). Dynamic Assessment of Sentence Structure (DASS): Design and evaluation of a novel procedure for assessment of syntax in children with language impairments. *International Journal of Language and Communication Disorders, 47*(3), 285–299.

Haynes, C. & Naidoo, S. (1991). *Children with Specific Speech and Language Impairment*. London: Mac Keith.

Henderson, S. E. & Sugden, D. A. (1992). *Movement Assessment Battery for Children*. Sidcup, UK: Psychological Corporation.

Henry, L. A., Messer, D. J. & Nash, G. (2012). Executive functioning in children with specific language impairment. *Journal of Child Psychology and Psychiatry, 53*(1), 37–45.

Hill, E. L. (1998). A dyspraxic deficit in specific language impairment and developmental coordination disorder? Evidence from hand and arm movements. *Developmental Medicine and Child Neurology, 40*, 388–395.

——(2001). Non-specific nature of specific language impairment: A review of the literature with regard to concomitant motor impairments. *International Journal of Language and Communication Disorders, 36*(2), 149–171.

Hill, E. L., Bishop, D. V. M. & Nimmo-Smith, I. (1998). Representational gestures in developmental co-ordination disorder and specific language impairment: Error-types and the reliability of ratings. *Human Movement Science*, 17, 655–678.

Hill, P. R., Hogben, J. H. & Bishop, D. M. (2005). Auditory frequency discrimination in children with specific language impairment. *Journal of Speech, Language, and Hearing Research, 48*(5), 1136–1146.

Hoff, E. & Naigles, L. (2002). How children use input to acquire a lexicon. *Child Development, 73*(2), 418–433.

Johnson, C. J., Beitchman, J. H. & Brownlie, E. B. (2010). Twenty-year follow-up of children with and without speech-language impairments: Family, educational, occupational, and quality of life outcomes. *American Journal of Speech-Language Pathology, 19*, 51–65.

Karmiloff-Smith, A. (1998). Development itself is the key to developmental disorders. *Trends in Cognitive Sciences, 2*(10), 389–398.

Kjelgaard, M. M. & Tager-Flusberg, H. (2001). An investigation of language impairment in autism: Implications for genetic subgroups. *Language and Cognitive Processes, 16*(2–3), 287–308.

Krassowski, E. & Plante, E. (1997). IQ variability in children with SLI: Implications for use of cognitive referencing in determining SLI. *Journal of Communication Disorders, 30*, 1–9.

Law, J., Lee, W., Roulstone, S., Wren, Y., Zeng, B. & Lindsay, G. (2012). *What Works: Interventions for Children and Young People with Speech, Language and Communication Needs*. London: Department for Education.

Martin, G. E., Klusek, J., Estigarribia, B. & Roberts, J. E. (2009). Language characteristics of individuals with Down Syndrome. *Topics in Language Disorders, 29*(2), 112–132.

Marton, K. (2008). Visuo-spatial processing and executive functions in children with specific language impairment. *International Journal of Language and Communication Diorders, 43*(2), 181–200.

Mawhood, L., Howlin, P. & Rutter, M. (2000). Autism and developmental receptive language disorder – a comparative follow up in early adult life: I – cognitive and language outcomes. *Journal of Child Psychology and Psychiatry, 41*, 547–559.

McArthur, G. & Bishop, D. V. M. (2004). Frequency discrimination deficits in people with specific language impairment: Reliability, validity, and linguistic correlates. *Journal of Speech, Language, and Hearing Research, 47*(3), 527–541.

Miller, C. A., Kail, R., Leonard, L. & Tomblin, J. B. (2001). Speed of processing in children with specific language impairment. *Journal of Speech, Language, and Hearing Research, 44*, 416–433.

Molfese, V. J., Modglin, A. & Molfese, D. L. (2003). The role of environment in the development of reading skills: A longitudinal study of preschool and school-age measures. *Journal of Learning Disabilities, 36*(1), 59–67.

Noble, K. G., McCandliss, B. D. & Farah, M. J. (2007). Socioeconomic gradients predict individual differences in neurocognitive abilities. *Developmental Science, 10*(4), 464–480.

Owen, S. E. & McKinlay, I. A. (1997). Motor difficulties in children with developmental disorders of speech and language. *Child: Care, Health and Development, 23*, 315–325.

Paul, R. (1996). Clinical implications of the natural history of slow expressive language development. *American Journal of Speech-Language Pathology, 5*, 5–21.

——(2001). *Language Disorders from Infants through Adolescence: Assessment and Intervention.* Philadelphia, PA: Mosby.

Paul, R. & Cohen, D. (1984). Outcome of severe disorders of language acquisition. *Journal of Autism and Developmental Disorders, 14*, 405–421.

Powell, R. P. & Bishop, D. V. M. (1992). Clumsiness and perceptual problems in children with specific language impairment. *Developmental Medicine and Child Neurology, 34*, 755–765.

Pruitt, S. & Oetting, J. (2009). Past tense marking by African-American English speaking children reared in poverty. *Journal of Speech, Language, and Hearing Research, 52*(1), 2–15.

Rapin, I. & Allen, D. (1983). Developmental language disorders: Nosologic considerations. In U. Kirk (ed.), *Neuropsychology of Language, Reading, and Spelling* (pp. 155–184). New York: Academic Press.

Rapin, I. & Dunn, M. (2003). Update on the language disorders of individuals on the autistic spectrum. *Brain & Development, 25*, 166–172.

Reilly, S., Tomblin, B., Law, J., McKean, C., Mensah, F. K., …Wake, M. (in press; 2014) Specific Language Impairment: A convenient label for whom? *International Journal of Language and Communication Disorders.*

Rescorla, L., Dahlsgaard, K. & Roberts, J. (2000). Late-talking toddlers: MLU and IPSyn outcomes at 3;0 and 4;0. *Journal of Child Language, 27*, 643–664.

Rice, M. L. (2000). Grammatical symptoms of specific language impairment. In D. M. V. Bishop & L. B. Leonard (eds), *Speech and Language Impairments in Children: Causes, Characteristics, Intervention and Outcome* (pp. 17–34). New York, NY: Psychology Press.

Rice, M. L., Wexler, K. & Cleave, P. L. (1995). Specific language impairment as a period of extended optional infinitive. *Journal of Speech, Language, and Hearing Research, 38*(4), 850–863.

Rice, M. L., Tomblin, J. B., Hoffman, L., Richman, W. A. & Marquis, J. (2004). Grammatical tense deficits in children with SLI and non-specific language impairment: Relationships with nonverbal IQ over time. *Journal of Speech, Language, and Hearing Research, 47,* 816–834.

Roberts, M. Y. & Kaiser, A. P. (2011). The effectiveness of parent-implemented language interventions: A meta-analysis. *American Journal of Speech-Language Pathology, 20,* 180–199.

Robinson, R. J. (1991). Causes and associations of severe and persistent specific speech and language disorders in children. *Developmental Medicine and Child Neurology, 33,* 943–962.

Rosen, S. (2003). Auditory processing in dyslexia and specific language impairment: Is there a deficit? What is its nature? Does it explain anything? *Journal of Phonetics, 31,* 509–527.

Rosen, S., Adlard, A. & van der Lely, H. K. (2009). Backward and simultaneous masking in children with grammatical specific language impairment: No simple link between auditory and language ability. *Journal of Speech, Language, and Hearing Research, 52*(2), 396–411.

Rowe, M., Raudenbush, S. W. & Goldin-Meadow, S. (2012). The pace of vocabulary growth helps predict later vocabulary skill. *Child Development, 83*(2), 508–525.

Stanton-Chapman, T. L., Chapman, D. A., Bainbridge, N. L. & Scott, K. G. (2002). Identification of early risk factors for language impairment. *Research in Developmental Disabilities, 23,* 390–405.

Stark, R. E. & Tallal, P. (1981). Selection of children with specific language deficits. *Journal of Speech and Hearing Disorders, 46,* 114–180.

Stevens, C., Sanders, L. & Neville, H. (2006). Neurophysiological evidence for selective auditory attention deficits in children with specific language impairment. *Brain Research, 1111,* 143–152.

Stevens, C., Lauinger, B. & Neville, H. (2009). Differences in the neural mechanisms of selective attention in children from different socioeconomic backgrounds: An event-related brain potential study. *Developmental Science, 12*(4), 634–646.

Tallal, P. (1980). Auditory temporal perception, phonics and reading disabilities in children. *Brain and Language, 9,* 182–198.

Tamis-LeMonda, C. S., Bornstein, M. H. & Baumwell, L. (2001). Maternal responsiveness and children's achievement of language milestones. *Child Development, 72*(3), 748–767.

Tanner, E. M. & Finn-Stevenson, M. (2002). Nutrition and brain development: Social policy implications. *American Journal of Orthopsychiatry, 72*(2), 182–193.

Thomas, M. S. C. & Karmiloff-Smith, A. (2002). Residual normality: Friend or foe? *Behavioural and Brain Sciences, 25*(6), 772–780.

Thomas, M. S. C & Knowland, V. (2014). Modelling mechanisms of persisting and resolving delay in language development. *Journal of Speech, Language, and Hearing Research, 57*(2), 467–483.

Tomblin, J. B. (1997). Epidemiology of specific language impairment: Prenatal and perinatal risk factors. *Journal of Communication Disorders, 30*(4), 325–344.

Tomblin, J. B., Freese, P. & Records, N. (1992). Diagnosing specific language impairment in adults for the purpose of pedigree analysis. *Journal of Speech, Language, and Hearing Research, 35,* 832–843.

Tomblin, J. B., Records, N. L., Buckwalter, P., Zhang, X. & Smith, E. (1997). Prevalence of specific language impairment in kindergarten children. *Journal of Speech, Language, and Hearing Research, 40,* 1245–1260.

Ullman, M. T. & Pierpoint, E. I. (2005). Specific Language Impairment is not specific to language: The procedural deficit hypothesis. *Cortex, 41*, 399–433.

van der Lely, H. K. J. (1997). Language and cognitive development in a Grammatical SLI boy: Modularity and innateness. *Journal of Neurolinguistics, 10*, 75–107.

van der Lely, H., Rosen, S. & Adlard, A. (2004). Grammatical language impairment and the specificity of cognitive domains: Relations between auditory and language abilities. *Cognition, 94*(2), 167–183.

van Weerdenburg, M., Verhoeven, L. & van Balkam, H. (2006). Towards a topology of specific language impairment. *Journal of Child Psychology and Psychiatry, 47*(2), 176–189.

Ward, S. (1999). An investigation into the effectiveness of an early intervention method for delayed language development in young children. *International Journal of Language and Communication Disorders, 34*, 243–264.

Westerlund, M., Bergkvist, L., Lagerberg, D. & Sundelin, C. (2002). Comorbidity in children with severe developmental language disability. *Acta Paediatrica, 91*, 529–534.

Whitehurst, G. J. & Fischel, J. E. (1994). Early developmental language delay: What if anything should the clinician do about it? *Journal of Child Psychology and Psychiatry, 35*, 613–648.

Williams, D., Stott, C. M., Goodyer, I. M. & Sahakian, B. J. (2000). Specific language impairment with or without hyperactivity: Neuropsychological evidence for frontostriatal dysfunction. *Developmental Medicine and Child Neurology, 42*(6), 368–375.

Williams, D., Botting, N. & Boucher, J. (2008). Language in autism and specific language impairment: Where are the links? *Psychological Bulletin, 134*, 944–963.

World Health Organization (2008). *ICD-10: International statistical Classification of Diseases and Related Health Problems.* New York, NY: World Health Organization.

Wright, B. A., Lombardino, L. J., King, W. M., Puranik, C. S., Leonard, C. M. & Merzenich, M. M. (1997). Deficits in auditory temporal and spectral resolution in language-impaired children. *Nature, 387*, 176–178.

9

COMORBIDITY IN NEURO-DEVELOPMENTAL DISORDERS

Evidence from ADHD

Sinead Rhodes

9.1 Introduction

Attention Deficit Hyperactivity Disorder (ADHD) is a common neurodevelopmental disorder that shows high rates of co-occurrence, known as comorbidity, with other disorders such as Autism Spectrum Disorders (ASD: see Chapter 7 for a detailed discussion) and disruptive behaviour disorders. Diagnostic systems rely on categorical decisions; comorbidity is even more marked when symptoms are considered on a dimensional basis. The presence of co-occurring symptoms or disorders is a feature of most, if not all, neurodevelopmental disorders and can be described as 'the rule not the exception' (Youngstrom, Arnold & Frazier, 2010). Comorbidity influences the broad psychological profile of individuals with disorders including cognitive, social and behaviour profiles. An understanding of the effect of comorbidity is therefore vital to interpreting research where the inference is that the child shows sole symptoms of a specific disorder. Most studies do not differentiate individuals with ADHD in relation to the presence or absence of other disorders such as ASD (Taurines et al., 2012). In this chapter, ADHD will be used to illustrate the influence of comorbidity on the psychological profiles of children with neurodevelopmental disorders. The review is not exhaustive and focusses at the level of cognition and behaviour, without significant reference to biological and/or genetic factors. Areas of functioning within those levels are also selective for brevity, e.g. language development is not covered. The review of the literature will emphasise a need for future research to fully characterise their sample in relation to the range of comorbidities participants may show and in order to fully understand their psychological profile.

9.2 ADHD: psychological profile

ADHD is the most common pervasive developmental disorder among school-aged children (Woo & Keatinge, 2008). The disorder is characterised by persistent symptoms of inattention, hyperactivity and impulsivity that impact negatively on many aspects of functioning and development including family, social and academic areas of a child's life (Biederman, 2005) and are evident in at least two settings, typically school and home. ADHD is common with a worldwide prevalence of around 5.3 percent for children and adolescents (Polanczyk, de Lima, Horta, Biederman & Rohde, 2007) with estimates in the UK ranging between 3 and 9 per cent (NICE, 2008). ADHD often continues into adulthood with an estimated 2 to 4 per cent of adults still presenting with significant symptoms (e.g. Fayyad et al., 2007). ADHD and the associated problem behaviours are a significant issue for our wider society, as well as for families and schools (e.g. Johnston & Ohan, 2005).

ADHD is a heterogeneous disorder with no single explanatory risk factor (Banaschewski et al., 2005; Coghill, Nigg, Rothenberger, Sonuga-Barke & Tannock, 2005). It is now clear that ADHD is associated with multiple structural and functional alterations throughout the brain and a broad range of cognitive and social impairments (Coghill et al., 2005; Uekermann et al., 2010). It is also now generally accepted that both genetic and environmental influences contribute to causality and that their effects are inter-independent. Heritability is estimated at around 0.76 and there are clear familial associations (Faraone et al., 2005). It is a clinically heterogeneous disorder with high rates of comorbidity with a range of psychiatric and neurodevelopmental conditions (Rommelse et al., 2009; Willcutt, Sonuga-Barke, Nigg & Sergeant, 2008).

In studies with clinical samples of ADHD children, it has been reported that between one-quarter and one-third show symptoms of ADHD in the absence of other disorders (24 per cent: Rhodes, Coghill & Matthews, 2005; 32 per cent: Takeda, Ambrosini, deBerardinis & Elia, 2012), and therefore, the presence of a comorbid disorder is really the norm rather than the exception. There appears to be an important overlap with other psychiatric, and in particular neurodevelopmental, disorders; especially oppositional defiant disorder (ODD)/conduct disorder (CD), ASD, and developmental co-ordination disorder (DCD), but also anxiety (see Chapter 14), depression, bipolar disorder and schizophrenia (Rommelse et al., 2009; Smoller et al., 2013; Yoshimasu et al., 2012). Such comorbidity effects psychological functioning. Crucially, children with ADHD and comorbid conditions tend to be more impaired in their daily functioning, have poorer outcomes, and show greater difficulties in a range of psychological areas than children with ADHD alone (Biederman et al., 1996; Connor et al., 2003; Gillberg et al., 2004; Rommelse et al., 2009; Spencer, 2006).

Current causal models of cognitive function suggest that ADHD is not characterised by a single cognitive impairment and is instead associated with multiple neuropsychological 'endophenotypes' including various aspects of executive functions, delay aversion, temporal processing and response variability (Castellanos, Sonuga-Barke, Milham & Tannock, 2006; Kasper, Alderson & Hudec, 2012; Rhodes, Coghill & Matthews, 2004, 2005; Rhodes, Park, Seth & Coghill, 2012; Willcutt et al., 2008). Accumulating evidence suggests that there is significant causal heterogeneity in ADHD (Coghill et al., 2005) with altered functioning of dopaminergic and noradrenergic pathways across multiple neural networks including the prefrontal cortex and connecting areas. Executive functions are, in particular, consistently implicated in ADHD with impaired function observed across core areas of inhibition, working memory, and set-shifting, in addition to planning deficits (Gau & Shang, 2010; Rhodes et al., 2005). Emotionally salient aspects of executive function have also been implicated such as decision making and risk taking (Groen, Gaastra, Lewis-Evans & Tucha, 2013), referred to as 'hot' executive functions in the literature. Executive function profiles in ADHD have been shown to be highly sensitive to the presence of comorbid disorders and are indeed a core feature of other neurodevelopmental disorders (e.g. ASD). The nature of how this co-occurrence influences executive function profiles will be addressed later in this chapter.

Neuropsychological heterogeneity exists and while ADHD samples show consistent impairments in executive functions, delay aversion, temporal processing and response variability as a group, more in-depth analyses have revealed that there is significant individual variation and not all children with the disorder will show impairments in each of these areas (e.g. Coghill, 2010; Fair, Bathula, Nikolas & Nigg, 2012). It has been argued, however, that typically developing children could be classified into distinct neuropsychological profiles and that the heterogeneity observed in ADHD samples falls within this normal variation (Fair et al., 2012). Heterogeneity can also be linked to the presence or absence or severity of inattentive or hyperactive/impulsive symptoms. While ADHD combined subtype (whereby children show both inattentive and hyperactive/impulsive symptoms) is the most common diagnosis, research samples may also include children with the inattentive or the hyperactive/impulsive subtype only. This distinction is important because there is some evidence that inattention but not hyperactivity/impulsivity is associated with working memory impairment (Martinussen, Hayden, Hogg-Johnson & Tannock, 2005) and delay aversion is more consistently linked to hyperactivity/impulsivity but not inattention (Sonuga-Barke, Dalen & Remington, 2003). A further reason for this heterogeneity could of course reflect the presence of comorbid conditions, which will vary considerably amongst ADHD children; this point will be returned to in the later section on the influence of comorbidity on the cognitive profile of ADHD.

Research on social cognition in ADHD is much more limited than cognitive/neuropsychological functioning. This is surprising given the high rate of comorbidity between ADHD, ASD and Williams syndrome (Gillberg et al., 2004; Rhodes, Riby, Park, Fraser & Campbell, 2010; Rhodes, Riby, Matthews & Coghill, 2011; Taurines et al., 2012), and the growing literature on atypical social cognition in these neurodevelopmental disorders (e.g. Riby, Hancock, Jones & Hanley, 2013; see Chapter 12 for a full discussion). Most researchers who have examined psychological functioning in ADHD samples have focussed on cognitive aspects of functioning to the neglect of aspects of social cognition, such as theory of mind (TOM) and affect perception (Uekermann et al., 2010). Although limited, the available research suggests impairments in the perception of emotional prosody and faces, empathy, and TOM in ADHD samples (Dickstein & Castellanos, 2012; Uekermann et al., 2010). Some evidence for impaired identification of affective prosody has been reported (Corbett & Glidden, 2000) and other research has reported impairments in facial affect recognition and identification of threat-related emotional expressions (Sinzig, Morsch & Lehmkuhl, 2008b; Williams et al., 2008). Evidence for TOM impairment in ADHD samples is inconsistent with some reporting impairment (Buitelaar, Van der Wees, Swaab-Barneveld & Van der Gaag, 1999; Sodian, Hulsken & Thoermer, 2003) and others reporting no differences between ADHD and control samples (Charman, Carroll & Sturge, 2001; Dyck, Ferguson & Schochet, 2001). Evidence for social cognitive impairments in ADHD is generally mixed and further research is required to investigate if inconsistent findings relate to use of samples with different subtypes of ADHD (Uekermann et al., 2010). There also remains the possibility that the presence of comorbid conditions, in particular the presence or absence of ASD traits, is responsible for this inconsistency. While some of the research in this area has not examined comorbidities (e.g. Corbett & Glidden, 2000), others directly compare ADHD samples to those with ADHD and comorbid ASD (e.g. Buitelaar et al., 1999; Dyck et al., 2001; Sinzig, Morsch, Bruning, Schmidt & Lehmkuhl 2008a, Sinzig et al., 2008b; Tye et al., 2013a, 2013b). The influence of this comorbidity on the social cognitive profile of children with ADHD will be an important focus of the current chapter and particular focus will be given to research papers that have compared both disorders with the inclusion of the additive disorder.

The current chapter review is not exhaustive and will focus specifically on the comorbidity between ADHD with ASD and with the disruptive behaviour disorders ODD/CD as the more common examples of comorbid conditions observed in children with ADHD (Rommelse et al., 2009). The current chapter will first examine broader issues relating to comorbidity conceptually before exploring the cognitive and social cognitive literatures relating to these specific conditions when comorbid with ADHD.

9.3 Comorbidity in neurodevelopmental disorders

The term 'comorbidity' was first introduced to refer to the co-occurrence of two separate disorders (Feinstein, 1970), a co-occurrence that is higher than would be expected by chance (Banaschewski, Neale, Rothenberger & Roessner, 2007). Children with one neurodevelopmental disorder commonly show symptoms of another disorder. Clinicians and researchers employ a number of different techniques to decide which diagnosis is primary, or the core diagnosis (Youngstrom et al., 2010); such as on the basis of which arose first developmentally, which led to the child being referred to the clinical service, or in relation to severity. Children with ADHD, in particular, show very high rates of symptoms of other disorders to the point that calls into question the diagnostic systems (DSM and ICD) used to characterise the disorder. Diagnostic systems (i.e. DSM, ICD) rely on categorical decisions; co-occurrence is even more marked when disorders are considered on a dimensional basis with many individuals with a diagnosed developmental disorder showing 'sub-clinical' symptoms of another disorder (e.g. five inattention symptoms of ADHD; whereas six symptoms are required for a confirmed clinical diagnosis). For the purposes of this chapter, comorbidity will be defined on a categorical approach; given it is the norm in the literature.

Comorbidity has been attributed to various causes including those of an 'artifactual' and 'non-artifactual' basis (Banaschewski et al., 2007; Caron & Rutter, 1991; Neale & Kendler, 1995). Artifactual comorbidity may arise for a number of reasons; including overlapping diagnostic criteria (Caron & Rutter, 1991) or because they are part of a 'clinical' (rather than epidemiological) sample. An example of the latter has been illustrated in the case of ADHD and paediatric bipolar disorder (Youngstrom et al., 2010); the non-specificity of ADHD symptoms such as poor concentration and impulsiveness are common features of several other disorders including bipolar disorder. Other possibilities include use of categorical labels where dimensions are more appropriate (Youngstrom et al., 2010), and referral or ascertainment biases whereby untrained raters may be more likely to diagnose ADHD symptoms in children with another disorder (Banaschewski et al., 2007). However, these possibilities are unlikely to fully account for comorbidity; population-based epidemiological studies have shown that neurodevelopmental and psychiatric disorders cluster within the same individual more than would be expected by chance (Angold, Costello & Erkanli, 1999; Caron & Rutter, 1991; Costello, Foley & Angold, 2006; Galanter & Leibenluft, 2008; Klein & Riso, 1993; Neale & Kendler, 1995).

A number of non-artifactual based reasons have been proposed to explain comorbidity (Caron & Rutter, 1991; Banaschewski et al., 2007; Neale & Kendler, 1995). A common suggestion in the literature, referred to as 'phenocopy' or 'phenomimicry' (Bishop, 2010), is the possibility that comorbidity arises when symptoms of a disorder cause or mimic the symptoms of another disorder. This could occur, for example, if motor tics were mistaken as excessive motor activity and interpreted as ADHD symptoms (Banaschewski et al., 2007). Another possibility is that the disorders share a common underlying etiology. A comorbid condition may represent a separate disorder, and be a phenotypically distinct subtype with each of the three disorders representing an independent disorder (e.g. ADHD, ASD, ADHD + ASD). A more common view is that the co-occurrence reflects an additive component of two separate diagnoses that could represent a 'true' comorbidity. A number of researchers and theorists in developmental disorders have considered, and in some cases applied, these hypotheses to the study of ADHD and comorbid conditions (Angold et al., 1999; Banaschewski et al., 2007; Caron & Rutter, 1991; Gillberg et al., 2004; Rhodes et al., 2012). Later in the chapter, research findings in the area of cognition and social cognitive functioning will be examined to determine whether they fit best within a distinct or additive subtype account. In order to fully examine this, research will be drawn on where ADHD samples without comorbidity are compared with samples with comorbidity (ODD/CD or ASD). Some studies have used 2x2 designs with

ADHD samples with and without the comorbid condition (e.g. ADHD, ADHD + ODD, ODD: Rhodes et al., 2012; and ADHD, ADHD + ASD, ASD: Tye et al., 2013a, 2013b) to examine and disentangle the psychological profile in ADHD and comorbid conditions. While only a limited number of studies have incorporated such a design, the next section of the chapter will draw on these wherever possible to help elucidate the influence of comorbidity on psychological functioning in neurodevelopmental disorders.

9.4 ADHD and comorbidity

ADHD is commonly comorbid with a range of other conditions (Gillberg et al., 2004; Rommelse et al., 2009; van Steensel, Bögels & de Bruin, 2013), including both neurodevelopmental disorders (e.g. ASD) and other psychological disorders (e.g. bipolar disorder). Children with ADHD with comorbid problems compared to those with ADHD without comorbid problems appear to have a more severe form of ADHD. Rommelse et al. (2009) reported that having a more severe form of ADHD was associated with having more severe oppositional defiant behaviours, higher levels of anxiety, more autistic traits and more severe motor co-ordination and reading problems. Children with ADHD with comorbid problems are also often more impaired in their daily functioning, and have a poorer long-term prognosis (Bauermeister et al., 2007; Biederman et al., 1996; Connor et al., 2003; Gadow et al., 2009; Gillberg et al., 2004).

The most common disorders to co-occur with ADHD are: ODD/CD (Rhodes et al., 2004), ASD (Jang et al., 2013; Rommelse, Geurts, Franke, Buitelaar & Hartman 2011; Taurines et al., 2012; Tye et al., 2013a, 2013b), specific language impairment (SLI) (Williams, Stott, Goodyer & Sahakian, 2000), and Tic disorder (Banaschewski et al., 2007). Children and adults with Williams syndrome (WS) also commonly show symptoms of ADHD (Rhodes et al., 2010, 2011). WS is a rare genetic disorder (for a detailed discussion see Chapter 12) and therefore, the commonality does not work the other way around (most children with ADHD do not have WS). Thus, while ADHD symptoms are highly prevalent in WS, this comparison will not form a key focus of the current chapter. For brevity, the current chapter will focus on the disorders that most commonly co-occur with ADHD, namely disruptive behaviour disorders (ODD, CD) and ASD, and for which comparisons of functioning are available in the literature. Significant variability in the co-occurrence of these disorders is observed across studies. Nonetheless, their co-occurrence is generally very high across studies. Reports on the co-occurrence of ADHD and ODD/CD vary from 42 per cent to as much as 90 per cent (e.g. Angold et al., 1999; Bauermeister et al., 2007; Gillberg et al., 2004; Jensen, Martin & Cantwell, 1997; Rhodes et al., 2005). A focus on the comorbidity between ADHD and ASD may seem somewhat surprising given that a dual diagnosis of ASD and ADHD was precluded within DSM-IV. Their co-occurrence, while close but not quite as high as ODD/CD, is common with reports varying from 45 per cent to as high as 87 per cent (Ames & White, 2011;

Clark, Feehan, Tinline & Vostanis, 1999; de Bruin, Ferdinand, Meester, de Nijs & Verheij, 2007; Gillberg et al., 2004). Non-clinical sample studies within the general population suggest a lower rate of co-occurrence with 28 per cent of children with ASD having comorbid ADHD (Simonoff et al., 2008). Nevertheless, co-occurrence is still clearly high between the two disorders and accumulating evidence suggests significant clinical, genetic and cognitive overlap between ADHD and ASD (Rommelse et al., 2011). Accordingly, DSM-5 recognises the high rates of comorbidity of these two disorders and no longer precludes their co-occurrence.

9.5 Influence of comorbidity on psychological profile of children with ADHD

The neuropsychological literature on ADHD over the last fifteen years or so has predominantly focussed on executive functions to explain the cognitive difficulties of children with ADHD. Executive function impairments are not specific to ADHD however, and indeed impairments in a number of aspects of executive functions have been documented in children with ASD and ODD/CD. Researchers have consistently reported executive function impairments in children with ASD, with the most consistent characterisation focussed on attention shifting and planning impairments (Corbett, Constantine, Hendren, Rocke & Ozonoff, 2009; Pellicano, 2007). Children with ADHD tend to show a broader executive function impairment profile (e.g. impairments across more areas of executive function), including working memory (Rhodes et al., 2004, 2005, 2012) and inhibitory control (Sinzig et al., 2008a). Inhibitory impairment has been much more inconsistently reported in ASD samples (Happé, Booth, Charlton & Hughes, 2006; Corbett et al., 2009; Taurines et al., 2012). While both ADHD and ASD samples appear to show executive function impairment therefore, the specific profile appears to be different between the two disorders.

Such differences in executive function impairment between ADHD and ASD raise the question of how the presence of both conditions influences this profile. While few studies have examined ADHD samples with and without comorbid ASD, the available studies provide inconsistent evidence. Nydén et al. (2010) examined executive function profiles in adults with ADHD, ASD and ADHD + ASD. The authors reported similar planning performance on a Tower of London task across all groups. In contrast, another study has suggested differences in the specific profile of the two disorders with an additive effect observed in the comorbid condition. Sinzig et al. (2008a) compared children (aged six to eighteen years) with ADHD, ADHD + ASD, ASD, and typically developing children on tests of inhibition, working memory, flexibility and planning. Children in the ADHD group showed inhibition and working memory impairments, while children with ASD showed difficulties in planning. The children with comorbid ADHD and ASD performed the same as those in the ADHD group supporting the idea of an additive effect of the comorbid diagnoses on executive function performance. As well as contrasting with the findings of Nydén et al. (2010), it should also be noted that several studies have reported planning impairments in children with ADHD including those with large, well-characterised and drug naïve samples (Kempton et al., 1999; Rhodes et al., 2005). Inconsistent findings may relate to the age of the participant samples as Nydén et al.'s (2010) findings are reported in an adult group. A recent study examined a range of discrete aspects of executive function (attention orienting, inhibition, conflict monitoring and response preparation) while recording ERPs in children with ADHD, ADHD + ASD, ASD, and typically developing children (Tye et al., 2013a). The authors reported dissociation in the executive function profile of children with ADHD and ASD; children with ADHD showed impaired attention orienting and inhibitory control, whereas children with ASD showed impaired conflict monitoring and response preparation. Children with both ADHD and ASD generally showed an additive profile with impairments observed for both disorders. Collectively, research in this area suggests differences in the executive function profiles of ADHD and ASD with a composite of the difficulties observed in the comorbid condition, thus supporting additive models of comorbidity.

Research on other aspects of functioning known to be impaired in ADHD, with ADHD and ASD samples, is highly limited. However, there is some evidence that the marked delay aversion impairment seen in ADHD samples is not observed in ASD samples. Antrop et al. (2006) reported no difference in choice in small immediate and large delayed rewards between children with ASD and typically developing children. Demurie, Roeyers, Baeyens & Sonuga-Barke (2011) examined the effect of reward on performance of a reaction time task (adapted version of the Monetary Incentive Delay task) in children with ADHD, ASD, and controls and reported that both children with ADHD and ASD responded faster for monetary than social rewards. The findings suggest that both children with ADHD and children with ASD are less motivated in settings where social rewards can be gained. A further study conducted by the same authors (Demurie, Roeyers, Baeyens & Sonuga-Barke, 2012), however, showed that children with ASD were similar to typically developing children in performance on a hypothetical monetary temporal discounting task, while children with ADHD discounted future rewards at a higher rate than typically developing children. Taurines et al. (2012) concluded that while most studies include aberrant reward processing in ASD as well as ADHD, the impairment in ASD samples may be less than the deficit observed in ADHD samples. Research in this area is limited and precise conclusions about the effects of comorbidity on reward processing await further experimentation.

A number of researchers have now examined the effects of comorbid disruptive behaviour disorders on the profile of children with ADHD. Most research studies that have examined cognitive functioning in children with ADHD with or without the presence of ODD/CD have focussed on inhibitory control. This research suggests that inhibitory impairments are not unique to ADHD but are also a feature of these disruptive behaviour conditions (Oosterlaan, Logan & Sergeant, 1998; Scheres, Oosterlaan & Sergeant, 2001).

Studies employing other executive function tasks are few in number and have produced inconsistent findings. Oosterlaan, Scheres & Sergeant (2005) examined verbal fluency, working memory and planning in children with ADHD while controlling for the presence of comorbid ODD/CD. The authors reported that ADHD was associated with impaired working memory and planning independent of ODD/CD. In contrast to this profile, the presence of ODD/CD was not associated with any impairment in executive functions. Van Goozen et al. (2004) examined working memory in children with a diagnosis of ODD/CD with and without comorbid ADHD and reported no significant impairments in working memory or other associated executive functions such as planning and inhibition. It is difficult to interpret these findings as it is highly unusual that the comorbid ADHD + ODD/CD group in the study did not show impairments in working memory or inhibition which have been consistently shown in the literature (e.g. Martinussen et al., 2005; Rhodes et al., 2004, 2005; Willcutt, Doyle, Nigg, Faraone & Pennington, 2005).

A more recent study contradicts the findings of Oosterlaan et al. (2005) and Van Goozen et al. (2004) in relation to the lack of impairment in children with disruptive behaviour disorders. Rhodes et al. (2012) compared children with ADHD, ADHD + ODD, and ODD and reported working memory impairment across the three groups with some differences between the groups. A comprehensive approach to the examination of memory across these groups enabled a detailed working memory profile for each of the groups. This study revealed that ODD was characterised by impaired working memory performance but that the disorder was more closely associated with verbal memory impairments than ADHD. Rhodes et al. (2012) concluded that ADHD and ODD have an additive effect on memory functioning and that the combination of ADHD + ODD represents a true comorbidity rather than a separate clinical entity. Children with ADHD + ODD were more consistently, and more severely, impaired across the various aspects of working memory than boys in either of the 'pure' groups. Similar findings for an additive effect are available in the literature. Rommelse et al. (2009) examined inhibition, attention shifting, as well as verbal and visuo-spatial working memory in a large sample of children with ADHD who had a variety of comorbid conditions. The authors reported that the interaction between ADHD and comorbid conditions (including ODD and ASD) did not have predictive value on their executive function profile beyond the independent effects of ADHD, suggesting that comorbidity results in an 'additive effect'.

Collectively these findings support the idea of comorbid conditions in ADHD as reflecting an additive combination of the two disorders, resulting in 'more of the same' (a more severe form of ADHD and comorbid problem) rather than a phenotypically distinct subtype. Further research is warranted across aspects of cognitive functioning, moving beyond executive function, to determine if this additive combination reflects the broad cognitive profile of ADHD.

Very few comparative studies have examined social cognitive functioning across ADHD and comorbid groups. Studies that have examined social cognitive functioning within ADHD samples suggest impairments in some areas and not others (Rommelse et al., 2011; Uekermann et al., 2010). There is still a highly limited literature comparing social cognition across ADHD and ASD samples

(Taurines et al., 2012). While it is well established that children with ASD show impairment in ToM (Baron-Cohen, Lesley & Frith, 1985; Happé, 1995), evidence for ToM impairments in ADHD samples across this limited literature is mixed. Nyden et al. (2010) compared adults with ADHD, ADHD + ASD, and ASD and reported no differences in ToM abilities between the groups. However, another comparative study reported that ToM impairments were observed in an ASD group but not an ADHD group (Dyck et al., 2001). Ames and White (2011) examined children with ASD on twelve tests of ToM and related the findings to ASD and ADHD symptoms provided by parents using semi-structured parental interviews. The authors reported that ToM abilities were more strongly associated with ASD than ADHD symptoms in individuals with ADHD + ASD (Ames & White, 2011). In a review of the literature, it was concluded that the weight of evidence suggests that children with ADHD do not show ToM impairments (Geurts, Broeders & Nieuwland, 2010).

Research studies examining other aspects of social cognitive functioning across ADHD and ASD samples, such as emotion recognition, have also produced some evidence for impaired function in ADHD children. Sinzig et al. (2008b) reported that children with ADHD and ADHD + ASD were impaired in facial affect recognition but the ASD-only group showed no impairment. A recent study used ERPs to examine responses to face and gaze direction in children with ADHD, ADHD + ASD, and ASD (Tye et al., 2013b). The authors reported that the disorders were associated with distinct abnormalities. Children with ASD showed abnormalities on the face-sensitive N170 component in relation to hemispheric distribution and processing of gaze direction. Children with ADHD in contrast showed a similar response to upright and inverted faces on the latency of the P1 component representing a reduced effect of face inversion. Children with both conditions showed an additive combination of both abnormalities. The findings of this study thus concur with executive function studies that have suggested that the co-occurrence of the disorders reflects a 'true' comorbidity rather than a distinct subtype.

9.6 Conclusions

The current review of the literature highlights the high rate of comorbidity of neurodevelopmental disorders like ADHD with other neurodevelopmental and psychiatric conditions. The presence of these conditions influences the psychological profile of children with the disorder, in areas including cognition and social cognitive functioning and beyond. Children with comorbid neurodevelopmental disorders, at least in the case of ADHD, appear to show 'more of the same' characteristics of both disorders. Most of the comparative disorder research studies provide evidence that the co-occurrence of disorders produces an additive effect or 'true' comorbidity. The current review points to a need for research studies to fully characterise their samples in relation to the range of comorbidities their participants are likely to show in order to fully understand their psychological profile.

Practical tips

1. *Recruitment and diagnosis*: Children with ADHD are typically recruited via clinical services or within the community (e.g. schools). Regardless of where children are recruited from, parent and teacher confirmation of ADHD is essential to confirm a diagnosis of ADHD. Assessment by way of psychiatric interview alongside questionnaire data from parents and teachers is ideal to ensure accurate diagnosis of both ADHD and common comorbid conditions.
2. *Comorbidity:* Children with a range of disorders, including the neurodevelopmental disorders Williams syndrome and ASD, and disruptive behaviour disorders ODD and CD are highly likely to show clinical or sub-clinical ADHD symptoms. The presence or absence of ADHD symptoms are likely to influence their psychological profile and should be recorded within research studies routinely.
3. *Variability:* Children with ADHD are highly heterogeneous on a range of psychological characteristics. The combination of group analyses across the sample, and individual-level analyses to examine within-group differences, are important to understand the condition.

References

American Psychiatric Association (2000). *Diagnostic and Statistical Manual of Mental Disorders* (4th ed.). Washington, DC: American Psychiatric Publishing.

——(2013). *Diagnostic and Statistical Manual of Mental Disorders* (5th ed.). Arlington, VA: American Psychiatric Publishing.

Ames, C. & White, S. (2011). Are ADHD traits dissociable from the autistic profile? Links between cognition and behaviour. *Journal of Autism and Developmental Disorders, 41*(3), 357–363.

Angold, A., Costello, E. J. & Erkanli, A. (1999). Comorbidity. *Journal of Child Psychology and Psychiatry, 40,* 57–88.

Antrop, I., Stock, P., Vert, S., Wiersema, J. R., Baeyens, D. & Roeyers, H. (2006). ADHD and delay aversion: The influence of non-temporal stimulation on choice for delayed rewards. *Journal of Child Psychology and Psychiatry, 47*(11), 1152–1158.

Banaschewski, T., Hollis, C., Oosterlaan, J., Roeyers, H., Rubia, K., Willcutt, E. & Taylor, E. (2005). Towards an understanding of unique and shared pathways in the psychopathophysiology of ADHD. *Development Science, 8*(2), 132–140.

Banaschewski, T., Neale, B. M., Rothenberger, A. & Roessner, V. (2007). Comorbidity of tic disorders and ADHD: Conceptual and methodological considerations. *European Child and Adolescent Psychiatry, 16,* 5–14.

Baron-Cohen, S., Leslie, A. M. & Frith, U. (1985). Does the autistic child have a theory of mind? *Cognition, 21,* 37–46.

Bauermeister, J. J., Shrout, P. E., Ramírez, R., Bravo, M., Alegría, M., Martínez-Taboas, A., ... Canino, J. (2007). ADHD correlates, comorbidity, and impairment in community and treated samples of children and adolescents. *Journal of Abnormal Child Psychology, 35,* 883–898.

Biederman, J. (2005). Attention-deficit hyperactivity disorder. *Biological Psychiatry, 57,* 1215–1220.

Biederman, J., Faraone, S. V., Milberger, S., Curtis, S., Chen, L., Marrs, A., … Spencer, T. (1996). Predictors of persistence and remission of ADHD: Results from a four-year prospective follow-up study of ADHD children. *Journal of the American Academy of Child and Adolescent Psychiatry, 35,* 343–351.

Bishop, D. V. M. (2010). Overlaps between autism and language impairment: phenomimicry or shared etiology? *Behaviour Genetics, 40(5),* 618–629.

Buitelaar, J. K., Van der Wees, M., Swaab-Barneveld, H. & Van der Gaag, R. J. (1999). Theory of mind and emotion recognition functioning in autistic spectrum disorders and in psychiatric control and normal children. *Development and Psychopathology, 11,* 39–58.

Caron, C. & Rutter, M. (1991). Comorbidity in child psychopathology: Concepts, issues and research strategies. *Journal of Child Psychology and Psychiatry, and Allied Disciplines, 32,* 1063–1080.

Castellanos, F. X., Sonuga-Barke, E. J. S., Milham, M. P. & Tannock, R. (2006). Characterizing cognition in ADHD: Beyond executive dysfunction. *Trends in Cognitive Sciences, 10,* 117–123.

Charman, T., Carroll, F. & Sturge, C. (2001). Theory of mind, executive function and social competence in boys with ADHD. *Emotional Behavioural Difficulties, 6,* 27–45.

Clark, T., Feehan, C., Tinline, C. & Vostanis, P. (1999). Autistic symptoms in children with attention deficit-hyperactivity disorder. *European Child and Adolescent Psychiatry, 8(1),* 50–55.

Coghill, D. R. (2010). *Heterogeneity in Hyperkinetic Disorder.* M.D. thesis, University of Dundee.

Coghill, D., Nigg, J., Rothenberger, A., Sonuga-Barke, E. & Tannock, R. (2005). Whither causal models in the neuroscience of ADHD? *Developmental Science, 8,* 105–114.

Connor, D. F., Edwards, G., Fletcher, K. E., Baird, J., Barkley, R. A. & Steingard, R. J. (2003). Correlates of comorbid psychopathology in children with ADHD. *Journal of the American Academy of Child and Adolescent Psychiatry, 42,* 193–200.

Corbett, B. & Glidden, H. (2000). Processing affective stimuli in children with attention-deficit/hyperactivity disorder. *Child Neuropsychology, 6,* 144–155.

Corbett, B. A., Constantine, L. J., Hendren, R., Rocke, D. & Ozonoff, S. (2009). Examining executive functioning in children with autism spectrum disorder, attention deficit hyperactivity disorder and typical development. *Psychiatry Research, 166,* 210–222.

Costello, E. J., Foley, D. L. & Angold, A. (2006). 10-year research update review: The epidemiology of child and adolescent psychiatric disorders: II. Developmental epidemiology. *Journal of the American Academy of Child and Adolescent Psychiatry, 45,* 8–25.

de Bruin, E. I., Ferdinand, R. F., Meester, S., de Nijs, P. F. & Verheij, F. (2007). High rates of psychiatric co-morbidity in PDD-NOS. *Journal of ASD and Developmental Disorders, 37,* 877–886.

Demurie, E., Roeyers, H., Baeyens, D. & Sonuga-Barke, E. (2011). Common alterations in sensitivity to type but not amount of reward in ADHD and autism spectrum disorders. *Journal of Child Psychology and Psychiatry, 52(11),* 1164–1173.

——(2012). Temporal discounting of monetary rewards in children and adolescents with ADHD and autism spectrum disorders. *Developmental Science, 15(6),* 791–800.

Dickstein, D. P. & Castellanos, F. X. (2012). Face processing in attention deficit/hyperactivity disorder. *Current Topics in Behavioural Neuroscience, 9,* 219–237.

Dyck, M. J. Ferguson, K. & Schochet, I. M. (2001). Do ASD spectrum disorders differ from each other and from non-spectrum disorders on emotion recognition tests? *European Child and Adolescent Psychiatry, 10,* 105–116.

Fair, D. A., Bathula, D., Nikolas, M. A. & Nigg, J. T. (2012). Distinct neuropsychological subgroups in typically developing youth inform heterogeneity in children with ADHD. *Proceedings of the National Academy of Sciences USA, 109,* 6769–6774.

Faraone, S. V., Perlis, R. H., Doyle, A. E., Smoller, J. W., Goralnick, J. J., Holmgrenm, M. A. & Sklar, P. (2005). Molecular genetics of attention-deficit/hyperactivity disorder. *Biological Psychiatry, 57,* 1313–1323.

Fayyad, J., De Graaf, R., Kessler, R., Alonso, J., Angermeyer, M., Demyttenaere, K., … Jin, R. (2007). Cross-national prevalence and correlates of adult attention-deficit hyperactivity disorder. *British Journal of Psychiatry, 190,* 402–409.

Feinstein, A. (1970). The pre-therapeutic classification of co-morbidity in chronic disease. *Journal of Chronic Diseases, 23,* 455–468.

Gadow, K. D., DeVincent, C. J. & Schneider, J. (2009). Comparative study of children with ADHD only, autism spectrum disorder + ADHD, and chronic multiple tic disorder + ADHD. *Journal of Attention Disorders, 12,* 474–485.

Galanter, C. A. & Leibenluft, E. (2008). Frontiers between attention deficit hyperactivity disorder and bipolar disorder. *Child and Adolescent Psychiatric Clinics of North America, 17,* 325–346.

Gau, S. S-F. & Shang, C-Y. (2010). Executive functions as endophenotypes in ADHD: Evidence from the Cambridge Neuropsychological Test Battery (CANTAB). *Journal of Child Psychology and Psychiatry, 51*(7), 838–849.

Geurts, H. M., Broeders, M. & Nieuwland, M. S. (2010). Thinking outside the executive functions box: Theory of mind and pragmatic abilities in attention deficit/hyperactivity disorder. *European Journal of Developmental Psychology, 7,* 135–151.

Gillberg, C., Gillberg, I. C., Rasmussen, P., Kadesjö, B., Söderström, H., Råstam, M., … Niklasson, L. (2004). Co-existing disorders in ADHD – implications for diagnosis and intervention. *European Journal of Child and Adolescent Psychiatry, 13,* 80–92.

Groen, Y., Gaastra, G. F., Lewis-Evans, B. & Tucha, O. (2013). Risky behavior in gambling tasks in individuals with ADHD – a systematic literature review. *PLoS One,* 8,9, e74909.

Happé, F. (1995). The role of age and verbal ability in the theory of mind task performance of subjects with autism. *Child Development, 663,* 843–855.

Happé, F., Booth, R., Charlton, R. & Hughes, C. (2006). Executive function deficits in autism spectrum disorders and attention-deficit/hyperactivity disorder: examining profiles across domains and ages. *Brain and Cognition, 61, 1,* 25–39.

Jang, J., Matson, J. L., Williams, L. W., Tureck, K., Goldin, R. L. & Cervantes, P. E. (2013). Rates of comorbid symptoms in children with ASD, ADHD, and comorbid ASD and ADHD. *Research in Developmental Disabilities, 34,* 2369–2378.

Jensen, P. S., Martin, D. & Cantwell, D. P. (1997). Comorbidity in ADHD: Implications for research, practice and DSM-V. *Journal of the American Academy of Child and Adolescent Psychiatry, 36,* 1065–1079.

Johnston, C. & Ohan, L. (2005). The importance of parental attributions in families of children with attention-deficit/hyperactivity and disruptive behavior disorders. *Clinical Child and Family Psychology Review, 8,* 167–182.

Kasper, L. J., Alderson, R. M. & Hudec, K. L. (2012). Moderators of working memory deficits in children with attention-deficit/hyperactivity disorder (ADHD): a meta-analytic review. *Clinical Psychology Review, 32,* 605–617.

Kempton, S., Vance, A., Maruff, P., Luk, E., Costin, J. & Pantelis, C. (1999). Executive function and attention deficit hyperactivity disorder: Stimulant medication and better executive function performance in children. *Psychological Medicine, 29,* 527–538.

Klein, D. N. & Riso, L. P. (1993). Psychiatric disorders: Problems of boundaries and comorbidity. In C. G. Costello (ed.), *Basic Issues in Psychopathology* (pp. 19–66). New York: Guilford Press.

Martinussen, R., Hayden, J., Hogg-Johnson, S. & Tannock, R. (2005). A meta-analysis of working memory impairments in children with attention-deficit/hyperactivity disorder. *Journal of the American Academy of Child and Adolescent Psychiatry, 44,* 377–384.

Neale, M. C. & Kendler, K. S. (1995). Models of comorbidity for multifactorial disorders. *American Journal of Human Genetics, 57*(4), 935–953.

NICE (2008). *Attention Deficit Hyperactivity Disorder (CG72).* London: National Institute for Health and Care Excellence.

Nydén, A., Niklasson, L., Stahlberg, O., Anckarsater, H., Wentz, E., Rastam, M. & Gillberg, C. (2010). Adults with autism spectrum disorders and ADHD neuropsychological aspects. *Research in Developmental Disabilities, 31,* 1659–1668.

Oosterlaan, J., Logan, G. D. & Sergeant, J. A. (1998). Response inhibition in AD/HD, CD, comorbid AD/HD+CD, anxious and normal children: A meta-analysis of studies with the stop task. *Journal of Child Psychology and Psychiatry, 39,* 411–426.

Oosterlaan, J., Scheres, A. & Sergeant, J. A. (2005). Which executive functioning deficits are associated with AD/HD, ODD/CD and comorbid AD/HD + ODD/CD? *Journal of Abnormal Child Psychology, 33,* 69–85.

Pellicano, E. (2007). Links between theory of mind and executive function in young children with autism: Clues to developmental primacy. *Developmental Psychology, 43,* 974–990.

Polanczyk, G., de Lima, M. S., Horta, B. L., Biederman, J. & Rohde, L. A. (2007). The world-wide prevalence of ADGD: A systematic review and metaregression analysis. *American Journal of Psychiatry, 164,* 942–948.

Rhodes, S. M., Coghill, D. R. & Matthews, K. (2004). Methylphenidate restores visual memory, but not working memory function in attention deficit-hyperkinetic disorder. *Psychopharmacology, 175,* 319–330.

Rhodes, S. M., Coghill, D. R. & Matthews, K. (2005). Neuropsychological functioning in stimulant-naive boys with hyperkinetic disorder. *Psychological Medicine, 35,* 1109–1120.

Rhodes, S. M., Riby, D. M., Park, J., Fraser, E. & Campbell, L. E. (2010). Executive neuropsychological functioning in individuals with Williams syndrome. *Neuropsychologia, 48*(5), 1216–1226.

Rhodes, S. M., Riby, D. M., Matthews, K. & Coghill, D. R. (2011). ADHD and Williams syndrome: Shared behavioural and neuropsychological profiles. *Journal of Clinical and Experimental Neuropsychology, 33*(1), 147–156.

Rhodes, S. M., Park, J., Seth, S. A. & Coghill, D. R. (2012). A comprehensive investigation of memory functioning in ADHD and ODD. *Journal of Child Psychology and Psychiatry, 53*(2), 128–137.

Riby, D. M., Hancock, P. J. B., Jones, N. & Hanley, M. (2013). Spontaneous and cued gaze-following in ASD and Williams syndrome. *Journal of Neurodevelopmental Disorders, 5*(13), 1–11.

Rommelse, N. N., Altink, M. E., Fliers, E. A., Martin, N. C., Buschgens, C. J., Hartman, C. A., … Oosterlaan, J. (2009). Comorbid problems in ADHD: Degree of association, shared endophenotypes, and formation of distinct subtypes. Implications for a future DSM. *Journal of Abnormal Child Psychology, 37,* 793–804.

Rommelse, N. N., Geurts, H. M., Franke, B., Buitelaar, J. K. & Hartman, C. A. (2011). A review on cognitive and brain endophenotypes that may be common in autism spectrum disorder and attention deficit/hyperactivity disorder and facilitate the search for pleiotropic genes. *Neuroscience and Biobehavioural Reviews, 35,* 1363–1396.

Scheres, A., Oosterlaan, J. & Sergeant, J. (2001). Response execution and inhibition in children with AD/HD and other disruptive disorders: The role of behavioural activation. *Journal of Child Psychology and Psychiatry, 42,* 347–357.

Simonoff, E., Pickles, A., Charman, T., Chandler, S., Loucas, T. & Baird, G. (2008). Psychiatric disorders in children with autism spectrum disorders: Prevalence, comorbidity, and associated factors in a population-derived sample. *Journal of the American Academy of Child and Adolescent Psychiatry, 47,* 921–929.

Sinzig, J., Morsch, D., Bruning, N., Schmidt, M. H. & Lehmkuhl, G. (2008a). Inhibition, flexibility, working memory and planning in ASD spectrum disorders with and without comorbid ADHD symptoms. *Child and Adolescent Psychiatry and Mental Health, 2*(1), 4–16.

Sinzig, J., Morsch, D. & Lehmkuhl, G. (2008b). Do hyperactivity, impulsivity and inattention have an impact on the ability of facial affect recognition in children with ASD and ADHD? *European Child and Adolescent Psychiatry, 17*(2), 63–72.

Smoller, J. W. & Cross-Disorder Group of the Psychiatric Genomics Consortium (2013). Identification of risk loci with shared effects on five major psychiatric disorders: A genome-wide analysis. *The Lancet, 381*(9875), 1371–1379.

Sodian, B., Hulsken, C. & Thoermer, C. (2003). The self and action in theory of mind research. *Consciousness and Cognition, 12,* 777–782.

Sonuga-Barke, E. J., Dalen, L. & Remington, B. (2003). Do executive deficits and delay aversion make independent contributions to preschool attention-deficit/hyperactivity disorder symptoms? *Journal of the American Academy of Child and Adolescent Psychiatry, 42,* 1335–1342.

Spencer, T. J. (2006). ADHD and comorbidity in childhood. *Journal of Clinical Psychiatry, 67,* 27–31.

Takeda, T., Ambrosini, P. J., deBerardinis, R. & Elia, J. (2012). What can ADHD without comorbidity teach us about comorbidity? *Research in Developmental Disabilities, 33,* 419–425.

Taurines, R., Schwenck, C., Westerwald, E., Scahse, M., Siniatchkin, M. & Freitag, C. (2012). ADHD and ASD: Differential diagnosis or overlapping traits? A selective review. *Attention Deficit Hyperactivity Disorder, 4,* 115–139.

Tye, C., Asherson, P., Ashwood, K. L., Azadi, B., Bolton, P. & McLoughlin, G. (2013a). Attention and inhibition in children with ASD, ADHD and co-morbid ASD+ADHD: An event-related potential study. *Psychological Medicine 15,* 1–16.

Tye, C., Mercure, E., Ashwood, K. L., Azadi, B., Asherson, P., Johnson, M. H., … McLoughlin, G. (2013b). Neurophysiological responses to faces and gaze direction differentiate children with ASD, ADHD, and ASD+ADHD. *Developmental Cognitive Neuroscience, 5,* 71–85.

Uekermann, J., Kraemer, M., Abdel-Hamid, M., Schimmelmann, B. G., Hebebrand, J., Daum, I., … Kis, B. (2010). Social cognition in attention-deficit hyperactivity disorder (ADHD). *Neuroscience and Biobehavioural Reviews, 34,* 734–743.

Van Goozen, S. H. M., Cohen-Kettenis, P. T., Snoek, H., Matthys, W., Swaab-Barneveld, H. & van Engeland, H. (2004). Executive functioning in children: A comparison of hospitalised ODD and ODD/ADHD children and normal controls. *Journal of Child Psychology and Psychiatry, 45,* 284–292.

van Steensel, F. J. A., Bögels, S. M. & de Bruin, E. I. (2013). Psychiatric comorbidity in children with autism spectrum disorders: A comparison with children with ADHD. *Journal of Child and Family Studies, 22,* 368–376.

Willcutt, E. G., Doyle, A. E., Nigg, J. T., Faraone, S. V. & Pennington, B. F. (2005). Validity of the executive function theory of attention-deficit/hyperactivity disorder: A meta-analytic review. *Biological Psychiatry, 57,* 1336–1346.

Willcutt, E. G., Sonuga-Barke, E. J. S., Nigg, J. T. & Sergeant, J. (2008). Recent developments in neuropsychological models of childhood psychiatric disorders. In T. Banaschewski & L. A. Rohde (eds), *Biological Child Psychiatry. Recent Trends and Developments. Advances in Biological Psychiatry* (pp. 195–226). Basel: Karger.

Williams, D., Stott, C. M., Goodyer, I. M. & Sahakian, B. J. (2000). Specific language impairment with or without hyperactivity: Neuropsychological evidence for frontostriatal dysfunction. *Developmental Medicine and Child Neurology, 42,* 368–375.

Williams, L. M., Hermens, D. F., Palmer, D., Kohn, M., Clarke, S., Keage, H., … Gordon, E. (2008). Misinterpreting emotional expressions in attention-deficit/hyperactivity disorder: Evidence for a neural marker and stimulant effects. *Biological Psychiatry, 63*(10), 917–926.

Woo, S. M. & Keatinge, C. (2008). *Diagnosis and Treatment of Mental Disorders Across the Lifespan.* Hoboken, NJ: John Wiley.

Yoshimasu, K., Barbaresi, W. J., Colligan, R. C., Voigt, R. G., Killian, J. M., Weaver, A. L. & Katusic, S. K. (2012). Childhood ADHD is strongly associated with a broad range of psychiatric disorders during adolescence: A population-based birth cohort study. *Journal of Child Psychology and Psychiatry, 53*(10), 1036–1043.

Youngstrom, E. A., Arnold, L. E. & Frazier, T. W. (2010). Bipolar and ADHD comorbidity: Both artifact and outgrowth of shared mechanisms. *Clinical Psychology Science and Practice, 17*(4), 350–359.

10

GENETIC DISORDERS AS MODELS OF HIGH NEUROCOGNITIVE RISK

Evidence from Fragile X syndrome

Brianna Doherty, Andria Shimi and Gaia Scerif

10.1 Introduction

Neurodevelopmental disorders associated with an early genetic diagnosis ('genetic disorders' for brevity henceforth) and with high risk for later cognitive and behavioural difficulties provide models in which to study the neurodevelopmental mechanisms and origins of disorders that are currently defined only at the behavioural level and later in childhood (e.g. attention deficit/hyperactivity disorder: ADHD; Autism Spectrum Disorders: ASD). Here we aim to use the example of one such population, Fragile X syndrome (FXS), to illustrate a number of broad points that emerge from the study of genetic disorders. We begin, first, with a brief overview of FXS at multiple levels, from neuroscience to cognition and behaviour, with an emphasis on developmental stability and change. Secondly, we discuss evidence on variability in outcomes for affected individuals, even in the face of this monogenic disorder. We draw on recent longitudinal studies that aim to investigate what predicts variable outcomes in children with this monogenic disorder: these data emphasise the need to understand diverging developmental trajectories (see also Chapters 1 and 2 for a discussion) across children with the same diagnosis, by studying currently understudied factors such as predictors of greater risk, mechanisms of resilience, environmental protective influences and intervention. Having overviewed the emerging literature in FXS, we flag the potential role and some pragmatic considerations for this trajectory- and variability-focussed approach for other disorders of identified genetic aetiology in which within-group variability may not have been as heavily investigated, especially in a longitudinal context. Finally, we discuss the overlap and differences in social, behavioural and cognitive difficulties experienced by children with FXS with those of children with two very common functionally defined disorders, ADHD and ASD (for a detailed discussion of ADHD see Chapter 9; for ASD see Chapters 7 and 12).

10.2 Fragile X syndrome: an overview

Genetic disorders affect neurocognitive functioning from the outset of development, and the work on developmental disorders of this kind has highlighted the importance of investigating empirically the early developmental profile of each syndrome, rather than assuming a priori that the cognitive profile in adults is representative of earlier abilities (Karmiloff-Smith, 1998, and see Chapter 2 in this volume). So, while genetic disorders can provide unique insights into how relatively well-understood genetic modifications, molecular pathways and systems neuroscience changes influence cognition, these complex interactions cannot be fully understood outside a developmental context. This point is very clearly illustrated by monogenic disorders such as FXS: the syndrome is associated with striking attentional, memory and social cognition difficulties that are more severe than expected given overall developmental delay. For these socio-cognitive skills, infants, children, adolescents and adults with FXS perform more poorly than younger typically developing controls matched in terms of ability level. They also show a distinct profile of difficulties compared to individuals with Down syndrome (see Chapter 11) or other neurodevelopmental disorders of comparable IQ (for a brief review of these comparisons, please see Scerif and Steele, 2011). How does an understanding of the neurobiology of the syndrome enlighten the origin of these neurodevelopmental difficulties?

FXS is caused by the silencing of a single gene on the X chromosome. Therefore, in boys with the condition, the protein that is normally associated with this gene is absent or much reduced. As such, then, FXS provides an ideal model in which to study the effects of protein networks on the developmental trajectories of attentional control, memory and their impact in specific domains of cognition (e.g. social cognition) (see Belmonte & Bourgeron, 2006; Bourgeron, 2009; Scerif & Karmiloff-Smith, 2005; Walter, Mazaika & Reiss, 2009, for a treatment of this interdisciplinary argument). However, at all levels, crucial developmental considerations emerge. What follows is a brief overview of the wealth of information now available on FXS at all of these levels.

10.2.1 Genetic markers and patterns of inheritance

FXS is the most common inherited form of intellectual disability, with a prevalence of approximately 1 in every 4000 males and 1 in every 6000 females (Crawford, Acuña & Sherman, 2001). It is the result of a large trinucleotide CGG repeat expansion in the 5' untranslated region of the gene FMR1 at site Xq27.3. While individuals typically have approximately 30 CGG repeats, premutation carriers possess around 50–200 repeats, and individuals showing the full mutation have over 200 (Maddalena et al., 2001). For the purpose of the current treatment, here we focus primarily on outcomes in full mutation carriers, and refer to excellent recent overviews of the phenotype associated with the premutation (Bourgeois et al., 2009). Although premutation carriers do not show the full FXS phenotype, the pattern of inheritance typically involves women who carry the unstable premutation CGG repeat expansion conferring the full mutation to their sons and daughters. The large CGG repeat expansion in full mutation carriers causes epigenetic changes, including methylation of the FMR1 gene promoter, and subsequent transcriptional silencing of the FMR1 gene, which leads to a reduction of the gene product, Fragile X Mental Retardation Protein (FMRP) (Verkerk et al., 1991). As its prevalence suggests, males are often more affected than females. As FMR1 is located on the X chromosome, men who carry this expansion are more severely affected than women due to the presence of two X chromosomes and random X chromosome inactivation in females (Grigsby, Kemper, Hagerman & Myers, 1990). Physical features of FXS include large prominent ears, a long narrow face, flat feet, joint laxity and macro-orchidism (Hagerman, Van Housen, Smith & McGavran, 1984). However, these features are dependent upon physical maturation, and are not particularly telling in the first few years of life, whereas early delay in key cognitive and motor developmental milestones is most often what brings cases that are newly diagnosed within a family to the attention of clinicians (Bailey, Skinner, Hatton & Roberts, 2000).

10.2.2 Cellular phenotype and animal models

At the cellular level, FXS results in many anatomical and functional changes at the synaptic connections between neurons. Post-mortem examination of human brain tissue reveals dense, immature dendritic spines in neurons (Garber, Visootsak & Warren, 2008). Because the FMR1 gene is highly conserved across species (Verkerk et al., 1991), animal models, including rodent and drosophila, have allowed for further investigation of anatomical and functional changes due to the loss of FMRP. Fmr1 knockout (KO) mice show similar dense, immature dendritic spines as those observed in human patients (Grossman, Aldridge, Weiler & Greenough, 2006). Further work with mice has shown that FMRP selectively binds to mRNA in the post-synaptic spaces of dendritic spines, which represses synaptic translation by stalling ribosomal translocation. In response to synaptic activity, FMRP de-represses translation, thereby allowing for the synthesis of crucial synaptic plasticity proteins. Loss of FMRP therefore impairs this synaptic plasticity response, and because impairments in synaptic plasticity often correlate with learning and memory deficits, it has been suggested that such deficits are the main cause of the FXS phenotype. In particular, mGluR dependent long-term depression (LTD), a prominent form of synaptic plasticity, has been implicated as the neurological pathway involved in the observable symptoms (Bear, Huber & Warren, 2004). Indeed, mGluR LTD is altered in Fmr1 KO mice (Huber, Gallagher, Warren & Bear, 2002), and mGluR antagonists can rescue cognitive and behavioural deficits (Yan, Rammal, Tranfaglia & Bauchwitz, 2005), as well as rescue immature dendritic spine morphology (Michalon et al., 2012; Nakamoto et al., 2007). Such pharmacological interventions have instigated human clinical trials with drugs to target the mGluR LTD pathway, to some success (Berry-Kravis et al., 2009).

Although atypical synaptic function and anatomy are hallmarks of FXS models, when looking across studies with Fmr1 KO mice, these synaptic phenotypes are in fact transient and appear in short time windows in development, such that their effects are dependent upon the temporal expression of Fmr1 (Meredith, Dawitz & Kramvis, 2012). As such, although FXS is caused by a known genetic mutation, individual temporal expression dynamics in combination with the differing timing of environmental influences may be the driving forces for the heterogeneity in outcomes within groups of individuals with FXS, a point to which we turn later.

10.2.3 Systems neuroscience and human neuroimaging data

In addition to cellular studies, investigating FXS at the systems level has been fruitful in elucidating links between genes, brain and behaviour (see also Chapter 3 for a discussion of links between brain and behaviour in FXS). Deficits in working memory (WM), for example, correlate with abnormal brain activation in regions that are critical to those functions, as well as FMRP levels (Menon, Kwon, Eliez, Taylor & Reiss, 2000). FMRP has also been found to correlate with atypical recruitment of the dorso-striatal networks during attention and impulse control tasks, such that high levels of FMRP correlate with normal activity and function (Hoeft et al., 2007; Menon, Leroux, White & Reiss, 2004). These studies support the hypothesis that FMRP may be necessary for the brain to react to fast-changing environments, a requirement for WM and executive function tasks (Ross & Hoeft, 2009). Additionally, there is evidence that reduced FMRP is associated with reduced amygdala volume and activity during emotion processing tasks (Hessl et al., 2011). Beyond investigating functional activity in specific brain regions, recent work has suggested that an overall imbalance between excitation and inhibition across the brain contributes to the FXS phenotype. Support for this hypothesis comes through investigating levels of excitatory and inhibitory neurochemicals by magnetic resonance spectroscopy (MRS), including GABA and glutamate (D'Hulst et al., 2006). This balance is so critical to optimal brain functioning, that, unsurprisingly, it has large though regionally specific effects across the brain, and throughout development. A number of recent structural imaging studies have recently targeted very young children with FXS (Haas et al., 2009; Hoeft, Lightbody & Hazlett, 2008; Hoeft et al. 2010, 2011), highlighting how early diagnosis in FXS can allow for an investigation of very early neural markers of atypical brain development. For example, Hoeft et al. (2010) examined grey and white matter volumes over a two-year period in one- to three-year-old boys with FXS. They found areas of the brain in which grey matter volumes were either enlarged (caudate, thalamus and fusiform gyri) or reduced (cerebellar vermis) at both time-points, suggesting some relatively stable regional effects of FXS. However, there were also regions for which initial grey matter volume was similar to controls (orbital gyri, basal forebrain and thalamus), but then increased in size in FXS. White matter volume of fronto-striatal regions was greater in FXS compared with controls from the first time-point, and differences increased over time. Further semi-longitudinal work investigating individuals nine to twenty-two years old supports these findings (Bray et al., 2011). Persistent differences that demonstrate similar growth trajectories between participants with FXS and controls were again present in the caudate, as well as aberrant growth trajectories in the PFC that mirrored aberrant development in measures of executive control. As a whole, therefore, these results pinpoint how reduced FMRP differentially affects brain regions, and how structural (and perhaps functional) abnormalities of different brain regions in FXS develop differently over time. This is perhaps not surprising, given that synaptic maturation is a dynamic process that occurs in waves throughout development, and it is possible that different brain structures undergo this process at different times. These studies again emphasise time-dependent effects of FMR1 silencing and the importance of both pre- and post-natal critical windows of brain development, as the ones we discussed above in the context of animal models of the condition. Significantly, these studies support the possibility of future targeted therapy based on regional structural differences that offer insight into the temporal nature of reduced FMRP specific to an individual.

10.2.4 Cognitive and behavioural phenotype

Although variable in presentation, individuals with the full FXS mutation show a characteristic behavioural and cognitive profile across development. Males typically demonstrate severe intellectual impairment, with an average IQ of 40. However, some individuals with incomplete FMR1 inactivation may be more moderately affected (Merenstein et al., 1996). Males also show characteristic communication impairments, including significant language deficits and social difficulties that are often accompanied by problems with anxiety (see Chapter 14), hyperactivity, inattention, impulsivity and hyperarousal (Baumgardner, Reiss, Freund & Abrams, 1995). Females tend to be less affected, with moderate to no intellectual impairment as well as social difficulties that are more likely to be accompanied with emotional difficulties, including anxiety or depression (Freund & Reiss, 1991). Behavioural and cognitive symptoms occur in early infancy, with parents expressing concern for their children between nine and thirteen months on average. However, professional confirmation of delay is not typically made until between 21 and 24 months on average, and a full diagnosis of FXS does not occur until an average of 32 and 35 months, although there is considerable variability and sometimes diagnosis is not made until much later (Bailey et al., 2000; Bailey, Skinner & Sparkman, 2003). Between nine and twelve months, sensory-motor atypicalities, including decreased object play, increased leg stereotypies, and atypical posturing can correctly classify an infant with the FXS phenotype with 72.7 per cent accuracy (Baranek et al., 2005). Infants with FXS also demonstrate poor response inhibition (Scerif, Cornish, Wilding, Driver & Karmiloff-Smith, 2004, 2007), as well as poor control of eye movements (Scerif et al., 2005), and prolonged visual attention to objects (Roberts, Hatton, Long, Anello & Colombo, 2011a). School children and adolescents are similarly characterised by poor response inhibition (Sullivan et al.,

2007) and atypical visual attention (Hooper, Hatton & Baranek, 2000; Munir, Cornish & Wilding, 2000a, 2000b). In addition, increasing executive difficulties are presented, including memory impairments (Lanfranchi, Cornoldi & Drigo, 2009). These difficulties continue into adulthood, with the most marked cognitive impairments in executive functions, as well as visual-spatial attention difficulties (Cornish, Munir & Cross, 2001).

10.3 Fragile X syndrome: longitudinal insights into variable outcomes in a monogenic disorder

Recent studies focussed in particular on attentional control in FXS and have highlighted two critical points about the cognitive phenotype of individuals with the full mutation. Firstly, differences in attentional biases modify cognitive development from the outset for children with this genetic disorder, and therefore must be studied directly, rather than inferred from adult data, both by comparing younger and older individuals (Cornish, Scerif & Karmiloff-Smith, 2007; Scerif et al., 2004, 2005, 2007), and longitudinally (Cornish, Cole, Longhi, Karmiloff-Smith & Scerif, 2012, 2013; Scerif, Longhi, Cole, Karmiloff-Smith & Cornish, 2012). Secondly, even in monogenic disorders like FXS, there is substantial variability in outcomes across individuals, as illustrated by individual differences in eye-movement control patterns for toddlers with FXS between one and three years of age (Scerif et al., 2005). For example, when assessed with a very simple infant-friendly modification of the antisaccade task (modelled after Johnson, 1995), at the group level toddlers and young children with FXS differed from younger typically developing control children matched to them in mental age: unlike their younger counterparts, children with FXS did not decrease looking to a suddenly appearing peripheral stimulus. This finding is consistent with inhibitory control deficits that are measured through manual responses for older children with FXS (e.g. Scerif et al., 2004; Munir et al., 2000a). Of note, performance on this task was highly variable for all, but not predicted by mental age in children with FXS, in contrast to controls. There is also variability in how abilities change longitudinally over developmental time in individuals with the disorder (Cornish et al., 2012, 2013; Scerif et al., 2012). We review in greater detail, in turn, what novel implications have emerged from longitudinal studies of trajectories in FXS, and from the study of predictors of variability in FXS.

10.3.1 The importance of tracing developmental trajectories

Recent theoretical advances in the study of neurodevelopmental disorders have highlighted the need to go beyond group comparisons in the study of neurodevelopmental disorders, and instead trace trajectories of functioning within groups of affected individuals, by for example, plotting numerical or linguistic functioning against individuals' verbal or non-verbal ability level (e.g. Thomas et al., 2009; see also Chapter 1). Essentially, this approach underscores the need for researchers in this field to study differences across individuals with a particular disorder. Of note, however, trajectories traced from performance at a single time-point are ultimately cross-sectional. The relative absence of studies tracking developmental change longitudinally for individual affected children is becoming increasingly evident. For example, even though the cross-sectional studies listed above (Cornish et al., 2007; Scerif et al., 2004, 2005, 2007) had already demonstrated striking attentional difficulties even when compared to much younger typically developing participants matched in terms of developmental level, it was not possible to establish whether the severity of these difficulties increased or remained stable over developmental time, because experimental tools available to investigate attention in younger and older individuals are often radically different and hard to compare directly. Beyond attentional profiles and changes alone, few studies have investigated longitudinal changes for any sensory or cognitive domain in individuals with the condition (e.g. see Baranek et al., 2008; Roberts et al., 2009; Skinner et al., 2005, for rare examples related on language and sensory development).

And yet, there are important unique insights that can only emerge from longitudinal data. In the context of attentional control, although significant delays are present in boys with FXS, recent longitudinal studies show that dynamic trajectories of delayed development occur, as opposed to developmental arrest. Using a combined cross-sectional and prospective longitudinal design, we tested early profiles of attention and WM impairment in FXS (Cornish et al., 2013). When investigated cross-sectionally, significant weaknesses emerged for boys with FXS, with no substantial improvement over chronological age. In contrast, longitudinal improvements for boys with FXS paralleled those in TD children. Therefore, cognitive attention and WM, although delayed in FXS, reveal developmental improvements. This particular study therefore confirmed previous cross-sectional findings that suggested deficits in attentional control and WM compared to what would be expected given developmental delay. However, children's longitudinal trajectories displayed improvements over developmental time that a simplistic cross-sectional comparison would have masked. The findings composed part of a much larger protocol of longitudinal assessment for young boys with FXS. Other dependent measures, including non-verbal intelligence, displayed a similar pattern of unique insights generating from longitudinal data: for example, cross-sectional trajectories of non-verbal brief IQ scores, measured with the Leiter International Performance Scale – R (Roid & Miller, 1997) suggested a potential plateau, if not a decline in performance in older compared to younger individuals, whereas longitudinal trajectories measured with growth scores (an analogue of raw scores that takes into account repeated presentations and item difficulty) instead suggested a small but significant improvement over development (Cornish et al., 2012).

Beyond attention, although much of the work on neurocognitive phenotypes in FXS has focussed on high-level cognitive control functions, some studies with adults (Van der Molen et al., 2012) and infants (Farzin, Whitney, Hagerman & Rivera, 2008) suggest that atypical lower level visual perception, including stimulus detection generally, and contrast and motion detection specifically, may underlie visual spatial attention impairments. However, this is still debated. Again, longitudinal data would be critical in understanding whether low-level perceptual processing differences may over time lead to atypical higher-level processing.

10.3.2 Predictors of variable outcomes in individuals with monogenic disorders

In addition to the striking group-level impairments we reviewed above, clinicians and researchers working with individuals with FXS acknowledge equally clear individual differences in outcomes, with some individuals much more severely affected by inattention than others, and others much less inattentive, even in the context of equivalent IQ. This is because IQ or level of ability (mental age) alone are not very good predictors of attentional differences in this group (e.g. Scerif et al., 2005).

As part of a large longitudinal study described above, we assessed visual, auditory, and multimodal attention in young boys with FXS, aged between four and ten years of age when we first saw them, and twelve months later (Scerif et al., 2012). We also measured poor behaviour in FXS through standardised teacher questionnaires targeting dimensions that are relevant to ADHD symptoms (e.g. the Conners Teacher Rating Scales; Conners, 1997). At the group level, children with FXS attended less well than mental-age matched typically developing boys and experienced greater difficulties with auditory compared to visual stimuli. In addition, unlike typically developing children, they did not benefit from multimodal information. Most importantly from the perspective of individual differences within the group of boys with FXS, early visual attention markers were significant predictors of their later ADHD symptomatology, underscoring the need to dissect what drives differing developmental trajectories for individual children within this seemingly homogeneous group. Interestingly, the visual and auditory modality may differ in how they differentiate children within this sample: while visual attention was a significant longitudinal predictor of ADHD symptoms (Scerif et al., 2012), it was auditory attention that instead predicted later symptoms related to ASD (Cornish et al., 2012). These different patterns and trajectories suggest that attentional difficulties need not be considered a single monolithic entity: attention to visual and auditory stimuli can capture distinguishable characteristics of behaviour in FXS (and perhaps by extension in other neurodevelopmental disorders). A plausible hypothesis is that individual differences across the two modalities differentiate because, at least for this group, key elements of social cognition (tapped by overall ASD-symptomatology) hinge on oral communication, whereas inattention and hyperactivity in a classroom setting (an ADHD dimension) may be driven by visual over-stimulation or ineffective regulation. This hypothesis could be tested through a systematic investigation of which attentional dimensions (e.g. auditory or visual) relate more closely to which aspects of ASD or ADHD symptomatology (e.g. communication, repetitive behaviours, inattention or hyperactivity).

Of note, evidence of variability also highlights that, despite the high risk, FXS is not associated with certainty of impairment. Indeed, a number of children with FXS function rather well, despite carrying the full mutation. These good outcomes are not easily accounted for by mosaicism or X inactivation, because variability is striking even amongst boys with FXS who do not have the additional unaffected X that may act as a protective factor for girls with the full mutation. What protects these children from risk? Positive environmental influences, such as a rich home environment or well-coordinated intervention may act as protective factors. Indeed, there is evidence that a rich home environment, but not overall FMRP level, predicts adaptive behaviour in boys with FXS (e.g. Dyer-Friedman et al., 2002; Glaser et al., 2003). Young children with a diagnosis of FXS may therefore provide a very interesting model in which to investigate early predictors of risk and resilience, and early predictors of declining or improving neurocognitive trajectories. This argument has indeed been made for infants who are at high familial risk for ASD. Not all infants at high risk for ASD (who have an older sibling who has been diagnosed, and therefore possess more genetic risk: see discussion in Chapters 4 and 7) go on to receive a diagnosis. Studying these infants longitudinally may allow for the discovery of protective factors in development, as discussed in earlier chapters of this volume. Indeed, the prevalence of ASD in infants with an older sibling with ASD is approximately 20 per cent (Ozonoff et al., 2011), not dissimilar to estimates of 25 to 68 per cent prevalence of ASD in FXS (Bailey et al., 1998; Hernandez et al., 2009; Rogers, Wehner & Hagerman, 2001). Understanding why both a significant proportion of young siblings of children with ASD and of boys with FXS do not meet diagnostic criteria for ASD might shed some light onto these protective factors. We return to this point in a later section.

10.4 Implications for the study of other genetic disorders: a call for longitudinal consortia

Longitudinal trajectories and variability are notoriously hard to study in rare genetic disorders: the low prevalence tends to mean that sample sizes for individual studies is small and participants are widely spread geographically, resulting in long-distance travel for either researchers or many of the participating families. At best, therefore, most published studies have focussed on group comparisons: comparisons to typically developing individual controls selected along various dimensions. It is also very hard to recruit a large number of individuals in a restricted age or ability range, the ideal scenario for designing a longitudinal study. Moreover, there are also practical difficulties in assessing participants multiple times, starting from the substantial limitations in funding and in the typical length of grants. Why, therefore, should researchers investigating rare neurodevelopmental disorders strive to investigate longitudinal change and within-group variability?

Through the coverage of what has recently been uncovered in FXS, we hope to have pointed to two key unique sources of information that can only be gained through large longitudinal studies. First, advances have been made by tracing age-related trajectories of developmental disorders, rather than only group comparisons (see Thomas et al., 2009, for an extended treatment of the approach and methods). However, cross-sectional trajectories ultimately may not recapitulate longitudinal change, and change needs to be tested empirically (see Cornish et al., 2013). Second, longitudinal data are necessary in order to go beyond correlates of cognitive functioning at each time-point (e.g. correlating attentional control with behaviour in the classroom) to testing temporal predictors of later outcomes (e.g. early attentional control predicting later classroom behaviour, see Scerif et al., 2012) or predictors of change for later outcomes (e.g. the extent to which early abilities predict improvements in a later given function; see Steele, Scerif, Cornish & Karmiloff-Smith, 2013, for this argument in the context of longitudinal predictors of literacy in Williams syndrome and Down syndrome). Of note, ultimately even longitudinal data analyses hinge on correlations, albeit with a temporal dimension, and causality is therefore going to be assessed most clearly through a combination of longitudinal and intervention approaches. A further additional unique benefit would emerge in the context of cross-syndrome comparisons, a topic that is beyond the scope of the current chapter (see Scerif & Steele, 2011, for a summary of suggestions we made in this regard and see Chapter 2). We shall only briefly mention that longitudinal cross-syndrome comparisons could ultimately be extremely powerful in uncovering shared and unique pathways of risk across neurodevelopmental disorders that share some similarities in behavioural presentations (see Scerif & Wu, 2014, for a more detailed treatment of this argument; this is also at the core of recent cross-syndrome infant studies, see D'Souza et al., 2013).

In turn, the unique outcomes of prospective longitudinal studies mean that researchers in this area should try to overcome their practical obstacles to implement them. But how would we go about doing so given the practical difficulties? We can see at least one practical solution to this conundrum: more and more researchers investigating rare genetic disorders should form consortia, sharing common measures from common participant pools, especially when these participants are followed longitudinally. This has already started to happen across multiple countries, although a strong drive for these studies has been clinical pharmacological trials, rather than detailed neurocognitive assessment (e.g. Berry-Kravis et al., 2009). Ultimately, these collaborations will facilitate the establishment of prospective longitudinal cohorts, ideally starting to investigate neurocognitive outcomes and variability from diagnosis. This work would fill a theoretical need (understanding shared and distinct developmental pathways to difficulties), but also the important clinical and societal requirement of providing early diagnosed children, their families, and clinicians with much more information on early trajectories of change, and isolating predictors of later outcomes that could be targeted more effectively by early intervention. Large-scale collaborations and consortia have a highly successful precedent in the study of infant siblings at risk (e.g. ASD, Elsabbagh & Johnson, 2010; Elsabbagh et al., 2012): these studies may provide researchers investigating rare genotypes the practical mould for shaping their future research. Are there, in turn, implications of work on rare genotypes like FXS, for the study of functionally defined disorders like ASD? It is to these that we now turn.

10.5 Implications for functionally defined disorders: promise, caveats and potential solutions

One marked feature of the FXS cognitive and behavioural phenotype is the high risk for developmental difficulties, including Autism Spectrum Disorders (ASD)- and Attention Deficit Hyperactivity Disorder (ADHD)-like symptoms. Approximately 50 to 90 per cent of people with FXS demonstrate symptoms of ASD, including poor eye contact, hand flapping, hand biting, perseveration in speech and tactile defensiveness (Bailey et al., 1998; Baumgardner et al., 1995; Kerby & Dawson, 1994), and 25 to 68 per cent of individuals with FXS also meet the diagnosis for ASD (Bailey et al., 1998; Hernandez et al., 2009; Rogers et al., 2001). Additionally, FXS is the most common genetic cause of ASD, with approximately 1 to 2 per cent of individuals with ASD carrying the full FXS mutation (Hatton et al., 2006). With regards to ADHD, approximately 70 per cent of individuals with FXS fulfil the ADHD diagnosis (Turk, 1998), making ADHD the most commonly diagnosed comorbid condition in FXS (Tranfaglia, 2011). Despite the high risk for ASD and ADHD, behavioural outcomes are variable, which makes investigation of the factors involved in individual differences in these symptoms of high theoretical and clinical interest. What pushes developmental trajectories in many children with FXS to present with social and cognitive control difficulties akin to those experienced by children with ASD and ADHD, while some children with FXS do not exhibit these difficulties? Given that the average age of diagnosis is comparable to early ASD diagnosis, and much sooner than ADHD diagnosis (typically confirmed in the early school years), FXS affords the opportunity of studying high-risk cases from early in development. This promise of genetic disorders with an early diagnosis is not unique to FXS: disorders like Williams syndrome are also characterised by high risk for ADHD symptoms (Rhodes, Riby, Matthews & Coghill, 2011), for example, and receive a very early diagnosis.

However, the promise of insights from genetic disorders that, like FXS, are diagnosed early and carry a high risk for ASD or ADHD is not without debate. Does ASD/ADHD co-diagnosed with FXS represent a categorically distinct disorder, or is it the severe end of a continuum of cognitive impairment and behavioural difficulties? This question is paramount in decisions regarding the development of effective behavioural and pharmacological treatments that address the core impairments in ASD/ADHD and FXS, particularly stimulant medication in the case of ADHD. For ASD, many attempts have been made to investigate this question behaviourally. Although some studies have found similar profiles of ASD behaviours in individuals with FXS and individuals with idiopathic ASD (Bailey et al., 1998), others argue that behavioural profiles are distinct between groups (Kaufmann et al., 2004; McDuffie, Thurman, Hagerman & Abbeduto, 2014). For example, McDuffie and colleagues (2014) compared individuals with idiopathic ASD and individuals with FXS using three matching criteria: chronological age match regardless of comorbidity (such that some individuals in the FXS group did and others did not meet the diagnostic criteria for ASD), diagnostic match (chronological age match, and all FXS participants were diagnosed with ASD), and severity match (all former restrictions, and matched for severity of ASD). These groups were then compared based on theirs scores on the ADI-R, a diagnostic tool with scores for various behaviours within three categories: reciprocal social interaction, communication, and restricted interests and stereotyped behaviours. Their results indicate several significant differences in scores for specific behaviours between idiopathic ASD and co-morbid FXS and ASD, including social smiling and complex behaviours. These behavioural studies are problematic, however, in that they match individuals based on ASD severity, or ASD diagnostic criteria, which are behaviourally defined, and then compare groups based on behaviourally defined ASD symptomatology and measures of adaptive behaviours, which leads to circular reasoning.

These problems may be overcome by focussing on neurobiological and molecular variation between FXS and ASD or ADHD. For example, in the context of ASD, the way of investigating this question is asking why genetically defined FXS would lead to ASD-like symptoms. The main theory comes from studies that have found that many of the targets of FMRP are the products of genes implicated in ASD (Darnell et al., 2011), which has led researchers to suggest that FXS leads to ASD via downstream mechanisms of FMRP. More recent work with patients has strengthened this claim by modelling how FMRP targets not only contribute to ASD, they do so via several distinct aetiologies. These aetiologies include single, rare, highly penetrant disruptions in a subgroup of embryonically expressed FMRP targets, as well as multiple less penetrant disruptions with cumulative effects in a subgroup of FMRP targets up-regulated in adolescence and adulthood (Steinberg & Webber, 2013). Within this framework, FMR1 silencing would put individuals with FXS at greater risk for ASD if accompanied by other hits on its downstream targets that are also involved in risk for ASD. The reverse must also be asked, however – why does non-idiopathic ASD, which may or may not result from genetic disruption downstream of FMRP, share symptoms with genetically defined FXS? Molecular work with animal models is beginning to shed light on this question. A recent study with a common ASD mouse model, the NLGN3 KO mouse, has demonstrated the same synaptic phenotype as in FXS (Baudouin et al., 2012). Therefore, despite distinct aetiologies, FXS and one example of non-syndromic ASD share a core neurobiological phenotype, which may allow for shared therapeutic intervention. Furthermore, researchers suggest that this idea of shared genetic and neural mechanisms is supported by behavioural work. For example, Rogers et al. (2001) found two subgroups of children with FXS between 21 and 48 months, one group who performed similarly to children with developmental delay but not ASD, and another that performed similarly to a group with idiopathic ASD. They argue that this arises because the FXS mutation procures high risk, but additional mutations work synergistically to result in ASD. Despite these examples of shared genetic and neural mechanisms, there are many other examples of functional and anatomical differences between individuals with FXS and individuals with idiopathic ASD, which supports the contrasting idea that ASD symptoms in FXS may be distinct from non-syndromic ASD (Hall, Lightbody, Hirt, Rezvani & Reiss, 2010). Further work is required to distinguish between these competing theories. Although variation in the behavioural profiles of individuals with FXS, FXS and ASD, and idiopathic ASD complicates individualised therapy based on behavioural assessments, investigating the genetic and cellular mechanism of ASD risk in FXS may allow for a better understanding of comorbidity and the heterogeneous presentation of symptoms, as well as allow for possible targeted therapeutic interventions based on biological differences.

This potential resolution to the debate is also exemplified by studying the overlap in mechanisms for hyperactivity and inattention mechanisms in ADHD and FXS. ADHD is associated with both functional and structural abnormalities of a distributed right lateralised corticostriatal network implicated in inhibitory control (see Chapter 9 for a detailed discussion), highly overlapping with that implicated by functional imaging studies of inhibitory control difficulties in FXS (e.g. Hoeft et al., 2007). Early reports of localised structural abnormalities have been complemented by large-scale studies of cortical development (Shaw et al., 2007). Longitudinal studies of these abnormalities have also highlighted how differences in prefrontal cortical thickness across patients with ADHD predict later clinical outcome (Shaw et al., 2006). Functional abnormalities of these circuits are well established too: fMRI studies using classical inhibitory control tasks (e.g. gonogo task, stop-signal reaction time) show reduced activation of inferior prefrontal cortex and caudate nucleus compared to healthy age-matched controls (Durston et al., 2003), a finding that overlaps with the abnormalities measured in FXS (Hoeft et al., 2007).

Electrophysiological studies also suggest that children with ADHD differ from controls at multiple time-points in the information-processing cascade leading to the inhibition of a response or when resolving conflict (Liotti, Pliszka, Perez, Kothmann & Woldorff, 2005). Again, these findings have been mirrored in recent electrophysiological findings in adolescents and adults with FXS (Van der Molen et al., 2012). At the level of neurotransmission, the involvement of striatal circuits in ADHD is heavily supported by the fact that methylphenidate (MPH), a dopamine reuptake inhibitor, alleviates symptoms of the disorder in the majority of affected cases (Volkow, Wang, Fowler & Ding, 2005). MPH is indeed the most efficient pharmacological treatment for resolving ADHD symptoms in FXS (Roberts et al., 2011b). Intriguingly, recent work from genome-wide association studies of ADHD has revised considerably perspectives on key genes associated with ADHD (Franke, Neale & Faraone, 2009). Rather than the expected dopaminergic candidates emerging as significantly associated with ADHD risk, genes involved in neurodevelopmental networks for neurite outgrowth seem to be more prominent (Poelmans, Pauls, Buitelaar & Franke, 2011). These suggestions are also consistent with recent evidence from the study of rare copy-number variants (CNVs) in ADHD, suggesting that intrinsic neurotransmitter systems, and more specifically metabotropic glutamatergic pathways, may be involved in ADHD risk (Elia et al., 2012). These pathways overlap with those compromised in FXS, suggesting at least one neural pathway of risk for hyperactivity/inattention that is shared in 'idiopathic' ADHD and FXS. Similar mechanistic overlap and differences have been studied in the context of disorders with other identified genetic aetiology (e.g. Tuberous Sclerosis and ASD symptomatology, Tye & Bolton, 2013).

As a whole, then, the high risk for ADHD- and ASD-like symptoms in FXS has attracted much interest. Within a developmental context, this high risk has the potential for tracing developmental trajectories to poor outcomes, like a confirmed diagnosis of ADHD, well before this would be normally possible in the typical population. One might be able to recruit and follow young children with FXS before they settle into patterns of behavioural difficulties, and eventually better tailor intervention. Targeted intervention would be driven by understanding what modifiable protective factors (e.g. environmental input, home environment and teaching practices) lead young children with the same condition not to present with later difficulties. However, this approach has many caveats, the major one of which surrounds the debate about whether ADHD and ASD symptoms in FXS are similar or different to those in idiopathic cases of ADHD and ASD. We suggest that a focus on overlapping or distinct neural mechanisms may help advance this debate, especially if it takes into account potential differences in timing.

10.6 Conclusions

Here we used the example of FXS to illustrate a number of broad points that emerge from the study of genetic disorders. We overviewed what is known about the genotype, neuroscience, cognition and behaviour of individuals with FXS, emphasising the developmental nature of the disorder. Critically, recent longitudinal data emphasise variability in outcomes for affected individuals, even in the face of this monogenic disorder: these findings emphasise the need to understand diverging developmental trajectories, predictors of greater risk, mechanisms of resilience, and environmental protective influences. As a whole, we argue that disorders of known genetic origin, including FXS, present biologically well-understood models in which to study high risk of impairment for common functionally defined disorders, like ADHD and ASD. Critically, however, this approach needs to be inspired by the developmental cognitive neuroscience of each disorder, in order to understand trajectories leading to good or poor outcome, and their overlap/differences across disorders.

Practical tips

1. *Measuring within-group variability.* Even in monogenic, and therefore seemingly homogeneous groups, high variability is the norm. Ultimately, collecting

sufficiently large sample sizes to study predictors of variability in the rarest genetic disorders will require consortia and collaborations across research groups. In addition, and more pragmatically, consider using or developing measures that are as sensitive as possible to variability within a group of individuals, and not just robust on group-level comparisons, to ensure capturing the range of ability within the target group. Standardised tools developed for typically developing individuals might be highly problematic at the low end of ability, with floor effects truncating individual differences.

2. *Measuring atypical and typical trajectories longitudinally.* Following change longitudinally, when possible, can be highly informative. Practically speaking, while this is relatively easier to implement for affected individuals and their families, typically developing controls are much harder to follow longitudinally. However, do not be tempted not to study controls as much as your target population: for many developing neurocognitive functions we have far lesser insight of 'typical development' than case–control designs might suggest.

3. *Measuring early development.* Starting early in development is critical if your aim is to isolate predictors of risk and resilience, but, practically speaking, fewer measures may be available to assess young individuals or those who are very severely affected. Practical progress can be made by considering now sophisticated-looking measures that have been developed for young and pre-verbal children, although, again, their role as predictors of later development has yet to be established.

References

Bailey, D. B., Jr, Mesibov, G. B., Hatton, D. D., Clark, R. D., Roberts, J. E. & Mayhew, L. (1998). Autistic behavior in young boys with Fragile X syndrome. *Journal of Autism and Developmental Disorders, 28*(6), 499–508.

Bailey, D. B., Skinner, D., Hatton, D. & Roberts, J. (2000). Family experiences and factors associated with the diagnosis of fragile X syndrome. *Journal of Developmental and Behavioral Pediatrics, 21*(5), 315–321.

Bailey, D. B., Skinner, D. & Sparkman, K. L. (2003). Discovering Fragile X syndrome: Family experiences and perceptions. *Pediatrics, 111*(2), 407–416.

Baranek, G. T., Danko, C. D., Skinner, M. L., Bailey, D. B., Jr, Hatton, D. D., Roberts, J. E. & Mirrett, P. L. (2005). Video analysis of sensory-motor features in infants with fragile X syndrome at 9–12 months of age. *Journal of Autism and Developmental Disorders, 35*(5), 645–656.

Baranek, G. T., Roberts, J. E., David, F. J., Sideris, J., Mirrett, P. L., Hatton, D. D. & Bailey, D. B. Jr. (2008). Developmental trajectories and correlates of sensory processing in young boys with fragile X syndrome. *Physical and Occupational Therapy in Pediatrics, 28*(1), 79–98.

Baudouin, S. J., Gaudias, J., Gerharz, S., Hatstatt, L., Zhou, K., Punnakkal, P., … Scheiffele, P. (2012). Shared synaptic pathophysiology in syndromic and nonsyndromic rodent models of autism. *Science, 338*(6103), 128–132.

Baumgardner, T. L., Reiss, A. L., Freund, L. S. & Abrams, M. T. (1995). Specification of the neurobehavioral phenotype in males with fragile X syndrome. *Pediatrics, 95*(5), 744–752.

Bear, M. F., Huber, K. M. & Warren, S. T. (2004). The mGluR theory of fragile X mental retardation. *Trends in Neurosciences, 27*(7), 370–377.

Belmonte, M. K. & Bourgeron, T. (2006). Fragile X syndrome and autism at the intersection of genetic and neural networks. *Nature Neuroscience, 9*(10), 1221–1225.

Berry-Kravis, E., Hessl, D., Coffey, S., Hervey, C., Schneider, A., Yuhas, J., ... Hagerman, R. (2009). A pilot open label, single dose trial of fenobam in adults with fragile X syndrome. *Journal of Medical Genetics, 46*(4), 266–271.

Bourgeois, J. A., Coffey, S. M., Rivera, S. M., Hessl, D., Gane, L. W., Tassone, F., ... Hagerman, R. J. (2009). A review of Fragile X premutation disorders: Expanding the psychiatric perspective. *Journal of Clinical Psychiatry, 70*(6), 852–862.

Bourgeron, T. (2009). A synaptic trek to autism. *Current Opinion in Neurobiology, 19*(2), 231–234.

Bray, S., Hirt, M., Jo, B., Hall, S. S., Lightbody, A. A., Walter, E., ... Reiss, A. L. (2011). Aberrant frontal lobe maturation in adolescents with fragile X syndrome is related to delayed cognitive maturation. *Biological Psychiatry, 70*(9), 852–858.

Conners, C. K. (1997). *Conners' Rating Scales–Revised: Technical Manual.* North Tonawanda, NY: Multi-Health Systems.

Cornish, K. M., Munir, F. & Cross, G. (2001). Differential impact of the FMR-1 full mutation on memory and attention functioning: A neuropsychological perspective. *Journal of Cognitive Neuroscience, 13*(1), 144–150.

Cornish, K., Scerif, G. & Karmiloff-Smith, A. (2007). Tracing syndrome-specific trajectories of attention across the lifespan. *Cortex, 43*(6), 672–685.

Cornish, K., Cole, V., Longhi, E., Karmiloff-Smith, A. & Scerif, G. (2012). Does attention constrain developmental trajectories in fragile X syndrome? A 3-year prospective longitudinal study. *American Journal of Intellectual Development and Disability, 117*(2), 103–120.

——(2013). Mapping developmental trajectories of attention and working memory in fragile X syndrome: Developmental freeze or developmental change? *Development and Psychopathology, 25*(2), 365–376.

Crawford, D. C., Acuña, J. M. & Sherman, S. L. (2001). FMR1 and the fragile X syndrome: Human genome epidemiology review. *Genetics in Medicine: Official Journal of the American College of Medical Genetics, 3*(5), 359–371.

Darnell, J. C., Van Driesche, S. J., Zhang, C., Hung, K. Y. S., Mele, A., Fraser, C. E, ... Darnell, R. B. (2011). FMRP stalls ribosomal translocation on mRNAs linked to synaptic function and autism. *Cell, 146*(2), 247–261.

D'Hulst, C., De Geest, N., Reeve, S. P., Van Dam, D., De Deyn, P. P., Hassan, B. A. & Kooy, R. F. (2006). Decreased expression of the GABAA receptor in fragile X syndrome. *Brain Research, 1121*(1), 238–245.

D'Souza, D., Kyjonková, H., Johnson, M. H., Gliga, T., Kushnerenko, E., Scerif, G., Karmiloff-Smith, A. & the BASIS team (2013). Are early neurophysiological markers of ASD syndrome-specific? Preliminary results from a cross-syndrome study, International Society for Autism Research's Annual Meeting, IMFAR 2013, San Sebastian, Spain.

Durston, S., Tottenham, N. T., Thomas, K. M., Davidson, M. C., Eigsti, I. M., Yang, Y. H., ... Casey, B. J. (2003). Differential patterns of striatal activation in young children with and without ADHD. *Biological Psychiatry, 53*(10), 871–878.

Dyer-Friedman, J., Glaser, B., Hessl, D., Johnston, C., Huffman, L. C., Taylor, A., ... Reiss, A. L. (2002). Genetic and environmental influences on the cognitive outcomes of children with fragile X syndrome. *Journal of the American Academy of Child and Adolescent Psychiatry, 41*(3), 237–244.

Elia, J., Glessner, J. T., Wang, K., Takahashi, N., Shtir, C. J., Hadley, D., ... Hakonarson, H. (2012). Genome-wide copy number variation study associates metabotropic glutamate receptor gene networks with attention deficit hyperactivity disorder. *Nature Genetics, 44*(1), 78–113.

Elsabbagh, M. & Johnson, M. H. (2010). Getting answers from babies about autism. *Trends in Cognitive Sciences, 14*(2), 81–87.

Elsabbagh, M., Mercure, E., Hudry, K., Chandler, S., Pasco, G., Charman, T., ... BASIS Team (2012). Infant neural sensitivity to dynamic eye gaze is associated with later emerging autism. *Current Biology, 22*(4), 338–342.

Farzin, F., Whitney, D., Hagerman, R. J. & Rivera, S. M. (2008). Contrast detection in infants with fragile X syndrome. *Vision Research, 48*(13), 1471–1478.

Franke, B., Neale, B. M. & Faraone, S. V. (2009). Genome-wide association studies in ADHD. *Human Genetics, 126*(1), 13–50.

Freund, L. S. & Reiss, A. L. (1991). Cognitive profiles associated with the fra(X) syndrome in males and females. *American Journal of Medical Genetics, 38*(4), 542–547.

Garber, K. B., Visootsak, J. & Warren, S. T. (2008). Fragile X syndrome. *European Journal of Human Genetics, 16*(6), 666–672.

Glaser, B., Hessl, D., Dyer-Friedman, J., Johnston, C., Wisbeck, J., Taylor, A. & Reiss, A. (2003). Biological and environmental contributions to adaptive behavior in fragile X syndrome. *American Journal of Medical Genetics A*, 117A(1), 21–29.

Grigsby, J. P., Kemper, M. B., Hagerman, R. J. & Myers, C. S. (1990). Neuropsychological dysfunction among affected heterozygous fragile X females. *American Journal of Medical Genetics, 35*, 28–35.

Grossman, A. W., Aldridge, G. M., Weiler, I. J. & Greenough, W. T. (2006). Local protein synthesis and spine morphogenesis: Fragile X syndrome and beyond. *Journal of Neuroscience, 26*(27), 7151–7155.

Haas, B. W., Barnea-Goraly, N., Lightbody, A. A., Patnaik, S. S., Hoeft, F., Hazlett, H., ... Reiss, A. L. (2009). Early white-matter abnormalities of the ventral frontostriatal pathway in fragile X syndrome. *Developmental Medicine and Child Neurology, 51*(8), 593–599.

Hagerman, R. J., Van Housen, K., Smith, A. C. & McGavran, L. (1984). Consideration of connective tissue dysfunction in the fragile X syndrome. *American Journal of Medical Genetics, 17*(1), 111–121.

Hall, S. S., Lightbody, A. A., Hirt, M., Rezvani, A. & Reiss, A. L. (2010). Autism in fragile X syndrome: A category mistake? *Journal of the American Academy of Child and Adolescent Psychiatry, 49*(9), 921–933.

Hatton, D. D., Sideris, J., Skinner, M., Mankowski, J., Bailey, D. B., Roberts, J. & Mirrett, P. (2006). Autistic behavior in children with fragile X syndrome: Prevalence, stability, and the impact of FMRP. *American Journal of Medical Genetics Part A, 140A*(17), 1804–1813.

Hernandez, R. N., Feinberg, R. L., Vaurio, R., Passanante, N. M., Thompson, R. E. & Kaufmann, W. E. (2009). Autism spectrum disorder in fragile X syndrome: A longitudinal evaluation. *American Journal of Medical Genetics Part A, 149A*(6), 1125–1137.

Hessl, D., Wang, J. M., Schneider, A., Koldewyn, K., Le, L., Iwahashi, C., … Rivera, S. M. (2011). Decreased Fragile X mental retardation protein expression underlies amygdala dysfunction in carriers of the Fragile X premutation. *Biological Psychiatry*, *70*(9), 859–865.

Hoeft, F., Hernandez, A., Parthasarathy, S., Watson, C. L., Hall, S. S. & Reiss, A. L. (2007). Fronto-striatal dysfunction and potential compensatory mechanisms in male adolescents with fragile X syndrome. *Human Brain Mapping*, *28*(6), 543–554.

Hoeft, F., Lightbody, A. A. & Hazlett, H. C. (2008). Morphometric spatial patterns differentiating boys with fragile X syndrome, typically developing boys, and developmentally delayed boys aged 1 to 3 years. *Archives of General Psychiatry*, *65*(9), 1087–1097.

Hoeft, F., Carter, J. C., Lightbody, A. A., Hazlett, H. C., Piven, J. & Reiss, A. L. (2010). Region-specific alterations in brain development in one- to three-year-old boys with fragile X syndrome. *Proceedings of the National Academy of Sciences of the United States of America*, *107*(20), 9335–9339.

Hoeft, F., Walter, E., Lightbody, A. A., Hazlett, H. C., Chang, C., Piven, J. & Reiss, A. L. (2011). Neuroanatomical differences in toddler boys with Fragile X syndrome and idiopathic autism. *Archives of General Psychiatry*, *68*(3), 295–305.

Hooper, S. R., Hatton, D. D. & Baranek, G. T. (2000). Nonverbal assessment of IQ, attention, and memory abilities in children with fragile-X syndrome using the Leiter-R. *Journal of Psychoeducational Assessment*, *18*(3), 255–267.

Huber, K. M., Gallagher, S. M., Warren, S. T. & Bear, M. F. (2002). Altered synaptic plasticity in a mouse model of fragile X mental retardation. *Proceedings of the National Academy of Sciences of the United States of America*, *99*(11), 7746–7750.

Johnson, M. H. (1995). The inhibition of automatic saccades in early infancy. *Developmental Psychobiology*, *28*(5), 281–291.

Karmiloff-Smith A. (1998). Development itself is the key to understanding developmental disorders. *Trends in Cognitive Sciences*, *2*(10), 389–398.

Kaufmann, W. E., Cortell, R., Kau, A. S. M., Bukelis, I., Tierney, E., Gray, R. M., …. Stanard, P. (2004). Autism spectrum disorder in fragile X syndrome: Communication, social interaction, and specific behaviors. *American Journal of Medical Genetics*, *129A*(3), 225–234.

Kerby, D. S. & Dawson, B. L. (1994). Autistic features, personality, and adaptive behavior in males with the fragile X syndrome and no autism. *American Journal of Mental Retardation*, *98*(4), 455–462.

Lanfranchi, S., Cornoldi, C. & Drigo, S. (2009). Working memory in individuals with fragile X syndrome. *Child Neuropsychology*, *15*(2), 105–119.

Liotti, M., Pliszka, S. R., Perez, R., Kothmann, D. & Woldorff, M. G. (2005). Abnormal brain activity related to performance monitoring and error detection in children with ADHD. *Cortex*, *41*(3), 377–388.

Maddalena, A., Richards, C. S., McGinniss, M. J., Brothman, A., Desnick, R. J., Grier, R. E., … Quality Assurance Subcommittee of the Laboratory Practice Committee (2001). Technical standards and guidelines for fragile X: The first of a series of disease-specific supplements to the Standards and Guidelines for Clinical Genetics Laboratories of the American College of Medical Genetics. Quality Assurance Subcommittee of the Laboratory Practice Committee. *Genetics in Medicine: Official Journal of the American College of Medical Genetics*, *3*(3), 200–205.

McDuffie, A., Thurman, A. J., Hagerman, R. J. & Abbeduto, L. (2014). Symptoms of autism in males with Fragile X syndrome: A comparison to nonsyndromic ASD using current ADI-R scores. *Journal of Autism and Developmental Disorders, 44*(1), 1–13.

Menon, V., Kwon, H., Eliez, S., Taylor, A. K. & Reiss, A. L. (2000). Functional brain activation during cognition is related to FMR1 gene expression. *Brain Research, 877*(2), 367–370.

Menon, V., Leroux, J., White, C. D. & Reiss, A. L. (2004). Frontostriatal deficits in fragile X syndrome: relation to FMR1 gene expression. *Proceedings of the National Academy of Sciences of the United States of America, 101*(10), 3615–3620.

Meredith, R. M., Dawitz, J. & Kramvis, I. (2012). Sensitive time-windows for susceptibility in neurodevelopmental disorders. *Trends in Neurosciences, 35*(6), 335–344.

Merenstein, S. A., Sobesky, W. E., Taylor, A. K., Riddle, J. E., Tran, H. X. & Hagerman, R. J. (1996). Molecular-clinical correlations in males with an expanded FMR1 mutation. *American Journal of Medical Genetics, 64*(2), 388–394.

Michalon, A., Sidorov, M., Ballard, T. M., Ozmen, L., Spooren, W., Wettstein, J. G., … Lindemann, L. (2012). Chronic pharmacological mGlu5 inhibition corrects Fragile X in adult mice. *Neuron, 74*(1), 49–56.

Munir, F., Cornish, K. M. & Wilding, J. (2000a). A neuropsychological profile of attention deficits in young males with fragile X syndrome. *Neuropsychologia, 38*(9), 1261–1270.

——(2000b). Nature of the working memory deficit in Fragile-X Syndrome. *Brain and Cognition, 44*(3), 387–401.

Nakamoto, M., Nalavadi, V., Epstein, M. P., Narayanan, U., Bassell, G. J. & Warren, S. T. (2007). Fragile X mental retardation protein deficiency leads to excessive mGluR5-dependent internalization of AMPA receptors. *Proceedings of the National Academy of Sciences of the United States of America, 104*(39), 15537–15542.

Ozonoff, S., Young, G. S., Carter, A., Messinger, D., Yirmiya, N., Zwaigenbaum, L., … Stone, W. L. (2011). Recurrence risk for autism spectrum disorders: A Baby Siblings Research Consortium study. *Pediatrics, 128*(3), e488–e495.

Poelmans, G., Pauls, D. L., Buitelaar, J. K. & Franke, B. (2011). Integrated genome-wide association study findings: Identification of a neurodevelopmental network for Attention Deficit Hyperactivity Disorder. *American Journal of Psychiatry, 168*(4), 365–377.

Rhodes, S. M., Riby, D. M., Matthews, K. & Coghill, D. R. (2011). Attention-deficit/hyperactivity disorder and Williams syndrome: Shared behavioural and neuropsychological profiles. *Journal of Clinical and Experimental Neuropsychology, 33*(1), 147–156.

Roberts, J. E., Mankowski, J. B., Sideris, J., Goldman, B. D., Hatton, D. D., Mirrett, P. L., … Bailey, D. B. Jr. (2009). Trajectories and predictors of the development of very young boys with fragile X syndrome. *Journal of Pediatric Psychology, 34*(8), 827–836.

Roberts, J. E., Hatton, D. D., Long, A. C. J., Anello, V. & Colombo, J. (2011a). Visual attention and autistic behavior in infants with Fragile X syndrome. *Journal of Autism and Developmental Disorders, 42*(6), 937–946.

Roberts, J. E., Miranda, M., Boccia, M., Janes, H., Tonnsen, B. L. & Hatton, D. D. (2011b). Treatment effects of stimulant medication in young boys with fragile X syndrome. *Journal of Neurodevelopmental Disorders, 3*(3), 175–184.

Rogers, S. J., Wehner, D. E. & Hagerman, R. (2001). The behavioral phenotype in fragile X: Symptoms of autism in very young children with fragile X syndrome, idiopathic autism, and other developmental disorders. *Journal of Developmental and Behavioral Pediatrics, 22*(6), 409–417.

Roid, G. H. & Miller, L. J. (1997). *Leiter International Performance Scale–Revised*. Wood Dale, IL: Stoelting Col.

Ross, J. & Hoeft, F. (2009). Gene, brain, and behavior relationships in fragile X syndrome: Evidence from neuroimaging studies. *Developmental Disabilities Research Reviews, 15*(4), 343–352.

Scerif, G. & Karmiloff-Smith, A. (2005). The dawn of cognitive genetics? Crucial developmental caveats. *Trends in Cognitive Sciences, 9*(3), 126–135.

Scerif, G. & Steele, A. (2011). Neurocognitive development of attention across genetic syndromes: Inspecting a disorder's dynamics through the lens of another. *Progress in Brain Research, 189*, 285–301.

Scerif, G. & Wu, R. (2014). Developmental disorders. In A. C. Nobre & S. Kastner (eds), *The Oxford Handbook of Attention* (pp. 893–926). Oxford: Oxford University Press.

Scerif, G., Cornish, K., Wilding, J., Driver, J. & Karmiloff-Smith, A. (2004). Visual search in typically developing toddlers and toddlers with Fragile X or Williams syndrome. *Developmental Science, 7*(1), 116–130.

Scerif, G., Karmiloff-Smith, A., Campos, R., Elsabbagh, M., Driver, J. & Cornish, K. (2005). To look or not to look? Typical and atypical development of oculomotor control. *Journal of Cognitive Neuroscience, 17*(4), 591–604.

Scerif, G., Cornish, K., Wilding, J., Driver, J. & Karmiloff-Smith, A. (2007). Delineation of early attentional control difficulties in fragile X syndrome: Focus on neurocomputational changes. *Neuropsychologia, 45*, 1889–1898.

Scerif, G., Longhi, E., Cole, V., Karmiloff-Smith, A. & Cornish, K. (2012). Attention across modalities as a longitudinal predictor of early outcomes: The case of fragile X syndrome. *Journal of Child Psychology and Psychiatry, 53*(6), 641–650.

Shaw, P., Lerch, J., Greenstein, D., Sharp, W., Clasen, L., Evans, A. … Rapoport, J. (2006). Longitudinal mapping of cortical thickness and clinical outcome in children and adolescents with attention-deficit/hyperactivity disorder. *Archives of General Psychiatry, 63*(5), 540–549.

Shaw, P., Eckstrand, K., Sharp, W., Blumenthal, J., Lerch, J. P., Greenstein, D., … Rapoport, J. L. (2007). Attention-deficit/hyperactivity disorder is characterized by a delay in cortical maturation. *Proceedings of the National Academy of Sciences of the United States of America, 104*(49), 19649–19654.

Skinner, M., Hooper, S., Hatton, D. D., Roberts, J., Mirrett, P., Schaaf, J., … Bailey, D. B. Jr. (2005). Mapping nonverbal IQ in young boys with fragile X syndrome. *American Journal of Medical Genetics A, 132A*(1), 25–32.

Steele, A., Scerif, G., Cornish, K. & Karmiloff-Smith, A. (2013). Learning to read in Williams syndrome and Down syndrome: Syndrome-specific precursors and developmental trajectories. *Journal of Child Psychology and Psychiatry, 54*(7), 754–762.

Steinberg, J. & Webber, C. (2013). The roles of FMRP-regulated genes in Autism Spectrum Disorder: Single- and multiple-hit genetic etiologies. *The American Journal of Human Genetics, 93*(5), 825–839.

Sullivan, K., Hatton, D. D., Hammer, J., Sideris, J., Hooper, S., Ornstein, P. A. & Bailey, D. B. (2007). Sustained attention and response inhibition in boys with fragile X syndrome: Measures of continuous performance. *American Journal of Medical Genetics. Part B, Neuropsychiatric Genetics, 144B*(4), 517–532.

Thomas, M. S. C., Annaz, D., Ansari, D., Scerif, G., Jarrold, C. & Karmiloff-Smith., A. (2009). Using developmental trajectories to understand genetic disorders. *Journal of Speech, Language and Hearing Research, 52*, 336–358.

Tranfaglia, M. R. (2011). The psychiatric presentation of Fragile X: Evolution of the diagnosis and treatment of the psychiatric comorbidities of Fragile X syndrome. *Developmental Neuroscience, 33*(5), 337–348.

Turk, J. (1998). Fragile X syndrome and attentional deficits. *Journal of Applied Research in Intellectual Disabilities, 11*(3), 175–191.

Tye, C. & Bolton, P. (2013). Neural connectivity abnormalities in autism: Insights from the Tuberous Sclerosis model. *BMC Medicine, 11,* 55–59.

Van der Molen, M. J. W., Van der Molen, M. W., Ridderinkhof, K. R., Hamel, B. C. J., Curfs, L. M. G. & Ramakers, G. J. A. (2012). Auditory and visual cortical activity during selective attention in fragile X syndrome: A cascade of processing deficiencies. *Clinical Neurophysiology: Official Journal of the International Federation of Clinical Neurophysiology, 123,* 720–729.

Verkerk, A. J. M. H., Pieretti, M., Sutcliffe, J. S., Fu, Y.-H., Kuhl, D. P. A., Pizzuti, A., ... Warren, S. T. (1991). Identification of a gene (FMR-1) containing a CGG repeat coincident with a breakpoint cluster region exhibiting length variation in fragile X syndrome. *Cell,* 65(5), 905–914.

Volkow, N. D., Wang, G. J., Fowler, J. S. & Ding, Y. S. (2005). Imaging the effect of methylphenidate on brain dopamine: New model on its therapeutic actions for attention-deficit/hyperactivity disorder. *Biological Psychiatry, 57*(11), 1410–1415.

Walter, E., Mazaika, P. K. & Reiss, A. L. (2009). Insights into brain development from neurogenetic syndromes: Evidence from Fragile X syndrome, Williams syndrome, Turner syndrome and Velocardiofacial syndrome. *Neuroscience, 164*(1), 257–271.

Yan, Q. J., Rammal, M., Tranfaglia, M. & Bauchwitz, R. P. (2005). Suppression of two major Fragile X syndrome mouse model phenotypes by the mGluR5 antagonist MPEP. *Neuropharmacology, 49*(7), 1053–1066.

11

EXPERIMENTAL DIFFICULTIES IN NEURODEVELOPMENTAL DISORDERS

Evidence from Down syndrome

Harry Purser

11.1 Introduction

A description of Down syndrome (DS) was first given by John Langdon Down in 1866 (Langdon Down, 1866). DS has a prevalence of approximately 5 in every 10,000 live births (Steele & Stratford, 1995) and results from an extra copy, or part-copy, of chromosome 21. Several physical characteristics are associated with DS, including a relatively small buccal cavity, a relatively large tongue, and shorter than average height. Children with DS often have a congenital heart abnormality, the most common being an atrial septal defect ('hole in the heart'). In addition, hearing loss affects the majority of people with DS and this population is prone to recurrent ear infections as young children (see Gibson, 1978).

11.1.1 Neurodevelopment

In utero, the brains of individuals with DS are characterised by cerebellar hypoplasia (below-normal number of neurons) and a relatively short frontal lobe (Winter, Ostrovsky, Komarniski & Uhrich, 2000). Compared with typically developing (TD) infants, those with DS continue to show the emergence of neuroanatomical differences. These include local differences such as a reduced size of the brainstem and cerebellum, and global differences such as delayed myelination and a reduction in the number of cortical granular neurons (Nadel, 1999). By the age of 35 years, there tend to be signs of certain neuropathological characteristics that are common to those seen in Alzheimer's disease, including neurofibrillary tangles and amyloid plaques (Arai, Suzuki, Mizuguchi & Takashima, 1997), although it should be noted that the exact degenerative pattern of neuropathology seen in DS shows some clear differences to the one seen in Alzheimer's disease (Allsop, Kidd, Landon & Tomlinson, 1986).

11.1.2 Cognitive profile

At the cognitive level of description, individuals with DS tend to have IQ scores in the range of 30 to 70, and show particular difficulties with expressive language (e.g. Chapman, 1997). Within the domain of expressive language, both vocabulary and narrative syntax, in particular, tend to be delayed relative to the general level of cognitive ability (Chapman, Seung, Schwartz & Kay-Raining Bird, 1998). The mean length of utterance (MLU) in morphemes or words can be used as a measure of expressive language: the MLUs of children and adolescents with DS have been found to be lower than both those of TD children matched on non-verbal ability (Chapman, Schwartz & Kay-Raining Bird, 1991; Chapman et al., 1997) and mental-age (MA) matched control participants with other intellectual impairments (e.g. Rosin, Swift, Bless & Vetter, 1988).

In contrast, word comprehension is typically more advanced than would be predicted by overall level of cognitive functioning (Chapman et al., 1991), and can exceed that of TD children of similar MA or MLU (see Barrett & Diniz, 1989). Comprehension of grammar, however, appears to be a relative weakness in DS (e.g. Chapman, 1995; Chapman et al., 1991; Fowler, 1990; Laws & Bishop, 2003). For example, Laws and Bishop (2003) showed that adolescents with DS attained markedly low scores on the Test for the Reception of Grammar (TROG; Bishop, 1983).

Although children with DS improve with age on measures of cognitive and adaptive abilities, these changes occur at a slower rate than that seen in their TD peers, resulting in a decline on standardised scores (Hodapp & Zigler, 1999). Mirroring these improvements, most children with DS show consistent increases in academic attainments throughout their school years, with advances in basic reading and numeracy, and more modest increases in basic writing ability (Turner & Alborz, 2003).

11.1.3 Attention/motivation

One area of cognition that is expected to have a widespread impact on educational prowess is attention (e.g. Scholtens, Rydell & Yang-Wallentin, 2013). Atypicalities have been found in a variety of attentional functions, each of which might be expected to impact on the ability to be successful in cognitive tasks. Adults with DS often direct their attention to irrelevant aspects of a display, or only to particular parts of a display (House & Zeaman, 1959, 1960), such that only a limited amount of information can be processed. Infants with DS, too, are less likely than MA-matched controls to look at a new toy when it is presented, requiring a shift of attention to the toy (Landry & Chapieski, 1989).

Breckenridge and colleagues (Breckenridge, Braddick, Anker, Woodhouse & Atkinson, 2013) assessed children and adolescents with DS and Williams syndrome on a newly developed attentional battery, the ECAB (Early Childhood Attention Battery; Atkinson, Braddick & Breckenbridge, 2010). Both groups were impaired relative to MA norms on a range of attention tasks, including visual search, visuospatial (motor) inhibition, and attentional flexibility. Sustained attention, however, was a relative strength for both groups, with the DS group scoring particularly well on a test of auditory sustained attention, in which participants must be vigilant to detect a rarely occurring auditory stimulus.

Closely related to attention are 'executive functions', which are thought to underlie control of attention (e.g. Posner & Petersen, 1990). In another study comparing participants with DS and Williams syndrome, where each group was a mixture of children, adolescents and adults, Costanzo et al. (2013) found evidence of particular difficulties in attentional shifting (comparable to the flexibility tasks used by Breckenridge and colleagues, 2013, above) in the DS group. The DS group fared more poorly than MA-matched TD controls on tests of verbal, but not visual, inhibition, and on both verbal and visual shifting. Critically, both disorder groups did markedly worse than TD controls on a measure of auditory sustained attention, but did not differ from each other. Furthermore, none of the groups differed on a visual sustained attention task.

These results stand in contrast to the superior auditory sustained attention found in DS by Breckenridge et al. (2013), above. It is possible that the differences owe to the different age compositions in the two studies, but this is not at all clear. Certainly, the particular auditory sustained attention tests used by each research group seem broadly similar. Taking these two studies together, people with DS appear to have particular difficulties with attentional flexibility relative to MA-matched control participants, but more research seems to be needed to establish the cognitive profile in terms of other aspects of attention.

A related, but less well described, aspect of the DS phenotype is motivation. There is a body of evidence indicating that intrinsic motivation – the doing of an activity for its inherent satisfactions rather than for some separable consequence (e.g. Ryan & Deci, 2000) – may be a problem area for people with DS. Children and adolescents with DS tend to abandon difficult or impossible tasks more readily than controls (Kasari & Freeman, 2001; Pitcairn & Wishart, 1994; Wishart & Duffy, 1990). By way of illustration, Wishart (1993) investigated the possible use of 'avoidance strategies' when confronted with demanding activities in children with DS aged five or younger. A wide variety of avoidance behaviours were observed in classroom-style tasks, but there were two features common to the behaviours. First, they were generally maintained until they had the desired effect: breaking off the activity. Second, they tended to involve the use of the child's developing social skills. It was reported that a particularly frequent strategy was to engage eye contact with the experimenter in the midst of the experimental presentation, such that successful performance on the trial was highly unlikely. Describing a visual search task, Wishart noted that:

> [c]hildren would in any case often not go on to search at all, despite the fact that there was a very limited number of possible hiding places, all within very easy reach. Many simply sat back, maintaining eye contact, smiling and refusing to do anything until the tester moved on to some other task.
>
> *(Wishart, 1993, p. 51)*

There is some evidence that similar kinds of avoidance behaviours persist in older children, defaulting to social engagement strategies when faced with nontrivial tasks (Kasari & Freeman, 2001).

Taken together, these studies indicate that a lack of intrinsic motivation may impair task performance of young people with DS, leading to an underestimation of underlying levels of ability and, more importantly, to poorer educational attainments. This introduces the main theme of this chapter, namely that the scores of people with DS on tests and assessments designed to measure particular abilities may be limited by demands that are not 'central' to the test or assessment. In other words, an individual with DS who achieves a low score might do so for different reasons than a TD individual, even if the test is well designed for the typical population.

11.1.4 Long-term memory

Clearly, any academic advancement involves learning, which will depend heavily on long-term memory: the very notion of a 'learning disability', then, raises the possibility that individuals with DS might have difficulties in this area. Indeed, several studies have provided evidence that individuals with DS have a deficit in long-term memory function. Some of these studies have included verbal list-learning tasks, in which participants are tested repeatedly on the same list of words, with a learning trial between each test (Carlesimo, Marotta & Vicari, 1997; Pennington, Moon, Edgin, Stedron & Nadel, 2003). In these tasks, any improvement in recall across tests is taken as evidence of long-term learning.

In each of these studies, the participants with DS learned fewer words in total than the control participants. Moreover, both Pennington et al. (2003) and Vicari, Bellucci and Carlesimo (2000) found that the adolescents with DS also showed clear deficits on non-verbal long-term learning tasks (though see Carlesimo et al., 1997). Other studies have used the Rivermead Behavioural Memory Test (Wilson, Cockburn & Baddeley, 1985), a battery that was designed to assess memory skills related to 'everyday' functioning. Such studies have suggested that adults with DS show particularly poor performance on a long-term verbal recall component of the battery, but relatively better performance on a long-term visual recognition task (e.g. Hon, Huppert, Holland & Watson, 1998; Wilson & Ivani-Chalian, 1995). However, no statistics were presented in either study to evaluate this comparison. Moreover, none of the above long-term memory studies provided comparable assessments of both long-term recall and recognition memory for both visual and verbal information.

More recently, Jarrold, Baddeley and Phillips (2007) assessed long-term memory among mixed-age samples of people with DS and Williams syndrome. The assessments were made using the Doors and People battery (Baddeley, Emslie & Nimmo-Smith, 1994), which does provide measures of both long-term recall and recognition of both verbal and visual information. Since many studies of short-term memory (STM) in DS have investigated memory in both the verbal and visuospatial domains, it is worth considering this long-term memory study in more detail. Recall of verbal information was assessed with the People subtest: participants were required to learn the names of four individuals depicted in photographs. Participants were tested on the same four names (both forenames and surnames) across trials and were reminded of any names they had forgotten before the next trial. The Shapes subtest was used to assess recall of visual material: the procedure was similar in structure to that of the People subtest, but instead of recalling names, participants were required to learn to draw four complex shapes from memory. There was also an initial copying phase, with no memory load, in order that participants' drawing skills could be taken into account. The performance of these intellectually impaired participants was standardised for age and level of intellectual ability against that of a large sample of TD children. The verbal recall performance of the DS group was no poorer than predicted by participants' general levels of verbal ability. In contrast, the DS group showed evidence of particular problems with the visual recall task. However, the DS group had no particular difficulty on the visual recognition task, raising the possibility that this apparent deficit may have been due to more general task demands, if one accepts that the difference between recall and recognition is simply a difference in the availability of cues (e.g. Tulving, 1976).

11.1.5 Short-term memory

Despite appearing to have no verbal long-term memory deficit, individuals with DS tend to exhibit poor verbal STM (Marcell & Armstrong, 1982), although such a deficit is not observed in all individuals (e.g. Vallar & Papagno, 1993). Marcell and Armstrong (1982) found that a group of children and adolescents with DS performed less well on the Auditory than the Sequential Memory subtest of the Illinois Test of Psycholinguistic Abilities (cf. Bilovsky & Share, 1965). They subsequently compared this group to a sample of TD children, using more comparable visual and auditory STM tasks. The auditory test used was the forward digit span task, in which a list of items is verbally presented, to be repeated back immediately in correct serial order. The visual test was identical, except that the digits were instead presented on a series of cards. This TD group showed a clear recall advantage for auditorily presented lists of digits over visually-presented ones. However, when the DS group was assessed on the same two tasks, no such auditory advantage was found. It is worth noting here that according to many models of working memory (e.g. Baddeley, 1986), phonological information can be stored in verbal STM regardless of its mode of presentation, i.e. visually presented memoranda may be spontaneously recoded into phonological memory, while verbally presented material will gain 'automatic' access to verbal STM. However, there is considerable evidence that children less than seven years old do not spontaneously recode visually presented verbal material into a phonological form (e.g. Conrad, 1971; Henry, 1991).

In view of this, and the evidence that adolescents with DS are unlikely to rehearse (Jarrold, Baddeley & Hewes, 2000; see below), such a modality manipulation may be argued to provide an appropriate comparison of verbal and visuospatial STM (see Jarrold, Purser & Brock, 2006). Could this lack of auditory advantage for the DS group be explained by a non-central task demand? One simple explanation would be poor hearing. Clearly, one cannot correctly output an item from memory that was not correct at the input to that memory system. Audiological research has indicated the presence of mild to moderate hearing problems in the majority of individuals with DS (e.g. Brooks, Wooley & Kanjilal, 1972). To answer this, Jarrold and Baddeley (1997) investigated the relationship between hearing ability and phonological memory performance in children and adolescents with DS. Participants were tested on a modified version of the McCormick Toy Discrimination Test (McCormick, 1977), which assesses comprehension of single spoken words, thereby providing an indirect measure of their auditory sensitivity; no reliable relationship between hearing ability and digit span performance was found.

11.1.6 Taking forward the issue of specificity

This impairment of phonological memory does not seem to result from hearing problems, but could it reflect some general impairment of STM, rather than being specific to *verbal* STM? Numerous STM studies of TD adults have shown that auditory presentation affords better retention than does visual presentation (e.g. Craik, 1969). This modality effect has also been found in children aged between five and ten, using various experimental procedures (e.g. Dilley & Paivio, 1968). Jarrold and Baddeley (1997) measured the digit and Corsi spans of children and adolescents with DS and receptive vocabulary-matched controls. The Corsi span task is a visuospatial analogue of the digit span test in which participants watch an experimenter tap out a sequence of spatial locations, then attempt to reproduce that sequence (Corsi, 1972). The participants with DS achieved higher Corsi spans than digit spans. This 'reverse modality effect' has been replicated (Laws, 2002; Jarrold, Baddeley & Phillips, 2002; Purser & Jarrold, 2005), and many other studies have failed to find the normal modality effect in DS. Recently, Naess, Lyster, Hulme, and Melby-Lervåg (2011) have demonstrated the robustness of this verbal STM deficit using a meta-analytical approach. Taken together, these studies indicate that individuals with DS have a *selective* deficit in verbal STM.

A somewhat different, and better-controlled approach to this notion of selectivity has been taken by Brock and Jarrold (2005). In their study, a mixed-age DS group and TD controls were tested on a digit reconstruction task. In this task, participants were auditorily presented with sequences of digits, and were then required to respond by pressing the digits in correct serial order on a touch-screen display. Only the relevant digits were displayed on the screen, and each one disappeared as it was selected. In this way, only order errors could be made on the task. In addition to this verbal serial order reconstruction task, participants were assessed on a conventional test of digit span. Furthermore, there were four background measures: performance on a closely-matched visuospatial serial order reconstruction task, reaction time on a simple digit identification task, non-verbal MA and receptive vocabulary. A hierarchical regression showed that the DS group performed significantly more poorly than the control group on both measures of verbal STM, even after variation in the four background measures had been accounted for. This finding clearly supports the view that people with DS have a selective deficit in verbal STM.

Several features of the study's procedure strengthen this conclusion. First, the verbal and non-verbal tasks were very closely matched, so that group differences in performance across tasks could not readily be attributed to group differences in articulation, motivation or motor control. Second, the inclusion of the digit identification task allowed participants to be screened out if they could not consistently match auditorily presented numbers to their graphical tokens, regardless of whether this resulted from hearing problems or poor knowledge of numbers. Furthermore, the results from the digit identification task provided evidence that visual search speed was unlikely to underlie group differences.

11.1.7 An impairment of the phonological loop?

A specific verbal STM deficit of this form can be readily characterised in terms of an impairment of the phonological loop component of Baddeley's (1986) working memory model. The working memory model consists of three components: the phonological loop, the visuospatial sketchpad and the central executive. According to this framework, the phonological loop consists of a short-term store, of limited capacity, that stores temporally labile information in a phonological code. Auditorily presented memoranda gain direct access to this store, and can be refreshed by a sub-vocal articulatory rehearsal process, such that items can be held in the store indefinitely. However, this articulatory rehearsal mechanism also serves the function of translating visually presented material into a phonological code. The visuospatial sketchpad is a limited-capacity store of visuospatial material, concerned with memoranda such as colour, location and shape. The third component, the central executive, acts to direct attention and coordinate the activity of the other components.

The finding that individuals with DS have poor verbal STM has prompted many researchers to suggest that the syndrome may be associated with an impairment of the phonological loop (e.g. Varnhagen, Das & Varnhagen, 1987). However, the locus of such an impairment could be either the rehearsal process or the phonological store. If rehearsal were at fault, then the deficit might not really be one of storage at all, but of articulation (motor control).

However, research has suggested that the deficit is not, in fact, caused by a dysfunction of articulatory rehearsal (e.g. Jarrold et al., 2000). One marker of rehearsal is the word length effect in verbal STM (Baddeley, Thompson & Buchanan, 1975). This is the phenomenon that more words of a shorter duration can be recalled than those of a longer duration, implying that the ability to recall a list of items correctly depends on the time taken to rehearse or output that list. In view of this, it has been suggested that poor articulation rates underlie the phonological memory problems seen in DS, because this would make rehearsal less efficient (Kay-Raining Bird & Chapman, 1994). Articulatory problems are, indeed, associated with DS (see Gibson, 1978), and articulation problems are known to give rise to verbal STM difficulties in other disorders (see Hulme & Roodenrys, 1995). However, Jarrold and colleagues found that a group of children and adolescents with DS had comparable articulation rates to those of a group of MA matched individuals with moderate learning difficulties, measured by the time taken to repeat pairs of words as rapidly as possible (Jarrold et al., 2000). Moreover, the two groups showed similar word-length effects. Despite this, the DS group demonstrated significantly lower verbal memory span and covarying out articulation rate did not affect the size of this deficit in the DS group. Furthermore, correlational analysis indicated that articulation speed did not predict STM performance in either group (see also Jarrold, Cowan, Hewes & Riby, 2004). Finally, in a further experiment, a probed recall procedure was used to examine word-length effects, in light of the potential confound of output decay; in serial recall, the more slowly a participant outputs a response list, the more degraded by decay will be the items yet to be verbalised (Cowan et al., 1992; Henry, 1991; Jarrold et al., 2000). Probing was found to eliminate word-length effects in both groups, providing additional evidence that neither group was rehearsing (cf. Henry, 1991). Together, these results indicate that neither the DS group nor the controls in that study were rehearsing, and thus count against articulatory rehearsal problems as an explanation for the specific verbal STM deficit in DS.

Instead, two studies by Purser and Jarrold (2005, 2010) converge on the idea that the STM deficit associated with DS might owe to a limited capacity. Both studies involved presenting four-item lists in tasks that tapped verbal STM; in each, adolescents and young adults with DS showed particular difficulty with earlier serial positions, consistent with the notion of a limited capacity. In Purser and Jarrold (2010), phonologically-coded storage was evident only at serial position 4, suggesting that individuals with DS might have a verbal short-term memory capacity of only one item. It should be considered, however, that the task was difficult, which may have encouraged participants to attempt to retain only the relatively distinct final item, resulting in an underestimation of verbal short-term memory capacity (children and adolescents with DS tend to have a digit span of at least two to three items; Jarrold et al., 2002).

11.1.8 The broader influence of STM

A specific deficit can have widespread developmental consequences, leading to failure on tasks that measure other areas of ability: a deficit in verbal short-term, or phonological, memory may have a broader influence on cognitive development than merely restricting memory for sequences of numbers and words. Baddeley and colleagues (Baddeley, Gathercole & Papagno, 1998; Gathercole & Baddeley, 1990) have collected a body of evidence indicating a role for phonological memory in language comprehension, vocabulary acquisition and in learning to read. Gathercole and Baddeley (1990) assessed the phonological skills of three groups of children: one with disordered language development, one control group matched on non-verbal intelligence, and a further control group matched on verbal ability. The language-disordered children performed significantly more poorly on verbal STM tasks than both of the control groups, suggesting a specific deficit in phonological memory. However, the language-disordered children showed clear effects of phonological similarity – the phenomenon that lists made up from similar-sounding items are recalled less well than lists in which the items do not sound similar (e.g. Wickelgren, 1965a, 1965b) – and of word length. Further experiments indicated that neither phonological skills nor articulatory problems were likely to underlie the poor verbal STM performance shown by the language-disordered group. Gathercole and Baddeley (1993) proposed that, instead, an impairment of phonological storage could underpin this deficit in verbal STM and play a key role in the deviant language development seen in such children.

Chapman and colleagues (Chapman, Kay-Raining Bird & Schwartz, 1990; Chapman, Miller, Sindberg & Seung, 1996) have investigated the predictors of 'fast mapping' skill in the learning of new words, in children and adolescents with DS. Participants were presented with novel words (nonwords) for novel referents one or more times in an incidental learning situation. Although no reliable differences were found between the performance of participants with DS and MA matched controls when only a single novel word was presented (Chapman et al., 1990), learning deficits were apparent in a DS group when a greater number of words was presented (Chapman, Miller, Sindberg & Seung, 1996). Participants were assessed on both the comprehension and production of the novel words, along with tests of verbal STM and syntax comprehension. A regression analysis showed that performance on the comprehension test predicted fast mapping in comprehension, whereas verbal STM predicted fast mapping in production. These results indicate a relationship between verbal STM and expressive vocabulary learning for both children and adolescents with DS and also TD children.

More recently, Mosse and Jarrold (2011), using carefully controlled tasks, found no evidence of a word-learning deficit in a mixed-age DS group relative to TD individuals matched for receptive vocabulary, using demanding production (expression) procedures. The authors argued that this is inconsistent with the notion that verbal STM is the sole determinant of new word learning. They suggested that, instead, there might be an additional route to vocabulary acquisition, namely a domain-general process involving long-term memory for serial order, by repeated presentation. Although it would be premature to accept this conclusion firmly, the above studies illustrate the fact that the specificity of a deficit depends on how it is defined and measured. Individuals with DS seem only to struggle with new word learning, relative to controls, when heavier demands are made on phonological memory. The take-home message for parents and teachers would be to keep to one new word at a time when teaching pupils with DS. Does the literature offer any insights into the impact of phonological memory on language more generally?

11.1.9 Verbal STM and expressive language

Laws (2004) investigated the contributions of phonological memory, language comprehension and hearing to expressive language abilities in children and adolescents with DS. Among the measures of phonological memory were nonword repetition, where a single nonword is auditorily presented on each trial and the participant is required to repeat it, and digit span. Nonwords of different numbers of syllables are used, in order to vary memory load. Word repetition was also assessed, in order to estimate speech ability. Language comprehension was measured using the TROG (Bishop, 1983), in which participants are required to select a target picture to match a phrase or sentence spoken by the experimenter. In one measure of expressive language, participants were shown a wordless picture book and instructed to tell the story using the pictures as cues and their narratives were recorded. MLUs in morphemes were calculated from these recordings. Hearing was also assessed, using pure tone audiometry.

Hearing was found not to contribute significantly to the expressive language scores of participants who provided an intelligible narrative. Nonword repetition scores were found to correlate significantly with MLUs, even when the effect of word repetition had been partialled out. This led Laws (2004) to suggest that phonological memory is related to expressive language, but not merely because the measures of both required spoken output. However, digit span (traditionally viewed as a measure of phonological memory, perhaps a purer one than nonword repetition) did *not* correlate significantly with MLUs, which clearly requires explanation.

Laws (2004) suggested that a third factor, such as knowledge of phonotactic structure, might have mediated the relationship between nonword repetition and expressive language. An alternative explanation, perhaps, is simply that articulatory (speech output) demands mediated the relationship between nonword repetition and expressive language. Whatever the case, the nature of the relationship between verbal STM and expressive language is not yet clear. This rather convoluted example serves to show how difficult it can be to interpret the relationships between measures when each measure involves multiple cognitive demands.

11.2 The purity of our cognitive measures

For researchers who wish to investigate the relationships between, and perhaps statistical independence of, a range of cognitive functions, a key challenge is to identify so-called 'clean' (as opposed to 'dirty') tasks. In other words, tasks that measure what they are designed to measure, without measuring other things, too. But how realistic is this aim? Much of the STM research above has been painstaking in its attempts to eradicate non-central task demands from its memory measures. However, it is not clear that all test designers have been quite as successful in this regard. The next section will be concerned with analysing the task demands of some of the most commonly used tests in developmental disorder research, with a view to highlighting difficulties of interpreting task performances of people with DS.

11.2.1 Raven's Coloured Progressive Matrices

Raven's Coloured Progressive Matrices test (RCPM, Raven, Raven & Court, 1998), is used almost ubiquitously as a measure of non-verbal intelligence in developmental research. The test is a series of 30 multiple-choice puzzles, in which participants are shown either a series of images with one missing, or a whole image with a piece missing, and must select the missing image or piece from a set of six possible answers. The test is intended to be a measure of fluid, or unlearned, intelligence (Raven et al., 1998), which is intimately related to Spearman's *g* factor of general intelligence (Spearman, 1904). The notion has more recently been exposited by Cattell as 'an expression of the level of complexity of relationships which an individual can perceive and act upon when he does not have recourse to answers to such complex issues already sorted in memory' (Cattell, 1971, p. 99).

However, there may be a little more to it: it might be instructive to consider what the task requires in more detail. Participants must attend to the whole puzzle in order to construe it fully and then they must select the correct answer from a pool that includes five distractors. Could these task demands pose a problem for participants with DS? Recall from above that House and Zeaman (1959, 1960) found that adults with DS often direct their attention only to particular aspects of a visual display, or to irrelevant parts of it, in such a way that only a limited amount of information can be processed. In line with this, an investigation into RCPM performance by Gunn and Jarrold (2004) found that individuals with DS were more likely than RCPM-matched TD controls to select 'Difference' responses in the task, which either feature no pattern of any kind, or have no direct relevance to the target pattern. This suggests that individuals with DS were failing to attend fully either to the target picture or to the response set, as House and Zeaman (1959, 1960) might have predicted. Relatedly, the motivational issues reported by Wishart (1993) and Kasari and Freeman (2001) above indicate that young people with DS might invoke (social) avoidance strategies when faced with difficult items. The author of this chapter can attest that such strategies are frequently encountered when administering the RCPM, not only with children, but also sometimes with adolescent and adult participants.

Considering these points, then, a participant with DS may attain a particular score on the RCPM either because they answered to the best of their ability, with incorrect responses reflecting items that they were simply unable to compute, or the score may reflect some combination of ability and also attentional and motivational factors. On balance, it may be more plausible to accept the latter possibility, in which case performance on RCPM may be limited by attention or motivation rather than by Spearman's *g* factor for some participants with DS.

11.2.2 British Picture Vocabulary Scale

After RCPM, perhaps the second most commonly encountered test in developmental disorder research is the British Picture Vocabulary Scale (BPVS;

Dunn, Dunn, Styles & Sewell, 2009; the USA version is the Peabody Picture Vocabulary Test [PPVT, Dunn & Dunn, 1997]). The BPVS is designed to assess receptive vocabulary: lexicosemantic knowledge relevant to comprehension, rather than language production. On a given trial, the participant is shown a page with four pictures; the experimenter says a word to the participant, who must respond by pointing to the picture that best illustrates the spoken word. For example, the participant might hear 'castle' and must select the picture of a castle, with distractor pictures of other types of building. In a sense, this test is intended to measure something that stands in stark contrast to RCPM: 'crystallised' knowledge in a specific domain, rather than a general, knowledge-independent cognitive ability. So, how pure a measure of vocabulary might we expect it to be, when administered to a participant with DS? As with RCPM, the task demands will now be considered more closely. Participants must first attend to the word spoken by the experimenter and hold it in mind while analysing the four pictures, before selecting the answer that best illustrates the word.

The astute reader might have spotted that there is a similar set of potential problems here as were found with RCPM: first, the failure to attend fully to the set of pictures, or perhaps to focus only on a single part of the display (a single picture), either of which could entail an incorrect response. Second, the motivational issue: failing to respond at all as the task becomes harder. Again the author of this chapter has encountered these behaviours countless times. However, there are further issues with the BPVS. Recall from above that Jarrold et al. (2000) found evidence indicating that children and adolescents with DS appear not to rehearse memoranda after hearing them: they do not refresh them in STM, using sub-vocal speech. In the absence of rehearsal, and with a distracting activity (examining the pictures), forgetting might be expected to occur rapidly due to decay processes, within two seconds or so (e.g. Baddeley, 1986). It should be noted here that this would also be a concern for TD children under the age of seven, who also do not tend to rehearse spontaneously (Henry, 1991).

It could be countered that participants could perhaps retrieve the single verbal item, after all, because some theorists require interference of temporally close stimuli for forgetting to occur, rather than time-based decay (see Lewandowsky & Oberauer, 2009). In any case, one could also counter that the target word might simply be retrieved from long-term memory. However, this presents another possible challenge: the most robust finding in the executive function literature, outlined above, was that some kind of attentional shifting would put people with DS at a relative disadvantage. It was noted above that the task requires holding the word in mind while analysing the four pictures, before selecting the answer that best illustrates the word. This would seem to involve shifting attention back and forth between retrieving the verbal representation, in one modality, and perceiving the pictures in another (visual) modality. Therefore, there is some reason to be concerned that a deficit in attentional shifting could lead to a poorer outcome than would otherwise be possible on the BPVS.

11.2.3 Test for Reception of Grammar

Another frequently encountered language assessment is the TROG (the current version is TROG-2, Bishop, 2003). The task is similar in format to the BPVS: the participant is presented with a set of four pictures and then hears a *sentence*, spoken by the experimenter, and must then point to the picture that best illustrates the sentence. The task was designed to be sensitive to comprehension of syntax, rather than vocabulary; correspondingly, all the sentences employed are formed of words with low age-of-acquisition and high frequency (with the expectation that the words would be known by all native English-speaking participants).

Every concern raised for the BPVS applies equally to the TROG: poor task performance could arise from attending only to a subset of the pictures, from motivational factors, or from attentional switching. However, there is a particular concern about the TROG that eclipses these: judging the syntax of a sentence requires holding the words of the sentence in mind in the exact order in which they were heard. *Prima facie*, this appears to be very similar to the demands of a verbal STM task, with memory demands increasing as the number of words separating subject and object increases. As expounded in this chapter, one of the defining aspects of the DS cognitive phenotype is a profound and specific verbal STM deficit. Unfortunately, Laws (2004) did not report the correlation between TROG and digit span scores. The relationship between verbal STM and sentence comprehension is not yet clear in typical development, but it appears that the two are related when sentences are more complex (see Kidd, 2013, for a recent review). What counts as 'complex' might be rather different for people with DS compared with TD individuals, given the robust findings of poor receptive grammar (Chapman, 1995; Chapman et al., 1991).

As might be expected on the basis of the above, and mentioned near the start of the chapter, individuals with DS do score very poorly on the TROG (Laws & Bishop, 2003). It does seem, however, that these low scores could be due, at least in part, to limiting cognitive and behavioural factors that are not specific to syntax.

11.2.4 Phonological awareness tasks

There are several popular tests of phonological awareness. One is initial sound detection, where participants attempt to match a target picture to one of a number of response pictures on the basis of sharing the same initial sound (e.g. 'Which starts with the same sound as bee – table, bed or sun?'). Another is phoneme deletion, which is presented in a similar fashion; the task involves deciding which of a number of pictures would match the sound of the target picture following a particular deletion (e.g. 'If d is removed from deer, which would match – door, eye or ear?'). Yet another is rhyme detection, in which participants attempt to decide which of a number of response pictures rhymes with a target picture. This time, the main concern is that such tasks might make a verbal STM demand that would be problematic for participants with DS, given that the verbal stimuli must be held in mind while a judgement about them is made.

Phonological awareness does appear to be another area of difficulty for people with DS. Roch and Jarrold (2008) assessed the phonological awareness skills of children and young adults with DS, and reading-matched TD controls, with all three of the paradigms in the paragraph above. Although the DS group performed more poorly than controls on each phonological awareness task, the DS group demonstrated particular difficulties on the rhyme detection test, in line with other studies (Cardoso-Martins, Michalick & Pollo, 2002; Snowling, Hulme & Mercer, 2002; see also Naess, Melby-Lervåg, Hulme & Lyster, 2012).

Brock and Jarrold (2004) found that verbal STM in adolescents and young adults with DS was associated with another aspect of phonological awareness, phonemic discrimination, using a task in which participants were auditorily presented with pairs of words or nonwords and then asked to respond as to whether the two items were the same or different. However, this association would be expected, given the apparent STM load. More recently, Purser and Jarrold (2013) ran a comparable study with adolescents and young adults with DS, using a phonemic discrimination task designed to minimise memory load. In this task, participants were shown two pictures side-by-side (e.g. Pig and Pin) on a touch-screen and heard a word (either *pig* or *pin*) and had to touch the picture that matched the word. Rather than holding and manipulating at least two words in mind, participants had only to correctly match one word to a picture. The DS group actually performed markedly better on the discrimination task than non-verbal-matched controls, but markedly worse than the same participants on a STM task that used the same stimuli. This serves to bring home the importance of considering verbal STM demands for DS research.

11.3 Conclusions

The early part of this chapter was concerned with the specificity of apparent cognitive deficits in DS. So versed in the language of task demands, the reader was then presented with a task demand analysis of some common tasks in developmental disorder research, viewing them through the lens of the would-be DS researcher. It was seen that cognitive tests might not, in all cases, be very pure measures of the abilities that they are designed to test. In developmental disorder research, it is critically important to consider whether non-central task demands might limit, or be likely to limit, the performance of a given participant group.

Practical tips

1. Phonological memory is poor, so avoid such memory demands (if non-central) at all costs. Are your instructions brief, self-contained sentences? Are you checking that they have been understood? Does success at your task require

holding more than one thing in mind? If so, could you use visual support to reduce memory load?

2. Expressive language can be a problem, so do not require verbal responses, or at least keep verbal requirements to a minimum. Could participants point or use a touch-screen? If verbal response is necessary, are the possible responses as short and distinct as possible?

3. Visual attention seems to be a problem, so avoid complex visual displays or presentations. Can you make the stimuli more distinct? Is it possible to simplify the presentation? When testing, are you checking to make sure that the participant is looking where they should be looking?

4. Motivation appears to be an issue, at least for some age groups. Are you encouraging them enough? If using a computer, are you up at the screen with the participant, or are you sitting behind them, playing on your smartphone? It is imperative that you do all you can to motivate your participant. Difficulty appears to be a root cause of giving up, so have you fully considered points 1 to 3?

References

Allsop, D., Kidd, M., Landon, M. & Tomlinson, A. (1986). Isolated senile plaque cores in Alzheimer's disease and Down's syndrome show differences in morphology. *Journal of Neurology, Neurosurgery and Psychiatry, 49,* 886–927.

Arai, Y., Suzuki, A., Mizuguchi, M. & Takashima, S. (1997). Developmental and aging changes in the expression of amyloid precursor protein in Down syndrome brains. *Brain Development, 19,* 290–294.

Atkinson, J., Braddick, O. & Breckenbridge, K. (2010). Components of attention in normal and atypical development, *Journal of Vision, 10,* 492.

Baddeley, A. D. (1986). *Working Memory.* New York: Oxford University Press.

Baddeley, A. D., Thompson, N. & Buchanan, M. (1975). Word length and the structure of short-term memory. *Journal of Verbal Learning and Verbal Behaviour, 14,* 575–589.

Baddeley, A. D., Emslie, H. & Nimmo-Smith, I. (1994). *The Doors and People Test: A Test of Visual And Verbal Recall and Recognition.* Bury St. Edmunds: Thames Valley Test Company.

Baddeley, A. D., Gathercole, S. & Papagno, C. (1998). The phonological loop as a language learning device. *Psychological Review, 105,* 158–173.

Barrett, M. D. & Diniz, F. A. (1989). Lexical development in mentally handicapped children. In M. Beveridge, G. Conti-Ramsden & I. Leudar (eds), *Language and Communication in Mentally Handicapped People* (pp. 3–32). London: Chapman & Hall.

Bilovsky, D. & Share, J. (1965). The ITPA and Down's syndrome: An exploratory study. *American Journal of Mental Deficiency, 70,* 78–82.

Bishop, D. V. M. (1983). *Test for Reception of Grammar.* Published by the author and available from Age and Cognitive Performance Research Centre, University of Manchester.

——(2003). *The Test for Reception of Grammar, version 2 (TROG-2).* London: Pearson Assessment.

Breckenridge, K., Braddick, O., Anker, S., Woodhouse, M. & Atkinson, J. (2013). Attention in Williams syndrome and Down's syndrome: Performance on the new early childhood attention battery. *British Journal of Developmental Psychology, 31,* 257–269.

Brock, J. & Jarrold, C. (2004). Language influences on verbal short-term memory performance in Down syndrome: Item and order recognition. *Journal of Speech, Language and Hearing Research, 47,* 1334–1346.

——(2005). Serial order reconstruction in Down syndrome: Evidence for a selective deficit in verbal short-term memory. *Journal of Child Psychology and Psychiatry, 46,* 304–316.

Brooks, D. N., Wooley, H. & Kanjilal, G. C. (1972). Hearing loss and middle ear disorders in patients with Down Syndrome (Mongolism). *Journal of Mental Deficiency Research, 16,* 21–29.

Cardoso-Martins, C., Michalick, M. F. & Pollo, T. C. (2002). Is sensitivity to rhyme a developmental precursor to sensitivity to phoneme? Evidence from individuals with Down syndrome. *Reading and Writing: An Interdisciplinary Journal, 15,* 439–454.

Carlesimo, G. A., Marotta, L. & Vicari, S. (1997). Long-term memory in mental retardation: Evidence for a specific impairment in subjects with Down's syndrome. *Neuropsychologia, 35,* 71–79.

Cattell, R. B. (1971). *Abilities: Their Structure, Growth, and Action.* New York: Houghton Mifflin.

Chapman, R. S. (1995). Language development in children and adolescents with Down syndrome. In P. Fletcher & B. MacWhinney (eds), *Handbook of Child Language* (pp. 641–663). Oxford, UK: Blackwell.

——(1997). Language development in children and adolescents with Down syndrome. *Mental Retardation and Developmental Disabilities Research Reviews, 3,* 307–312.

Chapman, R. S., Kay-Raining Bird, E. & Schwartz, S. E. (1990). Fast mapping of novel words in event contexts by children with Down syndrome. *Journal of Speech and Hearing Disorders, 55,* 761–770.

Chapman, R. S., Schwartz, S. E. & Kay-Raining Bird, E. (1991). Language skills of children and adolescents with Down syndrome: I. Comprehension. *Journal of Speech and Hearing Research, 34,* 1106–1120.

Chapman, R. S., Miller, S., Sindberg, H. & Seung, H.-K. (1996). Fast mapping of novel words by children and adolescents with Down syndrome: Relation to auditory memory. Poster presented at the Symposium for Research on Child Language Disorders, Madison, WI, June 8, 1996.

Chapman, R. S., Seung, H.-K., Schwartz, S. E. & Kay-Raining Bird, E. (1998). Language skills of children and adolescents with Down syndrome: II. Production deficits. *Journal of Speech, Language and Hearing Research, 41,* 861–873.

Conrad, R. (1971). The chronology of the development of covert speech in children. *Developmental Psychology, 5,* 398–405.

Corsi, P. H. (1972). *Human Memory and the Medial Temporal Region of the Brain.* Unpublished doctoral dissertation, McGill University.

Costanzo, F., Varuzza, C., Menghini, D., Addona, F., Gianesini, T. & Vicari, S. (2013). Executive functions in intellectual disabilities: A comparison between Williams syndrome and Down syndrome. *Research in Developmental Disabilities, 34,* 1770–1780.

Cowan, N., Day, L., Saults, J. S., Keller, T. A., Johnson, T. & Flores, L. (1992). The role of verbal output time in the effects of word length on immediate memory. *Journal of Memory and Language, 31,* 1–17.

Craik, F. I. M. (1969). Modality effects in short-term storage. *Journal of Verbal Learning and Verbal Behaviour, 8,* 658–664.

Dilley, M. G. & Paivio, A. (1968). Pictures and words as stimulus and response items in paired-associate learning of young children. *Journal of Experimental Child Psychology, 6,* 231–240.

Dunn, L. M. & Dunn, D. M. (1997). Peabody picture vocabulary test, 3rd edition. Circle Pines, MN: American Guidance Service.

Dunn, L. M., Dunn, D. M., Styles, B. & Sewell, J. (2009). *British Picture Vocabulary Scale III.* Windsor, UK: NFER-Nelson.

Fowler, A. E. (1990). Language abilities in children with Down syndrome: Evidence for a specific syntactic delay. In D. Cicchetti & M. Beeghly (eds), *Children with Down Syndrome: A Developmental Perspective* (pp. 302–328). Cambridge: Cambridge University Press.

Gathercole, S. E. & Baddeley, A. D. (1990). Phonological memory deficits in language disordered children: Is there a causal connection? *Journal of Memory and Language, 29,* 336–360.

——(1993). *Working Memory and Language.* Hove, UK: Lawrence Erlbaum Associates.

Gibson, D. (1978). *Down's Syndrome: The Psychology of Mongolism.* Cambridge: Cambridge University Press.

Gunn, D. & Jarrold, C. (2004). Raven's matrices performance in Down syndrome: Evidence of unusual errors. *Research in Developmental Disabilities, 25,* 443–457.

Henry, L. A. (1991). The effects of word length and phonemic similarity in young children's short-term memory. *The Quarterly Journal of Experimental Psychology, 43A,* 35–52.

Hodapp, R. M. & Zigler, E. (1999). Intellectual development and mental retardation: Some continuing controversies. In M. Anderson (ed.), *The Development of Intelligence* (pp. 295–308). London, UK: University College Press.

Hon, J., Huppert, F. A., Holland, A. J. and Watson, P. (1998). The value of the Rivermead Behavioural Memory Test (Children's Version) in an epidemiological study of older adults with Down's syndrome. *British Journal of Clinical Psychology, 37,* 15–29.

House, B. J. & Zeaman, D. (1959). Position discrimination and reversals in low-grade retardates. *Journal of Comparative and Physiological Psychology, 52,* 564–565.

——(1960). Visual discrimination learning and intelligence in defectives of low mental age. *American Journal of Mental Deficiency, 65,* 51–58.

Hulme, C. & Roodenrys, S. (1995). Practitioner review: Verbal working memory development and its disorders. *Journal of Child Psychology and Psychiatry, 36,* 373–398.

Jarrold, C. & Baddeley, A. D. (1997). Short-term memory for verbal and visuospatial information in Down's syndrome. *Cognitive Neuropsychiatry, 2,* 101–122.

Jarrold, C., Baddeley, A. D. & Hewes, A. K. (2000). Verbal short-term memory deficits in Down syndrome: A consequence of problems in rehearsal? *Journal of Child Psychology and Psychiatry, 40,* 233–244.

Jarrold, C., Baddeley, A. & Phillips, C. E. (2002). Verbal short-term memory in Down syndrome: A problem of memory, audition, or speech? *Journal of Speech, Language and Hearing Research, 45,* 531–544.

Jarrold, C., Cowan, N., Hewes, A. K. & Riby, D. M. (2004). Speech timing and verbal short-term memory: Evidence for contrasting deficits in Down syndrome and Williams syndrome. *Journal of Memory and Language, 51,* 365–380.

Jarrold, C., Purser, H. R. M. & Brock, J. (2006). Short-term memory in Down syndrome. In T. P. Alloway & S. Gathercole (eds), *Working Memory and Neurodevelopmental Conditions* (pp. 239–266). Hove, UK: Psychology Press.

Jarrold, C., Baddeley, A. D. & Phillips, C. (2007). Long-term memory for verbal and visual information in Down syndrome and Williams syndrome: Performance on the Doors and People Test. *Cortex, 43,* 233–247.

Kasari, C. & Freeman, S. F. (2001). Task-related social behaviour in children with Down syndrome. *American Journal of Mental Retardation, 106,* 253–264.

Kay-Raining Bird, E. & Chapman, R. S. (1994). Sequential recall in individuals with Down syndrome. *Journal of Speech and Hearing Research, 37,* 1369–1380.

Kidd, E. (2013). The role of verbal working memory in children's sentence comprehension: A critical review. *Topics in Language Disorders, 33,* 208–223.

Landry, S. H. & Chapieski, M. L. (1989). Joint attention and infant toy exploration: Effects of Down syndrome and prematurity. *Child Development, 60,* 103–118.

Langdon Down, J. (1866). Observations on an ethnic classification of idiots. *Clinical Lectures and Reports of the London Hospital, 3,* 259–262.

Laws, G. (2002). Working memory in children and adolescents with Down syndrome: Evidence from a colour memory experiment. *Journal of Child Psychology and Psychiatry, 43,* 353–364.

——(2004). Contributions of phonological memory, language comprehension and hearing to the expressive language of adolescents and young adults with Down syndrome. *Journal of Child Psychology and Psychiatry, 45,* 1085–1095.

Laws, G. & Bishop, D. V. M. (2003). A comparison of language abilities in adolescents with Down syndrome and children with specific language impairment. *Journal of Speech, Language and Hearing Research, 46,* 1324–1339.

Lewandowsky, S. & Oberauer, K. (2009). No evidence for temporal decay in working memory. *Journal of Experimental Psychology: Learning, Memory & Cognition, 35,* 1545–1551.

McCormick, B. (1977). The Toy Discrimination Test: An aid for screening the hearing of children above a mental age of two years. *Public Health, London, 91,* 67–69.

Marcell, M. M. & Armstrong, V. (1982). Auditory and visual sequential memory of Down syndrome and nonretarded children. *American Journal of Mental Deficiency, 87,* 86–95.

Mosse, E. K. & Jarrold, C. (2011). Evidence for preserved novel word learning in Down syndrome suggests multiple routes to vocabulary acquisition. *Journal of Speech, Language and Hearing Research, 54,* 1137–1152.

Nadel, L. (1999). Down syndrome in cognitive neuroscience perspective. In H. Tager-Flusberg (ed.), *Neurodevelopmental Disorders: Contributions to a New Framework from the Cognitive Neurosciences* (pp. 187–221). Cambridge, MA: MIT Press.

Naess, K.-A. B., Lyster, S.-A. H., Hulme, C. & Melby-Lervåg, M. (2011). Language and verbal short-term memory skills in children with Down syndrome: A meta-analytic review. *Research in Developmental Disabilities, 32,* 2225–2234.

Naess, K.-A. B., Melby-Lervåg, M., Hulme, C. & Lyster, S.-A. H. (2012). Reading skills in children with Down syndrome: A metaanalytic review. *Research in Developmental Disabilities, 33,* 737–747.

Pennington, B. F., Moon, J., Edgin, J., Stedron, J. & Nadel, L. (2003). The neuropsychology of Down syndrome: Evidence for hippocampal dysfunction. *Child Development, 74,* 75–93.

Pitcairn, T. K. & Wishart, J. G. (1994). Reactions of young children with Down's syndrome to an impossible task. *British Journal of Developmental Psychology, 12,* 485–490.

Posner, M. I. & Petersen, S. E. (1990). The attention system of the human brain. *Annual Review of Neuroscience, 13,* 25–42.

Purser, H. R. M. & Jarrold, C. (2005). Impaired verbal short-term memory in Down syndrome reflects a capacity limitation rather than atypically rapid forgetting. *Journal of Experimental Child Psychology, 91*, 1–23.

——(2010). Short- and long-term memory contributions to immediate serial recognition: Evidence from serial position effects. *Quarterly Journal of Experimental Psychology, 63*, 679–693.

——(2013). Poor phonemic discrimination does not underlie poor verbal short-term memory in Down syndrome. *Journal of Experimental Child Psychology, 115*, 1–15.

Raven, J., Raven, J. C. & Court, J. H. (1998). *Coloured Progressive Matrices*. Oxford: Oxford University Press.

Roch, M. & Jarrold, C. (2008). A comparison between word and non-word reading in Down syndrome: The role of phonological awareness. *Journal of Communication Disorders, 41*, 305–318.

Rosin, M. M., Swift, E., Bless, D. & Vetter, D. K. (1988). Communication profiles of adolescents with Down syndrome. *Journal of Childhood Communication Disorders, 12*, 49–64.

Ryan, R. M. & Deci, E. L. (2000). The darker and brighter sides of human existence: Basic psychological needs as a unifying concept. *Psychological Inquiry, 11*, 319–338.

Scholtens S., Rydell, A.-M. & Yang-Wallentin, F. (2013). ADHD symptoms, academic achievement, self-perception of academic competence and future orientation: A longitudinal study. *Scandinavian Journal of Psychology, 54*, 205–212.

Snowling, M. J., Hulme, C. & Mercer, R. C. (2002). A deficit in rime awareness in children with Down syndrome. *Reading and Writing: An Interdisciplinary Journal, 15*, 471–495.

Spearman, C. (1904). 'General intelligence', objectively determined and measured. *American Journal of Psychology, 15*, 201–293.

Steele, J. & Stratford, B. (1995). Present and future possibilities for the UK population with Down's syndrome. *American Journal of Mental Deficiency, 86*, 465–472.

Tulving, E. (1976). Ecphoric processes in recall and recognition. In J. Brown (ed.), *Recognition and Recall* (pp. 37–73). London: Wiley.

Turner, S. & Alborz, A. (2003). Academic attainments of children with Down's Syndrome: A longitudinal study. *British Journal of Educational Psychology, 73*, 563–583.

Vallar, G. & Papagno, C. (1993). Preserved vocabulary acquisition in Down's syndrome: The role of phonological short-term memory. *Cortex, 29*, 467–483.

Varnhagen, C. K., Das, J. P. & Varnhagen, S. (1987). Auditory and visual memory span: Cognitive processing by TMR individuals with Down syndrome or other etiologies. *American Journal of Mental Deficiency, 91*, 398–405.

Vicari, S., Bellucci, S. & Carlesimo, G. A. (2000). Implicit and explicit memory: A functional dissociation in persons with Down syndrome. *Neuropsychologia, 38*, 240–251.

Wickelgren, W. A. (1965a). Acoustic similarity and retroactive interference in short-term memory. *Journal of Verbal Learning and Verbal Behaviour, 4*, 53–61.

——(1965b). Short-term memory for phonemically similar lists. *American Journal of Psychology, 78*, 567–574.

Wilson, B., Cockburn, J. & Baddeley, A. D. (1985). *The Rivermead Behavioural Memory Test*. Titchfield: Thames Valley Test Company.

Wilson, B. A. & Ivani-Chalian, R. (1995). Performance of adults with Down's syndrome on the children's version of the Rivermead Behavioural Memory Test: A brief report. *British Journal of Clinical Psychology, 34*, 85–88.

Winter, T. C., Ostrovsky, A. A., Komarniski, C. A. & Uhrich, S. B. (2000). Cerebellar and frontal lobe hypoplasia in fetuses with trisomy 21: Usefulness as combined sonographic markers. *Radiology, 214*, 533–538.

Wishart, J. G. (1993). Learning the hard way: Avoidance strategies in young children with Down syndrome. *Down Syndrome Research and Practice, 1*, 47–55.

Wishart, J. G. & Duffy, L. (1990). Instability of performance on cognitive tests in infants and young children with Down's syndrome. *British Journal of Educational Psychology, 60*, 10–22.

12

EYE-TRACKING AND NEURO-DEVELOPMENTAL DISORDERS

Evidence from cross-syndrome comparisons

Mary Hanley

12.1 Introduction

The aim of this chapter is to provide an overview of how eye-tracking techniques have been used to inform our understanding of neurodevelopmental disorders. The use of eye-tracking techniques in psychology is a relatively new, but steadily growing research method. The rise in the popularity of this technique is due to the many advantages it offers to the study of attention and cognitive processing, coupled with the widening availability and accessibility of the technology. In the neurodevelopmental disorders literature, eye-tracking has most commonly been applied to explore the social deficits in Autism Spectrum Disorders (ASD). In this chapter, I will consider how it has been used to compare the social attention profiles of ASD and Williams syndrome (WS). As a detailed account of ASD is provided earlier in this book (see Chapter 7), I will begin with an overview of WS, and issues relevant to carrying out research with individuals with WS before discussing eye-tracking techniques and insights gained from comparing social attention in ASD and WS.

12.2 Williams syndrome

WS is a genetic neurodevelopmental disorder that impacts upon an individual's physical, cognitive and behavioural functioning. It was first identified in the 1960s by the cardiologists Williams, Barrat-Boyes and Lowe (1961), through a study of four children with aortic stenosis (a specific heart defect involving narrowing of the arteries), who also had learning disabilities and distinctive facial appearances (Bellugi, Wang & Jernigan, 1994; Williams et al., 1961). Before the availability of genetic testing, the disorder was diagnosed phenotypically on the basis of this characteristic triad (Bellugi, Klima & Wang, 1996). It is now diagnosed using FISH testing (fluorescent in situ hybridization) according to its genetic hallmark: the hemizygous deletion of approximately 26–28 genes on chromosome 7q11.23, including the gene for elastin (ELN) (Bellugi, Mills, Jernigan, Hickok & Galaburda, 1999; Eisenberg, Jabbi & Berman, 2010). Elastin is responsible for tissue elasticity and its deletion underlies many of the physical characteristics of WS (Morris & Mervis, 2000). Although we are much better now at recognising and diagnosing WS, it remains a relatively rare disorder. It occurs sporadically within the population, with a reported prevalence of between 1 in 7,500 (Stromme, Bjornstad & Ramstad, 2002) and 1 in 20,000 (Morris, Demsey, Leonard, Dilts & Blackburn, 1998).

Since its identification by Williams et al. (1961), our understanding of WS has developed considerably. It is now recognised as a multi-system disorder that includes not only serious physical and medical difficulties (e.g. heart defects) but also a unique pattern of strengths and difficulties within cognition and behaviour (Bellugi et al., 1994; Riby & Porter, 2010). While relative strengths with language and relative weaknesses with visuospatial processing characterise the cognitive profile in WS, a very friendly, empathetic, and sociable nature characterises the behavioural profile (Riby & Porter, 2010; Tager-Flusberg & Sullivan, 2000). In fact, one of the most striking characteristics of people with WS is their strong desire for social interaction (Jones et al., 2000). The unique cognitive and behavioural profile in WS has provided the impetus for a growing body of research on this genetic neurodevelopmental disorder, in the hope that WS may offer 'a new window to the organisation and adaptability of the normal brain' (Lenhoff, Wang, Greenberg & Bellugi, 2006, p. 68). One avenue for research has been to compare WS and ASD, due to the opposing nature of the social phenotypes associated with both neurodevelopmental disorders (hypersociability in WS vs. social withdrawal in ASD; Brock, Einav & Riby, 2008). Eye-tracking has been an important tool used to gain insights into atypical social behaviour through this cross-syndrome comparison. Before this eye-tracking evidence is reviewed, a brief overview of the cognitive profile in WS is discussed.

12.2.1 Cognitive profile in WS

Although early accounts of the cognitive profile in WS indicated a profile of spared/impaired abilities, it is now considered in terms of relative strengths in aspects of verbal abilities and relative weaknesses with visuospatial abilities (Karmiloff-Smith et al., 1997). In the context of overall mild to moderate learning disability (mean full scale intelligence quotient [FSIQ] 55, range 40–100; Martens, Wilson & Reutens, 2008) individuals with WS have relative strengths in the verbal/language domain (mean verbal IQ 63, range 45–109; Martens et al., 2008), and profound difficulties in the visuospatial domain (mean performance IQ 55, range 41–75; Martens et al., 2008). IQ tests that involve less spatial ability components tend to provide slightly higher estimates of IQ in WS (e.g. mean scores of 66 on the Kaufman Brief Intelligence Test, K-BIT; Kaufman & Kaufman,

2004; Morris & Mervis, 1999), highlighting the impairments individuals with WS have in this domain, and how care should be taken in relation to cognitive testing in WS. It must be noted that there is much individual variability in cognitive functioning in WS, even within the language and visuospatial domains (Porter & Coltheart, 2005). Furthermore, the discrepancy between language and visuospatial ability is often small and does not apply across the board (Brock, 2007).

Within the language domain, the picture is by no means clear – individuals with WS have an uneven profile of language abilities. For example, relative strengths have been reported for speech production, phonological short-term memory, receptive vocabulary and grammatical abilities (Bellugi, Bihrle, Jernigan, Trauner & Doherty, 1990; Brock, 2007). However, language acquisition is delayed (Mervis, Robinson, Rowe, Becerra & Klein-Tasman, 2003b) and difficulties have been reported with pragmatics (Laws & Bishop, 2004; for full review of language in WS, see Brock, 2007). In the visuospatial domain, the picture is somewhat more straightforward – individuals with WS have profound and robust impairments on tasks measuring visuospatial construction (Bellugi, Lichtenberger, Jones, Lai & St. George, 2000), and show a local processing bias similar to younger typically developing (TD) children (Georgopoulos, Georgopoulos, Kuz & Landau, 2004).[1]

An important aspect of cognition in WS relevant to research design is that ADHD is a common co-morbid diagnosis (64 per cent; Leyfer, Woodruff-Borden, Klein-Tasman, Fricke & Mervis, 2006; for a discussion on ADHD see Chapter 9), and although relatively under-researched, issues with attention and executive functions have been reported in WS. Difficulties with disengaging attention and visual orienting have been reported (Cornish, Scerif & Karmiloff-Smith, 2007), as well as difficulties with planning, working memory and inhibition (Rhodes, Riby, Park, Fraser & Campbell, 2010; Greer, Riby, Hamilton & Riby, 2013).

In sum, although individuals with WS function in the mild to moderate learning disability range, researchers need to be aware of the uneven profile of abilities in this population. Due to certain strengths with language, individuals with WS will often seem more capable than they actually are, and care needs to be taken in experimental design around task instructions and matching procedures. Although there is no golden rule for participant matching, it is advisable to match to more than one comparison group (for a detailed discussion on matching see Chapter 1) – for example, a mental age matched and a chronological age matched group, or TD and a developmental disorder comparison group. Matching for specific task-relevant abilities is preferable to using global ability measures based on batteries that tap a range of abilities (Farran & Jarrold, 2003). Finally, of particular relevance to eye-tracking research, consideration needs to be given to experimental setup (e.g. location of experimenter in relation to eye tracker and participant) and task length. Individuals with WS will easily get distracted, particularly by the presence of other people, and if the experimenter's face is in view they will prefer to look at it rather than the eye-tracking screen (Jones et al., 2000; Mervis et al., 2003a).

12.2.2 Williams syndrome as the opposite of autism – cross-syndrome comparison

Individuals with WS are known for their sociable, friendly, outgoing personalities and here again, they show unique syndrome-specific behaviour. They have a strong desire for social interaction, a clear interest in looking at others' faces, and show little restraint towards unfamiliar people (Jones et al., 2000; Mervis et al., 2003a). Coupled with cognitive impairments, these behavioural traits make them a socially vulnerable group (Riby, Kirk, Hanley & Riby, 2014). The striking hypersociability seen in WS is often contrasted with the aloofness and social withdrawal typically seen in ASD (Asada & Itakura, 2012). ASD is behaviourally defined in terms of social and communicative impairments and the presence of repetitive interests and behaviour (American Psychiatric Association, 2013). The classic phenotype of ASD is characterised by lack of social engagement, but social functioning difficulties are significant even for those with the disorder who are 'socially interested' (Wing & Gould, 1979). Although they do share some similarities in respect of communication and socio-cognitive impairments (Asada & Itakura, 2012), it is due to the apparent contrast of sociability in ASD and WS that they are often considered as opposites on a spectrum of atypical social functioning (Brock et al., 2008).

The most common comparison method in neurodevelopmental disorder research involves matching developmental disorder groups to TD children on the basis of age and cognitive ability, which can indicate the typicality of the behaviour or process under investigation. However, this cannot indicate the 'uniqueness' of an atypicality, and whether it is the result of having a specific disorder, or of having a neurodevelopmental disorder more generally (Burack, Iarocci, Flanagan & Bowler, 2004). Cross-syndrome comparison is a very useful tool for unpicking syndrome specificity, and can help to unravel the relationships between underlying processes and behaviour (see also Chapter 2 for discussion of cross-syndrome comparisons). WS and ASD have been used as a cross-syndrome comparison to elucidate the 'neurocognitive mechanisms that underlie human social behaviour' (Tager-Flusberg, Plesa Skwerer & Joseph, 2006, p. 175). An important avenue for research has been to compare the typicality of attention to social information in WS and ASD.

12.3 Why study social attention?

Social attention broadly refers to how we attend to social information, including people and faces, and thus largely refers to visual attention. Studying social attention is important as looking at faces provides a key source of learning from birth, and is at the heart of some important early socio-developmental milestones (e.g. gaze following, joint attention; von Hofsten & Gredebäck, 2009). It remains a crucial input throughout development, as the majority of our socialisation is mediated by faces (especially by information portrayed by the eyes) and it is important for mental state attribution (Klin, 2008; Baron–Cohen, Wheelwright & Joliffe, 1997). It is also important to pick up on socio-communicative cues from faces in order to adapt our social behaviour appropriately during interaction (Hanley, Riby, Caswell, Rooney & Back, 2013). Indeed, there is considerable evidence that our brains are adapted to be 'social', through regions and networks that are specialised for processing social information (e.g. the amygdala, superior temporal gyrus, the medial prefrontal cortex; Senju & Johnson, 2009; for a discussion of the neurological profiles in WS and ASD see Chapters 3 and 4). Thus, exploring attention to social information in WS and ASD may offer insight into the basis of human social behaviour, as well as furthering understanding of these disorders and identifying areas for intervention.

Anecdotally, we know that people with WS and ASD respond to faces very differently, with an intense interest in faces in WS and a relative lack of interest or avoidance of faces in ASD. Face processing studies have confirmed atypicalities in WS and ASD that relate to their respective social phenotypes. Face processing is a well-documented atypicality in ASD (Gepner, de Gelder & de Schonen, 1996), evidenced by a lack of an inversion effect on face recognition (Langdell, 1978), impairments when using information from the upper half of the face (Riby, Doherty-Sneddon & Bruce, 2009), and problems with emotion/mental state recognition (Celani, Battachi & Arcidiacono, 1999). In WS, aspects of face processing are a relative strength (e.g. face recognition; Bellugi et al., 1994), while at the same time involving atypical strategies (relying on internal face features for unfamiliar face matching; Riby, Doherty-Sneddon & Bruce, 2008a). Some face processing studies suggest that individuals with WS show greater competence with interpreting gaze cues and emotional expressions than individuals with ASD (Riby, Doherty-Sneddon & Bruce, 2008b), indicating that greater social interest in WS may aid socio-communicative skill development, with the opposite relationship in ASD.

Although face processing research has been extremely informative, one limitation is that highly structured lab tasks are unlikely to reveal the exact processes underlying atypical social behaviour in everyday life. Real-world social interaction, where individuals with WS and ASD experience their greatest difficulties, is unstructured and fluid (Klin, Jones, Schultz, Volkmar & Cohen, 2002a). This is where eye-tracking techniques offer distinct advantages to exploring the roots of atypical social behaviour in WS and ASD. They provide a rich quantifiable measure of social interest and attention, capturing an individual's spontaneous gaze behaviour to social information as opposed to relying solely on performance indicators based on accuracy. In other words, an in-depth analysis of how someone carried out a task as opposed to whether they passed or failed it. Tasks measuring spontaneous gaze behaviour to social stimuli circumvent the need for complex task instructions, which is an advantage when working with a neurodevelopmental disorder population who have language impairments. Importantly, eye-tracking offers the opportunity to create experiments that replicate the demands of natural social interaction, enhancing ecological validity and the likelihood of identifying processes key to real-world social behaviour. It provides a fine-grained temporal and spatial analysis of what a participant looks at, when and for how long – giving an online measure of social information processing as a participant engages in a task (Benson & Fletcher-Watson, 2011). Consequently, this method can help to pinpoint where atypicalities arise in social interaction, whether it be the amount of time spent attending to social information, speed of detecting key social information or the integration of verbal and non-verbal cues for example (Klin et al., 2002a). Before insights from eye-tracking studies of WS and ASD is discussed, the kinds of eye-tracking techniques currently in use will be considered.

12.4 Eye-tracking methods and the exploration of social attention

Prior to the advent of eye-tracking technology, researchers interested in measuring gaze behaviour relied on less precise methods, such as coding of looking behaviour through retrospective analysis of home videos (Adrien et al., 1993). Eye-tracking provides accurate indexes of attention, through the measurement of well-defined movements of the eyes, such as fixations and saccades. Saccades are rapid eye movements that move the eyes towards a point of fixation (Gilchrist, 2011). As the focus of this chapter is on social information processing, I will mainly be referring to patterns of visual fixation. A fixation is a period of relative stability in visual pursuit, where the fovea (or centre of gaze) is focussed on a specific area and information can be processed (Henderson, 2003). Actively controlling the centre of gaze is critical for visual processing, as visual acuity is sharpest at the fovea and the quality of visual information declines rapidly from the centre of gaze to the rest of the retina (Henderson, 2003). Therefore, the analysis of visual fixation patterns gives a precise quantification of what information has been selected for processing.

How do eye trackers measure eye movements? The most common method of eye-tracking uses video-based infra-red technology with desktop mounted systems.[2] An infra-red beam is shone on the eyes, while a video camera recording the eyes (typically positioned under a stimulus presentation screen) captures the position of the centre of the pupil and the corneal reflex. The corneal reflex is a white dot reflected out from the eye, the position of which changes with head position and thus it is used to take account of head position while tracking the eye. Before eye movement recording begins, a calibration procedure must take place to ensure accurate determination of the gaze position in relation to a specific stimulus. For most video-based eye-tracking systems stimuli are presented on a computer screen, the dimensions and location of which are known to the eye-tracking system. The process of calibration involves asking the participant to look at known locations on the screen (e.g. a dot programmed to appear in specific locations), while the eye tracker records the position of the eye at each location.

The calibration process is key for accurate tracking of the gaze position, and several factors can affect it. Lighting conditions in the room where testing takes place is important, and a good deal of natural light tends to aid the calibration process. Lighting levels should be kept constant between calibration and data collection, including lighting levels in the room and also the luminance levels of the stimuli within the calibration and the experiment. For example, calibrating to a white background but using stimuli that are very dark in colour will impact the accuracy of the eye movement data. This is because of how the pupil changes in size in response to very dark or very bright colours. If there are drastic changes in pupil size it will affect the accuracy of the data. Although eye trackers can compensate for some head movements, any significant changes in the participant's position between calibration and data recording will also affect accuracy. Due to the various factors that can affect the accuracy of calibration, it is advisable to incorporate a validation procedure into the experiment before data recording begins. From the participant's point of view it looks like an extension of the calibration, i.e. more dots to look at. For the experimenter however, it is possible to see the live gaze position as the participant looks at specified locations, and the eye tracker will compute the deviation between the known locations and the gaze position. Using threshold values according to the systems tracking accuracy, it is possible to determine whether the system is tracking the participant accurately. It is fair to say that this is often the trickiest part of eye-tracking, and it is arguably the most important part, because it ensures the validity of the data.

Once an accurate calibration has been achieved, eye movement recording can begin. Output from the eye tracker comes in the form of x and y coordinates for the pupil position in relation to the stimulus. Different eye trackers will sample at different rates (i.e. produce different amounts of x and y coordinates per second), but generally speaking the higher the sampling rate the better. Modern screen-mounted eye trackers are available at a range of sampling rates: 60 Hz (ASL D6; www.asleyetracking.com); 250 Hz (CRS High speed VET; www.crsltd.com); 300 Hz (Tobii TX300; www.tobii.com); 500 Hz (SMI RED500; www.smivision.com). Head-mounted or mobile eye trackers tend to sample at slower rates: Tobii glasses 30 Hz (www.tobii.com); SMI eye-tracking glasses 60 Hz (www.smivision.com). However, the technology is developing rapidly, and there are eye-trackers available that sample as fast as 2000 Hz (Eyelink 1000; www.sr-research.com), and head-mounted eye trackers that sample as fast as 500 Hz (Eyelink II; www.sr-research.com). Whatever the system, once the raw data has been obtained algorithms will be applied to the data to define when fixations, saccades and blinks have taken place. Fixation algorithms are typically based on maximum movement thresholds for minimum periods of time (Duchowski, 2007); e.g. a minimum time of 80 ms within a specified area of pixels or degrees of the visual angle.

Modern eye-tracking procedures are non-invasive, and for desktop eye-tracking, the experience for the participant is nothing more than looking at a computer screen. The technology has vastly improved in a short space of time, becoming more user-friendly, requiring less constrained setups (e.g. no need for bite bars), greater ability to compensate for participant movements, easier to calibrate and faster sampling rates. One of the most important advances for researchers working with neurodevelopmental disorder groups is the increasing portability of modern eye trackers, enabling researchers to carry out eye-tracking research in schools, and importantly to access rare neurodevelopmental disorders groups such as those with WS.

12.5 Eye-tracking insights into Autism and Williams syndrome

So, what insights have eye-tracking studies of social attention revealed about ASD and WS? Considerably more research has been carried out using eye-tracking to explore the social deficits in ASD than in WS. A lot of this work has focussed on whether there is a fundamental difficulty with sampling and using information portrayed by the eyes in ASD. It has been suggested that a lack of attention to social information from birth (particularly from the eyes) may play a significant role in the development of ASD by derailing social learning and therefore, may be a diagnostic marker (Dawson et al., 2004; Klin, 2008; Senju & Johnson, 2009). In the first study to address this, Pelphrey et al. (2002) showed how less time looking at the core features of the face, and particularly the eyes, characterised the scanning patterns of five participants with ASD compared to TD controls. Since then, a range of eye-tracking studies have replicated reduced fixation times on eyes and faces by participants with ASD, showing how pertinent social information is not prioritised for attention in ASD (Corden, Chilvers & Skuse, 2008; Riby & Hancock, 2009a; Riby & Hancock, 2009b; Norbury et al., 2009; Klin, Jones, Schultz, Volkmar & Cohen, 2002b; Nakano et al., 2010; Speer, Cook, McMahon & Clark, 2007). Corden et al. (2008) showed how this can be problematic for 'reading faces', as their participants with Asperger syndrome (AS) showed less fixation time on the eyes of faces expressing emotion, which predicted poorer fear recognition. Importantly, reduced eye gaze has also been found when participants with ASD viewed more naturalistic presentations of social information, such as images depicting interaction (Hanley, McPhillips, Mulhern & Riby, 2012; Riby & Hancock, 2008), and dynamic clips of social interaction (Klin et al., 2002b; Nakano et al., 2010). While typical individuals prioritise social information for attention, individuals with ASD prefer to attend to non-social information such as objects and information from the background of scenes (Klin et al., 2002b; Nakano et al., 2010).

Some studies have indicated that when individuals with ASD attend to faces, they show a bias for looking at mouths (Jones, Carr & Klin, 2008; Klin et al., 2002b). Klin et al. (2002b) showed how high-functioning adults with ASD fixated significantly less on the eyes of characters involved in complex dynamic social interaction, but significantly more on their mouths by comparison to controls. This bias for looking at the mouth was predictive of better social competence for participants with ASD. The authors suggested that there might be benefits to focussing on mouths, possibly by relying on speech as an inroad to understanding social interaction. A mouth bias has also been found in ASD during emotion discrimination. Using the 'bubbles technique' Spezio et al. (2007) showed that when judging whether a face was happy or afraid, participants with ASD neglected information from the eyes and focussed on information from the mouth. Thus, such a bias may not be reflective of reliance on speech, but on a source of socio-communicative information other than the eyes.

Collectively, these findings provide insights into the difficulties that individuals with ASD have in social interaction, corroborating anecdotal reports of difficulties with eye contact and highlighting where problems may arise in interaction. For example, following and understanding information from the eyes is important for understanding 'meaning' in social interactions (as is the case when trying to understand what another person is thinking or feeling). As a further example, problems may arise in relation to a bias to fixate on mouths. Although it may provide a means of compensating for reduced eye fixation, it may also lead to literal interpretation of language due to over-reliance on what is said and neglect of the non-verbal information that moderates the meaning of what is said (e.g. as in the case of sarcasm; Klin et al., 2002b). Indeed, reduced fixation time to eyes by individuals with ASD has been found to correlate with greater social disability in ASD (Klin et al., 2002b; Speer et al., 2007), and increased fixation on mouths has been found to correlate with social/communicative competence (Norbury et al., 2009; Klin et al., 2002b). This is quite important, as much psychological research on ASD such as on core cognitive deficits, does not show relationships between performance and ASD symptomatology (Pellicano, Maybery, Durkin & Maley, 2006). It must be noted however, that there have been some inconsistencies in this literature, where several studies report typical social gaze in ASD (Fletcher-Watson, Leekam, Benson, Frank & Findlay, 2009; Freeth, Chapman, Ropar & Mitchell, 2010; van der Geest, Kemner, Verbaten & van Engeland, 2002). The implications of this will be considered in the next section.

Although a considerably smaller literature, insights from eye-tracking studies involving individuals with WS paint a very different picture. An unusual bias for looking at others' eyes has been found in WS using eye-tracking. Porter, Shaw and Marsh (2010) found that individuals with WS spent much longer attending the eye regions of emotionally expressive faces than TD controls. However, it was not the case that the eyes captured their attention faster than typical individuals. They were also found to have difficulties recognising basic emotions, linking atypical over-attending to the eyes with problems with emotion recognition in WS (Porter et al., 2010). Williams, Porter and Langdon (2013) also found a bias in WS for attending to social information (images of people) for longer than in typical development. However, they did find that the presentation of social information (centrally or non-centrally presented) impacted upon the typicality of visual fixation patterns. In other words, when social information was presented non-centrally, prolonged gaze was not reported, indicating that problems with attentional disengagement may contribute to atypical social gaze in WS.

Eye-tracking studies comparing the typicality of social attention in ASD and WS to the same stimuli provide the starkest contrast of the divergence in social attention linking to their divergent social phenotypes. Through a series of eye-tracking studies, Riby and Hancock (2008, 2009a, 2009b) and Riby, Hancock, Jones and Hanley (2013) have used eye-tracking techniques to compare individuals with ASD and WS on measures of attentional preferences in social scenes and clips of social interaction, attention capture by faces, and the use of gaze cues to identify targets. Importantly, participants with WS and ASD were not compared directly given the obvious difficulties with appropriate matching. Thus, it is the typicality of their gaze that was compared – each developmental disorder group was matched to separate typical comparison groups.[3] Using images depicting social interaction, Riby and Hancock (2008) found that attentional preferences in ASD and WS contrasted with each other. Whereas participants with WS spent more time than typical groups fixating faces in scenes, particularly the eyes, participants with ASD spent less time than typical groups fixating faces and eyes. They replicated this cross-syndrome pattern when participants viewed dynamic clips of interaction involving human actors (Riby & Hancock, 2009a). In a further study, Riby and Hancock (2009b) explored the basis of characteristic over- and under-attending to social information in WS and ASD by using eye-tracking to measure how faces captured and held attention in these groups. Across two experiments using different sets of images containing faces[4] they found that participants with ASD were slower to fixate faces, had shorter fixations on the faces on average, and spent less time overall fixating the faces (Riby & Hancock, 2009b). The opposite pattern was observed in WS, with longer overall time spent looking at faces and longer average fixations on faces. However, the participants with WS did not detect the faces faster than typical comparisons, indicating that the social bias in WS may be more likely to do with difficulties disengaging from faces (Riby & Hancock, 2009b; Williams et al., 2013).

As well as emphasising the contrasting nature of social attention in these groups, Riby et al. (2013) have shown how these social attention atypicalities link to the socio-cognitive difficulties associated with WS and ASD. In this study, eye-tracking was used to measure how individuals with WS and ASD attended to and then used an actor's gaze cues. Images of actors directing their gaze to an object in the context of everyday scenes (e.g. actor looking at one cup out of three in a kitchen scene) were shown to participants under two conditions. In the first condition, spontaneous gaze patterns were recorded while participants viewed the images without any instruction. In a second condition, participants were cued to detect the target of the actor's gaze in each scene. When viewing the scenes without instruction, participants with ASD viewed the face, eyes, as well as the correct and plausible targets for less time than typical comparison participants. When instructed to decide what the actor was looking at, they increased their gaze to face, but not to the correct target, and were still looking less at these regions than the TD group. For participants with WS, the characteristic over-attending to faces and eyes was seen in the spontaneous viewing condition, but less looking at the correct or plausible targets in comparison to TD participants. When cued, time attending faces did not change from the uncued condition, and participants with WS were still spending more time fixating faces than typical comparisons. However, time spent attending the correct and plausible targets increased. Interestingly, although both groups changed their gaze behaviour in response to the instruction, they were less accurate at naming what the actor was looking at in comparison to their typical control groups. Thus, the characteristic social attention atypicalities of over-attending to social information in WS and under-attending in ASD leads to a lack of spontaneous gaze following and a reduced ability to gaze follow when required (Riby et al., 2013).

12.5.1 Summary of insights for WS and ASD in relation to social attention

In relative terms, much more research has been carried out using eye-tracking to explore the atypical social phenotype in ASD than in WS. The majority of this research highlights a profile of reduced social interest in ASD that is related to poor social functioning and impaired socio-cognitive skills, and increased social interest in WS, but not better socio-cognitive outcomes. This research shows how over-attending and under-attending to social information is problematic for using socio-communicative information. In terms of underlying neurofunction, it points to the role of the amygdala in atypical social behaviour in ASD and WS. The amygdala is implicated in the processing of social and emotional information as a central part of the social brain, and is particularly important for processing information from the eyes (Kawashima et al., 1999). Abnormalities of the amygdala have been linked to both WS and ASD (Baron-Cohen et al., 2000; Jawaid, Schmolck & Schulz, 2008), and directly linked to the atypical processing of socio-emotional information through studies of patients with amygdala damage (Adolphs et al., 2005). Using eye-tracking and magnetic resonance imaging (MRI), functioning of the amygdala has been directly linked to reduced eye fixation in ASD, indicating that eye fixation is aversive in ASD due to hyper-arousal (Dalton et al., 2005). Such evidence suggests that social development is derailed in ASD early in infancy by the aversive experience of eye contact due to hyper-arousal of the amygdala, leading to an atypical social behavioural profile characterised by reduced social interest and poor social cognitive expertise. The opposite could thus also be true for WS, where hypo-arousal leads to over-attending to social information (Haas et al., 2010) and failure to disengage from socio-emotional information and use it properly, contributing to the atypical social profile seen in WS (Triesch, Teuscher, Deák & Carlson, 2006).

Although it would be tempting based on the eye-tracking evidence above to endorse the notion that ASD and WS are indeed opposites (potentially underpinned by amygdala abnormalities), new evidence is emerging to suggest more overlap between these disorders than previously thought.[5]

12.6 The question of within-syndrome heterogeneity and overlap between ASD and WS

Although the majority of social attention studies in ASD find reduced eye gaze, there are some important exceptions. Individuals with ASDs have shown typical attention allocation when viewing isolated emotional faces (Van der Geest, Kemner, Verbaten & van Engeland, 2002) and social scenes (Fletcher-Watson et al., 2009; Freeth et al., 2010). Furthermore, a bias to mouths is by no means a consistent finding in ASD (Norbury et al., 2009; Rice, Moriuchi, Jones & Klin, 2012). Arising from such inconsistencies has been much debate about the impact of ecological validity on social gaze in ASD, with the suggestion that as stimuli more closely replicate realistic social information (e.g. more complex, dynamic, including visual and verbal information), atypicalities in ASD become clearer. Some have suggested that it is the multi-sensory nature of social interaction that poses problems for people with ASD, particularly the integration of information from different modalities (Kemner & van Engeland, 2003). A study by Speer et al. (2007) supports this, as they found atypical scanning by participants with ASD only to dynamic clips of social interaction, and not to static images or dynamic clips of only one person. That being said, the only study to have used eye-tracking methods with participants with ASD during real-life interaction does not report attention allocation atypicalities (Nadig, Lee, Singh, Bosshart & Ozonoff, 2010). Some evidence suggests that as well as sensory complexity, social complexity is important. Hanley et al. (2012) found that the same participants with AS showed typical scanning of isolated faces and atypical scanning of the same faces in the context of static scenes depicting social interaction. It is generally accepted that choice of stimuli is a very important consideration in this kind of research, and that stimuli that are less realistic, are less likely to capture attention reflective of real-life. Although important, stimuli differences alone cannot account for differences between reported gaze typicalities/atypicalities.

Autism Spectrum Disorders collectively represent an extremely heterogeneous group of individuals, with wide-ranging presentations of affectedness in terms of social and communicative competence, and presence of repetitive behaviours (Volkmar, Lord, Bailey, Schultz & Klin, 2004). In their early descriptions of ASD, Wing and Gould (1979) outlined three behavioural phenotypes in children with ASD – aloof, passive, and socially active but odd. These phenotypes captured the range of social engagement styles characteristic of individuals with ASD, emphasising that while some avoid social interaction or seem completely indifferent to it, others seek it out albeit in inappropriate ways. Cognitive ability also varies greatly along the spectrum, ranging from intellectual disability to average or above average ability (Joseph, Tager-Flusberg & Lord, 2002). Thus, heterogeneity in participant characteristics such as these are likely to have contributed to reported inconsistencies, especially given that sample sizes in eye-tracking literature tend to be very small (but see Rice et al., 2012; for a detailed discussion of heterogeneity in WS see Chapter 7). The idea that atypical attention to faces and particularly eyes is related to subtypes within the ASD spectrum has already been mooted (Benson & Fletcher-Watson, 2011, p. 718).

Rice et al. (2012) have considered the interplay between cognitive subtypes and social attention patterns in ASD. Using a large sample (N = 109) of children with ASD varying in overall ability (FSIQ range 75–118), Rice et al. (2012) explored the relationship between signatures of atypical social attention and social disability (measured using the ADOS) between subgroups of children with ASD defined by their cognitive profile (VIQ > NVIQ; NVIQ > VIQ; high even FSIQ; low even FSIQ). Participants were shown dynamic clips of social interaction and, although a pattern of reduced eye gaze, reduced mouth gaze, and increased object gaze characterised the viewing preferences of all subgroups with ASD, there were different patterns of association with social functioning between the different subgroups. A relationship between more looking to objects and higher social disability was most commonly found across the subgroups, but an interesting divergence was reported between the group with discrepantly high VIQ (VIQ > PIQ) and the group with high even FSIQ (no discrepancy between VIQ and PIQ). More looking to the mouth was related to less social disability in the VIQ > PIQ group, with the opposite pattern in the high even FSIQ group. For the latter only, more looking to the eyes was related to less social disability. This indicated that for children with ASD whose clear cognitive strength was in the verbal domain, honing in on the source of verbal information was beneficial for social processing. However, for children with good verbal and non-verbal skills, honing in on verbal information alone was not beneficial but using other socio-communicative information was, such as from the eyes. This work by Rice et al. (2012) represents an important advance in the literature on eye-tracking in neurodevelopmental disorders, paving the way for future research using large samples to look at clustering of subtypes and fixation patterns, and future research should look at not only cognitive subgroups, but also social subgroups.

Similar issues are also coming to light in relation to WS. In an eye-tracking study exploring emotional expression judgement from faces, Kirk, Hocking, Riby, and Cornish (2013) did not find prolonged gaze to faces and eyes in WS, and did find that less time spent looking at eyes was related to more anxiety as measured by the Spence Children's Anxiety Scale (SCAS; Spence, 1998). Hanley et al. (2013) carried out a similar study, looking at attention during mental state recognition in WS. Although mental state recognition ability in WS was broadly in line with previous research (at the level of verbal mental age matched TD children), scanning patterns revealed less looking to the eyes than TD participants. Less looking at the eyes was related to a poorer social functioning for participants with WS on a measure of ASD symptoms (Social Responsiveness Scale; Constantino & Gruber, 2005).

Despite its known genetic origin, WS too involves considerable heterogeneity (Porter & Coltheart, 2005), and recent behavioural evidence suggests that WS and ASD share more overlap than might be expected from classic descriptions of both disorders. A number of studies have shown phenotypic overlap between WS and ASD using diagnostic assessments such as the Autism Diagnostic Observation Schedule (Klein-Tasman, Mervis, Lord & Phillip, 2007; Lincoln, Searcy, Jones & Lord, 2007; Lord, Rutter, DiLavore & Risi, 1999). Klein-Tasman et al. (2007) reported that 8 out of 29 participants with WS exceeded cut-off for reciprocal social interaction difficulties on the ADOS. Lincoln et al. (2007) showed that 3 out of 27 individuals with WS met criteria for co-morbid ASD diagnosis. This indicates that there are social-behavioural subtypes in WS that deviate from the classic hypersociable one. Recent eye-tracking evidence supports the idea that the classic characterisation of individuals with WS involving prolonged face gaze does not apply to all with the condition (Hanley et al., 2013). For future research exploring the underpinnings of social behaviour, it may be more useful to look at the overlap between WS and ASD, rather than focussing on the ways in which individuals with these conditions seem to be opposites. For example, recent behavioural genetics research has been looking at case studies comparing individuals with the classic WS profile to individuals with WS with an ASD-like behavioural profile to understand the genotype to social phenotype relationships (Karmiloff-Smith et al., 2012). This is insightful as it shows how even though both individuals have a diagnosis of WS because of their genetic deletion, subtle variations in the nature of their genetic deletions lead to very different behavioural presentations, with one individual fitting the more classically sociable WS profile and the other individual meeting criteria for an ASD diagnosis. Eye-tracking techniques may be particularly beneficial here in furthering behavioural genetic research because of the advantages they offer to capturing and quantifying social phenotypes in ASD and WS that may be mapped onto specific genotypes (Asada & Itakura, 2012).

12.7 Conclusions

In this chapter, the usefulness of eye-tracking as an experimental tool when working with individuals with neurodevelopmental disorder groups has been discussed. It offers many advantages over traditional behavioural experimental methods (e.g. no need for complex verbal instructions), provides precise data on attention (sometimes too much data!), and provides an online measure of processing. A limitation of eye-tracking methods is that they cannot tell us how the brain uses the information it receives (Boraston & Blakemore, 2007). Although an exciting advantage to eye-tracking methods is the possibility of using them along with neurofunctional techniques, in practice this is difficult and has not been achieved often in neurodevelopmental disorders (but see Dalton et al., 2005). With widening availability of MEG and MRI compatible eye trackers, future research in this area holds much promise for unearthing how the brain uses the precise information it receives.

Although eye-tracking methods have the potential to help us answer many questions about attention and processing, it can be a difficult tool to calibrate, especially with children and individuals with neurodevelopmental disorders. Thus, the explanatory potential of eye-tracking research can be constrained by the sample sizes, and this has been highlighted as an issue throughout this chapter. However, modern eye trackers are much easier to use, and the technology is improving all the time. This will enable larger-scale eye-tracking studies, such as Rice et al. (2012), and cluster analyses of eye-tracking data which may help to delineate subgroups of individuals according to their attention patterns (Nakano et al., 2010).

The research discussed in this chapter is concerned with capturing and quantifying social attention and understanding how it relates to atypical social behaviour. However, it could be argued that the essence of what is social largely eludes the majority of the studies discussed here – because the difference between passively looking at social information on a screen and engaging in social interaction is significant. The demands of social interaction are completely different (e.g. engaging in mutual gaze, turn-taking in conversation), and we know that ecological validity of stimuli has an impact upon attention preferences (Hanley et al., 2012; Speer et al., 2007). Recent work has begun using eye-tracking methods during real social interaction in typical adults (Freeth, Foulsham & Kingstone, 2013) as well as including children with and without ASD (Nadig et al., 2010). Although the logistics of using eye-tracking methods in real interaction are more complex than desktop-mounted eye-tracking, this is a really important avenue for future research as potential models on the role of atypical social attention in developmental disorders will only have theoretical and clinical utility if they apply to social gaze behaviour in real life.

In terms of models of social attention in ASD, it has been postulated that atypical social attention early in development could derail social learning, having a cascading impact upon development. In other words reduced attention to faces leads to less social experience and atypicalities of social perception and social cognition, and is therefore causal (at least to some degree) in the core social deficits of ASD (South, Schultz & Ozonoff, 2011). The majority of eye-tracking work in children and adults supports this outcome, but work in infancy is lacking and somewhat inconclusive thus far (see also Chapter 7). There have been reports of reduced eye gaze in toddlers with ASD (Jones et al., 2008), and in infants at risk for ASD using eye-tracking (siblings of children with a diagnosis of ASD; Merin, Young, Ozonoff & Rogers, 2007), and there have also been contradictory reports. A follow-up to Merin et al. (2007) showed that these measures were not a reliable indicator of ASD, as lower rates of eye contact did not predict ASD symptoms, and three children who did not show reduced eye gaze as infants went on to receive a diagnosis of ASD (Young, Merin, Rogers & Ozonoff, 2009). However, recent eye-tracking work by Jones and Klin (2013) adds exciting and significant insights into ASD relevant markers of gaze behaviour in infancy, by showing that social gaze behaviour changes in important ways early in infancy, and that it is the pattern of change that is significant to the development of ASD. They found that very early in infancy social attention patterns were very similar between infants at high risk and low risk for developing ASD. However, between two and six months, eye fixation declined in infants who went on to be diagnosed with ASD. This is a very significant piece to the puzzle of how social attention atypicalities may play a role in ASD, and highlights the importance of exploring the developmental time course of gaze behaviour in a detailed way (Jones & Klin, 2013). Much more research is needed in this area, particularly in terms of longitudinal work and a focus on developmental trajectories in typical and neurodevelopmental populations, and with cross-syndrome comparisons.

A lot has been learned about neurodevelopmental disorders using eye-tracking in a relatively short space of time. As the technology improves and access to it widens, it is clear that the field of eye-tracking research on neurodevelopmental disorders will be exciting going forward. It will be critically important that researchers endeavour to use this tool not only to explore the typicality of gaze behaviour but to understand syndrome specificity. In this chapter, I have focussed on the cross-syndrome comparison of ASD and WS, to provide insights into atypical social behaviour. However, other cross-syndrome comparisons using eye-tracking are revealing insights into social development, by comparing individuals with Fragile X syndrome to WS (Williams, Porter & Langdon, 2013), and children with Specific Language Impairment (SLI) to ASD (Hosozawa, Tanaka, Shimizu, Nakano & Kitazawa, 2012). Cross-syndrome comparison involving SLI and ASD using eye-tracking is also being used to explore language development (Kelly, Walker & Norbury, 2013). It will be critical that future research focusses on understanding how social attention operates in the real world. It will also be important that more effort is concentrated on moving beyond capturing attention patterns alone to looking at how the brain is using the visual information it selects for processing. Finally, more prospective longitudinal work focussing on the developmental time course of gaze behaviour will be vital for pinpointing the precise role of attention/social attention for outcome in neurodevelopmental disorders.

Practical tips

1. Plan your experimental setup carefully, so that you can monitor the participants as they carry out the task, but so that you are not in their view and therefore a distraction. This is particularly important when working with people with WS.
2. Try to set up in a place with good lighting, preferably with ample natural light to aid the eye-tracking process.
3. Include a validation procedure before beginning data collection to ensure the accuracy of the eye movement data and also between trials to ensure consistency of eye movement data.
4. Due consideration of stimuli is needed when designing experiments to explore social attention in lab-based studies, particularly if trying to capture attention patterns reflective of everyday life.

Notes

1 For a review of visuospatial processing difficulties in WS, see Farran and Jarrold (2003).
2 Eye-tracking techniques can be broadly categorised in three ways: 1) coil systems that track eye movements by way of special contact lenses, which is a particularly invasive method; 2) electrical occulography methods which track changes in the electrical field when the eyes move, measured by electrodes placed around the eyes; 3) video-based systems that track the pupil position in relation to a stimulus. Due to the fact that the studies discussed in this chapter use a video-based method, the discussion of eye-tracking techniques will focus on this method.
3 In Riby and Hancock (2008, 2009a) participants with WS and ASD were matched separately to two TD comparison groups, one for CA and one for non-verbal ability. In Riby and Hancock (2009b) and Riby et al. (2013), participants with WS and ASD were matched separately to a group of TD participants on the basis of non-verbal ability.

4 In experiment 1, images were natural scenes with incongruently embedded faces. In experiment 2, images containing faces that had been divided into squares and scrambled (with one square always containing an entire face) were used.

5 It should also be noted that models of hypo-arousal of the amygdala have also been put forward to explain social attention atypicalities in ASD, where hypo-arousal leads to failure to orient to social information due to lack of positive reward associated with eye contact (Dawson, Webb & McPartland, 2005).

References

Adolphs, R., Gosselin, F., Buchanan, T. W., Tranel, D., Schyns, P. & Damasio, A. R. (2005). A mechanism for impaired fear recognition after amygdala damage. *Nature, 433*, 68–72.

Adrien, J. L., Lenoir, P., Martineau, J., Perrot, A., Hameury, L. & Larmande, C. (1993). Blind ratings of early symptoms of autism based upon family home videos. *Journal of the American Academy of Child and Adolescent Psychiatry, 32*(3), 617–626.

American Psychiatric Association. (2013). *Diagnostic and Statistical Manual Of Mental Disorders (5th ed.).* Arlington, VA: American Psychiatric Publishing.

Asada, K. & Itakura, S. (2012). Social phenotypes of autism spectrum disorders and Williams syndrome: Similarities and differences. *Frontiers in Psychology, 3*, 247.

Baron-Cohen, S., Wheelwright, S. & Joliffe, T. (1997). Is there a 'language of the eyes'? Evidence from normal adults, and adults with autism or Asperger syndrome. *Visual Cognition, 4*, 311–331.

Baron-Cohen, S., Ring, H. A., Bullmore, E. T., Wheelwright, S., Ashwon, C. & Williams, S. C. R. (2000). The amygdala theory of autism. *Neuroscience and Biobehavioral Reviews, 24*, 355–364.

Bellugi, U., Bihrle, A., Jernigan, T. L., Trauner, D. & Doherty, S. (1990). Neuropsychological, neurological, and neuroanatomical profile of Williams syndrome. *American Journal of Medical Genetics, 6*, 115–125.

Bellugi, U., Wang, P. P. & Jernigan, T. L. (1994). Williams syndrome: An unusual neuropsychological profile. In S. Broman & J. Grafman (eds), *Atypical Cognitive Deficits in Developmental Disorders: Implications for Brain Function* (pp. 23–56). Hillsdale, NJ: Lawrence Erlbaum Associates.

Bellugi, U., Klima, E. S. & Wang, P. P. (1996). Cognitive and neural development: Clues from genetically based syndromes. In D. Magnussen (ed.), *The Lifespan Development of Individuals: A Synthesis of Biological and Psychological Perspectives* (pp. 223–243). New York: Cambridge University Press.

Bellugi, U., Mills, D., Jernigan, T. L., Hickok, G. & Galaburda, A. (1999). Linking cognition, brain structure and brain function in Williams syndrome. In H. Tager-Flusberg (ed.), *Neurodevelopmental Disorders* (pp. 111–136). Cambridge: MIT Press.

Bellugi, U., Lichtenberger, L., Jones, W., Lai, Z. & St. George, M. (2000). The neurocognitive profile of Williams syndrome: A complex pattern of strengths and weaknesses. *Journal of Cognitive Neuroscience, 12*, 7–29.

Benson, V. & Fletcher-Watson, S. (2011). Eye movements in autism. In S. Liversedge, I. Gilchrist & S. Everling (eds), *Oxford Handbook of Eye Movements*, Chapter 39 (pp. 709–730). Oxford, UK: Oxford University Press.

Boraston, Z. & Blakemore, S. J. (2007). The application of eye-tracking in the study of autism. *Journal of Physiology, 581*, 893–898.

Brock, J. (2007). Language abilities in Williams syndrome: A critical review. *Developmental Psychopathology, 19*, 97–127.

Brock, J., Einav, S. & Riby, D. M. (2008). The other end of the spectrum? Social cognition in Williams syndrome. In V. Reid & T. Striano (eds), *Social Cognition: Development, Neuroscience and Autism*, Chapter 18 (pp. 281–300). Oxford: Blackwell.

Burack, J. A., Iarocci, G., Flanagan, T. & Bowler, D. (2004). On mosaics and melting pots: Conceptual considerations of comparison and matching strategies. *Journal of Autism and Developmental Disorders, 34*, 65–73.

Celani, G., Battachi, M. W. & Arcidiacono, L. (1999). The understanding of the emotional meaning of facial expressions in people with autism. *Journal of Autism and Developmental Disorders, 29*, 57–66.

Constantino, J. N. & Gruber, C. P. (2005). *Social Responsiveness Scale*. Los Angeles, CA: Western Psychological Services.

Corden, B., Chilvers, R. & Skuse, D. (2008). Avoidance of emotionally arousing stimuli predicts social-perceptual impairment in Asperger's syndrome. *Neuropsychologia, 46*, 137–147.

Cornish, K., Scerif, G. & Karmiloff-Smith, A. (2007). Tracing syndrome-specific trajectories of attention across the life-span. *Cortex, 43*, 672–685.

Dalton, K. M., Nacewicz, B. M., Johnstone, T., Schaefer, H. S., Gernsbacher, M. A., Goldsmith, H. H., … Davidson, R. J. (2005). Gaze fixation and the neural circuitry of face processing in autism. *Nature Neuroscience, 8*, 519–526.

Dawson, G., Toth, K., Abbott, R., Osterling, J., Munson, J., Estes, A. & Liaw, J. (2004). Early social attention impairments in autism: Social orienting, joint attention, and attention to distress. *Developmental Psychology, 40*, 271–283.

Dawson, G., Webb, S. J. & McPartland, J. (2005). Understanding the nature of face processing impairment in autism: Insights from behavioral and electrophysiological studies. *Developmental Neuropsychology, 27*, 403–424.

Duchowski, A. T. (2007). *Eye Tracking Methodology, Theory and Practice*. London: Springer.

Eisenberg, D. P., Jabbi, M. & Berman, K. F. (2010). Bridging the gene-behavior divide through neuroimaging deletion syndromes: Velocardiofacial (22q11.2 Deletion) and Williams (7q11.23 Deletion) syndromes. *NeuroImage, 53*, 857–869.

Farran, E. K. & Jarrold, C. (2003). Visuospatial cognition in Williams syndrome: Reviewing and accounting for the strengths and weaknesses in performance. *Developmental Neuropsychology, 23*, 173–200.

Fletcher-Watson, S., Leekam, S. R., Benson, V., Frank, M. C. & Findlay, J. M. (2009). Eye-movements reveal attention to social information in autism spectrum disorder. *Neuropsychologia, 47*, 248–257.

Freeth, M., Chapman, P., Ropar, D. & Mitchell, P. (2010). Do gaze cues in complex scenes capture and direct the attention of high functioning adolescents with ASD? Evidence from eye-tracking. *Journal of Autism and Developmental Disorders, 40*, 534–547.

Freeth, M., Foulsham, T. & Kingstone, A. (2013). What affects social attention? Social presence, eye contact and autistic traits. *PLoS One, 8(1)*. doi: 10.1371/journal.pone.0053286

Georgopoulos, M.-A., Georgopoulos, A. P., Kuz, N. & Landau, B. (2004). Figure copying in Williams syndrome and normal subjects. *Experimental Brain Research, 157*, 137–146.

Gepner, B., de Gelder, B. & de Schonen, S. (1996). Face processing in autistics: Evidence for a generalised deficit? *Child Neuropsychology, 2(2)*, 123–139.

Gilchrist, I. D. (2011). Saccades. In S. Liversedge, I. Gilchrist & S. Everling (eds), *Oxford Handbook of Eye Movements*, Chapter 5 (pp. 85–94). Oxford, UK: Oxford University Press.

Greer, J., Riby, D. M., Hamilton, C. & Riby, L. (2013). Attentional lapse and inhibition control in adults with Williams Syndrome. *Research in Developmental Disabilities, 34*, 4170–4177.

Haas, B. W., Hoeft, F., Searcy, Y. M., Mills, D., Bellugi, B. & Reiss, A. (2010). Individual differences in social behavior predict amygdala response to fearful facial expressions in Williams syndrome. *Neuropsychologia, 48*, 1283–1288.

Hanley, M., McPhillips, M., Mulhern, G. & Riby, D. M. (2012). Spontaneous attention to faces in Asperger syndrome using ecologically valid static stimuli. *Autism, 17*, 754–761.

Hanley, M., Riby, D. M., Caswell, S., Rooney, S. & Back, E. (2013). Looking and thinking: How individuals with Williams syndrome make judgements about mental states. *Research in Developmental Disabilities, 34*, 4466–4476.

Henderson, J. M. (2003). Human gaze control during real-world scene perception. *Trends in Cognitive Science, 7*, 498–504.

Hosozawa, M., Tanaka, K., Shimizu, T., Nakano, T. & Kitazawa, S. (2012). How children with specific language impairment view social situations: An eye tracking study. *Paediatrics, 129*, 1453–1460.

Jawaid, A., Schmolck, H. & Schulz, P. E. (2008). Hypersociability in Williams syndrome: A role for the amygdala? *Cognitive Neuropsychiatry, 13*, 338–342.

Jones, W. & Klin, A. (2013). Attention to eyes is present but in decline in 2–6-month-old infants later diagnosed with autism. *Nature, 504*, 427–431.

Jones, W., Bellugi, U., Lai, Z., Chiles, M., Reilly, J., Lincoln, A. & Adolphs, R. (2000). Hypersociability in Williams syndrome. *Journal of Cognitive Neuroscience, 12*, 30–46.

Jones, W., Carr, K. & Klin, A. (2008). Absence of preferential looking to the eyes of approaching adults predicts level of social disability in 2-year-old toddlers with autism spectrum disorder. *Archives of General Psychiatry, 65*, 946–954.

Joseph, R. M., Tager-Flusberg, H. & Lord, C. (2002). Cognitive profiles and social-communicative functioning in children with autism spectrum disorder. *Journal of Child Psychology and Psychiatry, 43*, 807–821.

Karmiloff-Smith, A., Grant, J., Berthoud, I., Davies, M., Howlin, P. & Udwin, O. (1997). Language and Williams syndrome: How intact is intact? *Child Development, 68*, 246–262.

Karmiloff-Smith, A., Broadbent, H., Farran, E. K., Longhi, E., D'Souza, D., Metcalfe, K., … Sansbury, F. (2012). Social cognition in Williams syndrome: Genotype/phenotype insights from partial deletions. *Frontiers in Psychology, 3*, 1–8.

Kaufman, A. S. & Kaufman, N. L. (2004). *Kaufman Brief Intelligence Test (2nd ed.)*. Circle Pines, MN: American Guidance Service, Inc.

Kawashima, R., Sugiura, M., Kato, T., Nakamura, A., Hatano, K., Ito, K., … Nakamura, K. (1999). The human amygdala plays an important role in gaze monitoring: A PET study. *Brain, 122*, 779–783.

Kelly, D., Walker, R. & Norbury, C. F. (2013). Deficits in volitional oculomotor control align with language status in autism spectrum disorders. *Developmental Science, 16*, 56–66.

Kemner, C. & van Engeland, H. (2003). Autism and visual fixation. *American Journal of Psychiatry, 160*, 1358–1359.

Kirk, H., Hocking, D., Riby, D. M. & Cornish, K. (2013). Linking social behaviour and anxiety to attention to emotional faces in Williams syndrome. *Research in Developmental Disabilities, 34*, 4608–4616.

Klein-Tasman, B. P., Mervis, C. B., Lord, C. & Phillip, K. (2007). Socio-communicative deficits in young children with Williams syndrome: Performance on the autism diagnostic observation schedule. *Child Neuropsychology, 13*, 444–467.

Klin, A. (2008). In the eye of the beholden: Tracking developmental psychopathology. *Journal of the American Academy of Child and Adolescent Psychiatry, 47*, 362–363.

Klin, A., Jones, W., Schultz, R., Volkmar, F. & Cohen, D. (2002a). Defining and quantifying the social phenotype in autism. *American Journal of Psychiatry, 159*, 895–908.

——(2002b). Visual fixation patterns during viewing of naturalistic social situations as predictors of social competence in individuals with autism. *Archives of General Psychiatry, 59*(9), 809–816.

Langdell, T. (1978). Recognition of faces: An approach to the study of autism. *Journal of Child Psychology and Psychiatry, 19*, 255–268.

Laws, G. & Bishop, D. M. V. (2004). Pragmatic language impairment and social deficits in Williams syndrome: A comparison with Down's syndrome and specific language impairment. *International Journal of Language & Communication Disorders, 39*, 45–64.

Lenhoff, H. M., Wang, P. P., Greenberg, F. & Bellugi, U. (2006). Williams syndrome and the brain [Electronic version]. *Uncommon Genius, Scientific American, 31*, 11–15.

Leyfer, O. T., Woodruff-Borden, J., Klein-Tasman, B. P., Fricke, J. S. & Mervis, C. B. (2006). Prevalence of psychiatric disorders in 4–16-year-olds with Williams syndrome. *American Journal of Medical Genetics Part B – Neuropsychiatric Genetics, 141*, 615–622.

Lincoln, A. J., Searcy, Y. M., Jones, W. & Lord, C. (2007). Social interaction behaviours discriminate young children with autism and Williams syndrome. *Journal of the American Academy of Child and Adolescent Psychiatry, 46*, 323–331.

Lord, C., Rutter, M., DiLavore, P. C. & Risi, S. (1999). *Autism Diagnostic Observation Schedule-WPS (ADOS-WPS)*. Los Angeles, CA: Western Psychological Services.

Martens, M. A., Wilson, S. J. & Reutens, D. C. (2008). Research review: Williams syndrome: a critical review of the cognitive, behavioural, and neuroanatomical phenotype. *The Journal of Child Psychology and Psychiatry, 49*, 576–608.

Merin, N., Young, G. S., Ozonoff, S. & Rogers, S. J. (2007). Visual fixation patterns during reciprocal social interaction distinguish a sub-group of 6-month-old infants at-risk for autism from comparison infants. *Journal of Autism and Developmental Disorders, 37*, 108–121.

Mervis, C. B., Morris, C. A., Klein, T., Bonita, P., Bertrand, J., Kwitny, S., Appelbaum, L. G. & Rice, C. E. (2003a). Attentional characteristics of infants and toddlers with Williams syndrome during triadic interactions. *Developmental Neuropsychology, 23*, 243–268.

Mervis, C. B., Robinson, B. F., Rowe, M. L., Becerra, A. M. & Klein-Tasman, B. P. (2003b). Language abilities of individuals with Williams syndrome. *International Review of Research in Mental Retardation, 27*, 35–81.

Morris, C. & Mervis, C. (1999). Williams syndrome. In S. Goldstein & C. Reynolds (eds), *Handbook of Neurodevelopmental and Genetic Disorders in Children* (pp. 55–90). New York: Guildford.

——(2000). Williams syndrome and related disorders. *Annual Review of Genomics and Human Genetics, 1*, 461–484.

Morris, C. A., Demsey, S. A., Leonard, C. O., Dilts, C. & Blackburn, B. L. (1998). Natural history of Williams syndrome: Physical characteristics. *The Journal of Pediatrics, 113*, 318–326.

Nadig, A., Lee, I., Singh, L., Bosshart, K. & Ozonoff, S. (2010). How does the topic of conversation affect verbal exchange and eye gaze? A comparison between typical development and high-functioning autism. *Neuropsychologia, 48*, 2730–2739.

Nakano, T., Tanak, K., Endo, Y., Yamane, Y., Yamamoto, T., Nakano, Y., … Kitazawa, S. (2010). Atypical gaze patterns in children and adults with autism spectrum disorders dissociated from developmental changes in gaze behaviour. *Proceedings of the Royal Society B – Biological Science, 277*, 2935–2943.

Norbury, C. F., Brock, J., Cragg, L., Einav, S., Griffiths, H. & Nation, K. (2009). Eye-movement patterns are associated with communicative competence in autistic spectrum disorders. *The Journal of Child Psychology and Psychiatry, 50*, 834–842.

Pellicano, E., Maybery, M., Durkin, K. & Maley, A. (2006). Multiple cognitive capabilities/ deficits in children with an autism spectrum disorder: 'Weak' central coherence and its relationship to theory of mind and executive control. *Development and Psychopathology, 18*, 77–98.

Pelphrey, K. A., Sasson, N. J., Reznick, J. S., Paul, G., Goldman, B. D. & Piven, J. (2002). Visual scanning of faces in autism. *Journal of Autism and Developmental Disorders, 32*(4), 249–261.

Porter, M. A. & Coltheart, M. (2005). Cognitive heterogeneity in Williams syndrome. *Developmental Neuropsychology, 27*, 275–306.

Porter, M. A., Shaw, T. & Marsh, P. J. (2010). An unusual attraction to the eyes in Williams–Beuren syndrome: A manipulation of facial affect while measuring face scanpaths. *Cognitive Neuropsychiatry, 15*(6), 505–530.

Rhodes, S. M., Riby, D. M., Park, J., Fraser, E. & Campbell, L. E. (2010). Executive neuropsychological functioning in individuals with Williams syndrome. *Neuropsychologia, 48*, 1216–1226.

Riby, D. M. & Hancock, P. J. B. (2008). Viewing it differently: Social scene perception in Williams syndrome and autism. *Neuropsychologia, 46*, 2855–2860.

——(2009a). Looking at movies and cartoons: Eye-tracking evidence from Williams syndrome and autism. *Journal of Intellectual Disability Research, 53*(2), 169–218.

——(2009b). Do faces capture the attention of individuals with Williams syndrome or Autism? Evidence from tracking eye movements. *Journal of Autism and Developmental Disorders, 39*(3), 421–431.

Riby, D. M. & Porter, M. A. (2010). Williams Syndrome. In J. Holmes (ed.), *Advances in Child Development and Behaviour* (pp. 163–209). Burlington, VT: Academic Press.

Riby, D. M., Doherty-Sneddon, G. & Bruce, V. (2008a). Atypical unfamiliar face processing in Williams syndrome: What can it tell us about typical familiarity effects? *Cognitive Neuropsychiatry, 13*, 47–58.

——(2008b). Exploring face perception in disorders of development: Evidence from Williams syndrome and autism. *Journal of Neuropsychology, 2*, 47–64.

——(2009). The eyes or the mouth? Feature salience and unfamiliar face processing in Williams syndrome and autism. *The Quarterly Journal of Experimental Psychology, 62*, 189–203.

Riby, D. M., Hancock, P. J. B., Jones, N. & Hanley, M. (2013). Spontaneous and cued gaze-following in autism and Williams syndrome. *Journal of Neurodevelopmental Disorders, 5*, 13. doi: 10.1186/1866-1955-5-13.

Riby, D. M., Kirk, H., Hanley, M. & Riby, L. M. (2014). Stranger danger awareness in Williams syndrome. *Journal of Intellectual Disability Research, 58*, 572–582.

Rice, K., Moriuchi, J. M., Jones, W. & Klin, A. (2012). Parsing heterogeneity in autism spectrum disorders: visual scanning of dynamic social scenes in school-aged children. *Journal of the American Academy of Child and Adolescent Psychiatry, 51*, 238–248.

Senju, A. & Johnson, M. H. (2009). The eye contact effect: Mechanisms and development. *Trends in Cognitive Science, 13*, 127–134.

South, M., Schultz, R. T. & Ozonoff, S. (2011). Social cognition in ASD. In D. Fein (ed.) *The Neuropsychology of Autism* (pp. 225–242). New York, NY: Oxford University Press.

Speer, L. L., Cook, A. E., McMahon, W. M. & Clark, E. (2007). Face processing in children with autism: Effect of stimulus contents and type. *Autism, 11*, 265–277.

Spence, S. H. (1998). A measure of anxiety symptoms among children. *Behaviour Research and Therapy, 36*, 545–566.

Spezio, M. L., Adolfs, R., Hurley, R. S. E. & Piven, J. (2007). Abnormal use of facial information in high-functioning autism. *Journal of Autism and Developmental Disorders, 37*, 929–939.

Stromme, P., Bjornstad, P. G. & Ramstad, K. (2002). Prevalence estimation of Williams syndrome. *Journal of Child Neurology, 17*, 269–271.

Tager-Flusberg, H. & Sullivan, K. (2000). A componential view of theory of mind: Evidence from Williams syndrome. *Cognition, 76*, 59–90.

Tager-Flusberg, H., Plesa Skwerer, D. & Joseph, R. (2006). Model syndromes for investigating social cognitive and affective neuroscience: A comparison of autism and Williams syndrome. *Social Cognitive and Affective Neuroscience, 1*, 175–182.

Triesch, J., Teuscher, C., Deák, G. O. & Carlson, E. (2006). Gaze following: Why (not) learn it? *Developmental Science, 9*, 125–147.

Van der Geest, J. N., Kemner, C., Verbaten, M. N. & van Engeland, H. (2002). Gaze behavior of children with pervasive developmental disorder toward human faces: A fixation time study. *Journal of Child Psychology and Psychiatry and Allied Disciplines, 43*(5), 669–678.

Volkmar, F., Lord, C., Bailey, A., Schultz, R. T. & Klin, A. (2004). Autism and pervasive developmental disorders. *Journal of Child Psychology and Psychiatry, 45*, 135–170.

Von Hofsten, C. & Gredebäck, G. (2009). The role of looking in social cognition: Perspectives from development and autism. In T. Striano & V. Reid (eds), *Social Cognition. Development, Neuroscience, and Autism* (1st ed.) (pp. 237–253). West Sussex: Wiley-Blackwell.

Williams, J., Barrat-Boyes, B. & Lowe, J. (1961). Supravalvar aortic stenosis. *Circulation, 24*, 1311–1381.

Williams, T. A., Porter, M. A. & Langdon, R. (2013). Viewing social scenes: A visual scan-path study comparing Fragile X syndrome and Williams syndrome. *Journal of Autism and Developmental Disorders, 43*, 1880–1894.

Wing, L. & Gould, J. (1979). Severe impairments of social interaction and associated abnormalities in children: Epidemiology and classification. *Journal of Autism and Developmental Disorders, 9*, 11–29.

Young, G. S., Merin, N., Rogers, S. J. & Ozonoff, S. (2009). Gaze behaviour and affect at 6 months: Predicting clinical outcomes and language development in typically developing infants and infants at risk for autism. *Developmental Science, 12*, 798–814.

PART III

Applied issues in neurodevelopmental disorders

13

USES OF NEW TECHNOLOGIES BY YOUNG PEOPLE WITH NEURO-DEVELOPMENTAL DISORDERS

Motivations, processes and cognition

Sue Fletcher-Watson and Kevin Durkin

13.1 Introduction

Technology is now pervasive in everyday life. The proliferation of the internet, the rise of mobile and touchscreen technologies, and the vast array of specialist software, such as apps, to go with them mean that we are rarely without some form of digital technology. Technology, as has always been the case, is not the preserve of adults, and this is even more pronounced since large touchscreen devices such as iPads have opened up accessibility to young children and to those with intellectual disabilities (Kagohara et al., 2013). These factors raise questions for developmental psychologists about whether technology can be harnessed to support people with neurodevelopmental disorders, but also about whether too much technology could be damaging (Durkin & Blades, 2009). The ubiquity of technology means that it is redundant to ask whether or not these groups should access technology – they do. Instead, we must turn our attention to when or how they use it, how they may benefit from it and what problems they may encounter. These are particularly important questions in respect of children with neurodevelopmental disorders.

Technology, for the purposes of this chapter, refers to computerised devices and accompanying software of all kinds. At the time of writing, this includes videogames played on specialised devices such as an Xbox or Playstation or found on the internet or in arcades. There are also iPads, iPhones and other touchscreen tablets and smartphones that run apps – these can be educational, functional (e.g. calendars), social (e.g. Facebook, FaceTime) or entertaining – and often more than one of these descriptors can apply. Most homes in the developed world now have a computer of some kind and internet access is very common (Rideout, Foehr & Roberts 2010; Warschauer & Matuchniak, 2010). Computers are used for academic or professional activities such as word processing, leisure such as online shopping, as well as social and entertainment functions. All of these mainstream technologies are being used by people with neurodevelopmental disorders. In addition, there are a number of disability-specific technologies which address a bewilderingly broad range of functions (for example, see Figure 13.1).

One issue that colours many discussions about the use of technology to support people with additional needs, especially children, is a widespread concern over 'screen time' as a potentially damaging influence in development. The latest good evidence that we have is from the Millennium Cohort Study in which parent-report data about over 11,000 children were analysed to look at how screen time at five years old predicted behavioural outcomes at seven years (Parkes, Sweeting, Wight & Henderson, 2013). No relationships were found between screen time and theoretically relevant outcomes such as hyperactivity/inattention, conduct problems, pro-social behaviour and peer relations. However, other authors have pointed out the need for further well-designed studies exploring the effects of screen time, especially in younger children (Thakkar, Garrison & Christakis, 2006).

Technology, and skills in using technology, offers much to people with additional support needs. They can provide cognitive and perceptual stimulation, alternative or supplementary modes of communication, means of making or strengthening connections within the peer community, opportunities for participation and a sense of normality, increased self-confidence, and well-being (Durkin, Boyle, Hunter & Conti-Ramsden, 2013). At the same time, technology can present challenges or barriers, including demands on technical ability, conceptual and vocabulary knowledge, motoric skills, as well as risks, such as the possibility of over-use, diversion from other activities, and exposure to unproductive or inappropriate contents. All of these considerations underscore why we need to

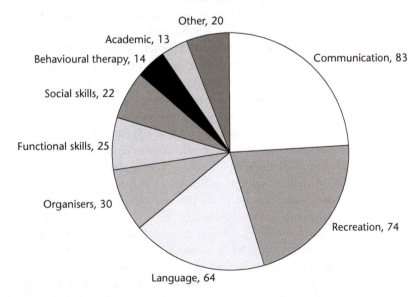

FIGURE 13.1 Apps targeted at the autism community, by functional category,* n = 345.
* Data downloaded from http://www.autismspeaks.org/autism-apps on 02.01.2013

learn more about how young people with neurodevelopmental disorders use contemporary technologies.

In addition, studies employing new technologies may provide us with insight into the theoretical underpinnings of diagnostic categories or personal profiles (Rajendran, 2013). How children with different symptoms use and learn from technology can provide insight into their cognitive, social and emotional characteristics, in much the same way that studies of reading development have provided understanding of wider developmental issues in cognitive and neuropsychology (Daneman & Carpenter, 1980; Altemeier, Abbott & Berninger, 2008). Technologies present rich and dynamic environments in which to collect detailed data about cognitive and perceptual processes and spontaneous preferences, meaning that with careful design it can be employed as a naturalistic research tool, providing multiple insights (Fletcher-Watson, 2014).

Thus, the goals of this chapter are to review how technologies are being or could be used by people with neurodevelopmental disorders and to consider the available evidence we have for best practice in this field. We will select for attention those studies that have greatest relevance for current practice and future research. We will focus on three main groups about whom we have more research-based knowledge than other exceptional populations: these are people with attention deficit hyperactivity disorder (ADHD: for a detailed discussion see Chapter 9), people with autism spectrum disorder (ASD; see also Chapter 7), and people with specific language impairment (SLI; see Chapters 5 and 8). This is not, of course, to imply that the issues under discussion are relevant only to individuals with these disorders. We hope that readers specialising in other disorders will also find themes reviewed here relevant to their own current practice and/or future research.

13.2 Attention Deficit/Hyperactivity Disorder and new technologies

Children with ADHD present interesting issues with respect to uses of new technologies. By definition, ADHD entails persistent and developmentally inappropriate patterns of inattention, hyperactivity and impulsiveness (Barkley, 2006; Hulme & Snowling, 2009). Individuals with high levels of ADHD symptomatology find it difficult to sustain attention and to disregard distractions; they are less likely to persist in difficult tasks at school and are at risk of poor reading and maths scores, grade repetition and poor educational outcomes (Loe & Feldman, 2007; Washbrook, Propper & Sayal, 2013; Zentall & Beike, 2012). Yet, the limited evidence available to date indicates that children with ADHD spend about the same amount of time playing videogames as typically developing children (TD; Bioulac, Arfi & Bouvard, 2008; Ferguson & Olson, 2014; Mazurek & Engelhardt, 2013; Shimoni, Engel-Yeger & Tirosh, 2010). There is some evidence to suggest that adolescents with ADHD spend more time using the internet than do TD adolescents (Ko, Yen, Yen, Chen & Chen, 2012). Parents often complain that it is difficult to persuade their child with ADHD to desist from these activities (Bioulac et al., 2008). Young people with ADHD sometimes report that they find videogames so absorbing that they become oblivious to all else (Meaux, Green & Broussard, 2009). Whether or not this is problematic or beneficial (it is an experience commonly reported by many players without ADHD, too; Wood, Griffiths, Chappell & Davies, 2004), it is different from their engagement with many other leisure activities, which tends to be less focussed and less sustained than that of typical youth (Shimoni et al., 2010).

If children with ADHD are using new technologies roughly as much as TD children, this raises a number of questions: What attracts them to these activities when they are unable to settle on many others? Are they able to concentrate more adequately in these contexts? Are their uses of the technologies similar to those of TD children? Do the technologies have potential benefits for these young people? Could the technologies be harmful to them?

13.2.1 Attractions of new technologies for young people with ADHD

TD children are attracted to new technologies for a range of reasons, including the skills, challenges and excitement of videogames, entertainment and relaxation via games and internet uses, the identity correlates of participating with peers in online and offline games, and the perceived importance to preadolescents and adolescents of social networking (Durkin, 2006; Ferguson & Olson, 2014). Many report mood-management or cathartic motives (Durkin & Aisbett, 1999; Ferguson & Olson, 2014). It is likely that at least some of these motivations are also pertinent for young people with ADHD, though relatively little research has been conducted to assess their motives per se. A specific strong motivation in this population may be that some uses of new technologies are appealing because they satisfy the children's need for rapid reinforcement (Durkin, 2010). Children with ADHD have an unusually high requirement for immediate reward (Luman, Oosterlaan & Sergeant, 2005; Sonuga-Barke, Taylor, Sembi & Smith, 1992).

Evidence from healthy adult participants suggests that during action videogame play striatal dopamine is released (Koepp et al., 1998). Dopamine is a neurotransmitter in the central nervous system known to be closely associated with reward-seeking behaviours (Luciana, Wahlstrom, Porter & Collins, 2012). Individuals with ADHD are believed to have a dysfunctional dopamine system (Sikström & Söderlund, 2007). Researchers have speculated that videogame play stimulates dopamine release in young people with ADHD (Han et al., 2009; Houghton et al., 2004; Sikström & Söderlund, 2007). Videogames offer scope for rapid and often enjoyable consequences of the player's actions and this may render them a particularly gratifying or even self-medicating environment (Han et al., 2009).

13.2.2 Cognitive performance, ADHD and new technologies

Videogames, apps, surfing the web, online social networking and peer coordination via mobiles draw on a range of cognitive and communicative abilities. We are in only the early stages of investigating these phenomena in TD individuals, and have even less evidence in respect of children with developmental disorders. However, it is clear, for example, that much videogame play involves complex cognitive and perceptual skills (Durkin, 2010; Greenfield, 2009; Spence & Feng, 2010). Executive functions (EF) are necessary for goal-directed behaviour such as planning a sequence of actions, initiating and modifying a course of events, ceasing specific behaviours when it is advantageous or prudential to do so; all of these are common demands of videogame play. Deficits in executive function have been reported for children with ADHD (Barkley, 2006; Pennington & Ozonoff, 1996; Rhodes, Coghill & Matthews, 2006). Hence, it is of interest to examine the cognitive dimensions of their game play and uses of other technologies.

Several studies have found evidence that children with ADHD can achieve satisfactory performance on some EF tasks when tested in motivating conditions (including computerised, game-like formats) that they fail to demonstrate on standardised tests (Morein-Zamir, Hommersen, Johnston & Kingstone, 2008). Lawrence et al. (2002) found that six- to twelve-year-old boys with ADHD were as able as TD participants to interrupt ongoing screen activity in the course of a platform game and to inhibit prepotent responses (for example, they could pause their character at critical moments in the face of imminent hazards). On the other hand, participants with ADHD showed less skilful adherence to rules governing spinning moves and more on-task affective exclamations and self talk during the games; these responses are indicative of difficulties in working memory. In a similar study, Lawrence et al. (2004) found that children with ADHD completed fewer challenges within a videogame than did TD comparison children, and their performances were associated with other indices of EF. Shaw, Grayson and Lewis (2005) obtained no difference between children with ADHD and TD comparisons on either the number of moves or of impulsive errors in videogame play. Bioulac et al. (2012) found that children with ADHD, who showed the expected lower (than TD controls) performance on a routine, computer-based ADHD assessment, did not differ from controls on several measures of videogame performance reflecting inhibitory skills.

The evidence to date indicates that children with ADHD can achieve satisfactory cognitive performances in videogames in respect of certain EFs but may also reflect some deficits in working memory (Durkin, 2010). The findings that, in videogames, children with ADHD do appear to be able to demonstrate inhibitory skills on a par with typical peers are of considerable importance in relation to theories of the disorder, which assume a global inhibitory impairment (Barkley, 2006). As pointed out by Bioulac et al. (2012), they suggest that inhibitory capacity in ADHD is amenable to contextual and motivational influences; in turn, it follows that gaming and related technologies may have potential as tools to support these children's learning and performance.

Fabio and Antonietti (2012) provide further support for this assumption in an experimental comparison of the effects of hypermedia instruction (delivered via a web browser, combining texts, pictorial illustrations, sounds and graphics) with those of traditional (teacher-delivered, primarily oral) instruction. Participants with

ADHD, aged twelve to fourteen years, showed superior learning and retention in the hypermedia condition. This condition was also more effective with TD participants, too, but notably the learning gap between ADHD and TD participants was reduced in the hypermedia condition. The authors conclude that students with ADHD can benefit from educational delivery via new technologies. This could reflect motivational, attentional and/or control of pace factors.

13.2.3 Are new technologies harmful to those with ADHD?

We do not have sufficient evidence to determine whether new technologies are harmful for children with ADHD. This is a vulnerable population and it might be anticipated that any risks associated with the activities that any media make available could be intensified among this group. In popular discussions, it is sometimes assumed that new technologies, such as videogames, foster short attention spans and promote undesirable behaviour (such as aggression). Indeed, it is sometimes speculated that videogames cause, or at least exacerbate, ADHD itself. There is little evidence to support these fears and some evidence to point to different conclusions.

Parkes et al. (2013) reported tentative evidence that children who played no videogames had increased levels of inattention/hyperactivity compared to children who played for moderate amounts of time. However, this effect was not robust in the face of adjustments for a range of covariates relating to family and child characteristics.

Ferguson and Olson (2014), in a large-scale study of American twelve- to thirteen-year-olds, found that children identified with clinically elevated attention deficit symptoms did not differ from peers without these problems in terms of their total time spent gaming, violent game exposure, social play or challenge motivation. However, children with elevated ADHD symptoms were more likely to endorse a catharsis motivation for playing videogames. This is consistent with the thesis that young people with ADHD use (or attempt to use) this medium in a self-regulatory way (Han et al., 2009; Houghton et al., 2004).

13.2.4 Summary

Children with ADHD appear to spend approximately the same amount of time playing videogames as do children with TD and to be attracted to them for much the same reasons. These reasons include the desire to be sociable and addressing the challenges that games present. There is some evidence to suggest that children with ADHD symptoms may find the rewards of gaming physiologically gratifying, and researchers have reported a slightly higher tendency among this group to report self-management strategies, including cathartic release, via gaming. Less is known about the use of other new technologies, such as apps and mobile phones, among those with ADHD but preliminary evidence indicates that these, too, are attractive to this population. Evidence indicates that children with ADHD can achieve superior cognitive performances in gaming and hypermedia contexts compared to their performance in standard tests. Researchers have attributed these outcomes to the strong motivational appeal of the technologies and the possibility that some demands may be tailored in ways that accommodate attentional difficulties. Despite occasional speculation, there is little evidence to date that use of new technologies is harmful to children with ADHD. In contrast, it has been argued that children's interest in these technologies should be exploited to foster their learning and behaviour.

13.3 Autism Spectrum Disorder and new technologies

Autism Spectrum Disorder (ASD) is diagnosed by the presence of difficulties in two domains: social interaction and communication; and repetitive and restricted behaviours (APA, 2013; see Chapters 7 and 12 for a discussion on the cognitive and behavioural profile of individuals with ASD). There is considerable evidence to support the assumption that many people with ASD have a preference for using technology, both as a leisure activity (Orsmond & Kuo, 2011; Mineo, Ziegler, Gill & Salkin, 2009; Shane & Albert, 2008) and in classrooms (Moore & Calvert, 2000; Williams, Wright, Callaghan & Coughlan, 2002). For example, Orsmond and Kuo (2011) found that the second most common discretionary activity of adolescents with ASD is computer use (watching television is the most common) – accounting for an average of about 50 minutes per day. Although there was a significant difference in computer use between those with and without intellectual disability (ID), nevertheless, 45 per cent of adolescents with ID still engaged in computer use. Nor was computer use longitudinally related to social impairments. These data indicate that engagement with computers does not seem to systematically vary across the spectrum of ASD profiles. However, it should also be noted that 49 per cent of adolescents in the study did not use computers at all, though a relationship with family status indicates this may have been driven by socio-economic factors rather than preference. While this seems to contradict evidence that computer ownership is common in developed countries, we hypothesise that parents may not allow access to a computer by adolescents with ASD if this is the only such device in the home, and a valuable possession.

13.3.1 Why do people with ASD favour technology?

Both of the diagnostic symptom domains of ASD can be theoretically referenced to explain the preference for people with ASD to use technology. For example, one logical interpretation is that people with ASD engage with technology so readily because it is a way to avoid the interpersonal contact that many find stressful or at least challenging (Watabe & Suzuki, 2013). Indeed, some adolescents with ASD prefer to use ostensibly highly social technologies, such as mobile phones, primarily for non-communicative purposes, such as playing electronic games (Durkin, Whitehouse, Jaquet, Ziatas & Walker, 2010b). Alternatively, we can posit that working with technology provides an opportunity to indulge a preference for repetition, predictability and routine that is harder to achieve in less tightly bound contexts. However, despite these hypothetical links, the reasons why people with ASD are both skilled in using technology and do so extensively is poorly understood at a psychological level. There is a need for further research mapping both spontaneous use of technology and experimental studies of computer use onto clinical profiles to further elucidate these underpinnings (e.g. Rajendran et al., 2011).

Existing studies showing preferences among people with ASD for using technology in their leisure time are supported by a new survey of parents of children with ASD (of all ages).[1] This online questionnaire enquires about technology use in the home. Results indicate both a wide variety and a high rate of technology use by people with ASD for many purposes, positive perceptions of the value of technology by parents but also concerns regarding over-use of technology (see Figure 13.2).

One of the major themes emerging from this study is that parents of children with ASD often feel guilty about the amount of time their child spends using technology. There is as yet no evidence to confirm or deny whether amount of technology use is detrimental to development in ASD. Virtual online worlds such as Second Life™ and web-based interactive gaming systems such as Club Penguin™, Minecraft™ or League of Legends™ are popular among children with ASD as they grow up and may provide a much desired and needed opportunity to

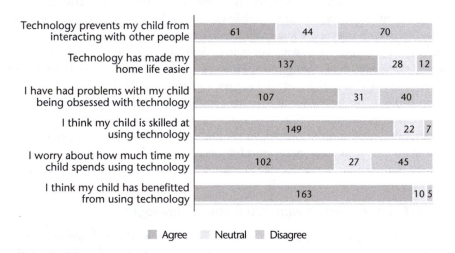

FIGURE 13.2 Parent responses in a survey of attitudes to technology use by children with autism.

socialise in a context which is comfortable to them (Fusar-Poli, Cortesi, Borgwardt & Politi, 2008), and to gain the kind of knowledge and expertise which converts into valuable playground currency.

13.3.2 Using novel technologies to support learning in ASD

There has been a recent flurry of reviews of this field that cover technology for academic learning (Pennington, 2010) and literacy (Ramdoss et al., 2011a) but also technology for more ASD-specific difficulties such as communication development (Ramdoss et al., 2011b) and social impairment (Ramdoss, Machalicek, Rispoli, Lang & O'Reilly, 2012). A meta-analysis incorporating fourteen technological intervention studies indicates a significant positive effect of technological intervention on target skills in ASD, which is unrelated to age and IQ of participants (Grynszpan, Weiss, Perez-Diaz & Gal, 2013). In addition, there are a number of studies that point to 'spin-off' benefits to working with technology that may be unexpected (see Fletcher-Watson, 2014, for examples). Rather than review this extensive literature again here, we select a handful of recent studies for further attention, which illustrate the breadth of effects of technological interventions for education.

Williams et al. (2002) explored whether children with ASD, aged three to five years and minimally verbal, would learn to read more readily using computer-assisted lessons compared with traditional teaching, using a cross-over design. In this sample of only eight children, there was some evidence that children learned more words during their computer-instruction phase than during their book-learning phase. However, the more striking findings came from observational data, which showed three times as much on-task time and twice as much language during computer instruction. There was also evidence of greater amounts of spontaneous gesture including pointing during the computer condition. These findings are echoed in similar studies using technology to target an academic skill, but observing knock-on effects on social communication and on-task behaviour (Alcorn et al., 2011; Bernard-Opitz, Sriram & Sapuan, 1999; Heimann, Nelson, Tjus & Gillberg, 1995; Hetzroni & Shalem, 2005; Tjus, Heimann & Nelson, 2001).

Working with older children (mean age = ten years), Hopkins and colleagues (2011) investigated whether groups of children with ASD with and without concurrent intellectual disability could be taught to become more expert at following gaze, recognising faces and interpreting emotions using a computer program, *FaceSay*. In this case the adoption of a computerised technique represents another of the strengths of this approach, which is the opportunity to present multiple exemplars of a type repeatedly and with consistent presentation style and degrees of variation. In the real world, while one might see a lot of faces, these are not well displayed for training purposes. The trained groups both demonstrated significant improvements in emotion recognition ability, and generalisation of skills to real-world social interactions. This well-designed study is part of a much larger body of work looking at face recognition and/or emotion recognition skills using computerised training (Bolte et al., 2002, 2006; Faja, Aylward, Bernier & Dawson, 2008; Faja et al., 2011; Golan & Baron-Cohen, 2006; Golan et al., 2010; LaCava, Rankin, Mahlios, Cook & Simpson, 2010; Silver & Oakes, 2001; Tanaka et al., 2010). A recent meta-analysis of a set of randomised controlled trials in this field demonstrated a positive overall effect on emotion recognition in people with ASD when trained in this way (Fletcher-Watson, McConnell, Manola & McConachie, 2014c).

13.3.3 Can technology be harnessed to target social interaction difficulties?

Computerised approaches have also been applied to the core social interactive difficulties associated with ASD, despite the fact that this might seem paradoxical. One excellent example of this work is the Secret Agent Society (Beaumont & Sofronoff, 2008) which combines individual computer-based training in social skills with group work and some parent guidance. This randomised controlled trial reports beneficial effects of the intervention, including teacher- and parent-report evidence of improvement of skills in real-world settings such as the playground and classroom. These skills were not directly observed but the integration of computer-assisted learning with real-world activities is gaining popularity and may represent best practice in this field (Golan & Baron-Cohen, 2006; Whalen et al., 2010).

Early intervention has long been considered to be important to support developmental progress among children with ASD (Woods & Wetherby 2003). The (relatively) recent proliferation of touchscreen technologies means that computerised therapeutic approaches can now be applied to very young children. Previously the challenge of mastering the interface was often a block to learning progress and a distraction when analysing results (e.g. Williams et al., 2002) and real-world rewards such as sweets were used to engage the children with the technology (e.g. Clark & Green, 2004; Hagiwara & Myles, 1999; Miller & Neuringer, 2000). However, new technologies such as iPads are helping to overcome this barrier (Kagohara et al., 2013). A recent randomised controlled trial of an iPad app for joint attention for children with ASD did not produce group level intervention effects on parent–child interaction but did indicate excellent, spontaneous engagement with the program even in children whose ability level was very low (Fletcher-Watson et al., 2014a, 2014b). Twenty-two of a sample of twenty-six children (85 per cent) reached the highest level of the game, of which all but one went on to repeat the game at least once more. Furthermore, there was no relationship between scores on a standardised test of ability (the Mullen Scales of Early Learning: Mullen, 1995) and engagement with the app.

Other ways of using technology to support people with ASD are founded on this assumption that technology may be, for a large proportion of the group, particularly motivating. For example, software designed for building social stories such as StoryMaker™, provides a way to present social stories (Kokina & Kern, 2010) on a touchscreen. However, this transition from paper to digital confers more advantages than a simple motivational edge – using a digital platform means that dozens, or even hundreds, of social stories can be held on one device and carried around at all times for use when needed. It is simple to create new stories using the built-in camera, embedded audio-recording and text captioning. Finally, the app can hold in one place the interfaces required to learn about the theory and practice of social stories, as well as to create and share the stories themselves. This system seems to offer a lot of benefits but research comparisons of social story apps and traditional paper versions have not yet been carried out. Another example of this principle in practice is the use of robots as a therapeutic partner where there is beginning to be evidence that working with a robot can enhance the social responsivity of a sub-set of children with ASD in a therapeutic setting (Diehl, Schmitt, Villano & Crowell, 2012). Finally, Farr and colleagues (Farr, Yuill & Raffle, 2010) have shown how the creativity embedded in tangible technologies can promote pretend play skills more effectively than low-tech alternatives such as Lego™ therapy.

Novel technologies have also been applied to address life skills or to provide adaptive support. For people with ASD who are non-verbal or minimally verbal, augmented and assisted communication technologies such as voice-output communication aids have proven accessible (for reviews see Mirenda, 2008; Mirenda & Iacono, 2009) and may reduce challenging behaviours (Schlosser, Blischak, Belfiore, Bartley & Barnett, 1998). This is another area in which modern technologies, such as the iPad and other tablets, are game-changing because they are so much more affordable and accessible to use than previous communication devices (Gillespie-Smith & Fletcher-Watson, 2014). Furthermore, mobile technologies can be applied to ameliorate social challenges as they arise, such as the PARLE system (Bishop, 2003), which was developed to help people with ASD or social anxiety translate metaphorical language when out and about.

13.3.4 Summary

Many children with ASD are especially attracted to screen-based technologies and, as a group, are relatively high users of them. This alone indicates that researchers and practitioners need to pay careful attention to this aspect of the children's lives and interests. Their patterns of use may reflect challenges that they experience in other domains (such as face-to-face interaction) as well as the inherent attractions of the diverse activities that can be undertaken, practised and revisited in a technological context. It is clear that computer programs have been very successfully employed to facilitate learning among people with ASD. Positive effects on target skills are widespread (though not guaranteed) but there is also evidence of greater on-task time and more language use by children with ASD receiving computer instruction. It has been shown that even areas of core social difficulty for individuals with ASD, such as face processing, emotion discrimination and social skills implementation, can be facilitated by careful computerised delivery. High levels of engagement can be won from children with low levels of ability who are otherwise difficult to enlist in structured activities.

13.4 Specific Language Impairment and new technologies

The issues relating to young people with Specific Language Impairment (SLI) and new technologies overlap with some of those already discussed but, not surprisingly, there are others tied more directly to language issues. SLI is a condition in which children have language abilities (expressive and/or receptive and/or pragmatic) significantly below those expected of their age level, yet in the presence of non-verbal IQ in the typical range and with no physical explanation such as hearing impairment (Conti-Ramsden & Durkin, 2011; see also Chapters 5 and 8 for a detailed description of SLI). Thus, crucial questions in this context include: To what extent do the language difficulties of children with SLI compromise their abilities to use new technologies? Do these young people find new technologies as attractive as do their TD peers, or do they find them aversive? Can new technologies be exploited to support these children's communicative needs? Are new technologies helpful or harmful to these children's educational attainments?

Again, we do not have exhaustive answers to these questions. Descriptive data on these children's patterns of technology and new media use are scant. Despite the fact that at the point of school entry approximately 7 per cent of children have SLI (Tomblin et al., 1997), making them one of the largest groups of children with a developmental disorder, they have been relatively neglected in research (Bishop, 2010). We do know that these children are likely to experience above average difficulties with traditional media. For example, their reading and writing skills often fall behind those of their TD peers (Mackie & Dockrell, 2004; Snowling, Bishop & Stothard, 2000; St. Clair, Durkin, Conti-Ramsden & Pickles, 2010). We know also that they are at greater risk of poorer educational outcomes (Conti-Ramsden, Durkin, Simkin & Knox, 2009), with less favourable post-school outcomes and occupational opportunities (Durkin, Fraser & Conti-Ramdsen, 2012; Durkin, Simkin, Knox & Conti-Ramsden, 2009b). Thus, connecting to the world around them is a multifaceted challenge for these children. It is important to ask how they connect within an increasingly technological world.

13.4.1 Patterns of use

Durkin, Conti-Ramsden, Walker and Simkin (2009a) compared educational versus interpersonal uses of home computers in seventeen-year-olds with and without a history of SLI. They measured frequency and ease of computer use. Adolescents with SLI, in common with TD adolescents, showed a preference for social and entertainment uses (compared to educational uses) of new media.

The social motivation is noteworthy because children and adolescents with SLI tend to experience more social difficulties, higher levels of shyness and have poorer quality friendships than do TD peers (Durkin & Conti-Ramsden, 2007; Wadman, Durkin & Conti-Ramsden, 2008). At the same time, they do desire to socialise (Wadman et al., 2008). Thus, their engagements with new technologies may in part reflect a search for ways to relate to others, including an interest in exploiting alternatives to conventional face-to-face relationships. Durkin, Conti-Ramsden and Walker (2010a) examined the extent to which the frequency of use of computer-mediated communication (e.g. email, MSN) could be predicted by linguistic and social factors in sixteen-year-olds with SLI. Severity of language impairment predicted extent of use of computer-mediated communication (CMC). Even so, the majority of adolescents with SLI were users of CMC. Analysis of motives showed that linguistic considerations (pace of communication, time to review messages, relaxed literacy rules) were more important to participants with SLI than to those without. Social factors, including shyness and desire to interact with peers, were also predictive of frequency of CMC use. Both SLI participants and TD comparisons were less shy online than offline. Adolescents who were less shy online were more frequent users of CMC. The authors argued that young people with language difficulties are able to find in CMC means of interaction that are attractive and helpful to them.

Young people with SLI do find aspects of new technologies difficult and their uses are not invariably the same as those of TD peers. For example, Durkin et al. (2009a) found that language and literacy skills predicted home use of educational computing. In general, adolescents with SLI engaged in educational computing less than did their TD peers. Some 30 per cent of those with SLI reported no uses of educational applications during a given week, compared to 8 per cent of those with TD. Participants with SLI expressed difficulties in using the information provided in educational applications, finding it too technical and involving too much text. They commented that they found it hard to read, write and spell when using these packages. Conti-Ramsden, Durkin and Walker (2010) found that adolescents with SLI reported higher levels of computer anxiety (discomfort and fear about computer use) than did TD peers and that language ability was negatively correlated with computer anxiety.

Adolescents with SLI also experience difficulties with aspects of mobile phone use. Again, lower language/literacy abilities are associated with less proficient use of this technology (Durkin, Conti-Ramsden & Walker, 2011). Adolescents with SLI tend to produce shorter texts and use less text language than do TD adolescents. At the same time, they are well aware of the benefits; social motives – the desire to keep in touch – predict the extent to which they use mobiles (Conti-Ramsden, Durkin & Simkin, 2010).

Relatively little research has addressed the uses of commercial videogames by young people with SLI (Durkin, 2010; Durkin et al., 2013). However, Durkin et al. (2009a) found that one respect in which adolescents with SLI exceeded TD adolescents was in playing offline games. Gaming was popular with both groups but, while 74 per cent of the TD adolescents reported this use, 88 per cent of adolescents with SLI did. There was no difference in the proportion of individuals in each group who played online games (approximately 66 per cent). It is possible that the greater level of use of offline games by those with SLI reflects a preference for less time-pressured activities than multiplayer online contexts afford. In turn this may reflect more time spent alone by those with SLI, due to their reticence and social difficulties. These questions await further research but it is clear that new technologies are integrated into the lives of young people with SLI in ways that reflect their limitations, potentialities, needs and interpersonal contexts.

13.4.2 Can new technologies be helpful to young people with SLI?

For some time, speech and language therapists have been interested in uses of new technologies in therapy and training for children with language impairments. Approaches using game-like, computer-based interventions have proven effective, though precisely how they contribute remains controversial (Gillam et al., 2008; Tallal, 2000). Just as in the ASD field above, there is also strong interest among the professionals in this area in the use of apps in the course of therapy and/or supplementary activities managed by caregivers (Kuster, 2012). Durkin and Conti-Ramsden (2014) reviewed related literature and argue that there is a strong case for the encouragement of constructive uses of new media by families of children with language impairments.

As noted above, adolescents with SLI tend to use educational applications of computers less extensively and less comfortably than do TD adolescents (Durkin et al., 2009a), though some persist. Durkin and Conti-Ramsden (2012) found that frequency of educational uses of computers by adolescents with SLI was associated positively with exam scores at seventeen years. Of course, correlational findings can be interpreted in various ways: it could be that the use of computers in this way confers benefits but it is also possible that those who are doing better in education will be more likely to elect to use educational materials. However, the participants were followed longitudinally and, after non-verbal ability (performance IQ) was controlled for statistically, frequency of educational uses at age seventeen contributed to the prediction of educational progress at age nineteen. This suggests that engagement with these features of new technologies is beneficial.

13.4.3 Summary

Children with SLI have been a relatively neglected group among young people with developmental disorders, and most of the extant research on this condition has been focussed, understandably, on their psycholinguistic and cognitive capacities. As the field has broadened, the implications of language impairment for other aspects of their lives, including social, behavioural and educational dimensions, have received increasing attention and in this context researchers have begun to examine how these children use new media. At least among adolescents, it is clear that they are interested in these technologies and, in common with TD adolescents, have a preference for social and entertainment uses compared to educational uses. Their language impairments and associated social characteristics do affect the frequency and ease with which they use new technologies, yet at the same time their desire to communicate and to socialise with peers provide motivations to explore the potentialities of new media.

13.5 Discussion issues

This brief review of the evidence pertaining to technology use demonstrates the wide variety in research that has been conducted with these different diagnostic groups and the pressing need for further studies to elucidate the effects of technology in development. Studies with people with ADHD have focussed on their use of videogames as a medium in which to explore EF, and have often demonstrated that computer gaming environments may be a zone in which the deficits normally associated with ADHD are alleviated. In the ASD literature, while there are studies describing spontaneous use of technology, the focus has been much more on how technologies can be created to address some of the learning and therapeutic needs of the population. And in SLI research, technological studies have revealed how the core difficulties associated with the condition are also reflected in leisure and educational activities including technology use.

One (seemingly) simple goal for researchers would be to reproduce across groups the kinds of studies that have been done so far within each syndrome group (either separately or ideally in comparative projects). For example, in ASD there is currently scant evidence of the kind available for SLI, exploring whether the social difficulties characteristic of the disorder are represented equally in their technology-mediated social interactions. Do people with ASD show atypical social behaviours in their Facebook status updates and comments, or on Twitter? And, drawing on the ADHD findings, we need to enhance our understanding of why people with ASD engage so much with technology – is there a neurological underpinning to this behaviour? Do people with ASD find in technology a place in which their deficits are alleviated? From the ASD literature, researchers in SLI and ADHD could both benefit from more attention to how bespoke technologies can be created to directly address the difficulties associated with the conditions. Can we create games (or modify existing commercial technologies) to train EF or produce computer-aided ways to learn which bypass or directly address the language impairments of SLI?

Another significant issue for researchers in the future is to respond to the very powerful concerns of the community. Despite evidence to the contrary, parents, practitioners and especially policy-makers often remain pessimistic about the effects of technology. Studies show that having fun can be a contributor to better learning (Della Sala & Anderson, 2012) and that indulging restricted interests may alleviate issues such as anxiety (Boulter, Freeston, South & Rodgers, 2013). Yet, there remains a powerful and vocal lobby that seems to assume that because technology is fun and captures the interest of children so powerfully, it must automatically be bad for them. There is a pressing need for good evidence-based assessment of associations with gaming and screen time more generally to alleviate the concerns of parents.

On the other hand, the accessibility of technologies raises new issues about their use in uncontrolled settings. Very expensive assisted communication devices are being replaced by commercially available tablets and apps such as Proloquo2Go™, meaning that parents of minimally verbal children with ASD are taking this decision into their own hands. Speech and language therapists and other practitioners are faced with a scenario where this key aspect of development is being modified by the introduction of a piece of technology that, once it has become the main form of communication, cannot be removed. There is preliminary evidence to support the use of assisted communication apps in ASD (Lubas, Mitchell & De Leo, 2014), but much more work needs to be done to explore the efficacy of this approach relative to other ASD-specific language learning methods, and to provide practitioners with the skills they need to advise parents on best practice in their use (Bradshaw, 2013).

Within the educational and therapeutic context, little is known about how to design technologies to be maximally appealing and accessible to people with additional needs (Frauenberger, Good, Alcorn & Pain, 2013; Frauenberger, Good & Keay-Bright, 2011) and in particular about how to match the right technological approach to the needs and preferences of the user. Theoretical models that have explanatory power to describe matching between technology and symptom clusters or behaviours would be valuable to inform progress in this field. This would also permit better correspondence between technology-based and 'live' or traditional teaching methods which, it is logical to assume, could provide the best balance between the motivational and flexible advantages of technology and the complexity and depth of an interpersonal learning environment.

One of the most powerful arguments in favour of using technology to support people with neurodevelopmental disorders (and their families) is in consideration of the benefits of use outside the intended, main learning outcome. We have discussed how videogaming may be a mechanism for peer acceptance and interaction as well as a respite from the challenges of the mainstream world. In addition, we would argue that there needs to be a significant shift in how we appraise human computer interaction skills themselves. If these abilities were valued in the same way as other routes to knowledge (e.g. reading) we might find the skills and preferences of people with ADHD or ASD being embraced more positively. For this reason, studies exploring the use of technology should measure not just effects on the target skill but also associated benefits such as effects on user well-being and self-confidence, or impact on the whole family context.

Of course, not everyone with a neurodevelopmental disorder uses technology or enjoys it. This then raises the question of what technology has to offer individuals who are less ready to participate. First, we would emphasise that in no cases should technology fully replace other learning or socialising methods. Children especially, but also teenagers and adults, benefit from a variety of experiences and healthy behaviours and face-to-face interactions should be part of the average day for most people. Second, we point out that technology can also provide a valuable support for families of people with additional needs. For example, families of children with rare syndromes such as Cornelia de Lange and Prader-Willi have formed online communities that provide support and can share the latest findings – some are even significant funders of research. Without these technology-mediated links, research into these very rare genetic syndromes would be virtually impossible. Technology also provides a way for the mainstream community to learn about neurodevelopmental disorders. People with ASD have been active in this area, using platforms such as YouTube to educate people about their experiences.

13.6 Conclusions

Researchers with an interest in the application of technologies to support people with neurodevelopmental disorders have a lot of work to do. Their findings will have powerful implications for the way in which parents and practitioners behave towards technology, and for how they feel about their child's use of technology. It is essential that we build a solid evidence base for best practice so that we can be confident about the parameters for positive technology use and exploit this engaging and sophisticated resource to benefit those with additional needs.

The research we have reviewed in this chapter has begun to address a number of important themes. These include: which technologies children will use spontaneously and what motivates them to do so; where young people encounter challenges and barriers in new technologies; the uses of technology in research for elucidating the strengths and weaknesses of a given disorder; and the uses of technology for the purposes of interventions. Much remains to be done.

Practical tips

1. *Examine associated benefits.* When measuring people's use of technology or evaluating the efficacy of a technology-based intervention don't focus simply on the core outcome, such as learning to read. Consider how the child engages with the technology and the effect this has on concentration, well-being, domestic life or peer relations. The power of using technology may well lie in these additional benefits rather than simply in progress in key skills.
2. *Take lessons from the research that has been done with other syndrome groups.* There is currently no consistent methodology or set of research questions that have been applied across syndromes. Key issues include: Why do people with neurodevelopmental disorders engage with technologies? How can technologies be designed to capitalise on strengths and scaffold areas of weakness? What do technology-based studies tell us about the underpinnings of diagnostic categories and personal profiles.
3. *Consider the longevity of your research.* Technologies develop at a remarkable rate which far outstrips academic progress. Design studies to provide understanding about the features of technology that promote positive outcomes so that the impact of your study will persist beyond the specific technological platform used.

Conflict of interest

Sue Fletcher-Watson was involved in development of an iPad and iPhone app for children with autism called FindMe, which is available for download from iTunes following licensing by a commercial partner. She will receive a royalty payment if paid downloads exceed a certain threshold.

Note

1   For details see http://www.dart.ed.ac.uk/technology-survey/

References

Alcorn, A., Pain, H., Rajendran, G., Smith, T., Lemon, O., Porayska-Pomsta, K., ... & Bernardini, S. (2011). Social communication between virtual characters and children with autism. *AIED LNAI, 6738*, 7–14.

Altemeier, L. E., Abbott, R. D. & Berninger, V. W. (2008). Executive functions for reading and writing in typical literacy development and dyslexia. *Journal of Clinical and Experimental Neuropsychology, 30*(5), 588–606.

American Psychiatric Association (2013). *DSM-5* (5th ed). Washington DC: American Psychiatric Association.

Barkley, R. A. (2006). *Attention Deficit Hyperactivity Disorder: A Handbook for Diagnosis and Treatment* (3rd ed.). New York: Guilford Press.

Beaumont, R. & Sofronoff, K. (2008). A multi-component social skills intervention for children with Asperger syndrome: The junior detective training program. *Journal of Child Psychology and Psychiatry, and Allied Disciplines, 49*, 743–753.

Bernard-Opitz, V., Sriram, N. & Sapuan, S. (1999). Enhancing vocal imitations in children with autism using the IBM speech viewer. *Autism, 3*(2), 131–147.

Bioulac, S., Arfi, L. & Bouvard, M. P. (2008). Attention deficit/hyperactivity disorder and video games: A comparative study of hyperactive and control children. *European Psychiatry, 23*, 134–141.

Bioulac, S., Lallemand, S., Rizzo, A., Philip, P., Fabrigoule, C. & Bouvard, M. P. (2012). Impact of time on task on ADHD patient's performances in a virtual classroom. *European Journal of Paediatric Neurology, 16*, 514–521.

Bishop, D. V. (2010). Which neurodevelopmental disorders get researched and why? *PLoS One, 5*(11), e15112.

Bishop, J. (2003). The internet for educating individuals with social impairments. *Journal of Computer Assisted Learning, 19*, 546–556.

Bolte, S., Feineis-Matthews, S., Leber, S., Dierks, T., Hubl, D. & Poutska, F. (2002). The development and evaluation of a computer-based program to test and to teach the recognition of facial affect. *International Journal of Circumpolar Health, 61*(Supplement 2), 61–68.

Bolte, S., Hubl, D., Feineis-Matthews, S., Prvulovic, D., Dierks, T. & Poutska, F. (2006). Facial affects recognition training in autism: Can we animate the fusiform gyrus? *Behavioural Neuroscience, 120*(1), 211–216.

Boulter, C., Freeston, M., South, M. & Rodgers, J. (2013). Intolerance of uncertainty as a framework for understanding anxiety in children and adolescents with autism spectrum disorders. *Journal of Autism and Developmental Disorders, 44*, 1–12.

Bradshaw, J. (2013). The use of augmentative and alternative communication apps for the iPad, iPod and iPhone: An overview of recent developments. *Tizard Learning Disability Review, 18*(1), 31–37.

Clark, K. M. & Green, G. (2004). Comparison of two procedures for teaching dictated-word/symbol relations to learners with autism. *Journal of Applied Behaviour Analysis, 37,* 503–507.

Conti-Ramsden, G. & Durkin, K. (2011). Specific language impairment. In D. Skuse, H. Bruce, L. Dowdney and D. Mrazek (eds), *Child Psychology and Psychiatry: Frameworks for Practice* (pp. 180–186). Chichester, UK: John Wiley & Sons.

Conti-Ramsden, G., Durkin, K., Simkin, Z. & Knox, E. (2009). Specific language impairment and school outcomes. I: Identifying and explaining variability at the end of compulsory education. *International Journal of Language and Communication Disorders, 44,* 15–35.

Conti-Ramsden, G., Durkin, K. & Simkin, Z. (2010). Language and social factors in the use of cell phone technology by adolescents with and without specific language impairment. *Journal of Speech, Language, and Hearing Research, 53,* 196–208.

Conti-Ramsden, G., Durkin, K. & Walker, A. J. (2010). Computer anxiety: A comparison of adolescents with and without a history of specific language impairment (SLI). *Computers & Education, 54,* 136–145.

Daneman, M. and Carpenter, P. A. (1980). Individual differences in working memory and reading. *Journal of Verbal Learning and Verbal Behavior, 19(4),* 450–466.

Della Sala, S. & Anderson, M. (2012). *Neuroscience in Education: The Good, the Bad, and the Ugly.* Oxford: Oxford University Press.

Diehl, J. J., Schmitt, L. M., Villano, M. & Crowell, C. R. (2012). The clinical use of robots for individuals with autism spectrum disorders: A critical review. *Research in Autism Spectrum Disorders, 6*(1), 249–262.

Durkin, K. (2006). Game playing and adolescents' development. In P. Vorderer & J. Bryant (eds), *Playing Video Games: Motives, Responses, and Consequences* (pp. 415–427). Mahwah, NJ: Erlbaum.

——(2010). Videogames and young people with developmental disorders. *Review of General Psychology, 14,* 122–140.

Durkin, K. & Aisbett, K. (1999). *Computer Games and Australians Today.* NSW, Australia: Office of Film and Literature Classification.

Durkin, K. & Blades, M. (2009). Young people and the media: Special issue. *British Journal of Developmental Psychology, 27*(1), 1–12.

Durkin, K. & Conti-Ramsden, G. (2007). Language, social behavior and the quality of friendships in adolescents with and without a history of Specific Language Impairment. *Child Development, 78,* 1441–1457.

——(2012). Frequency of educational computer use as a longitudinal predictor of educational outcome in young people with Specific Language Impairment. *PloS One, 7*(12), e52194.

——(2014). Turn off or tune in? What advice can SLTs, educational psychologists and teachers provide about uses of new media and children with language impairments? *Child Language Teaching and Therapy, 30,* 187–205.

Durkin, K., Conti-Ramsden, G., Walker, A. & Simkin, Z. (2009a). Educational and interpersonal uses of home computers by adolescents with and without Specific Language Impairment (SLI). *British Journal of Developmental Psychology, 27,* 197–217.

Durkin, K., Simkin, Z., Knox, E. & Conti-Ramsden, G. (2009b). Specific language impairment and school outcomes. II: Educational context, student satisfaction, and post-compulsory progress. *International Journal of Language and Communication Disorders, 44,* 36–55.

Durkin, K., Conti-Ramsden, G. & Walker, A. J. (2010a). Computer-mediated communication in adolescents with and without a history of specific language impairment (SLI). *Computers in Human Behavior, 26,* 176–185.

Durkin, K., Whitehouse, A., Jaquet, E., Ziatas, K. & Walker, A. J. (2010b). Cell phone use by adolescents with Asperger syndrome. *Research in Autism Spectrum Disorders, 4,* 314–318.

Durkin, K., Conti-Ramsden, G. & Walker, A. (2011). Txt Lang: Texting, textism use and literacy abilities in adolescents with and without specific language impairment. *Journal of Computer Assisted Learning, 27,* 49–57.

Durkin, K., Fraser, J. & Conti-Ramsden, G. (2012). School-age prework experiences of young people with a history of specific language impairment. *The Journal of Special Education, 45,* 242–255.

Durkin, K., Boyle, J., Hunter, S. & Conti-Ramsden, G. (2013). Video games for children and adolescents with special educational needs. *Zeitschrift für Psychologie, 221,* 79–89.

Fabio, R. A. & Antonietti, A. (2012). Effects of hypermedia instruction on declarative, conditional and procedural knowledge in ADHD students. *Research in Developmental Disabilities, 33,* 2028–2039.

Faja, S., Aylward, E., Bernier, R. & Dawson, G. (2008). Becoming a face expert: A computerized face-training program for high-functioning individuals with autism spectrum disorders. *Developmental Neuropsychology, 33*(1), 1–24.

Faja, S., Webb, S., Jones, E. A., Merkle, K., Kamara, D., Bavaro, J., … Dawson, G. (2011). The effects of face expertise training on the behavioural performance and brain activity of adults with high functioning autism spectrum disorders. *Journal of Autism and Developmental Disorders, 42,* 278–293.

Farr, W., Yuill, N. & Raffle, H. (2010). Social benefits of a tangible user interface for children with autistic spectrum conditions. *Autism, 14*(3), 237–252.

Ferguson, C. J. & Olson, C. K. (2014). Video game violence use among 'vulnerable' populations: The impact of violent games on delinquency and bullying among children with clinically elevated depression or attention deficit symptoms. *Journal of Youth and Adolescence, 43,* 127–136.

Fletcher-Watson, S. (2014). A targeted review of computer-assisted learning for people with autism spectrum disorder: Towards a consistent methodology. *Review Journal of Autism and Developmental Disorders, 1,* 87–100.

Fletcher-Watson, S., Petrou, A., Dicks, P., O'Hare, A., Pain, H. & McConachie, H. (2014a). A trial of an iPad intervention targeting social communication skills in children with autism. Submitted.

Fletcher-Watson, S., Hammond, S., Humphrey, A., Pain, H. & McConachie, H. (2014b). Developing an educational iPad app for pre-schoolers with autism: The participatory design and pilot testing process. Submitted.

Fletcher-Watson, S., McConnell, F., Manola, I. & McConachie, H. (2014c). Interventions based on the 'Theory of Mind' cognitive model for autism spectrum disorder (Review). *Cochrane Database of Systematic Reviews.* doi: 10.1002/14651858.CD008785.pub2

Frauenberger, C., Good, J. & Keay-Bright, W. (2011). Designing technology for children with special needs: Bridging perspectives through participatory design. *CoDesign, 7*(1), 1–28.

Frauenberger, C., Good, J., Alcorn, A. & Pain, H. (2013). Conversing through and about technologies: Design critique as an opportunity to engage children with autism and broaden research(er) perspectives. *International Journal of Child–Computer Interaction, 1,* 38–49.

Fusar-Poli, P., Cortesi, M., Borgwardt, S. & Politi, P. (2008) Second life virtual world: A heaven for autistic people? *Medical Hypotheses, 71*(6), 980–981.

Gillam, R. B., Loeb, D. F., Hoffman, L. M., Bohman, T., Champlin, C. A., Thibodeau, L., ... & Friel-Patti, S. (2008). The efficacy of Fast ForWord language intervention in school-age children with language impairment: A randomized controlled trial. *Journal of Speech, Language and Hearing Research, 51,* 97–119.

Gillespie-Smith, K. & Fletcher-Watson, S. (2014). Designing AACs for children with autism: Evidence from eye-tracking. *Journal of Augmentative and Alternative Communication,* DOI: 10.3109/07434618.2014.905635.

Golan, O. & Baron-Cohen, S. (2006). Systemizing empathy: Teaching adults with Asperger's syndrome or high functioning autism to recognize complex emotions using interactive multimedia. *Development and Psychopathology, 18,* 589–615.

Golan, O., Baron-Cohen, S., Ashwin, E., Granader, Y., McClintock, S., Day, K. & Leggett, V. (2010). Enhancing emotion recognition in children with autism spectrum conditions: An intervention using animated vehicles with real emotional faces. *Journal of Autism and Developmental Disorders, 40*(3), 269–279.

Greenfield, P. M. (2009). Technology and informal education: What is taught, what is learned. *Science, 323,* 69–71.

Grynszpan, O., Weiss, P. L., Perez-Diaz, F. & Gal, E. (2013). Innovative technology-based interventions for autism spectrum disorders: A meta-analysis. *Autism, 18,* 346–361.

Hagiwara, T. & Myles, B. S. (1999). A multimedia social story intervention: Teaching skills to children with autism. *Focus on Autism and Other Developmental Disabilities, 14,* 82–95.

Han, D. H., Lee, Y. S., Na, C., Ahn, J. Y., Chung, U. S., Daniels, M. A., ... Renshaw, P. F. (2009). The effect of methylphenidate on Internet video game play in children with attention–deficit/hyperactivity disorder. *Comprehensive Psychiatry, 50,* 251–256.

Heimann, M., Nelson, K. E., Tjus, T. & Gillberg, C. (1995). Increasing reading and communication skills in children with autism through an interactive multimedia computer program. *Journal of Autism and Developmental Disorders, 25,* 459–480.

Hetzroni, O. E. & Shalem, U. (2005). From logos to orthographic symbols: A multilevel fading computer program for teaching nonverbal children with autism. *Focus on Autism and Other Developmental Disabilities, 20,* 201–212.

Hopkins, I. M., Gower, M. W., Perez, T. A., Smith, D. S., Amthor, F. R., Casey-Wimsatt, F. & Biasini, F. J. (2011). Avatar assistant: Improving social skills in students with an ASD through a computer-based intervention. *Journal of Autism & Developmental Disorders, 41,* 1543–1555.

Houghton, S., Milner, N., West, J., Douglas, G., Lawrence, V., Whiting, K., Tannock, R. & Durkin, K. (2004). Motor control and sequencing of boys with attention deficit/hyperactivity disorder (ADHD) during computer game play. *British Journal of Educational Technology, 35,* 21–34.

Hulme, C. & Snowling, M. J. (2009). *Developmental Disorders of Language, Learning and Cognition.* Chichester, UK: Wiley-Blackwell.

Kagohara, D. M., van der Meer, L., Ramdoss, S., O'Reilly, M. F., Lancioni, G. E., Davis, T. N., … Sigafoos, J. (2013). Using iPods and iPads in teaching programs for individuals with developmental disabilities: A systematic review. *Research in Developmental Disabilities, 34*, 147–156.

Ko, C. H., Yen, J. Y., Yen, C. F., Chen, C. S. & Chen, C. C. (2012). The association between Internet addiction and psychiatric disorder: A review of the literature. *European Psychiatry, 27*, 1–8.

Koepp, M. J., Gunn, R. N., Lawrence, A. D., Cunningham, V. J., Dagher, A., Jones. T., … Grasby, P. M. (1998). Evidence for striatal dopamine release during a videogame. *Nature, 393*, 266–268.

Kokina, A. & Kern, L. (2010). Social story interventions for students with autism spectrum disorders: A meta-analysis. *Journal of Autism and Developmental Disorders, 40*, 812–826.

Kuster (2012). Internet: In search of the perfect speech-language app? Available at: http://www.asha.org/Publications/leader/2012/120403/Internet–In-Search-of-the-Perfect-Speech-Language-App/ (accessed October 2013).

LaCava, P. G., Rankin, A., Mahlios, E., Cook, K. & Simpson, R. L. (2010). A single case design evaluation of a software and tutor intervention addressing emotion recognition and social interaction in four boys with ASD. *Autism, 14*, 161–178.

Lawrence, V., Houghton, S., Tannock, R., Douglas, G., Durkin, K. & Whiting, K. (2002). ADHD outside the laboratory: Boys' executive function performance on tasks in videogame play and on a visit to the zoo. *Journal of Abnormal Child Psychology, 30*, 447–462.

Lawrence, V., Houghton, S., Douglas, G., Durkin, K., Whiting, K. & Tannock, R. (2004). Executive function and ADHD: A comparison of children's performance during neuropsychological testing and real-world activities. *Journal of Attention Disorders, 7*, 137–149.

Loe, I. M. & Feldman, H. M. (2007). Academic and educational outcomes of children with ADHD. *Journal of Pediatric Psychology, 32*, 643–654.

Lubas, M., Mitchell, J. R. & De Leo, G. (2014). Augmentative and alternative communication solutions and autism. In V. Patel, V. Preedy & C. Martin (eds), *Comprehensive Guide to Autism*, (pp. 1081–1096). Springer: New York.

Luciana, M., Wahlstrom, D., Porter, J. N. & Collins, P. F. (2012). Dopaminergic modulation of incentive motivation in adolescence: Age-related changes in signaling, individual differences, and implications for the development of self-regulation. *Developmental Psychology, 48*, 844–861.

Luman, M., Oosterlaan, J. & Sergeant, J. A. (2005). The impact of reinforcement contingencies on AD/HD: A review and theoretical appraisal. *Clinical Psychology Review, 25*, 183–213.

Mackie, C. & Dockrell, J. E. (2004). The nature of written language deficits in children with SLI. *Journal of Speech, Language and Hearing Research, 47*, 1469–1483.

Mazurek, M. O. & Engelhardt, C. R. (2013). Video game use in boys with Autism Spectrum Disorder, ADHD, or Typical Development. *Pediatrics, 132*, 260–266.

Meaux, J. B., Green, A. & Broussard, L. (2009). ADHD in the college student: A block in the road. *Journal of Psychiatric and Mental Health Nursing, 16*, 248–256.

Miller, N. & Neuringer, A. (2000). Reinforcing variability in adolescents with autism. *Journal of Applied Behaviour Analysis, 33*(2), 151–165.

Mineo, B., Ziegler, W., Gill, S. & Salkin, D. (2009). Engagement with electronic screen media among students with autism spectrum disorders. *Journal of Autism and Developmental Disorders, 39*(1), 172–187.

Mirenda, P. (2008). A back door approach to autism and AAC. *Augmentative and Alternative Communication, 24*(3), 220–234.

Mirenda, P. & Iacono, T. (2009). *Autism Spectrum Disorders and AAC*. Baltimore, MD: Paul H. Brookes.

Moore, M. & Calvert, S. (2000). Brief report: Vocabulary acquisition for children with autism: Teacher or computer instruction. *Journal of Autism and Developmental Disorders, 30*, 359–362.

Morein-Zamir, S., Hommersen, P., Johnston, C. & Kingstone, A. (2008). Novel measures of response performance and inhibition in children with ADHD. *Journal of Abnormal Child Psychology, 36*, 1199–1210.

Mullen, E. M. (1995). *Mullen Scales of Early Learning*. San Antonio, TX: Pearson.

Orsmond, G. I. & Kuo, H. (2011). The daily lives of adolescents with an autism spectrum disorder: Discretionary time use and activity partners. *Autism, 15*(5), 579–599.

Parkes, A., Sweeting, H., Wight, D. & Henderson, M. (2013). Do television and electronic games predict children's psychosocial adjustment? Longitudinal research using the UK Millennium Cohort Study. *Archives of Disease in Childhood, 98*(5), 341–348.

Pennington, B. F. & Ozonoff, S. (1996). Executive functions and developmental psychopathology. *Journal of Child Psychology and Psychiatry, 37*, 51–87.

Pennington, R. C. (2010). Computer-assisted instruction for teaching academic skills to students with autism spectrum disorders: A review of literature. *Focus on Autism and Other Developmental Disabilities, 25*(4), 239–248.

Rajendran, G. (2013). Virtual environments and autism: A developmental psychopathological approach. *Journal of Computer Assisted Learning, 29*(4), 334–347.

Rajendran, G., Law, A., Logie, R., Meulen, M., Fraser, D. & Corley, M. (2011). Investigating multitasking in high-functioning adolescents with autism spectrum disorders using the virtual errands task. *Journal of Autism and Developmental Disorders, 41*(11), 1445–1454.

Ramdoss, S., Lang, R., Mulloy, A., Franco, J., O'Reilly, M., Didden, R. & Lancioni, G. E. (2011a). Use of computer-based interventions to teach communication skills to children with autism spectrum disorders: A systematic review. *Journal of Behavioural Education, 20*, 55–76.

Ramdoss, S., Mulloy, A., Lang, R., O'Reilly, M., Sigafoos, J., Lancioni, G. E., … El Zein, F. (2011b). Use of computer-based interventions to improve literacy skills in students with autism spectrum disorders: A systematic review. *Research in Autism Spectrum Disorders, 5*, 1306–1318.

Ramdoss, S., Machalicek, W., Rispoli, M., Lang, R. & O'Reilly, M. (2012). Computer-based interventions to improve social and emotional skills in individuals with autism spectrum disorders: A systematic review. *Developmental Neurorehabilitation, 15*, 119–135.

Rhodes, S. M., Coghill, D. R. & Matthews, K. (2006). Acute neuropsychological effects of methylphenidate in stimulant drug-naïve boys with ADHD II – broader executive and non-executive domains. *Journal of Child Psychology and Psychiatry, 47*, 1184–1194.

Rideout, V. J., Foehr, U. G. & Roberts, D. F. (2010). Generation M^2: Media in the Lives of 8-to 18-Year-Olds. Menlo Park, CA: Henry J. Kaiser Family Foundation.

Schlosser, R. W., Blischak, D. M., Belfiore, P. J., Bartley, C. & Barnett, N. (1998). Effects of synthetic speech output and orthographic feedback on spelling in a student with autism: A preliminary study. *Journal of Autism and Developmental Disorders, 28*, 309–319.

Shane, H. & Albert, P. (2008). Electronic screen media for persons with autism spectrum disorders: Results of a survey. *Journal of Autism and Developmental Disorders, 38*, 1499–1508.

Shaw, R., Grayson, A. & Lewis, V. (2005). Inhibition, ADHD, and computer games: The inhibitory performance of children with ADHD on computerized tasks and games. *Journal of Attention Disorders, 8*, 160–168.

Shimoni, M. A., Engel-Yeger, B. & Tirosh, E. (2010). Participation in leisure activities among boys with attention deficit hyperactivity disorder. *Research in Developmental Disabilities, 31*, 1234–1239.

Sikström, S. & Söderlund, G. (2007). Stimulus-dependent dopamine release in attention-deficit/hyperactivity disorder. *Psychological Review, 114*, 1047–1075.

Silver, M. & Oakes, P. (2001). Evaluation of a new computer intervention to teach people with autism or Asperger syndrome to recognise and predict emotion in others. *Autism, 5*(3), 299–316.

Snowling, M., Bishop, D. V. M. & Stothard, S. E. (2000). Is preschool language impairment a risk factor for dyslexia in adolescence? *Journal of Child Psychology and Psychiatry, 41*, 407–418.

Sonuga-Barke, E. J. S., Taylor, E., Sembi, E. & Smith, J. (1992). Hyperactivity and delay aversion: I. The effect of delay on choice. *Journal of Child Psychology and Psychiatry, 33*, 387–398.

Spence, I. & Feng, J. (2010). Video games and spatial cognition. *Review of General Psychology, 14*, 92–104.

St. Clair, M. C., Durkin, K., Conti-Ramsden, G. & Pickles, A. (2010). Growth of reading skills in children with a history of specific language impairment (SLI): The role of autistic symptomatology and language related abilities. *British Journal of Developmental Psychology, 28*, 109–131.

Tallal, P. (2000). Experimental studies of language learning impairments: From research to remediation. In D. V. M. Bishop & L. B. Leonard (eds), *Speech and Language Impairments in Children: Causes, Characteristics, Intervention and Outcome* (pp. 131–155). Philadelphia, PA: Psychology Press.

Tanaka, J. W., Wolf, J. M., Klaiman, C., Koenig, K., Cockburn, J., Herlihy, L., … Schultz, R. (2010). Using computerized games to teach face recognition skills to children with autism spectrum disorder: The let's face it! program. *Journal of Child Psychology and Psychiatry, 51*(8), 944–952.

Thakkar, R. R., Garrison, M. M. & Christakis, D. A. (2006). A systematic review for the effects of television viewing by infants and preschoolers. *Pediatrics, 118*(5), 2025–2031.

Tjus, T., Heimann, M. & Nelson, K. E. (2001). Interaction patterns between children and their teachers when using a specific multi-media and communication strategy: Observations from children with autism and mixed intellectual disabilities. *Autism 5*(2), 175–187.

Tomblin, J. B., Records, N. L., Buckwalter, P., Zhang, X., Smith, E. & O'Brien, M. (1997). Prevalence of specific language impairment in kindergarten children. *Journal of Speech, Language and Hearing Research, 40*, 1245–1260.

Wadman, R., Durkin, K. & Conti-Ramsden, G. (2008). Self-esteem, shyness and sociability in adolescents with specific language impairment. *Journal of Speech, Language and Hearing Research, 51*, 938–952.

Warschauer, M. & Matuchniak, T. (2010). New technology and digital worlds: Analyzing evidence of equity in access, use, and outcomes. *Review of Research in Education, 34*(1), 179–225.

Washbrook, E., Propper, C. & Sayal, K. (2013). Pre-school hyperactivity/attention problems and educational outcomes in adolescence: Prospective longitudinal study. *The British Journal of Psychiatry, 203*, 265–271.

Watabe, T. & Suzuki, K. (2013). Internet communication of outpatients with Asperger's disorder or schizophrenia in Japan. *Asia-Pacific Psychiatry*. doi: 10.1111/appy.12108.

Whalen, C., Moss, D., Ilan, A. B., Vaupel, M., Fielding, P., MacDonald, K., ... Symon, J. (2010). Efficacy of TeachTown Basics computer-assisted intervention for the intensive comprehensive autism program in Los Angeles unified school district. *Autism, 14*(3), 179–197.

Williams, C., Wright, B., Callaghan, G. & Coughlan, B. (2002). Do children with autism learn to read more readily by computer assisted instruction or traditional book methods? *Autism, 6*(1), 71–91.

Wood, R. T., Griffiths, M. D., Chappell, D. & Davies, M. N. (2004). The structural characteristics of video games: A psycho-structural analysis. *CyberPsychology and Behavior, 7*, 1–10.

Woods, J. J. & Wetherby, A. M. (2003). Early identification of and intervention for infants and toddlers who are at risk for autism spectrum disorder. *Language, Speech, and Hearing Services in Schools, 34*(3), 180–193.

Zentall, S. S. & Beike, S. (2012). Achievement and social goals of younger and older elementary students: Response to academic and social failure. *Learning Disability Quarterly, 35*, 39–53.

14

ANXIETY IN NEURODEVELOPMENTAL DISORDERS

Phenomenology, assessment and intervention

Victoria Grahame and Jacqui Rodgers

14.1 General introduction

Neurodevelopmental disorders have been consistently associated with increased risk for emotional, behavioural and mental health difficulties. Tonge & Einfeld (2000) reported the rates of significant mental health difficulties, which negatively impacted on daily life, were between 40 and 50 per cent for children with intellectual disabilities. This rate is up to three times that reported for children with typical development (TD). The individual, family and societal implications of the presence of mental health difficulties amongst children with neurodevelopmental disorders are profound and parents, teachers and clinicians are increasingly seeking advice on ways to manage the distress that these co-occurring conditions bring.

Research highlights the long-term consequences of childhood mental health difficulties. For example, the presence of anxiety symptoms in adolescence is a significant predictor of social isolation, school refusal and the development of an anxiety disorder in adulthood indicating both the acute and long-term psychological, social and economic significance of childhood anxiety. As well as the impact on the children themselves, the presence of emotional difficulties in children with neurodevelopmental disorders is associated with additional parental stress over and above that associated with the disorder itself (Ly & Hodapp, 2005; Wood & Gadow, 2010). Indeed, mental health difficulties, such as anxiety, have been reported to be a more urgent problem for many children and their families than core features of the neurodevelopmental disorder (White et al., 2010).

There are some key questions that still remain to be answered in this field and much work remains to be done to obtain a clear understanding of the challenges and issues. Why are children with neurodevelopmental disorders particularly vulnerable to the development of mental health difficulties? What are the specific risk and protective factors for these children and young people? What are the best measures, tools, and diagnostic processes to use to identify co-occurring mental health difficulties and what are the most effective interventions?

Whilst a range of mental health difficulties has been reported in developmental disability populations, the most common difficulty appears to be anxiety. Anxiety disorders are also one of the most prevalent categories of psychopathology in typically developing children and adolescents (Fong & Garralda, 2005), with prevalence rates for children aged between nine and sixteen years old estimated at 9.9 per cent (Costello, Mustillo & Erkanli, 2003). Clark and Beck (2010) define anxiety as 'a complex cognitive, affective, physiological and behavioural response system ... activated when anticipated events or circumstances are deemed to be highly aversive because they are perceived to be unpredictable, uncontrollable events' (p. 5).

Anxiety can manifest in a number of different forms. The prevalence of different types of anxiety disorders reported in children with neurodevelopmental disorders varies across disorders and also across studies examining particular disorders, perhaps highlighting that it is important to consider diagnostic and measurement issues when thinking about these prevalence rates. We will discuss these issues in more detail later in this chapter.

14.2 Prevalence and types of difficulties

Relatively little is known about the experience of anxiety in children with neurodevelopmental disorders (Evans, Canavera, Kleinpeter, Maccubbin & Taga, 2005). Research has begun to assess the phenomenology of anxiety in a range of neurodevelopmental disorders, including Autism Spectrum Disorders (ASD), Prader-Willi syndrome (PWS), Fragile X syndrome (FXS), and Williams syndrome (WS) (Whitaker & Read, 2006).

As is the case for children with typical development, anxiety in children with neurodevelopmental disorders appears to be related to a range of factors, including age and level of cognitive functioning. White, Ollendick, Scahill, Oswald and Albano (2009) state that generally, younger children with ASD experience lower levels of anxiety compared to older children. Furthermore, Kuusikko et al. (2008) found that children with ASD reported increased social anxiety with age. In relation to cognitive functioning, there are mixed findings. Masi, Brovedani, Mucci and Favilla (2002) state higher levels of anxiety disorder in children with a learning disability. However, in a group of children with pervasive developmental disorder, Sukhodolsky et al. (2008) reported elevated levels of anxiety in those children who were rated as having higher cognitive functioning.

It is important to consider age and ability level together when undertaking and interpreting research with children with neurodevelopmental disabilities. For some children with neurodevelopmental disabilities mental age (MA), that is the age at which a child is performing intellectually, may not be synonymous with chronological age (CA), with potentially significant heterogeneity within samples. For example, within ASD some children will present with MA assessments which are congruent to their CA and some children will present with a MA which is lower than their chronological age. Thus, it is important to consider whether authors have taken this into account when reporting age related associations in their data.

Given the issues outlined here when considering whether anxiety in children with neurodevelopmental disorders is related to age and/or ability, we need to carefully consider how these constructs have been assessed: has age been considered in relation to chronological age or mental age and have assessments of intellectual functioning taken into account the potential for the presence of uneven cognitive profiles?

In summary, anxiety appears to be common in children with neurodevelopmental disorders, ability and age may influence the presence of anxiety and are important factors to explore in research in the area, but the exact nature of these influences is still to be determined and is likely to be influenced by the type of neurodevelopmental disorder under investigation and the ways in which age and ability are assessed. The next section explores the phenomenology of anxiety in individual neuro-developmental disorders.

14.2.1 Autism Spectrum Disorder (ASD)

ASDs are characterised by clinically significant, persistent deficits in social communication and interactions and the presence of restricted, repetitive patterns of behaviour, interests and activities (DSM-5; APA, 2013) (for a further description of ASD see Chapters 7 and 12). The increased risk for anxiety is well-documented in relation to ASD, where it has been the focus of much attention from the research community in recent years (Rodgers, Riby, Janes & Connolly, 2012; White et al., 2010). MacNeil, Lopes & Minnes (2009) reported that young people with ASD have higher levels of anxiety than typically developing children and comparable levels of anxiety to clinically anxious children. Van Steensel, Bogels and Perrin (2011) report a meta-analysis of 31 studies of young people with ASD and report prevalence rates of around 40 per cent for at least one comorbid anxiety disorder, markedly higher than the expected prevalence rates in typically developing children of around 9 per cent (Costello et al., 2003; for a further discussion on comorbidity see Chapters 7 and 9). Sukhodolsky, Bloch, Panza and Reichow (2013) in a meta-analysis of the use of cognitive behavioural therapy (CBT) for anxiety with children with ASD report the prevalence rates of different anxiety disorders within this population to range from 40 per cent to 84 per cent for any anxiety disorder, 8 per cent to 63 per cent for specific phobias, 5 per cent to 23 per cent for generalised anxiety, 13 per cent to 29 per cent for social anxiety, and 8 per cent to 27 per cent for separation anxiety disorders.

The notion that anxiety is an important issue in ASD is not a new idea. As early as 1943, Kanner highlighted an association between anxiety and features of ASD, and observed that an insistence on sameness and the repertoire of fixed behaviours and routines appeared to have a strong association with anxiety (Kanner, 1943, as cited in Gillott, Furniss & Walter, 2001, p. 277). Since then, the relationships between anxiety and a number of associated and core features of ASD have been investigated.

Anxiety has been associated with core ASD symptom severity, including impairments in social functioning (Bellini, 2004, 2006) and theory of mind deficits (Burnette et al., 2005; Meyer, Mundy, Van Hecke & Durocher, 2006). Importantly this work has highlighted the possibility of a reciprocal interaction between anxiety and ASD symptomatology (Wood & Gadow, 2010). According to this model, increased ASD symptom severity raises vulnerability to anxiety due to an increased likelihood of negative peer evaluation and a reduced ability to challenge anxious beliefs. Conversely, anxiety may exacerbate ASD symptomatology, as children increasingly avoid social interaction or attempt to manage their anxiety through engagement in restricted and repetitive behaviours. Thus, anxiety may exacerbate the features of ASD and may be experienced as more acutely distressing than the core symptoms of ASD themselves (White et al., 2010). Understanding the interactions between anxiety and core characteristics of the neurodevelopmental disorders under investigation is critical for the development of appropriate theoretical models to guide assessment and intervention.

Individuals with ASD frequently experience difficulties with sensory processing (Leekam, Nieto, Libby, Wing & Gould, 2007). These difficulties include a range of responses to sensory stimuli and may manifest as an avoidance of being touched, a restricted diet, avoidance of bright lights, or an aversive response to certain sounds. Sensory processing difficulties were included for the first time in the diagnostic criteria for ASD in DSM-5 (APA, 2013) as a symptom manifestation under the revised restricted and repetitive behaviours (RRB) sub-domain. A number of studies have identified two types of RRB; 'lower level' repetitive sensorimotor behaviours and 'higher level' insistence on sameness (Turner, 1999; Richler, Bishop, Kleinke & Lord, 2007) in ASD. The former group includes hand and body mannerisms such as flapping, repetitive use of objects and unusual sensory interests. 'Insistence on sameness' behaviours include compulsions, rituals, resistance to change and circumscribed interests (Richler et al., 2007). There is evidence for an association in ASD between anxiety disorders and both sensory atypicalities (Green & Ben-Sasson, 2010; Ben-Sasson et al., 2008; Lidstone et al., 2014), and the presence of repetitive and restricted behaviours, particularly the higher order insistence on sameness RRB (Rodgers et al., 2012). However, the exact nature of these relationships is still to be understood.

Despite the burgeoning literature on anxiety in ASD, detailing prevalence rates and describing associations between anxiety and core characteristics of the disorder, there is a paucity of explanatory models of the processes underlying anxiety for this population. Boulter et al. (2013) investigated the utility of considering the role of intolerance of uncertainty (IU) in understanding anxiety in ASD. IU is defined as a 'broad dispositional risk factor for the development and maintenance of clinically significant anxiety' (Carleton, 2012, p. 939) and involves the 'tendency to react negatively on an emotional, cognitive, and behavioural level to uncertain situations and events' (Buhr & Dugas, 2009, p. 216). Individuals who have IU find uncertain situations stressful and upsetting due to beliefs that unexpected events are negative and should be avoided. They have a tendency to interpret all ambiguous information as threatening and find it difficult to function in the face of uncertainty. The construct has a robust evidence base as an important variable in the onset and maintenance of anxiety in typical populations and the construct has some striking similarities with some of the core characteristics of ASD (Rodgers et al., 2012), especially restricted and repetitive behaviours such as insistence on sameness, inflexible adherence to routines, and difficulty tolerating change and unexpected events. Boulter et al. (2013) report significant relationships between IU and anxiety in children with ASD that were suggestive of a causal model indicating that IU mediates the relationship between ASD and anxiety. These findings provide an example of how theoretical frameworks developed with typically developing populations might provide inroads to developing a way to understand and characterise anxiety in children with neurodevelopmental disorders, which will ultimately enable the development of effective, theoretically robust and evidence-based treatments.

We have considered that young people with ASD may be predisposed to anxiety as a result of a range of ASD-specific factors and that anxiety can exacerbate some of the features of ASD (e.g. repetitive behaviours; Sofronoff, Attwood & Hinton, 2005; Rodgers et al., 2012). Thus, the anxiety symptom constellations (i.e. anxiety sub-types) experienced by young people with ASD may reflect the features of ASD with which they present. An understanding of those anxiety sub-types most common in young people with ASD may help shed further light on the bidirectional relationship between symptoms of anxiety and the features of ASD.

14.2.2 Williams syndrome

Williams syndrome (WS) is a neurodevelopmental disorder caused by the microdeletion of a sequence of genes on chromosome 7q11.23 (Hillier et al., 2003). It is estimated to occur once in every 20,000 births (Korenberg, Bellugi, Salandanan, Mills & Reiss, 2003). There is growing evidence that anxiety is associated with a diagnosis of WS (Riby et al., 2014; Rodgers et al., 2012). Woodruff-Borden, Kistler, Henderson, Crawford and Mervis (2010) examined the longitudinal course of anxiety disorders in 45 children and adolescents with WS and reported chronic, persistent anxiety in 51.1 per cent of the sample. The most common diagnoses were specific phobias and generalised anxiety disorder. Rodgers et al. (2012) reviewed research examining the prevalence and phenomenology of anxiety in WS and concluded that anxiety was one of the most common psychopathologies in this group, with specific phobia being one of the most commonly reported anxiety sub-types (see also Dodd & Porter 2009; Dykens 2003; Leyfer et al., 2006; Rodgers et al., 2012).

Dodd and Porter (2009) examined the influence of age on the presentation of anxiety sub-types in WS and reported prevalence of anxiety disorders to be similar across age. However, phobias were more common in children than in adults and generalised anxiety disorder (GAD) was not present in their child group, whereas 25 per cent of the adult group met criteria for GAD. Leyfer et al. (2006) also report GAD to be significantly higher in older children with WS. They report no age differences in the presence of specific phobias. With regard to the relationship between ability and anxiety in WS, Dimitropoulos, Ho, Klaiman, Koenig and Schultz (2009) found lower levels of anxiety in those individuals with higher IQ, and suggest that intelligence may be a protective factor against anxiety in WS. Leyfer et al. (2006), as well as Dodd and Porter (2009), did not report significant effects of cognitive functioning on anxiety in WS. Children with neurodevelopmental disorders may present with an uneven cognitive profile, with relative strengths in some areas and deficits in others (see discussion in Chapters 1 and 2). For example, most individuals with Williams syndrome (WS) meet the criteria for mild to moderate intellectual difficulties with verbal processing and certain aspects of language functioning (Mervis & Klein-Tasman, 2000) identified as relative strengths within their cognitive profile. Specific areas of deficit include non-verbal processing and visuospatial skills (Porter & Coltheart, 2006). Composite IQ scores may therefore mask differences in risk factors for anxiety related to specific areas of cognitive functioning. Porter, Dodd and Cairns (2009) found no significant effects of full scale IQ on anxiety, but did find increased internalising problems (which included anxiety) in those individuals with higher verbal skills and lower spatial abilities. Woodruff-Borden et al. (2010) reported that IQ was not significantly related to the presence of an anxiety disorder in a sample of individuals with WS. However, anxiety was associated with difficulties with inhibitory control of affect and behaviour. In a similar vein, Riby et al. (2014) explored the profiles of social behaviour and anxiety across a broad age range of individuals with WS. They report that nearly half of their participants were classified as highly anxious and over 80 per cent showed deficits in social functioning. Individuals with high anxiety were significantly more impaired in their social skills than those with lower levels of anxiety.

Similarly to that reported in ASD, some research suggests a relationship between fear and sensory hypersensitivity in WS, in particular noise sensitivity (Blomberg, Rosander & Andersson, 2006). Semel and Rosner (2003) report that children with WS frequently resist, avoid or show aversion to anything they foresee to potentially cause them sensitivity, which may suggest that they are experiencing anticipatory anxiety. An association has also been reported between the presence of restricted and repetitive behaviours and anxiety in WS (Rodgers et al., 2012). The recognition of the high rates of anxiety in people with WS is very recent and at the present time there are no evidence-based theoretical models regarding the causal mechanisms of anxiety for this clinical group.

14.2.3 Fragile X syndrome

Fragile X syndrome (FXS) is the most common hereditary cause of intellectual disability, occurring in 1 in 4,000 males and 1 in 8,000 females (Turner, Webb, Wake & Robinson, 1996; see also Chapter 10 for a detailed discussion of FXS).

Social anxiety is included as an aspect of the behavioural phenotype of FXS, alongside language impairments, repetitive behaviours and self-injury. Some individuals with FXS will also have a diagnosis of ASD (reports of prevalence range from between 15 and 60 per cent, with the range probably reflecting changes in diagnostic practices). Given the association between ASD and anxiety it is perhaps important to consider whether co-occurring FXS and ASD is associated with increased vulnerability to anxiety.

Cordeiro, Ballinger, Hagerman and Hessl (2011) examined the prevalence of anxiety disorders in a sample of 58 individuals with Fragile X syndrome and report that 86.2 per cent of males and 76.9 per cent of females with FXS met criteria for an anxiety disorder, with social phobia and specific phobia the most commonly diagnosed anxiety sub-types. Tranfaglia (2011) reported social phobia to be highly prevalent in FXS, affecting around 75 per cent of their sample. Social phobia in FXS is characterised by poor eye contact, gaze aversion, delays in the initiation of social interaction, and significant difficulties forming and maintaining friendships. The presence of social phobia in FXS has been linked with aberrant brain activity in neural circuitry associated with social cognition (Holsen, Dalton, Johnstone & Davidson, 2008; Watson, Hoeft, Garrett, Hall & Reiss, 2008).

Other aspects of the environment have also been reported as anxiety-provoking in FXS. Woodcock, Oliver and Humphreys (2008) report anxiety following changes to routines or expectations, suggesting that decreases in predictability (caused by change) are particularly aversive, perhaps mirroring the associations between intolerance of uncertainty and anxiety in ASD reported by Boulter et al. (2013). Symons, Clark, Hatton, Skinner and Bailey (2003) report an association between the presence of self-injurious behaviour in FXS and anxiety related to changes in routine. Woodcock et al. (2011) present some evidence of anxiety related to highly stimulating environments in FXS.

14.2.4 Prader-Willi syndrome

Prader-Willi syndrome (PWS) is a genetically determined disorder characterised by mild to moderate intellectual disability, which occurs in around 1 in 25,000 births (Whittington, Holland & Webb, 2001). The syndrome is characterised by a behavioural phenotype which includes the presence of obsessions and compulsions, usually emerging by the age of four years and subject to increased severity and rigidity with age (Dykens, 2004). The presence of obsessive compulsive symptoms is associated with considerable difficulties for families with a child with PWS, with levels of symptomatology reported as comparable to clinical samples of individuals with OCD (Dykens, Leckman & Cassidy, 1996). Compulsive characteristics include hoarding, arranging, ordering, rigid routines, insistence on sameness and skin picking (Wigren & Hansen, 2005). Obsessive behaviours are reported to include extreme 'just right' behaviours, the excessive desire for sameness, and the need for symmetry. Skin picking behaviours are reported to be particularly prevalent for individuals with PWS affecting up to 95 per cent of children and 80 per cent of adults with the condition. Morgan et al. (2010) investigated the phenomenology and correlates of skin picking in a sample of 67 young people with PWS and reported that severity of the behaviour was positively correlated with anxiety symptoms.

In a cross-syndrome comparison study, Woodcock et al. (2008) examined the associations between repetitive questioning, resistance to change, temper outbursts and anxiety in individuals with PWS and FXS and concluded that changes to routines and to expectations were aversive and resulted in negative emotional reactions in both groups. Furthermore, the use of repetitive questioning appeared to function similarly across groups and served to enhance predictability. When faced with changes in routine, individuals with PWS were more likely to express distress in the form of temper outbursts, whilst anxiety was expressed as repetitive behaviours and self-injury in FXS. Studies using a cross-syndrome comparison design like this one are particularly useful when trying to determine what features of a construct are specific to a particular disorder and what aspects may be shared phenomena across syndromes. Understanding syndrome specificity of symptoms can be especially important in the development of sensitive measures and tailored interventions.

14.2.5 Summary

The studies discussed here illustrate that there are potentially a number of factors that may place children with neurodevelopmental disorders at risk for developing anxiety disorders. Some of these factors are similar to those present in typically developing children, such as age, ability and difficulties with uncertainty, but there are also a number of factors which appear to be particularly important when considering anxiety in children with neurodevelopmental disorders. These include the presence of sensory atypicalities, for example in WS, and restricted and repetitive behaviours, such as in ASD, and difficulties processing information from the social world in FXS. Overall, research into the factors related to anxiety in children with neurodevelopmental disorders is significantly lacking. In particular, there is little mention of the reasons why some children do not develop anxiety.

14.3 The identification and assessment of anxiety in children with neurodevelopmental disorders

Accurate and reliable diagnosis of comorbid mental health disorders in children with neurodevelopmental disorders is of major importance. However, the assessment of children with these conditions is a complex and challenging task. Most of the studies discussed here used measures designed for assessing anxiety in TD children and the small sample sizes inherent in studies with specialist populations often preclude the evaluation of the psychometric properties of measures used with children with neurodevelopmental disorders. Measures designed for another population may not be sensitive to characteristics that are specific to the population under investigation. Therefore, the reliability and validity of these measures is questionable. Furthermore, current psychiatric classification systems are based on studies for which the presence of a neurodevelopmental disorder is an exclusion criterion. Acknowledging the inherent difficulties in utilising standardised measures developed with typical populations, the use of informant- (usually parent) based semi-structured interviews is common (Woodcock et al., 2008). These methods provide rich and comprehensive data but often lack evidence regarding the validity and reliability of coding schemes and may be subject to informant bias. Taking these issues into account, it is important to carefully consider measurement issues when considering research in this area.

A further challenge to accurate assessment and identification of mental health difficulties in neurodevelopmental disorders is that it is often very difficult to distinguish between core symptoms of a developmental disorder and comorbid mental health symptoms. This may be especially the case with regard to anxiety, where some of the features of anxiety (e.g. repetitive questioning or reassurance seeking) may overlap with some aspects of the developmental disability (e.g. repetitive speech in ASD/FXS or hypersociability as reassurance seeking in WS) leading to suspicion of and the diagnosis of, or even mis- or over-diagnosis of anxiety (Kuusikko et al., 2008). Conversely, there may be a tendency to attribute all psychiatric problems in children and adults with developmental disabilities to the disability itself (Lainhart, 1999). This tendency to overlook comorbid mental health problems in the presence of a disability is known as *diagnostic overshadowing* (MacNeil et al., 2009). The risk here is that symptoms, such as anxiety, may be viewed as 'less important' than the disability itself, or as an integral part of that disorder. This will hinder the ability to directly address the anxiety and may mean that it is even mismanaged.

Thirdly, information from multiple sources (e.g. parents, teachers and, where possible, the child themselves) is important in identifying mental health difficulties in all children (Leyfer et al., 2006). This triangulation of information is perhaps even more critical for children with neurodevelopmental disorders, who are often regarded as unreliable informants due to their intellectual level, lack of self-reflection and insight, and limited communication skills. Yet, the majority of studies rely on single informants (often parents). Parents are hugely important informants in the process of assessment, they are the experts with regard to their child and their role is central. However, parents may underestimate or under-report the number and severity of internalising symptoms for their child because they perhaps have become accustomed to their child's behaviour (Muris, Merckelbach & Sijsenaar, 1998) and, of course, informant reports are subject to bias, being dependent on the psychological needs and beliefs of the informant (McBrien, 2003). Kim, Szatmari, Bryson, Streiner and Wilson (2000) found that parents of children with neurodevelopmental disorders who are anxious and worried about their child's chances in the future reported more child anxiety and depression than parents who were not so worried. Consequently, parental reports may be influenced by parent characteristics, such as parental anxiety, and reflect parental attributions regarding child behaviour problems (Sukhodolsky et al., 2008). So, whilst parents should be involved in the assessment process, it is recommended that wherever possible assessments, whether they are for clinical or research purposes, are multimodal (e.g. clinical interview, rating scales, direct observation, physiological measurement), use multiple informants (e.g. parents, teachers, self-report), and use appropriate instrumentation (e.g. adequate reliability and validity, normative data for the population under investigation).

In summary, conceptualising and identifying mental health difficulties in children with neurodevelopmental disorders is difficult using existing methods. Existing diagnostic classificatory systems depend substantially on the self-reported, subjective experiences of the individuals being diagnosed, a methodology often not feasible for individuals with cognitive and communication impairments (Hill & Furniss, 2006). In addition, some symptoms of internalising disorders may overlap with features of the neurodevelopmental disorder itself, bringing into question the suitability of the methods used.

14.4 Interventions

As we have seen, there is growing evidence that the prevalence of anxiety in children with a range of neurodevelopmental disabilities is high. Identifying effective interventions for this at-risk group of children is therefore a priority. This section will focus on the use of evidence-based psychological interventions to tackle anxiety in children with neurodevelopmental disorders. Consideration will be given to the types of interventions available and the modifications that have been made in the delivery of the intervention to meet the needs of children with neurodevelopmental disorders.

14.4.1 Types of interventions available

Cognitive behaviour therapy (CBT) is a well-established, successful treatment for anxiety disorders in TD children and adults (Chorpita et al., 2011). CBT aims to intervene at three levels: cognitions (how to manage unhelpful thoughts); behaviours (managing the behavioural reactions to anxiety); and feelings (managing the emotional and physical sensations associated with anxiety). It is based on the theory that psychological or behavioural problems, such as anxiety, are primarily a product of maladaptive thoughts and therefore changing the way one thinks and behaves can lead to changes in how one feels (Stallard, 2002).

CBT needs to be suitably adapted for the cognitive profile of individuals with neurodevelopmental disabilities. This is because individuals with neurodevelopmental difficulties may have difficulties with some of the skills required for CBT, such as higher level language skills, understanding their own and others emotions (Farrant, Boucher & Blades, 1999), and may have specific impairments in social cognition and limited cognitive flexibility which would reduce the wide range of problem-solving strategies available and inhibit generalisation of learning from one situation to another

(Donoghue, Stallard & Kucia, 2011; Ozsivadjian & Knott, 2011). Modifications are therefore needed to the way in which CBT is delivered to address these issues. For example, using more concrete and visual strategies to explain concepts (reducing language demands), repetition and video modelling for hard-to-grasp concepts (Reaven et al., 2009), and providing explicit opportunities to practise and generalise new skills (Anderson & Morris, 2006; Sofronoff et al., 2005; Wood et al., 2009).

Adapted CBT has been shown in seven published randomised controlled trials (RCTs) to help reduce anxiety in high-functioning children with ASD aged eight to sixteen years (e.g. Chalfant, Rapee & Carroll, 2006; McConachie et al., 2013; Reaven et al., 2012; Sofronoff et al., 2005; Storch et al., 2013; Sung et al., 2011; Wood et al., 2009). The studies varied in approaches from six group sessions (Sofronoff et al., 2005) to sixteen group sessions (Sung et al., 2011), individual sessions (Wood et al., 2009) or a mixture of both (White et al., 2013). The studies used a wide range of CBT programmes including some widely available commercial programmes such as the *Cool Kids Anxiety Program* (Lyneham, Abbott, Wignall & Rapee, 2003), the *Coping Cat Program* (Kendall & Hedtke, 2006), *Exploring Feelings* (Attwood, 2004), *Facing Your Fears* (Reaven, Blakeley-Smith, Nichols & Hepburn, 2011). All studies adapted core components of CBT such as enhancing emotion recognition, developing coping strategies (e.g. relaxation, emotion regulation), and exposure work. The outcomes were generally positive, with most studies showing large effects and reporting significant reductions on at least one anxiety measure. However, group therapy showed more varied results than for individual therapy (Sofronoff et al., 2005; Sung et al., 2011; White et al., 2013). The types of modifications in the delivery of CBT varied and included techniques such as using visual schedules, incorporation of individuals' special interests, social skills instruction, ways to address poor attention and motivation, and using parents as co-therapists. Some studies developed their own manuals, whilst others adapted existing treatment manuals for typically developing children. However, further research is still needed to establish exactly what CBT modifications are most helpful in targeting anxiety in children with ASD, and whether the same treatment can be applied to younger and less able children. The studies also varied with regard to how the intervention was delivered, including both group and individual therapies, and whether parents were involved.

The literature for other developmental disabilities and CBT is more limited. There are however, a few single case studies that show promising preliminary support for adapted CBT in other neurodevelopmental disabilities. For example, Storch and colleagues developed an individualised twelve-week CBT programme to treat obsessive compulsive disorder (OCD) in young people with PWS aged five to seventeen years (Storch et al., 2011). The programme is flexible enough for therapists to tailor to the developmental needs of individual children, trains parents as co-therapists, and includes sessions on behaviours common in PWS such as negotiating food hoarding. Brown and Hooper (2009) report a case study detailing the use of Acceptance and Commitment Therapy (ACT)[1] and mindfulness techniques[2] to tackle anxiety and obsessive thoughts in a young person with a learning disability and highlight that the experiential nature of these approaches is perhaps more suitable to individuals with learning disabilities than traditional CBT because of the reduced reliance on verbal reasoning ability.

Indeed, there is an emergent evidence base for the use of mindfulness-based therapies to address difficulties with anxiety in individuals with neurodevelopmental disabilities. Hwang & Kearney (2103) report a systematic review of 12 studies using mindfulness techniques with individuals with mild to severe developmental disabilities and conclude that the technique holds promise as an accessible method of intervention for a range of psychological and behavioural difficulties in individuals with developmental disabilities.

There are a number of key issues to take into account when evaluating the literature which reports effectiveness of interventions in neurodevelopmental disabilities, including issues related to the methods of identification/assessment of anxiety in the sample, the suitability of the outcome measures used and the range of informants included in the study.

14.4.2 Adapting and modifying interventions

There are a number of ways in which intervention programmes can be adapted to meet the needs of individuals with neurodevelopmental disabilities. It is often useful to include parents, especially when working with younger and less able children with neurodevelopmental disabilities, because the child may struggle to express verbally that they are anxious. Yet, parents can find it difficult to infer which behaviours are driven by anxiety and which are due to neurodevelopmental difficulties. Participation of parents therefore may serve to enhance identification and understanding of presenting symptoms by both the clinician and the family. For example, it may be that behaviours interpreted by parents as non-compliance or anger are actually a manifestation of anxiety (e.g. a young person's refusal to go to school or refusal to leave the classroom at lunchtime). In a recent review, engaging actively with parents was one of the predominant trends in modifying CBT programmes for young people with ASD and anxiety (Moree & Davis, 2010). The inclusion of parents has a number of additional benefits such as increasing how techniques are generalised as parents are able to prompt and coach their children's use of skills at home and in other settings, and providing parents and children with a shared emotional vocabulary to discuss problems. For children with neurodevelopmental disorders this is particularly important given that they have difficulties generalising information across situations such as home, school and therapy.

The influence of parents' own anxieties and parenting behaviours on their child's emotions may also need to be considered. Parents of children with neurodevelopmental disabilities report more mental health problems than parents of children without disabilities (Hastings, 2002). Parent involvement may build their ability and confidence not just in understanding and managing their child's anxiety but also by improving their insight and management of their own anxiety.

An important component of any intervention for children with neuro-developmental disabilities and co-occurring anxiety is emotional literacy training. This will enable them to develop the prerequisite skills required to identify and label a range of emotions and identify situations or thoughts that may make them feel a certain way. Once this has been achieved, there is a greater possibility of successfully implementing talking therapies such as CBT. For example, interventions which focus upon changing reactions to trigger situations (such as worrying scenarios) are more likely to be successful if a child has the skills to label how they are feeling and monitor the effect of this upon their body and behaviour.

Social skills training is included in some treatment programmes for children with neurodevelopmental disabilities and co-occurring anxiety disorders. Issues with anxiety may increase social interaction impairments through avoidance of social situations (Beaumont & Sofronoff, 2008). Conversely, difficulties with social cognition (resulting from the core disorder) may actually contribute to the development of anxiety. For example, for young people who have an awareness of their social difficulties and that their interactions with peers are awkward, may become anxious in this type of social situation (White et al., 2009). Anxiety may therefore compound the overall social impairment experienced by children with neurodevelopmental disabilities, and potentially increase their vulnerability to bullying and teasing from peers among other risks (Sofronoff, Dark & Stone, 2011).

Emotional and Social Skills Training for Individuals with Williams syndrome (ESST-WS; Essau & Longhi, 2013) is a newly developed CBT programme designed specifically for young people with WS to help reduce anxiety symptoms. The programme includes two sessions on social skills training which are designed to target the difficulties children with WS often have in maintaining friendships and in social interactions. Children with WS are often described as hypersociable or overly friendly, in that they have no difficulty initiating social interactions but often lack social understanding (Semel & Rosner, 2003). For example, they may be very honest and say things that are true but do not have the awareness that this may make other people feel uncomfortable. The programme has not yet been fully evaluated on a large group of children but initial case study reports indicate that social skills training is a useful addition to CBT for young people with WS.

Similarly, for children and young people with ASD there are also a number of CBT programmes that incorporate social skills training with moderate to large effect sizes in the reduction of anxiety symptoms (White et al., 2009; Wood et al., 2009), providing further support for the idea that social skills training as part of an intervention programme for children and adolescents with neurodevelopmental disabilities can have additional benefits.

14.4.3 Summary

We have seen that there is growing evidence that psychosocial interventions can be effective in reducing anxiety symptoms in children and adolescents with neurodevelopmental disabilities. However, further research is needed to establish what adaptations are most effective in enhancing effectiveness and on a greater range of developmental disabilities. There are a number of adaptations to CBT interventions for children and adolescents with neurodevelopmental disability that can increase treatment effectiveness such as the inclusion of parents, social skills training and ensuring that the young people have the prerequisite skills necessary to engage in CBT such as identifying and labelling their own emotions.

14.5 Conclusions

In this chapter we examined the prevalence of anxiety disorders associated with a range of neurodevelopmental disorders. We considered how some of the core features of a neurodevelopmental disorder (such as sensory issues or difficulties with social cognition) might enhance vulnerability to anxiety and how in turn the presence of anxiety may serve to then exacerbate some of the core characteristics of the disorder (e.g. RRB or hypersociability). We have lamented the lack of robust models to explain this increased vulnerability to anxiety seen in these populations and considered why the development of theoretical frameworks is so important for assessment and intervention. We also spent some time considering the thorny issue of measurement, including some thoughts about the use of suitable outcome measures and who potential informants should be. Finally, we spent some time thinking about advances in the development of psychological interventions to tackle anxiety in individuals with neurodevelopmental disorders, and paid particular attention to the adaptation of programmes to make them more accessible and increase efficacy.

Practical tips

1. *Use multiple informants/sources of evidence.* Given that:
    a. individuals with neurodevelopmental disorders often find it difficult to recognise, understand and talk about their feelings;
    b. parenting a child with a neurodevelopmental disorder is associated with increased parental anxiety, which may in turn impact on the ways in which parental attributions of a child's emotional state are reached;
    c. mental health clinicians may have limited experience working with children with neurodevelopmental disabilities and will be primarily working with classification systems based on research from which individuals with a neurodevelopmental disability were excluded.
    Triangulation of evidence from multiple sources (child, parents, teacher, clinician, researcher) regarding the presentation of emotional difficulties is central to an accurate and valid description of the sample under investigation.
2. *Careful consideration of the suitability of outcome measures.* We have seen in this chapter that much of the research in this field uses outcome measures that were developed for typically developing individuals. This issue cannot be solved overnight and whilst more tailored measures are developed and/or

adapted, it is important to use the best available at the time of your study. Indeed, it may be that some of the measures developed for typically developing individuals work well in your sample – it is important to check, wherever possible, by evaluating the psychometric properties of the measure based on your data (e.g. cronbachs alpha, factor analysis). So carefully select the measures you think have the best pedigree to answer your question and then check how well they have performed with your sample by addressing issues related to reliability and validity. This will enable you to have more confidence in the validity and reliability of your findings.

3. *Careful consideration of the influence of age and ability and matching.* If your question relates to the influence of age or ability level on the presentation and nature of mental health difficulties or the effectiveness of an intervention then it is important to consider carefully how these constructs are assessed and reported for your sample. Is chronological age or mental age important (or both)? Do you need to take into account the possibility of the presence of an uneven cognitive profile in your sample (and therefore report verbal and/or performance based ability assessments instead of or as well as full scale IQ)?

For all of these recommendations there are no right and wrong answers, what is important is to take these factors into consideration and for the decision-making process to be influenced by your research question and the characteristics of the population under investigation.

Notes

1 ACT teaches individuals how to accept their internal experiences (thoughts, feelings, memories and physical sensations) rather than changing the content of these and how to commit to making behavioural changes.

2 Mindfulness is a psychological concept that teaches an individual how to focus their attention and awareness in the present moment, using techniques like meditation, breathing and yoga.

References

American Psychiatric Association (2013). *DSM-5* (5th ed). Washington, DC: American Psychiatric Association.

Anderson, S. & Morris, J. (2006). Cognitive behavior therapy for people with Asperger syndrome. *Behavioural and Cognitive Psychotherapy, 34*(1), 293–303.

Attwood, T. (2004). *Exploring Feelings: Cognitive Behaviour Therapy to Manage Anxiety.* (1st ed.). Texas: Future Horizons.

Beaumont, R. & Sofronoff, K. (2008). A multi-component social skills intervention for children with Asperger syndrome: The Junior Detective Training Program. *Journal of Child Psychology and Psychiatry, 49*(7), 743–753.

Bellini, S. (2004). Social skill deficits and anxiety in high-functioning adolescents with autism spectrum disorders. *Focus on Autism and Other Developmental Disabilities, 19*(2), 78–86.

——(2006). The development of social anxiety in adolescents with autism spectrum disorders. *Focus on Autism and Other Developmental Disabilities, 21*(3), 138–145.

Ben-Sasson, A., Cermak, S. A., Orsmond, G. I., Tager-Flusberg, H., Kadlec, M. B. & Carter, A. S. (2008). Sensory clusters of toddlers with autism spectrum disorders: Differences in affective symptoms. *Journal of Child Psychology and Psychiatry, 49*(8), 817–825.

Blomberg, S., Rosander, M. & Andersson, G. (2006). Fears, hyperacusis and musicality in Williams syndrome. *Research in Developmental Disabilities, 27*(1), 668–680.

Boulter, C., Freeston, M. H., South, M. & Rodgers, J. (2013). Intolerance of uncertainty as a framework for understanding anxiety in children and adolescents with Autism Spectrum Disorders. *Journal of Autism Developmental Disorders, 44,* 1391–1402.

Brown, F. & Hooper, S. (2009). Acceptance and commitment therapy (ACT) with a learning disabled young person experiencing anxious and obsessive thoughts. *Journal of Intellectual Disabilities, 13*(3), 195–201.

Buhr, K. & Dugas, M. J. (2009). The role of fear of anxiety and intolerance of uncertainty. *Behaviour Research and Therapy, 47*(1), 215–223.

Burnette, C. P., Mundy, P. C., Meyer, J. A., Sutton, S. K., Vaughan, A. E. & Charak, D. (2005). Weak central coherence and its relations to theory of mind and anxiety in autism. *Journal of Autism & Developmental Disorders, 35*(1), 63–73.

Carleton, R. N. (2012). The intolerance of uncertainty construct in the context of anxiety disorders: Theoretical and practical perspectives. *Expert Review of Neurotherapeutics, 12*(8), 937–947.

Chalfant, A. M., Rapee, R. & Carroll, L. (2006). Treating anxiety disorders in children with high functioning Autism Spectrum Disorders: A controlled trial. *Journal of Autism and Developmental Disability, 37*(10), 1842–1857.

Chorpita, B. F., Daleiden, E. L., Ebesutani, C., Young, J., Becker, K. D., Nakamura, B. J. & Starace, N. (2011). Evidence-based treatments for children and adolescents: An updated review of indicators of efficacy and effectiveness. *Clinical Psychology: Science and Practice, 18*(2), 154–172.

Clark, D. D. & Beck, A. T. (2010). *Cognitive Therapy of Anxiety Disorders: Science and Practice* (1st ed.). New York: The Guilford Press.

Cordeiro, L., Ballinger, E., Hagerman, R. & Hessl, D. (2011). Clinical assessment of DSM-IV anxiety disorders in fragile X syndrome: Prevalence and characterization. *Journal of Neurodevelopmental Disorders, 3*(1), 57–67.

Costello, E. J., Mustillo, S. & Erkanli, A. (2003). Prevalence and development of psychiatric disorders in childhood and adolescence. *Archives of General Psychiatry, 60*(1), 837–844.

Dimitropoulos, A., Ho, A., Klaiman, C., Koenig, K. & Schultz, R. (2009). A comparison of behavioural and emotional characteristics in children with Autism, Prader-Willi syndrome, and Williams syndrome. *Journal of Mental Health Research in Intellectual Disabilities, 2*(3), 220–243.

Dodd, H. F. & Porter, M. A. (2009). Psychopathology in Williams syndrome: The effect of individual differences across the life span. *Journal of Mental Health Research in Intellectual Disabilities, 2*(1), 89–109.

Donoghue, K., Stallard, P. & Kucia, K. (2011). The clinical practice of cognitive behavioural therapy for children and young people with a diagnosis of Asperger's Syndrome. *Journal of Clinical Child Psychology and Psychiatry, 16*(1), 89–102.

Dykens, E. M. (2003). Anxiety, fears, and phobias in persons with Williams syndrome. *Developmental Neuropsychology, 23*(1), 291–316.

——(2004). Maladaptive and compulsive behavior in Prader-Willi syndrome: New insights from older adults. *American Journal on Mental Retardation, 109,* 142–153.

Dykens, E. M., Leckman, J. F. & Cassidy, S. B. (1996). Obsessions and compulsions in Prader-Willi Syndrome. *Journal of Child Psychology and Psychiatry, 37*(1), 995–1002.

Essau, C. A. & Longhi, E. (2013). CBT intervention for anxiety in children and adolescents with Williams syndrome. In C. A. Essau & T. H. Ollendick (eds), *The Wiley-Blackwell Handbook of the Treatment of Childhood and Adolescent Anxiety* (pp. 559–574). Chichester, West Sussex: Wiley-Blackwell.

Evans, D. W., Canavera, K., Kleinpeter, L., Maccubbin, E. & Taga, K. (2005). The fears, phobias and anxieties of children with Autism Spectrum Disorders and Down syndrome: comparisons with developmentally and chronologically age matched children. *Child Psychiatry and Human Development, 36*(1), 3–26.

Farrant, A., Boucher, J. & Blades, M. (1999). Metamemory in children with autism. *Child Development, 70*(1), 107–131.

Fong, G. & Garralda, E. (2005). Anxiety disorders in children and adolescents. *Psychiatry, 4*(8), 77–81.

Gillott, A., Furniss, F. & Walter, B. (2001). Anxiety in high-functioning children with autism. *Autism, 5*(3), 277–286.

Green, S. A. & Ben-Sasson, A. (2010). Anxiety disorders and sensory over-responsivity in children. *Journal of Autism and Developmental Disorders, 40*(1), 1495–1504.

Hastings, R. P. (2002). Parental stress and behaviour problems of children with developmental disability. *Journal of Intellectual and Developmental Disability, 27*(3), 149–160.

Hill, J. & Furniss, F. (2006). Patterns of emotional and behavioural disturbance associated with autistic traits in young people with severe intellectual disabilities and challenging behaviours. *Research in Developmental Disabilities, 27*(5), 517–528.

Hillier, L. W., Fulton, R. S., Fulton, L. A., Graves, T. A., Pepin, K. H., Wagner-McPherson, C., ... Wilson, R. K. (2003). The DNA sequence of chromosome 7. *Nature, 424*(1), 157–164.

Holsen, L. M., Dalton, K. M., Johnstone, T. & Davidson, R. J. (2008). Prefrontal social cognition network dysfunction underlying face encoding and social anxiety in fragile X syndrome. *Neuroimage, 43*(3), 592–604.

Hwang, Y. S. & Kearney, P. (2013). A systematic review of mindfulness intervention for individuals with developmental disabilities: Long-term practice and long lasting effects. *Research in Developmental Disabilities, 34*(1), 314–326.

Kendall, P. C. & Hedtke, K. A. (2006). *Cognitive-Behavioral Therapy for Anxious Youth: Therapist Manual* (3rd ed.). Ardmore, PA: Workbook Publishing.

Kim, J. A., Szatmari, P., Bryson, S. E., Streiner, D. L. & Wilson, F. J. (2000). The prevalence of anxiety and mood problems among children with autism and Asperger syndrome. *Autism, 4*(2), 117–132.

Korenberg, J. R., Bellugi, U., Salandanan, L. S., Mills, D. L. & Reiss, A. L. (2003). Williams syndrome: A neurogenetic model of human behaviour. In: *Encyclopedia of the Human Genome* (1st ed.). London: The Nature Publishing Group.

Kuusikko, S., Pollock-Wurman, R., Jussilla, K., Carter, A. A., Mattila, M. L., Ebeling, H., ... Moilanen, I. (2008). Social anxiety in high-functioning children and adolescents with autism and Asperger syndrome. *Journal of Autism and Developmental Disorders, 38*(1), 1697–1709.

Lainhart, J. E. (1999). Psychiatric problems in individuals with autism, their parents and siblings. *International Review of Psychiatry, 11*(1), 278–298.

Leekam, S. R., Nieto, C., Libby, S. J., Wing, L. & Gould, J. (2007). Describing the sensory abnormalities of children and adults with autism. *Journal of Autism and Developmental Disorders, 37*(5), 894–910.

Leyfer, O. T., Folstein, S. E., Bacalman, S., Davis, N. O., Dinh, E. & Morgan, J. (2006). Comorbid psychiatric disorders in children with autism: Interview development and rates of disorders. *Journal of Autism and Developmental Disorders, 36*(1), 849–861.

Lidstone, J., Uljarevic, M., Sullivan, J., Rodgers, J., McConachie, H., Freeston, M. H., … Leekam, S. (2014). Relations among restricted and repetitive behaviours, anxiety and sensory features in children with autism spectrum disorders. *Research in Autism Spectrum Disorders, 8*, 82–92.

Ly, T. M. & Hodapp, R. M. (2005). Children with Prader-Willi syndrome vs. Williams syndrome: Indirect effects on parents during a jigsaw puzzle task. *Journal of Intellectual Disability Research, 49*(12), 929–939.

Lyneham, H. J., Abbott, M. J., Wignall, A. & Rapee, R. M. (2003). *The Cool Kids Family Program – Therapist Manual.* Sydney: Macquarie University.

McBrien, J. A. (2003). Assessment and diagnosis of depression in people with intellectual disability. *Journal of Intellectual Disability Research, 47*(1), 1–13.

McConachie, H., McLaughlin, E., Grahame, V., Taylor, H., Honey., E, Tavernor, L., … Le Couteur, A. (2013). Group therapy for anxiety in children with autism spectrum disorder. *Autism.* doi: 10.1177/1362361313488839 [epub ahead of print].

MacNeil, B. M., Lopes, V. A. & Minnes, P. M. (2009). Anxiety in children and adolescents with Autism Spectrum Disorders. *Research in Autism Spectrum Disorders, 3*(1), 1–21.

Masi, G., Brovedani, P., Mucci, M. & Favilla, L. (2002). Assessment of anxiety and depression in adolescents with mental retardation. *Child Psychiatry and Human Development, 32*(3), 227–237.

Mervis, C. B. & Klein-Tasman, B. P. (2000). Williams syndrome: Cognition, personality, and adaptive behavior. *Mental Retardation and Developmental Disabilities Research Reviews, 6*(2), 148–158.

Meyer, J. A., Mundy, P. C., Van Hecke, A. V. & Durocher, J. S. (2006). Social attribution processes and comorbid psychiatric symptoms in children with Asperger syndrome. *Autism: The International Journal of Research & Practice, 10*(4), 383–402.

Moree, B. N. & Davis, T. E. (2010). Cognitive-behavioural therapy for anxiety in children diagnosed with autism spectrum disorders: Modification trends. *Research in Autism Spectrum Disorders, 4*(1), 346–354.

Morgan, J. R., Storch, E. A., Douglas, W. W., Bodzin, D., Lewin, A. B. & Murphy, T. K. (2010). A preliminary analysis of the phenomenology of skin-picking in Prader-Willi syndrome. *Child Psychiatry and Human Development, 41*(4), 448–463.

Muris, P., Merckelbach, H. & Sijsenaar, M. (1998). Treating phobic children: Effects of EMDR. *Journal of Consulting and Clinical Psychology, 66*(1), 193–198.

Ozsivadjian, A. & Knott, F. (2011). Anxiety problems in young people with autism spectrum disorders: A case series. *Clinical Child Psychology and Psychiatry, 16*(1), 203–214.

Porter, M. A. & Coltheart, M. (2006). Global and local processing in Williams syndrome, autism, and Down syndrome: Perception, attention, and construction. *Developmental Neuropsychology, 30*(1), 771–789.

Porter, M. A., Dodd, H. & Cairns, D. (2009). Psychopathological and behavior impairments in Williams-Beuren syndrome: The influences of gender, chronological age, and cognition. *Child Neuropsychology, 15*(1), 1–16.

Reaven, J. A., Blakeley-Smith, A., Nichols, S., Dasari, M., Flanigan, E. & Hepburn, S. (2009). Cognitive-behavioral group treatment for anxiety symptoms in children with high-functioning autism spectrum disorders: A pilot study. *Focus on Autism and Other Developmental Disabilities, 24*(1), 27–37.

Reaven, J., Blakeley-Smith, A., Nichols, S. & Hepburn, S. (2011). *Facing Your Fears: Group Therapy for Managing Anxiety in Children with High-Functioning Autism Spectrum Disorders* (1st ed.). Baltimore, MD: Paul H. Brookes Publishing.

Reaven, J., Blakeley-Smith, A., Leuthe, E., Moody, E. & Hepburn, S. (2012). Facing your fears in adolescence: Cognitive-behavioral therapy for high-functioning autism spectrum disorders and anxiety. *Autism Research and Treatment*, 2012, 1–13.

Riby, D., Hanley, M., Kirk, H., Clark, F., Little, K., Fleck, R., Janes, E., ... Rodgers, J. (2014). The interplay between social functioning and anxiety in Williams syndrome. *Journal of Autism and Developmental Disabilities*, 44, 1220–1229.

Richler, J., Bishop, S. L., Kleinke, J. R. & Lord, C. (2007). Restricted and repetitive behaviors in young children with autism spectrum disorders. *Journal of Autism and Developmental Disorders*, 37(1), 73–85.

Rodgers, J., Riby, D. M., Janes, E. & Connolly, B. (2012). Anxiety and repetitive behaviours in autism spectrum disorders and Williams syndrome: A cross-syndrome comparison. *Journal of Autism and Developmental Disorders*, 42(2), 175–180.

Semel, E. & Rosner, S. R. (2003). *Understanding Williams syndrome: Behavioral* (1st ed.). Mahwah, NJ: Lawrence Erlbaum Associates.

Sofronoff, K. V., Attwood, T. & Hinton, S. (2005). A randomised controlled trial of a CBT intervention for anxiety in children with Asperger syndrome. *Journal of Child Psychology and Psychiatry*, 46(11), 1152–1160.

Sofronoff, K., Dark, E. & Stone, V. (2011). Social vulnerability and bullying in children with Asperger syndrome. *Autism*, 15(3), 355–372.

Stallard, P. (2002). *Think Good – Feel Good: A Cognitive Behaviour Therapy Workbook for Children and Young People*. Chichester: John Wiley.

Storch, E. A., Rahman, O., Morgan, J., Brauer, L., Miller, J. & Murphy, T. K. (2011). Case series of behavioural psychotherapy for obsessive-compulsive symptoms in youth with Prader-Willi Syndrome. *Journal of Developmental and Physical Disability*, 23, 359–368.

Storch, E. A., Arnold, E. B., Lewin, A. M., Nadeau, J., Jones, A. M., Mutch, P. J. & Murphy, T. K. (2013). The effect of cognitive-behavioral therapy versus treatment as usual for anxiety in children with autism spectrum disorders: A randomized, controlled trial. *Journal of American Academy of Child and Adolescent Psychiatry*, 52(1), 132–142.

Sukhodolsky, D. G., Scahill, L., Gadow, K. D., Arnold, L. E., Aman, M. G. & McDougle, C. J. (2008). Parent-rated anxiety symptoms in children with pervasive developmental disorders: Frequency and association with core autism symptoms and cognitive functioning. *Journal of Abnormal Child Psychology*, 36(1), 117–128.

Sukhodolsky, D. G., Bloch, M. H., Panza, K. E. & Reichow, B. (2013). Cognitive-behavioral therapy for anxiety in children with high-functioning autism: A meta-analysis. *Paediatrics*, 132(5), 1341–1350.

Sung, M., Ooi, Y. P., Goh, T. J., Pathy, P., Fung, D. S., Ang, R. P., ... Lam, C. M. (2011). Effects of cognitive-behavioral therapy on anxiety in children with autism spectrum disorders: A randomized controlled trial. *Child Psychiatry and Human Development*, 42(6), 634–649.

Symons, F. J., Clark, R. D., Hatton, D. D., Skinner, M. & Bailey, D. B. (2003). Self-injurious behavior in young boys with fragile X syndrome. *American Journal of Medical Genetics Part A*, 118(1), 115–121.

Tonge, B. & Einfeld, S. (2000). The trajectory of psychiatric disorders in young people with intellectual disabilities. *Australian and New Zealand Journal of Psychiatry*, 34(1), 80–84.

Tranfaglia, M. R. (2011). The psychiatric presentation of Fragile X: Evolution of the diagnosis and treatment of the psychiatric comorbidities of Fragile X syndrome. *Developmental Neuroscience*, 33(5), 337–348.

Turner, G., Webb, T., Wake, S. & Robinson, H. (1996). Prevalence of fragile X syndrome. *American Journal of Medical Genetics, 64*(1), 196–197.

Turner, M. (1999). Annotation: Repetitive behaviour in autism: A review of psychological research. *Journal of Child Psychology and Psychiatry, 40*(6), 839–849.

Van Steensel, F. J. A., Bogels, S. A. & Perrin, S. (2011). Anxiety disorders in children and adolescents with Autistic Spectrum Disorders: A meta-analysis. *Clinical Child and Family Psychology Review, 14*(3), 302–317.

Watson, C., Hoeft, F., Garrett, A. S., Hall, S. S. & Reiss, A. L. (2008). Aberrant brain activation during gaze processing in boys with fragile X syndrome. *Archives of General Psychiatry, 65*(11), 1315–1323.

Whitaker, S. & Read, S. (2006). The prevalence of psychiatric disorders among people with intellectual disabilities: An analysis of the literature. *Journal of Applied Research in Intellectual Disabilities, 19*(4), 330–345.

White, S. W., Ollendick, T., Scahill, L., Oswald, D. & Albano, A. M. (2009). Preliminary efficacy of a cognitive-behavioral treatment program for anxious youth with autism spectrum disorders. *Journal of Autism and Developmental Disorders, 39*(12), 1652–1662.

White, S. W., Albano, A. M., Johnson, C. R., Kasari, C., Ollendick, T., Klin, A. & Scahil, L. (2010). Development of a cognitive-behavioral intervention. *Clinical Child and Family Psychological Review, 13*(1), 77–90.

White, S. W., Ollendick, T., Albano, A., Oswald, D., Johnson, C., Southam-Gerow, M. A. & Scahill, L. (2013). Randomized controlled trial: Multimodal anxiety and social skill intervention for adolescents with Autism Spectrum Disorder. *Journal of Autism and Developmental Disorders*, 43(2), 382–394.

Whittington, J. E., Holland, A. J. & Webb, T. (2001). Prevalence and estimated birth incidence and mortality rate for people with Prader-Willi syndrome in one UK Health Region. *Journal of Medical Genetics, 38*(11), 792–798.

Wigren, M. & Hansen, S. (2005). ADHD symptoms and insistence on sameness in Prader-Willi syndrome. *Journal of Intellectual Disability Research, 49*(1), 449–456.

Wood, J. J. & Gadow, K. D. (2010). Exploring the nature and function of anxiety in youth with Autism Spectrum Disorders. *Clinical Psychology: Science and Practice, 17*(1), 281–292.

Wood, J. J., Drahota, A., Sze, K., Har, K., Chiu, A. & Langer, D. A. (2009). Cognitive behavioral therapy for anxiety in children with autism spectrum disorders: A randomized, controlled trial. *Journal of Child Psychology and Psychiatry, 50*(3), 224–234.

Woodcock, K., Oliver, C. & Humphreys, G. (2008). Associations between repetitive questioning, resistance to change, temper outbursts and anxiety in Prader-Willi and Fragile-X syndromes. *Journal of Intellectual Disability Research, 53*(3), 265–278.

——(2011). The relationship between specific cognitive impairment and behaviour in Prader-Willi syndrome. *Journal of Intellectual Disability Research, 55*(1), 152–171.

Woodruff-Borden, J., Kistler, D. J., Henderson, D. R., Crawford, N. A. & Mervis, C. B. (2010). Longitudinal course of anxiety in children and adolescents with Williams syndrome. *American Journal of Medical Genetics, 154*(1), 277–290.

INDEX